Digital Content Creation

new literacies

AND DIGITAL EPISTEMOLOGIES

Colin Lankshear, Michele Knobel,
and Michael Peters
General Editors

Vol. 46

PETER LANG
New York • Washington, D.C./Baltimore • Bern
Frankfurt • Berlin • Brussels • Vienna • Oxford

Digital Content Creation

Perceptions, Practices & Perspectives

Edited by Kirsten Drotner & Kim Christian Schrøder

PETER LANG
New York • Washington, D.C./Baltimore • Bern
Frankfurt • Berlin • Brussels • Vienna • Oxford

Library of Congress Cataloging-in-Publication Data

Digital content creation: perceptions, practices, and perspectives /
edited by Kirsten Drotner, Kim Christian Schrøder.
p. cm. — (New literacies and digital epistemologies ; v. 46)
Includes bibliographical references and index.
1. Information technology—Study and teaching—United States.
2. Computers—Study and teaching—United States.
3. Internet in education—United States. 4. Web 2.0.
I. Drotner, Kirsten. II. Schrøder, Kim Christian.
LB1028.5D553 371.33'44678--dc22 2010017873
ISBN 978-1-4331-0696-5 (hardcover)
ISBN 978-1-4331-0695-8 (paperback)
ISSN 1523-9543

Bibliographic information published by **Die Deutsche Nationalbibliothek.**
Die Deutsche Nationalbibliothek lists this publication in the "Deutsche Nationalbibliografie"; detailed bibliographic data is available on the Internet at http://dnb.d-nb.de/.

FSC
Mixed Sources
Product group from well-managed forests, controlled sources and recycled wood or fiber
Cert no. SCS-COC-002464
www.fsc.org
©1996 Forest Stewardship Council

Cover design by Jonas Drotner Mouritsen,
Chromascope, http://www.chromascope.dk/

The paper in this book meets the guidelines for permanence and durability of the Committee on Production Guidelines for Book Longevity of the Council of Library Resources.

Printed in the United States of America

Contents

II. Competence Formation through Digital Content Creation: Personal Voice or Commercial Coercion?

III. Institutional Ramifications of Digital Content Creation for Learning

IV. Studying Digital Content Creation: New Methodological Challenges

V. Perspectives for Media Education in the Age of Digital Content Creation

List of Figures and Tables

Chapter 1

Chapter 2

Chapter 4

Chapter 5

Chapter 7

Chapter 8

Chapter 9

Chapter 11

Chapter 12

Chapter 13

Chapter 15

Introduction

Digital Content Creation: Perceptions, Practices, and Perspectives

KIRSTEN DROTNER & KIM CHRISTIAN SCHRØDER

User generated content, digital content creation, participatory culture, digital creativities (Burn, 2009; Ito et al., 2009; Jenkins, 2006): there is no dearth of terms to describe the types of activities propelled in recent years by the rapid worldwide uptake of the Internet and mobile technologies in general and by Web 2.0 in particular. Social media is the shorthand often applied to these applications and tools, which hold the potential for users to shape and share content and socialize across time and space. Among the most widespread social media to generate and communicate content are wikis, social networking sites for "friending" such as Facebook, media sharing sites such as YouTube, and microblogging utilities such as with Twitter. Much has been made of the revolutionary social potential harnessed by users of social media, from educational turnarounds, to new forms of civic engagement and virtual citizenship and the formation of novel business models and markets.

The present volume takes stock of these developments through reasoned and robust studies of innovative uses of these new social media such as weblogs and wikis, online chat clients, digital games, and virtual world applications. From a variety of perspectives—including media and ICT studies (Information and Communications Technologies), education, psychology, anthropology, sociology, and cultural studies—the volume authors contribute to popular discourses and professional investigations in three capacities: analytical perspective, methodological approach, and empirical focus.

This analytical perspective is based on situated sociocultural practices and multimodal processes rather than on technological uptake or product distribution of social media (Earnshaw & Vince, 2001). This perspective is chosen to help balance and supplement existing investigations that are chiefly of a policy or a corporate nature. While these investigations often adopt a quantitative approach to large-scale data sets so as to document diversities in terms of age, ethnicity, class, gender, and region, the analytical perspective in the present volume invites more qualitative and explicitly contextualized approaches, allowing authors to unpick textual and social complexities and nuances. Indeed, several of this volume's authors are at pains to adopt a comprehensive approach that includes both textual and social dimensions, an approach that is recommended in the large body of media and ICT research, but not easily practiced.

Many, if not all, of the authors here use the young generation as their empirical focus, which is not surprising given the way in which this particular generation has pioneered the exploration of the Internet and mobile forms of creation and communication. Social media, with options to shape and share content, demonstrate the strongest growth among young Europeans' web uses (Livingstone & Haddon, 2009), and similar trends are documented in the USA (Lenhart & Madden, 2005). More specifically, many chapters in this volume analyze and evaluate these explorations with a view to learning, education, and competence formation. This focus is not only a result of young people being the center of attention—many of them are, after all, involved in one form of educational training or another; the focus is more centrally to do with ways in which digital media and, especially, creative forms of content creation are imbricated with prevailing discourses of wider social significance. Two of these are of particular relevance here, namely the policy discourse and the corporate discourse on digital media.

Policy Issues: Creating Knowledge Societies

The European Commission celebrated 2009 as the "European Year of Creativity and Innovation." The subtitle of the Commission's website (www.create 2009.europa.eu/) is "imagine, create, innovate," and this phrase is indicative of the rationale governing the Commission's initiative. As a joint enterprise of the Directorate-General for Education and Culture and the Directorate-General for Enterprise and Industry, the stated key message of the quoted phrase is that "creativity and innovation contribute to economic prosperity as well as to social and individual wellbeing" (European Commission, 2009a). Creativity is seen as a lever of Europe's economic competitiveness and as a catalyst of wider social participation and development (see also Sales & Fournier, 2007). The background reports, fueling arguments for the initiative, couple creativity, education, and culture as the joint foundations of economic innovation (e.g., European Commission, 2007; European Council, 2008).

Both here and in related EU strategies, digital technologies and digital media figure as transformative factors in fostering key competences of the twenty-first century. For example, the Learnovation project, 2007–2009, aims to investigate and document the potential of technology-enhanced learning to support innovation in Europe, which is seen as "the core outcome to achieve both competitiveness and social cohesion in Europe" (Learnovation, 2009). A similar link is evident in a European Commission recommendation in 2009 with the telling title, *On media literacy in the digital environment for a more competitive audiovisual and content industry and an inclusive knowledge society* (European Commission, 2009b, p. 1).

While important policy divergences remain as to the definition of ICT vis-à-vis digital media (Drotner, 2009), the European discourse is mirrored in many parts of the world and across widely different educational and social systems (overviews in e.g., Cheung, 2009; Fedorov, n. d.; Hart & Süss, 2002). In the USA, for example, The Partnership for 21st Century Skills is an advocacy organization that brings together stakeholders in education, business, and politics to help promote competences that are defined as "key to improving our nation's competitiveness a knowledge driven economy" (Partnership 2009: n. p.). Two board members of the Partnership define the core of these skills as learning and innovation, digital literacy, and life and career skills (Trilling & Fadel, 2009).

The recent discourse—coupling creativity, digital literacies, and knowledge economies and societies—clearly positions digital content creation as a means to an end, namely future-oriented competence formation. This position is at odds with established discourses to do with creativity, with learning and with media. Creativity has traditionally been defined as an individual ability with which, for example, gifted individuals such as artists and scientists are endowed. Today, this ability is seen to potentially include everybody, and it is defined as a social demand and a means of economic innovation. From being an inborn gift for the few, creativity has become a collective competence to be nurtured by virtually everybody and with digital content creation as a key lever.

This transformation must be seen in tandem with the way in which long-established discourses on education over the last decade have increasingly turned into a discourse on learning, putting pupils and processes at the core of discussion and empirical exploration. Many policy documents, including the EU documents quoted above, define digital technologies as catalysts of this development, by allowing for virtual and mobile forms of collaboration and interaction in problem solving, thus potentially changing teacher-pupil relations, the locations of learning and, some argue, even learning itself (Drotner, Jensen & Schrøder, 2008; Scardamalia & Bereiter, 2006; Salmon, 2004). The interlacing of digital media and pedagogical practices are routinely viewed through a lens of optimism, defining changes in terms of improvement and competence advancement.

Likewise, digital media is rapidly challenging established discourses of concern with media uses, particularly when it comes to children and teenagers. The recent worldwide upsurge of digital participation and creation is viewed as indication that users operate as active and engaged citizens and consumers, freely voicing their own concerns and shaping their own futures (Buckingham 2000, Ito et al., 2009). Such views easily resonate with deep-seated notions on individual freedom of expression; several major private foundations, not least in the USA, build on such notions in their formation of youth empowerment programs. For example, the Adobe Foundation's Adobe Youth Voices as of 2009 operates in 31 countries, offering training, grants, software, and employee volunteers from Adobe Systems Incorporated, all with a view to support "young people in and out of school and [encourage] the use of cutting-edge multimedia tools to communicate and share their ideas, demonstrate their potential, and take action where they live" (Adobe, 2009: n. p.).

The transforming discourses on creativity, education, and media serve to highlight persisting issues of power and purpose. Who are in a position to define what digital technologies are for and in what contexts? What should be the aims and outcomes of digital uses? What are the enablers and barriers of digital content creation in terms of textual modes, contextual framings, and institutional organization? Several chapters in this volume address these key questions and provide answers based on in-depth empirical studies.

Corporate Issues: Capitalizing on Knowledge Economies

Social media is a growth area of marketing, just as the sociocultural processes of content creation and communication offer new challenges and chances facing the corporate sector. The upsurge of wikis and blogs, podcasts, online gaming, and networking sites for friending has not only added to the already vast popularity of short message services (SMS) or multimedia messages (MMS) and web-based instant messaging (IM), these utilities and tools have equally fueled new corporate strategies for addressing existing customers and widen corporate markets for potential consumers. The barrage of bestselling manuals on e-marketing, social media marketing, and digital marketing, for example, testifies to the way in which the corporate trend latches onto existing discourses through which ICTs and mobile devices are hailed as innovative and personalized push media. These discourses are ultimately propelled by active users who are a far cry from the old-time groups of couch potatoes addressed by the push media of mass communication. While such easy oppositions are an equally far cry from the sobering nuances found in audience studies, they do serve as effective rhetorical correlations of social media, creativity, and innovation.

As noted, new alliances and partnerships are being formed between industry, policy-makers, and public stakeholders involved in the area of digital development. In overall terms, such partnerships are based on visions that digital technologies are formative for corporate economic gain. Knowledge economies, rather than knowledge societies, are at the core of interest. Based on this shared vision, two types of discourses are in operation when it comes to user digital content creation, depending on the definition of users as employees or consumers.

In work-related contexts, users participate in virtual dialogs and upload and share text and images as ways of solving problems or handling work-related tasks; for example, in on-the-job training. Many private companies have explicit procedures for accessing social software on the job such as online games, social networks sites, and text messaging. While comparative research evidence is still sparse, studies suggest that stricter corporate rules exist in North America than in, for example, Northern Europe (Mante, 2002).

Conversely, the leisure market for social software and user-generated content, a market that is almost entirely of a commercial nature, poses few restrictions for adults; and, when it comes to children and teenagers, self-regulation by the industry is generally proposed. These corporate views are lodged within discourses on children as being socially adept, media-savvy, and with little need for adult guidance, be it by parents, teachers, or professional counselors. Such notions easily pick up on and are nurtured by policy issues of democratic participation and advocacy for children's self-expression.

The co-articulation of these discourses speaks to particular tensions regarding user privacy and protection, not least young users; with institutional conditions to secure rights of expression, cultural experimentation, and social critique; and with boundaries of trust and loyalty on virtual markets where the user-consumer easily turns into co-producer and co-worker (van Dijk, 2009). Several chapters in the volume offer discussions of these dilemmas with insights gained through careful analysis and interpretation.

Positions for Scholarship

Digital content creation and social media is a field embroiled in a turbulent set of oppositions in the public and private domains. It is, therefore, of particular importance to carve out a position for scholarly voices that may speak to, and hopefully be heard by, several groups of actors. and decision-makers The present volume is premised on the usefulness of such endeavors. More specifically, it is galvanized by a wish to engage with controversial issues often inherent in the field without being partisan to one set of beliefs or behaviors. The volume authors share engagement based on theory-driven empirical studies. Their conceptual understanding and insight operate as a key to unravel empirical complexities. In a field with no easy answers or simple outcomes, we hope that our interventions will serve to unpick the complexities, highlight the nuances, and illuminate the pedagogical affordances of creative digital content creation and communication.

The Organization of the Book

The chapters that make up this book (with the exception of one) originate in the conference *Digital Content Creation: Creativity, Competence, Critique* hosted by the Danish Research Centre on Education and Advanced Media Materials (DREAM) in September 2008 (http://www.dream.dk/#/172495/) and are organized into five parts.

Part One, *Digital Content Creation: Creative Processes and Textual Re-appropriations* opens with Jonas Löwgren's chapter, "Designing for Collaborative Crossmedia Creation." Taking his point of departure in satirical audio-video mash-ups of mainstream media products, and strongly anchored in three cases of collaborative digital crossmedia creation, Löwgren discusses how professional scholar-designers can facilitate creative processes for social change and aesthetic expression among groups of everyday users/designers. On the basis of the three cases, Löwgren distills the motives for participating in crossmedia collaborative design, focusing on the urge to belong, establish identity, express one's self, and influence others and society. Provocatively—or commonsensically?—he suggests that it may make sense to forget about outcomes and to be solely concerned with the process of crossmedia content creation.

Chapter 2, "Wiki as Semiospheric Text: Students' Meaning-Making Practices as Authors and Consumers of Digital Texts" by Wilma Clark, analyzes the creative processes and textual re-appropriations of the science classroom that invites digital services such as wikis and social network sites to become central tools of learning, in the hands of teachers and 11- to 14-year-old students. Clark's analytical lens is Yuri Lotman's theory of "semiosphere," which sees cultural practices as spatial relationships and meaning-making processes in context. Empirically anchored in a science curriculum about fossil fuels, and including the level of detailed linguistic analysis of classroom interaction and of the students' creation of wikis, the chapter demonstrates how teachers and students have different perceptions of what constitutes "core," "periphery," and "boundary" learning discourses in the semiosphere of the digital science classroom. These differences appear to be due to the permeability of traditional science curricula, on the one hand, and the informal repertoires of the social digital spaces on the other, the latter leading to irreverent boundary-crossing contributions from students from time to time.

Chapter 3, Ola Erstad's "Content in Motion: Remixing and Learning with Digital Media," begins with a brief historical overview of the creative remixing processes of the artistic institutions of Dadaism, montage cinema and, more recently, musical sampling, before going on to develop the chapter's main concern of studying "content in motion" in school settings. From this perspective, it is the users and creators of digital content, and their remixing practices, that are in focus, not the content itself. Erstad considers, based on two case studies from classroom remixing processes in lower secondary school settings, how digital remixing processes may serve as new resources for school learning and how they may challenge conventional understandings of learning and education.

Section One concludes with a chapter by Simon Staffans and Annika Wiklund-Engblom, "Developing Crossmedia and Interactivity for Edutainment: Conclusions Drawn from 'The Space Trainees' Project." The authors continue the theme about designing crossmedia digital content, as they describe the development of a language-learning edutainment initiative in Finland called "The Space Trainees," which bridges digital television and Internet platforms. The respective roles played by the two media are discussed, and the importance of integrating design process and user research is emphasized through a seven-phase model of the integrated design/research process. Further, the chapter warns that no medium in a crossmedia strategy should be treated as merely an add-on. Instead, the user's desire to cross over between media should be not just natural, but logical.

Section Two, *Competence Formation Through Digital Content Creation: Personal Voice or Commercial Coercion?*, begins with John Hartley's chapter titled "Where Money and Meanings Meet: Theorizing the Emergence of New Values in Media and Education." Hartley discusses how recent developments in the commercial global media culture signalled by buzzwords such as social networks, consumer-created content, and multiplatform publication pose a challenge to education and to business models alike. From a media and cultural studies perspective, the author explores new theoretical frameworks required to grasp, and make the collective best of, these innovative processes in the creative realm. While cultural studies, for reasons both good and bad, have been practiced as a kind of "aversion therapy" against the commercial media culture, Hartley proposes a theoretical lens that is as much based on openness, creativity, and competence as on critique. Where money and meanings meet, therefore, is in consumer co-created innovation. Hartley argues that such a perspective is best pursued in the context of a "cultural science," a term originating with Raymond Williams and now appropriated by Hartley to guide us towards understanding how innovative digital literacies emerge from the nexus of commerce and learning.

In chapter 6, "Media Production and the Problem of Consumption," Becky Herr Stephenson explores the tensions between the construction of children as media consumers and producers, on the one hand, and the understanding of schools as spaces separate from consumption and responsible for producing a particular type of literate citizen on the other. The chapter draws from participant observation and interviews conducted during a multimedia project in a public middle school in the Los Angeles area, in which students were challenged to create a brief video documentary on obesity and junk food bans in schools, aiming to facilitate students' critical thinking about school politics and the students' own consumption. Although the project was successful in providing an alternative form of expression, the challenge of negotiating adult-driven and school-sanctioned discourses regarding consumption frustrated students and led to a lack of engagement with the project. The analysis thus highlights ways in which schools have to bridge the gap between adult-driven discourses and youth practices related to consumption, if these schools want to seriously open up opportunities for media literacy, creativity, and increased engagement in classroom media production.

Nina Haferkamp and Nicole C. Krämer's chapter "Creating a Digital Self: Impression Management and Impression Formation on Social Network Sites," describes how young people's self-presentations can be seen as expressions of their personal voice. The authors report from a qualitative study of the widespread kind of digital content creation that takes place when young people build their identities on social network sites in order to create a desired impression on other network members. The authors compare this production aspect with a look also at the participants' reception and evaluation of the profiles made by other users, reporting interesting gender differences in self-presentation techniques and a paradoxical discrepancy between people's own motives for self-presentation and the motives they ascribe to others.

In the book's third section, *Institutional Ramifications of Digital Content Creation for Learning*, the contributors present analyses of different aspects of the organizational challenges and opportunities resulting from inviting users, learners, and customers to communicate and learn through various forms of digital content creation.

Based on an extensive review of recent mainly British research into the practices and consequences of attempts to bring classrooms into the digital age, as well as on her own learning research, Angela McFarlane's chapter "Digital Creativity: Editing Versus Cheating and How You Learn the Difference" notes that in spite of prevalent raptures about digital learning benefits, convincing data on the impact of the pedagogical use of ICT on educational attainment remains illusive. She traces this situation to, among other things, the continuing predominance of "industrial" models of testable learning and the lack of pedagogical models that embrace the "creative" learning needs of what she terms the information age. As an alternative, she explores a constructivist model of learning in which the collaborative production, on- and offline, of student-generated content may lead to the kind of learning and skill development likely to equip individuals and groups to be socially and commercially successful in the information-rich culture. If framed in a manner that naturally encourages the students' critical reflection through the collaborative effort, McFarlane argues, concerns about widespread plagiarism in student work become unnecessary.

Annette Grønning's chapter, "Chat Interaction in Public and Commercial Domains," analyses two instant messaging guidance cases in Denmark and explores how this chat interaction is perceived by the interactants. The analytical framework comprises empirical data from the Danish portal on learning opportunities and professions (*UddannelsesGuiden*—The "Education Guide") and from the Danish part of IKEA's customer service, which are analyzed using Computer Mediated Discourse Analyses, with a focus on encounter structure, requests, and perception. Grønning finds that instant messaging sessions are a complement to or a substitute for more established media forms such as telephone consultations. Significantly, there may be an empowering dimension to instant messaging guidance services, which appear to lower the access threshold, especially for young males (some from minority ethnic backgrounds), who tend to shy away from guidance that uses face-to-face and telephone communicative channels.

In chapter 10, "Learning Spaces," Jenny Weight shifts to more abstract debates about appropriate pedagogical uses of networked technology and digital literacy in tertiary education towards grounded experiences in tertiary learning and teaching environments. She discusses her own experiments with networked and physical learning spaces and incorporates interview material from teachers and instructional designers at RMIT University, in order to identify complementarities and tensions between networked and physical learning and teaching environments. Through this analysis of what she terms "blended learning" in constructivist learning spaces, Weight throws an innovative glance at the potential conflicts between pedagogy and technologies, when the latter in the form of digital learning resources are introduced into educational environments without careful reflection about their reconcilability (or not) with learning objectives as well as with the teachers' digital competences.

Studying and evaluating digital content creation empirically is different from, for example, studying media reception in everyday life or as part of school-based learning processes, because the content creation process is a practical phenomenon likely to stretch over a longer period of time. The empirical study of digital production inside and outside the classroom, therefore, often requires experimentation with processual fieldwork methods that transcend participant observation and interview designs. In Section Four, *Studying Digital Content Creation: New Methodological Challenges*, we have collected a number of such inventive and experimental design-oriented studies of digital content production.

In chapter 11, "Negotiating Perspective in Social Video Environments," Ralph Barthel, Shaaron Ainsworth, and Mike Sharples report from a study of creative knowledge building through story creation from online video, based on video clips hosted on YouTube. The authors developed and evaluated the Video Pathways social video environment that supports knowledge building through perspective making and perspective taking in the video medium. The chapter describes the theoretical framework of their work on multi-path video and a pilot study that informed the design of Video Pathways. The authors outline the methodological challenges of studying knowledge building in a social video environment and describe how the combined quantitative and qualitative framework for evaluating the online learning experience should analyze both the collaborative activity (process), the resulting video narratives (conceptual artefacts), and the participants' experience of process and artefacts.

Daniel Spikol, in the chapter "Design Strategies for Developing Mobile Collaborative Learning Platforms," demonstrates how different methods used for the design and development of a series of mobile games called *Skattjakt* ("Treasure Hunt" in Swedish) offer new strategies and benefits with regard to the development and implementation of future learning activities. Theoretically, he takes his point of departure in the fact that mobile collaborative learning activities seem to provide benefits for the learners by giving them opportunities to discover, create, and develop new literacies by actively working and collaborating through new technologies. He points out how, although co-design practices and other design methods have been used extensively in educational research, the joint "design-oriented research" and "research-oriented design" process for designing learning activities to support collaboration across locations with mobile technologies raises new challenges. The active involvement (also stressed in Löwgren's chapter) of the teachers and the learners in the multi-stage iterative design process of these mobile games is usefully conceptualized through a meta-design framework to theory-driven digital design.

The chapter by Mikael Kivelä and Jarkko Myllări, "Digitally Mapping a Rhizome: Making Sense of Digital Content Creation Processes" explores the use of diverse and multimodal data to study digital content creation. The author's study is based on two studies conducted with 25 primary school pupils (aged 10–12) producing digital concept maps in two different school projects during spring and autumn 2008. The aim was to study the use of ICT skills acquired in informal learning settings in a formal classroom project and investigate the distribution of activities between physical and virtual environments. The data in question consisted of dual- and single-camera video recordings, capture animations from computer workstations, stimulated recall interviews, internal recordings, and log files of the IHMC CmapTools software and questionnaire data. In addition to its focus on research methodology, the chapter also contributes to more general issues of understanding digital content creation

In the book's last section, *Perspectives for Media Education in the Age of Digital Content Creation*, Norbert Wildermuth reminds us, in his chapter about "Empowerment: The Real Challenge of Digital Inclusion," that the information revolution has so far bypassed the majority of humankind and that across the globe there are striking imbalances, often labelled digital divides, in physical access to digital technologies and in the resources and skills necessary to become a digital citizen. Based on his long-term fieldwork on youth community media in two urban communities in Recife, Brazil, he explores the limits of policies and initiatives towards digital empowerment, noting that in many such communities, digital media projects are facing an almost overwhelming challenge coming from the omnipresent lure and threat of gang-related criminal activities. Considering what else, besides digital technologies, is needed for underprivileged individuals and communities to become part of a participative and inclusive society, Wildermuth argues that the focus should be on digital empowerment rather than on digital inclusion, that the digital media used may not be the most advanced kinds, and that empowerment initiatives should be followed by a large measure of patience.

David Buckingham in the book's last chapter asks provocatively "Do We Really Need Media Education 2.0?" as he discusses challenges to media education in the age of participatory media. As educators are facing the widespread dissemination of inexpensive and accessible digital tools for media production and more participatory forms of media—such as online gaming, blogging, and social networking—Buckingham succinctly assesses the implications of these developments for the practice of media education, in and beyond schools. While some argue that these new media require a paradigm shift, not merely in the curriculum of media education, but also in its pedagogy and suggest that we should be embracing the new forms of creativity that are provided here and moving beyond outdated critical perspectives, Buckingham rings a sobering note. While agreeing that media educators should be exploiting the possibilities of these new media, he warns that these educators also raise important ethical, political, and cultural questions and that we should not merely romanticise these developments as a form of technology-driven democratization or simply celebrate the opportunities for "informal learning" that they appear to provide.

Buckingham's argument is particularly apt, since it substantially echoes the vision that has governed our selection of contributions to this volume: There is a clear educational and democratic promise in the new forms of digital content creation, inside and outside of the classroom, but the realization of that promise will require more than technology alone.

References

Adobe Youth Voices. (2009). What is AYP? Retrieved 10 September, 2009 from http://youthvoices.adobe.com/about/what/

Buckingham, D. (2000). *The making of citizens: young people, news and politics*. Abingdon: Routledge.

Burn, A. (2009). *Making new media. Creative production and digital literacy*. New York: Peter Lang.

Cheung, C. K. (2009). *Media education in Asia*. Amsterdam: Springer.

van Dijk, J. (2009). Users like you? Theorizing agency in user-generated content, *Media, culture & society*, *31*(1): 41–58.

Drotner, K. (2009). Children and digital media: Online, on site, on the go. In J. Qvortrup, W. A. Corsaro, & Honig, M.S. (Eds.), *The Palgrave handbook of childhood studies* (pp. 360–73). London: Palgrave Macmillan.

Drotner, K., Jensen, H.S., & Schrøder, K.C. (Eds.). (2008). *Informal learning and digital media*. Newcastle: Cambridge Scholars Press.

Earnshaw, R., & Vince, J. (Eds.). (2001). *Digital content creation*. London: Springer-Verlag.

European Commission. (2007). *Communication from the commission to the European parliament, the council, the European economic and social committee and the committee of the regions on a European agenda for culture in a globalizing world*. Retrieved 10 September 2009 from http://eur-lex.europa.eu/LexUriServ/LexUriServ.do?uri=COM:2007:0242:FIN:EN:PDF

European Commission. (2009a). European year of creativity and innovation. Retrieved 10 September, 2009 from http://www.create2009.europa.eu/

European Commission. (2009b). Commission Recommendation 20.8.2009 on media literacy in the digital environment for a more competitive audiovisual and content industry and an inclusive knowledge society. Retrieved September 10, 2009, from ec.europa.eu/avpolicy/media_literacy/docs/recom/c_2009_6464_en.pdf.

European Council. (2008). Conclusions of the Council and of the Representatives of the Governments of the Member States, meeting within the Council of 22 May 2008 on promoting creativity and innovation through education and training (2008/C 141/10). Retrieved 10 September 2009 from eur-lex.europa.eu/LexUriServ/LexUriServ.do?uri=OJ:C:2008:141:0017:0020:EN:PDF

Fedorov, A. (n. d.). Media education in Russia: Current stage. Retrieved from edu.of.ru/mediaeducation/default.asp?ob_no=850

Hart, A., & Süss, D. (Eds.). (2002). *Media education in 12 European countries*. Zurich: The Swiss Federal Institute of Technology

Ito, Mizuko, et al. (2009). *Hanging out, messing around, and geeking out: Kids Living and Learning with new media*. Cambridge, MA: The MIT Press.

Jenkins, H. (2006). *Fans, bloggers, and gamers: Exploring participatory culture*. New York: New York University Press.

Learnovation. (2009). Homepage. Retrieved September 10, 2009, from www.elearningeuropa.info/learnovation.

Lenhart, A. & Madden, M. (2005). Teen content creators and consumers: Findings of the Pew Internet and American life project. Retrieved September 10, 2009, from www.pewinternet.org/~/media//Files/Reports/2005/PIP_Teens_Content_Creation.pdf.pdf

Livingston, S., & Haddon, L. (Eds.). (2009). *Kids online*. Bristol: Policy Press.

Mante, E. (2002). The Netherlands and the UK compared. In J. Katz & R. Aakhus (Eds.). *Perpetual contact: Mobile communication, private talk, public performance*. Cambridge: Cambridge University Press.

Partnership for 21st Century Skills. (2009). Overview. Retrieved September 10, 2009, from www.21stcenturyskills.org/index.php?option=com_content&task=view&id=195&Itemid=183#-what_21st.

Scardamalia, M., & Bereiter, C. (2006). Knowledge building: Theory, pedagogy, and technology. In K. Sawyer (Ed.), *Cambridge handbook of the learning sciences* (pp. 97–119). Cambridge, MA: Harvard University Press.

Sales, A., & Fournier, M. (Eds.). (2007). *Knowledge, communication and creativity*. London: Sage.

Salmon, G. (2004a). *E-moderating: The key to teaching and learning online*. Abingdon: RoutledgeFalmer.

Trilling, B., & Fadel, C. (2009). *21st century skills: Learning for life in our times*. Hoboken, NJ: Wiley.

I

Digital Content Creation

Creative Processes and Textual Reappropriations

1

Designing for Collaborative Crossmedia Creation

JONAS LÖWGREN

In the fall of 2004, Swedish producer and DJ Eric Prydz released the song *Call On Me* featuring Steve Winwood re-recording a sample from his own 1982 hit *Valerie*. The song made it to the top of the charts throughout Europe, partly thanks to the video Huse Monfaradi directed to go with the song. The video features an aerobics class of mostly women performing sexually suggestive gym routines in 1980s-inspired and more or less provocative outfits. The storyline in the video suggests a romance between the gym instructor and the sole man in the group. (To get the most out of this introduction, it might be worthwhile to watch the video before reading further. At the time of writing, a search for "Call On Me Eric Prydz" on YouTube.com will find the video.)

The video was exceptionally successful in terms of public demand—it was the most downloaded music video of all time in Australia; it won the mobile equivalent of a gold record in 2005, and it formed the basis for a feature-length DVD called *Pump It Up*, which features the dancers from *Call On Me* performing aerobics routines to popular dance music songs.

The video was also controversial due to its sexually explicit content—which led to the production of a censored version for daytime screenings—and its pornographic, somewhat Neanderthal-like gender perspective.

People in the Western world, notably those involved in various forms of amateur crossmedia production, noticed the controversy surrounding the *Call On Me* video, and some of them decided to take a stand. What is interesting for our purposes here is that they did so by creating mash-ups: satirical audio-video montages using references to the original video but subverting it in various ways.

Literally hundreds of *Call On Me* rip-offs, parodies, and mash-ups published on video sites such as YouTube and Google Video from 2005 onwards. Some were sophisticated, others crude; some were pure audio/video remixes, others featured new recorded material. The majority of them were designed as disapproving comments on the sexism and antiquated gender perspective of the original video.

For instance, there were several examples of gender swap where a group of men and a lone woman perform the aerobics routine from the original video in order to highlight the mono-gendered nature of the sexually suggestive motions and outfits in the original (see Figure 1).

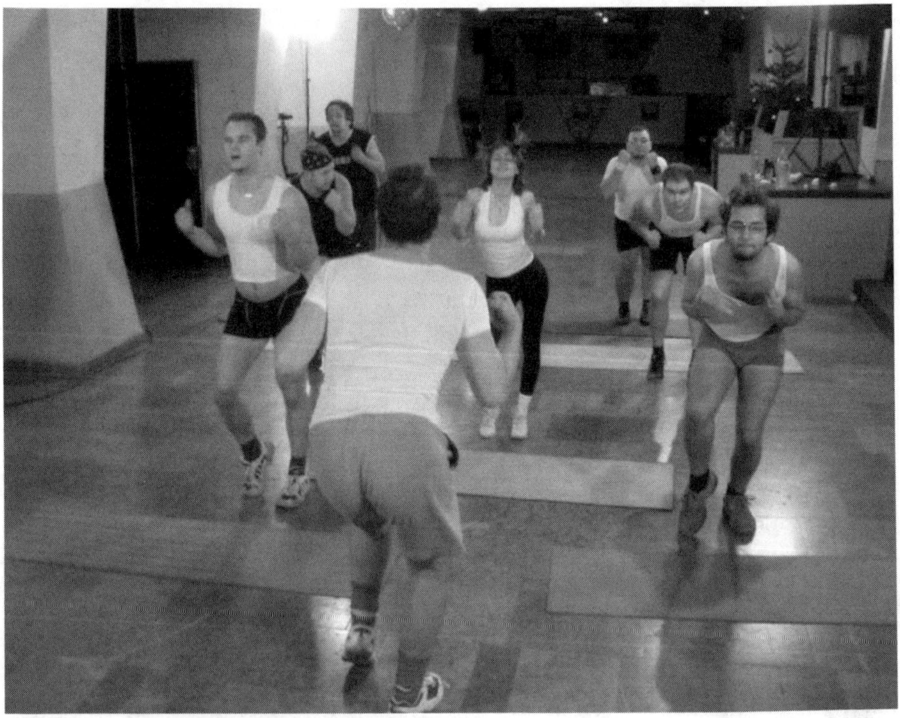

Figure 1: One of many Call On Me *gender-swap parodies, this one featuring students of Budapest Technical University.*

A more refined twist is illustrated in the *Call On Me/Brokeback Mountain* mash-up credited to "Director: Dan Colon" where the storyline is subverted into a lesbian romance between the gym instructor and one of the girls in the group.

And the list goes on, ranging from scatological audio additions to high-school performance remakes. A more exhaustive case study on the *Call On Me* mash-ups can be found in Löwgren (2007).

Choosing the *Call On Me* example to introduce this chapter was arbitrary—numerous examples of satirical mash-ups are circulating on the Internet—but the choice of satirical mash-ups was deliberate. As many observers have noted, we live in a time where the means for media production are more evenly distributed than ever before. Everybody with a personal computer and an Internet connection has the necessary tools to create and communicate their ideas; ideas that can also be communicated in media channels that only a decade ago were reserved for corporations and institutions.

We are talking about the phenomenon of debating a sexist music video by creating a mash-up video and distributing it in the very forum where the original video has its main circulation. The debate grows when more people add comments and their own mash-ups, which ultimately forms a social structure that is transient in its current topical focus but reasonably persistent in its underlying values. We may call it a structure of *collaborative crossmedia creation*.

The phenomenon and structures of collaborative crossmedia creation are arguably growing in importance, both as meaningful social practices engaging millions of people and as topics that deserve analytical treatment because they can teach us things about the new media in society. For this author, being a designer of digital products and services, collaborative crossmedia creation represents an emerging social practice to design for. Can my fellow designers and myself contribute positively to collaborative crossmedia creation and how it is practiced? Can we facilitate its introduction into new contexts? And how do we have to design in order to approach those goals?

The remainder of this chapter is devoted to such questions. After a discussion of the key differences between designing for collaborative crossmedia creation and more conventional design situations, I introduce three examples of designing for collaborative crossmedia creation. These examples address situations that are quite different in demographic as well as sociocultural terms, yet the designer experiences are reasonably coherent and certainly relevant beyond the individual cases. After a brief excursion into the more general question of what motivates people to participate in participatory media, the chapter closes with a summary of the key elements in a strategy of designing for collaborative crossmedia creation.

What Can a Designer Do?

This paper is written by an interaction designer who wants to design quality digital products and services. This task is challenging enough in traditional interaction design, yet somewhat manageable; we have explorative and empirical techniques to create a fairly reliable near-future image of our intended users, their wants and their needs, and the near-future use situations.

Designing for collaborative crossmedia creation is a completely different beast; the main difference is captured in the concept of *creative appropriation.*

It is certainly true in principle that no designer can control what happens to a product once it is released into actual use (Henderson & Kyng, 1991). Even products designed for highly specific uses end up being used in completely unanticipated ways—the texting (SMS) function of mobile phones is an obvious example. (As most of the readers undoubtedly know, the Short Message Service was originally conceived of as a protocol for the telecom network to send notifications to cell phone users, e.g., to indicate a waiting voicemail message.)

Some designers and design theorists see this as a problem to be attacked with new methodology, whereas for others it is merely a reflection of the nature of design, which is always about envisioning possible futures that can never be accurately predicted, only nudged in different directions. "[T]he effect of designing is to initiate change in man-made things," as Jones (1970, 1992) puts it in his seminal tome on design methodology.

The domain of collaborative crossmedia creation, however, is particularly challenging in this respect. The existing creative culture is more or less based on an ethos of taking existing tools and infrastructures, as well as "content," and combining them in new ways for new communicative purposes. There are strong historical connections to hacker cultures and open-source values, as seen in contemporary examples such as the Creative Commons movement as well as in older expressive practices such as *machinima.*

The practice of creating machinima draws upon the emergence of first-person shooter (FPS) computer games and has been around for as long as the games themselves. Simply put, the idea is to use the software created by the game producers for a completely different purpose, namely to produce animated films. The first examples of machinima film were created by people of high technical skill—since the first game engines had to be hacked in quite complicated ways in order to produce films—and generally drew on the aesthetic contrast between the hard-coded features of the game engine (character appearance and motions, props, settings, etc.) and the stories of the created films (see Figure 2).

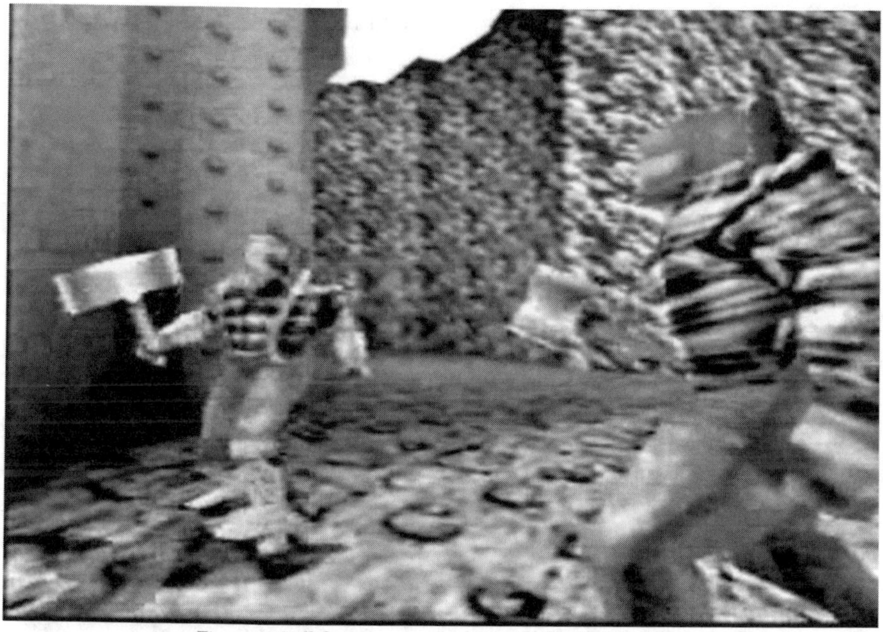

Figure 2: Still from Apartment Huntin' *by the ILL Clan.*

Game producers noted the creative energy of the machinima communities and responded by gradually opening their engines and providing tools geared more towards machinima production, culminating in the "game" *The Movies* by Lionhead Studios from 2005, which is, strictly speaking, not a game but rather a machinima production environment. The technical skill threshold was lowered accordingly and, quite predictably, the first machinima production to reach worldwide attention and prime media coverage was *The French Democracy*, a political piece on the socio-economic situation of immigrants and refugees in Paris. It was produced by Alex Chan (a.k.a. Koulamata) as a comment on the 2005 civil unrest of France, only a few weeks after *The Movies* was released, and is regarded by mainstream culture critics as an important step for machinima from computer-game in-jokes to contemporary issues and was compared by one critic with Mathieu Kassovitz's 1995 film *La Haine* rather than to previous machinima classics such as *Red vs. Blue* (Lee, 2006). The most important critical remarks, however, concern the obvious dissonance between the message of *The French Democracy* and the affordances of the production tool, which was clearly designed for a lighter style of film-making (see Figure 3).

What the practice of machinima illustrates so well—from making a lumberjack knock on a door by attacking it with his axe to making a wooden shack in the forest stand in for a power station in suburban Paris where two immigrant boys are killed—is how existing tools, technologies, and infrastructures are appropriated for communicative and expressive purposes way beyond what their designers might have envisioned. This kind of creative appropriation is the rule rather than the exception when it comes to the cultures of collaborative crossmedia creation.

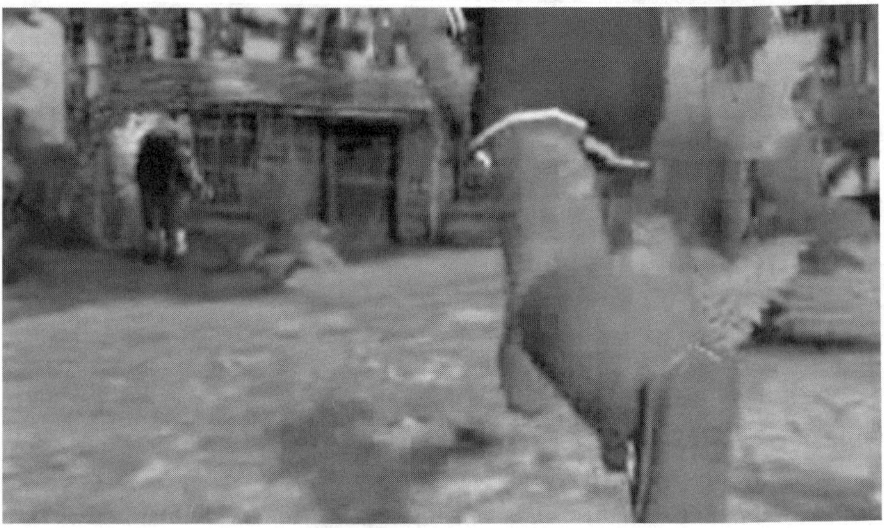

Figure 3: Still from The French Democracy.

Experimenting with the Mechanisms of Participatory Media

The "new media" with its increasingly even distribution of means for production and distribution, and hence a decreasingly clear boundary between producers and consumers, may be called *participatory media*. We have pointed out that the cultures of the participatory media are marked strongly by creative appropriation; it is also straightforward to establish that people's engagement in the participatory media is fundamentally social in its nature.

These two factors together suggest that the task of designing products and services for collaborative crossmedia creation must be understood as an ongoing process, a continuous interplay between "designers" and "users." In such processes, users contribute by acting out their insider knowledge of the practices constituting the creative communities they belong to. By participating in the design processes, users gain inspiration and means for new directions of collaborative crossmedia creation. Designers, on the other hand, contribute knowledge of participatory media tools and infrastructures and their social outcomes. What they can take away from the process, if they are looking carefully for it, are insights into the mechanisms of participatory media in actual use.

My colleagues and I have engaged in a number of such design projects, intended to initiate change in real participatory-media settings and, at the same time, help us learn more about the relations between new media products and services and their creative appropriation and use. In this section, I will summarize a few of those experiments with a focus on our insights into the mechanisms of participatory media.

Avatopia: Building a Community for Societal Change

The *Avatopia* project (Gislén & Löwgren, 2002; Gislén, Löwgren, & Myrestam, 2008) was initiated in 2001 as a collaboration between Animationens Hus, the Interactive Institute, the Swedish public-service TV broadcaster SVT, and a few other partners. The aim of the project was to create a voice in the public debate for young teenagers with the urge to change society for the better.

The project had two starting points. First, we realized that in order to approach the aim and build the discussion of what "changing society for the better" really means into the project itself, we would have to employ a deeply participatory design process. Second, we decided that the main media channels would be broadcast TV and the interactive web. The overall crossmedia concept was a spiral, where a small community would do things together on the web, and the community's actions would be disseminated to a much larger audience through broadcast TV, thus motivating new web community members to join as well as providing a channel to the public debate on societal change.

Throughout 2002, several task forces of handpicked teenagers worked with researchers and designers to develop a web-based avatar world for creative and communicative collaboration, the TV format, and the norms and practices of the Avatopia community. Here are some of the key decisions.

- The web forum would have to be highly visual to provide material for TV broadcast; the direction of a 3D avatar world was chosen.
- The avatar architecture would allow for collaborative animation tools even at the phone-modem bandwidths prevalent in domestic Internet connections at the time.
- The community would run crossmedia events to guide the use of the ani-

mation tools in the direction of, e.g., societal satire and commentary.

- The Avatopia community would be built from a seed of four mentor characters: people who had participated in the whole design process and who would be introduced to the TV audience through a series of trailers before launch, where the mentors would act as change agents together with other young people across Sweden. After launch, the mentors would be highly visible and active in the community, instilling Avatopia values by example rather than by rules.
- The connection from the web forum to broadcast TV would be performed by a staff editor at SVT, using the web forum as the field of journalistic inquiry and coverage (including reports, avatar interviews, live hearings, animation festivals, etc.). It would also be the responsibility of the staff editor to report in broadcast TV on real-world outcomes of Avatopia-initiated actions.

Avatopia was built in 2002–2003 and launched on the web and broadcast television in September 2003 (refer to Figure 4a, 4b, and 4c). It developed according to plan during the fall of 2003 and approached a point of maturity where formal longitudinal evaluations were planned to start. Unfortunately, the operation of Avatopia was linked to a small running cost for web hosting and a part-time SVT staff member. When SVT decided on a previously unanticipated budget cut by the end of

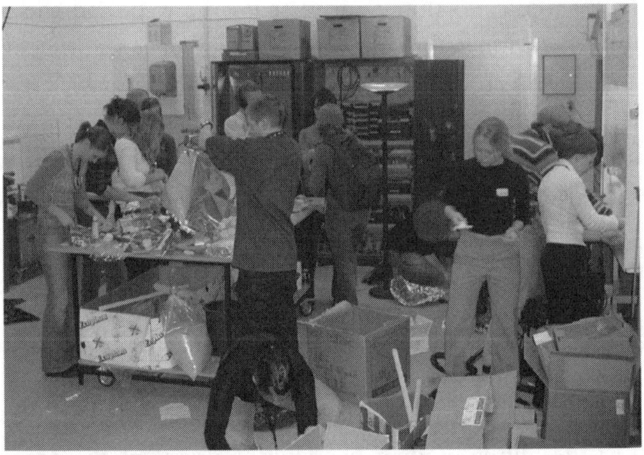

Figure 4a: A participatory design workshop.

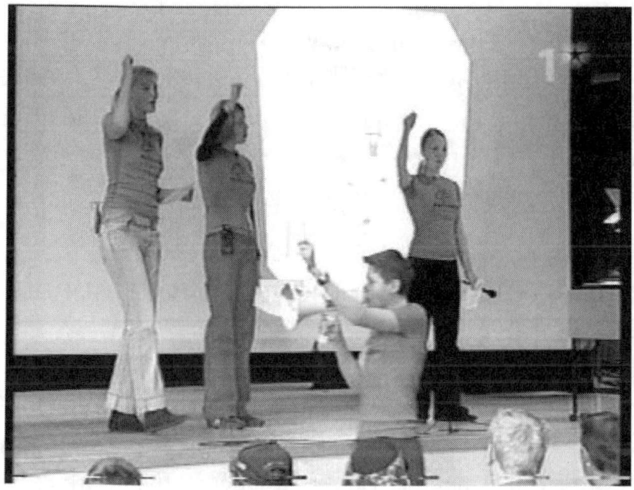

Figure 4b: A still from one of the TV trailers.

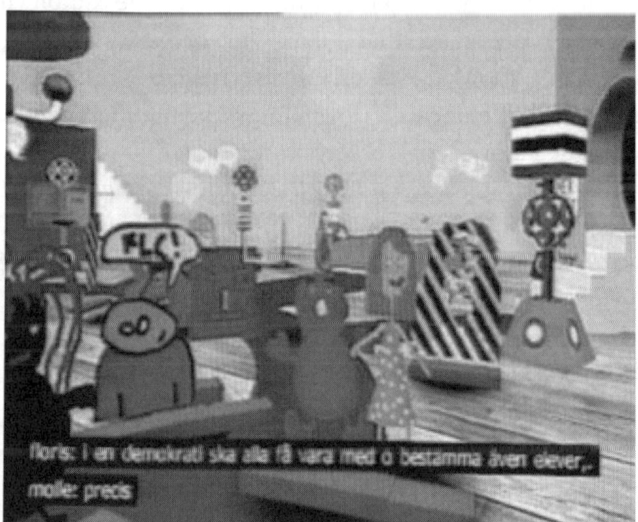

Figure 4c: A screenshot from the web forum.

2003, Avatopia was closed since it could not be defended as a core business activity.

In spite of the premature termination of the project, we had enough informal data to draw two conclusions. First, the notion of a crossmedia spiral was a workable way to conceptualize the relation between narrow and broad media channels. Second, we concluded that it is possible, albeit quite costly, to seed a collaborative community through a participatory design process.

Kliv: Nurturing the Management of Professional Knowledge in Health Care

The Kliv project (Björgvinsson & Hillgren, 2004), which ran 2001–2003, can be understood as an exercise in knowledge management in practice. Intensive care units in hospitals rely on a staff member's ability to operate the health care equipment. This ability is not evenly distributed, which may cause problems if, say, there is nobody on duty who knows how to use a certain kind of machine when a patient needs that particular machine. Moreover, the knowledge in question is experiential rather than formal, which means there needs to be an ongoing dialogue among staff members on new insights into better ways of using the equipment. The pace and organization of work is such that the dialogue necessary for maintaining and developing the shared knowledge is sometimes hampered.

Designers and PhD students Erling Björgvinsson and Per-Anders Hillgren entered into a participatory design process with the staff of the intensive care unit at Malmö University Hospital, examining the nature of professional knowledge in intensive care and exploring new ways of maintaining it. The tangible outcome of the project was a system where knowledgeable staff members could record short instructional videos on the use of certain equipment, and those videos would be tied to the equipment by barcode printouts and accessed later through PDAs extended with barcode readers (refer to Figure 5a and 5b). Other aspects of the system include organizational routines for reviewing and approving new instruction videos.

The relevance of Kliv as an example of collaborative crossmedia creation does not lie in its technical or organizational design, however. What makes it interesting for our purposes here is how it came to be used and what happened when variations of the idea were tested at other hospitals.

By the formal end of the project, the system was in place and a number of instructional videos had been produced. In subsequent years, it turned out that the system continued to be used—instruction videos were referred to as needed, their

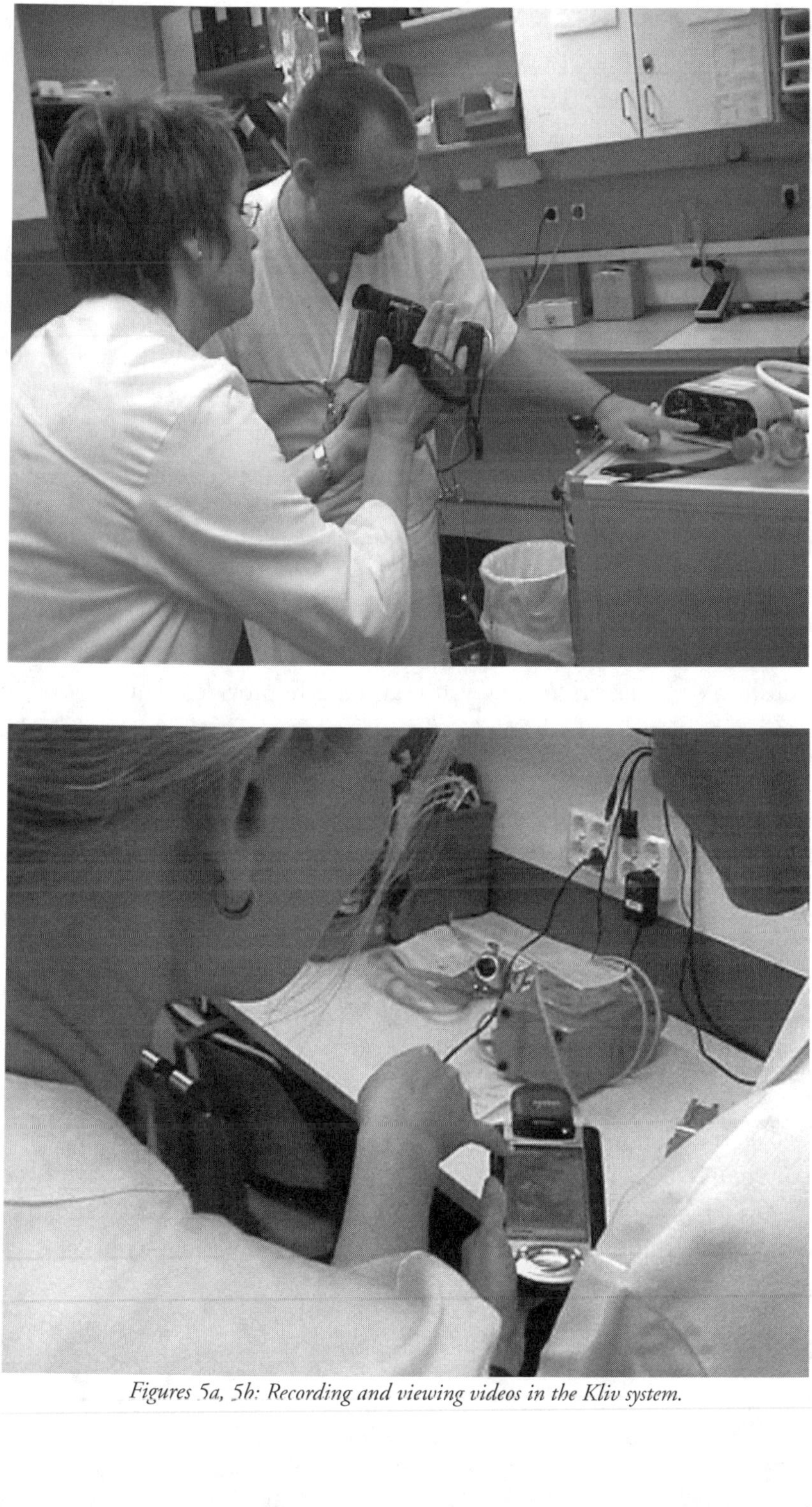

Figures 5a, 5b: Recording and viewing videos in the Kliv system.

contents were debated among the staff, new videos were made, and old videos were revised as the shared knowledge of the staff grew. In short, it worked the way every knowledge-management system is supposed to work (but not many do). In 2004, the system was nominated by the intensive-care unit staff to the national UsersAward competition and won first prize. The written nomination and the jury motivation for the prize did not mention the designers, however, which indicates the degree to which ownership of the system and the practices related to it were taken over by the medical staff.

The success of Kliv attracted the attention of health care administrations in counties outside Malmö. Unfortunately, in some cases it seems the technical system structure attracted the most interest. In one hospital, a system was built like Kliv with a video database and PDAs with barcode readers. It was decided that the instruction videos should be produced by the hospital's information office, which commissioned doctors to write medically correct scripts and actors to record the instructions in pedagogically correct ways. Needless to say, the resulting system was never used much.

For our present purposes, what the experiences from Kliv show is the possibility to form a persistent community around collaborative crossmedia creation, even dealing with matters as grave as life and death, provided that it is built on a foundation of shared meaning and authenticity.

Malmö New Media Living Lab and RGRA: Crossmedia Strategies

The final example in this section is an ongoing project, structured as a collaborative process mainly involving researchers, designers, media producers, and amateur creators.

In late 2007, Malmö New Media Living Lab was inaugurated with the mission of doing design-oriented research in collaboration with lead users and lead practices in new media. The lab is hosted by Inkonst, a center for young people's cultural activities in Malmö, together with Malmö University. Partners in the lab include companies in media and telecom as well as RGRA (The Voice and Face of the Streets), a movement aimed at involving young people in democratic processes and societal change through music, street art, and other urban-cultural forms of expression.

The work of the Living Lab began with concept development work for new kinds of new-media products and services related to Inkonst and its activities, including its club hosting. One concept emerging from the creative work was to offer music produced by RGRA members to passengers on city buses using Bluetooth transmission to cell phones. The idea was tested and found technically feasible, but it was also found that an unknown source pushing media onto your cell phone could be perceived as threatening.

At the Malmö City Festival in August 2008, the Living Lab organized live webcasting from five cell-phone cameras. RGRA people used the opportunity for local exposure in acting as reporters for the webcast.

A national public-service TV show is currently being planned, with RGRA spokesman Behrang Miri as the host and drawing on several innovative new-media concepts from the Living Lab to illuminate issues of segregation and urban culture in contemporary Sweden.

Finally, a project is underway in which the bus-music concept is deployed on Malmö city buses as a fully functional demonstrator, used by RGRA as a way to reach a larger audience. It is expected that the City Festival activities and broadcast TV presence will increase RGRA recognition to the level that its creative production will not be perceived as unknown by bus passengers, but rather as credible and desirable material.

To understand the point of this example, consider the Living Lab management as the designers and RGRA as the collaborative crossmedia creators. What the performed and planned activities above demonstrate is how several media channels are synchronized in order to approach RGRA's communicative goals. Specifically, the work of the Living Lab and RGRA so far has combined avant-garde live performances (clubs at Inkonst), mainstream public events and webcasting (Malmö City Festival), TV broadcasting and place-casting (the planned bus-music service).

Why Do People Participate in Participatory Media?

Before concluding with a discussion of how designers can in fact support collaborative crossmedia creation, it might be worthwhile to touch upon the more general question of why people participate in participatory media. Why do people:

- Upload their music to MySpace and their pictures to Flickr?
- Share BitTorrents of hand-ripped TV sitcoms?
- Contribute news reports to CurrentTV?
- Scribble a message on the palm of their hand, film it, and upload it to Youtube in response to MadV's initial *One World* video?
- Create dozens of machinima episodes?
- Talk for hours on Facebook with people they have never met?

- Micro-blog on Twitter during the train ride to work?

Not all kinds of participatory media participation fall within the realm of collaborative crossmedia creation, but a significant part does—as indicated by the examples above. Our experiments, together with the growing literature on online communication (Bolter & Grusin, 1999; Jenkins, 2006; Lunenfeld, 1999; Mayer, 1999; Porter, 2008; Wellman, 1999), form the basis for a number of insights, which can be summarized as follows:

> First, people generally participate in participatory media because of their urges to *belong*, to *express* themselves creatively, to establish *identity* and *status*, and to *influence* others and society. There is also a (highly legitimate) role in the participatory media that we might call the spectator—including lurkers in online fora as well as leeches in filesharing networks—who is driven primarily by individual motives and by the pleasure of gawking at strangers. This role, however, represents less active participation, and I will leave it out of the further discussion as its significance for collaborative crossmedia creation is of a more indirect nature.

Belonging (in the sense of sharing information, meaning, and values) has always been the main factor driving mass media consumption, but the participatory media add another dimension since the communication around the shared matter takes place in the medium itself. The way that belonging plays out in the participatory media is generally that a communication platform such as Facebook serves as the substrate for thousands of social constellations, larger and smaller, with various degrees of cohesion and persistence. Facebook and similar services are sometimes called "communities," which is largely incorrect. More accurately, they are infrastructures hosting a large number of communities or *tribes*, in the words of Maffesoli's (1996) sociological analysis of the breakup of mass culture (see also Godin, 2008, for a more contemporary discussion of emergent tribal structures and, specifically, their implications for consumerism and participatory media).

As the Kliv example and its failed rip-offs demonstrate, a high degree of shared meaning and shared experience is required for sustainable management of professional knowledge in the workplace. Similarly, Avatopia and Living Lab/RGRA are clear examples of tribal structures where members are prepared to commit themselves and their time for the benefit of other tribe members, fueled by a sense of shared concerns and goals.

Creative expression is in one sense a self-indulgent activity, but when the results are shared through participatory media, it is clear there are social motives at play. However, we must not jump to the conclusion that creative expression is done only for the eyes of others. The blogosphere is an interesting example here. A calculation of the number of blog posts published per day divided by the number of blog posts read per day would surely yield a ratio showing that average blog authors write for their own sake more than for their audiences. Knowing that the blog post can theoretically be seen by a billion people may be part of the attraction; the reality of the blogosphere anatomy is rather that it consists of millions of little tribes tied together by blog rings and RSS feeds, plus a few "massmedia blogs" read by large audiences. We should not forget that blogs started as web diaries, which are ultimately self-indulgent, and they remain diaries for many blog authors. For further consideration of the individual/social dimension of expression, a particularly illuminating analysis is offered by Gibbins and Reimer (1999), who maintain that expressivism is one of the key traits of postmodern life in relation to belonging as well as identity and influence.

Our own work demonstrates the significance of creative expression quite clearly: RGRA members engage in music-making, street art, and creative writing rather than in local political organizations and letters to newspaper editors; Avatopia members create animation, art, and public interventions rather than writing petitions; in the Kliv project, videomaking is seen as something more creative and inspirational than traditional knowledge-transfer activities, such as internal training, and that the videos are assessed by peers not only on factual veracity but also as communicative media products (Hillgren, 2006).

The need to work on our **identity**, how we are perceived by others, is a main force behind our engagement in fashion, public behavior, play, and many other activities. The participatory media are no exception in this regard. What makes them stand out is that they make it relatively easy to develop experimental identities unlike the one invoked by our physical appearance and demeanor (Turkle, 1995). Being judged by what you think and do, not by what you look like, has been a foundational value of the hacker cultures for many years (Blankenship, 1986)—and this is no coincidence. The relation to belonging is quite clear, as one of the functions of an identity is to identify one's own community affinities.

The openness of identity in the participatory media also has strong implications for status and the possibility to reach positions of power in particular tribes without being typecast by physical and material status conditions. Many tribes in the participatory media are meritocracies, which means that your position is determined by how good you are at performing what the tribe finds to be core activities. This holds equally for collaborative crossmedia creation, where your status in a particular tribe can be based on the quality of your creations.

A final reason for participating in participatory media, as well as for any type of public discourse, is the urge to **influence others** and to **influence society**. Having a trustworthy identity and adequate status are key preconditions for exerting influence within your tribe; external influence sometimes requires other strategies as well.

In our work, the social dynamics of identity and status in relation to influence are prevalent. For instance, the way in which the Avatopia design and launch process was set up—where key members of the design teams were introduced to larger audiences through the TV trailers and then assumed roles as mentors in the web community—was all about establishing the identity and status of the mentors in the community to the point where they could impart community values to newcomers. A similar strategy is illustrated in the way in which RGRA uses multiple coordinated channels for its work. The Kliv project demonstrates quite clearly the differences between a video made by a well-known colleague talking to her peers, and a video written by an authority and recorded by an actor. To paraphrase Argyris and Schön (1974), espoused-status and status-in-use have different meanings in any tribe.

How Can We Design for People to Collaborate and Create?

The work reported here suggests there are three areas through which the designer has the power to facilitate people's collaborative crossmedia creation: crossmedia infrastructures, expressive tools, and tribe values.

Designing a **crossmedia infrastructure** for collaborative creation entails stringing multiple media channels together over time, technically as well as organizationally. The two main channels of Avatopia are the avatar world and broadcast TV; stringing them together involved organizational work such as appointing a staff editor doing journalistic work in the avatar world and reporting it on TV, as well as production-related issues such as finding workable practices for broadcasting watchable TV from an avatar world. The ongoing Living Lab/RGRA work illustrates how the channel-mix changes over time as the crossmedia infrastructure evolves organically, from avant-garde live performances to mainstream public events to webcasting to TV broadcasting to place-casting.

Expressive tools sometimes entail designing custom means to make collaborative creation possible, such as the animation tools of the Avatopia avatar world. In other situations, expressive tools are already available, and the task for the designer is to identify them and make them work with the infrastructure. For example, the whole Kliv project was built from off-the-shelf components (consumer camcorders, standard barcode readers, PDA computers), and the designers found a way to put them into play within a specific process and infrastructure.

When it comes to **tribe values**, it would be pretentious to use the word "design." Here, the designer is rather a provider of initial directions and a facilitator of tribal processes being executed by the participants. In Avatopia, the act of design was to formulate the public-service intention of giving young teenagers a voice in societal change and to find the people to seed the community. What happened after that may have been facilitated by the designers, but it certainly wasn't designed in the conventional sense of the word. Similarly, the key design decision of the ongoing Living Lab/RGRA work was to initiate collaboration with RGRA and other partners based on shared values and goals for societal change, thus laying out an initial direction in which to channel subsequent efforts and resources.

A useful metaphor for understanding this conclusion might be to think of designing for collaborative crossmedia creation as the production of an improvisation performance. The producer sets the stage, provides the props, and hires the actors. Due to their affordances, the set and the props make it easier for the actors to do certain things and more difficult to do other things. The set and props guide an actor's actions and suggest initial directions. Selecting the actors to hire is based on what the producers knows about the actors, such as personalities and talents. The whole tone of the performance is influenced by the casting. But when the lights come on at the opening night, the producer can only sit back with the rest of the audience and see how the performance comes out.

It should also be noted for completeness that some recent work in interaction design theory is proposing similar perspectives also in design fields other than collaborative crossmedia creation. See, for example, the notion of emergent interaction formulated by Matthews, Stienstra, and Djajadiningrat (2008) in connection with their work on design for children's play.

To summarize our insights: In order to facilitate collaborative crossmedia creation, a designer can create infrastructures and tools and seed a tribe based on certain values. But the outcomes can never be "designed." In fact, it seems to make most sense not to think of outcomes at all, but rather think of ongoing processes, which the designer can influence through small interventions in the form of infrastructural features, tool capabilities, and directional values.

Acknowledgement

We are deeply indebted to all the young activists, health care professionals, and grassroots culture emancipators who have chosen to collaborate with my colleagues and myself over our years of crossmedia experimentations. None of this work and none of our insights would have been possible without you.

The project examples reported above were supported by research grants from Ungdomsrådet, Stiftelsen Framtidens Kultur, KK-stiftelsen and Vinnova.

References

Argyris, C., & Schön, D. (1974). *Theory in practice: Increasing professional effectiveness.* San Francisco: Jossey-Bass.

Björgvinsson, E., & Hillgren, P.-A. (2004). On-the-spot experiments within health care. In A. Clement & P. van den Besselaer (Eds.), *Proceedings of the eighth conference on participatory design* (PDC 04): Artful integration: interweaving media, materials, and practices (pp. 93–101). Retrieved January 16, 2009, from http://www.acm.org/dl

Blankenship, L. a.k.a. The Mentor (1986). Hacker's manifesto. *Phrack 1*(7), 3. Retrieved January 15, 2009, from http://www.phrack.org/issues.html?issue=7&id=3#article

Bolter, J., & Grusin, R. (1999). *Remediation: understanding new media.* Cambridge, MA: MIT Press.

Gibbins, J., & Reimer, B. (1999). *The politics of postmodernity: An introduction to contemporary politics and culture.* London: Sage.

Gislén, Y., & Löwgren, J. (2002). Avatopia: Planning a community for non-violent societal action. *Digital Creativity 13*(1), 23–37.

Gislén, Y., Löwgren, J., & Myrestam, U. (2008). Avatopia: A crossmedia community for societal action. *Personal & ubiquitous computing 12*, 289–297.

Godin, S. (2008). *Tribes: We need you to lead us.* London: Piatkus.

Henderson, A., & Kyng, M. (1991). There is no place like home: Continuing design in use. In J. Greenbaum & M. Kyng (Eds.), *Design at work: Cooperative design of computer systems,* Hillsdale, NJ: Lawrence Erlbaum, , pp. 219–240.

Hillgren, P.-A. (2006*). Ready-made-media-actions: Lokal produktion och användning av audiovisuella medier inom hälso-och sjukvården.* PhD dissertation 2006:07, Blekinge Institute of Technology. In Swedish. Retrieved January 16, 2009, from http://www.bth.se/fou

Jenkins, H. (2006). *Convergence culture: Where old and new media collide.* New York: New York University Press.

Jones, J. C. (1992). *Design methods* (2nd ed.). New York: Van Nostrand Reinhold. (Original work published 1970)

Lee, J. (2006). A different kind of French Revolution. Retrieved January 15, 2009, from http://www.popmatters.com/multimedia/reviews/f/french-democracy.shtml

Löwgren, J. (2007). Mashing the materials of digital culture: A case study of *Call On Me* videos. Retrieved January 15, 2009, from http://webzone.k3.mah.se/k3jolo/callOnMe/

Lunenfeld, P. (Ed.). (1999). *The digital dialectic: New essays on new media.* Cambridge, MA: MIT Press.

Maffesoli, M. (1996). *The time of the tribes: The decline of individualism in mass society* (D. Smith, Trans.). London: Sage. (Original work published 1988)

Matthews, B., Stienstra, M., & Djajadiningrat, T. (2008). Emergent interaction: Creating spaces for play. *Design Issues 24*(3), 58–71.

Mayer, P. (Ed.). (1999). *Computer media and communication: A reader.* Oxford: Oxford University Press.

Porter, J. (2008). *Designing for the social web.* Indianapolis, IN: New Riders.

Turkle, S. (1995). *Life on the screen: Identity in the age of the Internet.* New York: Simon & Schuster.

Wellman, B. (Ed.). (1999). *Networks in the global village: Life in contemporary communities.* Boulder, CO: Westview Press.

Web sites for organizations mentioned in the chapter

Creative Commons: http://www.creativecommons.org, accessed January 15, 2009.

Inkonst: http://www.inkonst.com, accessed January 15, 2009.

Malmö New Media Living Lab: http://malmolivinglab.se, accessed January 15, 2009.

RGRA: http://www.rgra.se, accessed January 15, 2009.

UsersAward: http://www.usersaward.se, accessed January 15, 2009.

2

Wiki as Semiospheric Text

Students' Meaning-Making Practices as Authors and Consumers of Digital Texts

WILMA CLARK

Young people's increasingly complex interactions with digital technologies in and beyond the school setting (Luckin et al., 2008) are generating a range of overlapping boundary spaces in the technology landscapes of young learners (Clark et al., 2009). The turn to complexity in the educational domain raises questions about the potential recontextualization of school culture generated by student technology-mediated, boundary-crossing activity in their authoring and consumption of digital texts in the school setting.

In recent years, there has been much debate around the use of digital technologies in the school setting, with topics ranging from digital technology's contribution as a tool for learning and collaborative knowledge building (Désilets & Paquet, 2006; Richardson, 2006) to digital technology's identification as a platform for new media literacies (Buckingham, 2007b; Livingstone, 2007). The participatory web (Jenkins et al., 2006) is reshaping ideas of what it means to be an author or consumer of content in the constantly evolving world of digital texts as a result of which new and complex practices and processes are emerging around young people's use of digital technologies.

Some researchers suggest that new developments in the use of digital technologies have rendered digital technology as a significant part of young people's everyday lives—from mobile phones to participation in online social networks (LSE,

2006; Boyd, 2007; Green and Hannon, 2007; Marchant, 2007). Other commentators have focused on the non-neutrality of technology (Bowers, 1988; Zhao et al., 2002) and the need for teachers and educational institutions to take into account the mediating role of technology in the "cultural milieu" that is educational practice (Bowers, 1998). In this complex web of digital cultures it is critical to understand the implications of the learner's digital worlds and the meaning-making potentials these worlds generate. Issues and ideas around the notion of the learner's learning context (Luckin, 2006) are becoming increasingly relevant as advances in technology reshape traditional learning spaces and literacies (Jewitt, 2006) with learners, teachers, and the institutions they belong to looking beyond the physical and pedagogic spaces of the classroom to contiguous contexts and cultures, in particular those mediated by digital technologies.

Previous research has turned to activity theory (Engeström, 1987), semiotics (Kress, 2004, 2007), multimodality (Jewitt, 2006, 2008; Kress & Bezemer, 2008) and cultural studies (Young, 2005; Buckingham, 2007a) as a means of exploring learning with digital technologies with a particular focus on interaction, meaning-making, and cultural contexts. However, the multidimensional, emergent nature of current technologies suggests that a more complex modelling system is needed to facilitate an understanding of the contexts and cultures at play in the technology-mediated classroom. This chapter addresses this challenge by applying a *semiospheric* approach to student boundary-crossing activities in the use of a wiki and YouTube in the UK secondary-school science classroom.

In the section that follows, the concept of *semiosphere* is outlined; it is discussed why and how it forms a useful system for modelling learner interactions with digital technologies across disparate contexts and cultures.

A Semiospheric Approach

The notion of *semiosphere* was first coined by the Russian semiotician Yuri Lotman in 1984 and defined by him as "that semiotic space which allows culture to dialogue with itself and to generate new meanings" (Lotman, 1990, 2005). The *semiospheric* framework is conceptual and focuses primarily on spatial relationships and meaning-making processes. The *semiosphere*, portrayed as the semiotic space of culture is further demarcated by the additional concepts of *core*, *periphery*, and the *notion of boundary*. Lotman's view of the meaning spaces of culture is an open, holistic one, and his framing of the concept of *semiosphere* is used to emphasize the notion of a semiotic continuum characterized by properties of continuity and discontinuity in semiotic space. As such, every culture comprises not only its own internal space but also its relation to external space or extra-culture. In this sense, the *semiosphere* may be regarded as being simultaneously local and global.

The perceived duality of the *semiospheric* approach (1) generates a boundary between the internal and external semiotic space created in the meeting of at least two contexts or cultures, and (2) maps the trajectory of meaning across semiotic space as communication traverses *core*, *periphery*, and *boundary*. As meaning flows across these spatial demarcations of the *semiosphere*, the semiotic value of the signs and representations utilized by participants in their negotiation of disparate sign systems (e.g., betwixt classroom and World Wide Web) are constantly remediated and reframed. It is through this lens that recent commentators have described Lotman's *semiosphere* as "the space of meaning-generation" (Kull, 2005) and as "a system that mediates the individual's relationship to their context" (Papastergiadis, 2002). The notion of context is particularly important for our understanding of students' meaning-making practices in their multi-discursive negotiation of curriculum, school, and digital cultures.

Lotman's conceptual framework is particularly useful in terms of its ability to demarcate the disparate meaning spaces at work in the technology-mediated classroom. In the empirical study discussed in this chapter, for example, students' interactions with a class wiki and their boundary-crossing activities as authors and consumers of digital texts are examined. In the study, the concept of *semiosphere* serves as a framing mechanism with which to map the proximity of students' meaning-making practices both to the *core* semiotic values of the science classroom as a particular knowledge domain and to any trajectory away from this *core* setting towards other *peripheral* values, e.g., those associated with non-contiguous technology-mediated contexts and cultures such as popular music, which do not sit easily with the established cultures of school or science classroom.

The study draws on two sets of data: a class wiki and a transcript of a video recording in which students' discuss a showcase of their wiki work at the end of an e-learning project. These data were used to explore the following research questions:

- What role do wikis play in students' contextualisation of knowledge in and beyond the school science classroom?
- What are the implications of "open learning spaces" such as wikis for the development of digital literacy practices in schools?

Framing Contexts and Cultures as Meaning Spaces

When applying a *semiospheric* lens to the meaning-making activity of participants in the empirical study outlined in this chapter, the background to the study forms a useful frame for understanding some key principles of Lotman's conceptualisation of *semiosphere*. For example, if the science curriculum and the science classroom as the principal location of learning are viewed as *core*, the introduction of the wiki may be viewed as a *peripheral* event in the sense that it bridges the internal space of the classroom and the external spaces of the World Wide Web (virtual) and other (physical) spaces inhabited by learners (e.g., the home), which leads to a resemiotisation of the *notion of boundary* as a hybrid space characterized by potentiality and alterity, i.e., open to alternative influences and audiences, which may be distinguished from the traditional closed and contained audience and purposes of the school setting.

Background

The study discussed in this chapter seeks to investigate students' meaning-making practices as authors and consumers of digital texts in a UK secondary-school science classroom. The study involved 25 11-year-old students (all female) and their teacher following the Key Stage 3 Science curriculum (aged 11–14). The study explored students' use of a wiki and related technologies in an e-learning project on the topic of fossil fuels.

The e-learning project was designed by the class teacher and was based on an existing scheme of work (curriculum plan) for Key Stage 3 Science. Beyond this, the traditional setup of the science class was remediated by the class teacher with a rearrangement of timetabling from a sequence of individual 50-minute lessons to a block of five. A shift from individual to collaborative and co-operative learning in self-selected groups facilitated rather than led by the teacher was also instigated. The focal point for most of the learning activity also shifted from classroom to wiki and from teacher to students.

Students' interactions with the wiki were analyzed on three levels: (1) negotiation, (2) consumption, and (3) production. The first—**negotiation**—focused on student interactions with the wiki as a cross-contextual learning space (e.g., between home and school, between curriculum and popular culture). The second—**consumption**—focused on student response to teacher-, other-, self-, and peer-generated texts and the meaning-making practices the students engaged in around these texts in the context of the science classroom and the e-learning project. The third—**production**—focused on student access to, selection, use, and remediation of a range of available digital texts and students' representations of fossil fuels as a topic of scientific interest. In the sections that follow, each of these levels is analyzed and discussed through the lens of Lotman's *semiosphere*.

Wiki as Semiosphere

Students' initial interactions with the class wiki occurred through a teacher's wiki project page (Figure 1). This page closely mirrored the school's scheme of work for Key Stage 3 Science, in particular, the topic area of fossil fuels and renewable energy. In addition to a clearly elaborated scientific knowledge domain, the scheme of work also suggests that the teacher draws on a distinct set of "semiotic strategies" (Klamer and van Heusden, 1996) with which to contextualize student learning based around learning objectives, learning activities, learning outcomes, and available resources. Activities incorporated in the scheme of work included a mixture of individual, collaborative, oral, written, audiovisual, practical and digital work. In this chapter, the impact of the "semiotic strategies" or "educational and cultural capital" (Buckingham and Willett, 2006) of the science classroom on the meaning potentials available to students are examined through the lens of Lotman's concept of *semiosphere*.

The Role of the Teacher in the Wiki

In the initial session of the e-learning project, the teacher introduced students to her wiki project page, linking content to curriculum goals, with a particular focus on activities, objectives, resources, and learning outcomes.

> T: If you've got onto the wiki site...you'll find an e-learning project ....You'll find an outline there of what you're going to do and what you're going to learn and there's a list of resources.

Here, the teacher works to reinforce the *core* semiotic values of the science classroom, presenting the wiki as a formal learning space designed to facilitate navigation of curriculum goals. This transformation of the e-learning project (in previous years delivered as a slideshow presentation) to a wiki-based project makes a significant impact on the learning space. The scheme of work is now explicitly presented in an open, holistic way that enables students to see and revisit the overarching narrative of the learning context at a glance, albeit in a condensed form. Whilst the teacher's oral communication appears highly directive, the content of her wiki page invites a more participatory relationship in the construction of knowledge, with students actively encouraged to contribute and extend the knowledge base in what is now portrayed as a common, shared, learning space.

Through the use of such semiotic strategies by the teacher, the implicit boundaries between teaching and learning are made transparent and permeable as students are afforded the opportunity to become co-participants in the pedagogic narratives underpinning the learning context. For example, students are invited to "add your own relevant resources." The word "relevant" is, however, used to qualify the *core* values of the wiki as a meaning-making space attached to the science classroom. This, in effect, serves to position students as co-teachers and teacher as co-learner in the construction of shared scientific discourse.

There were some interesting contradictions between the teacher's perception of how students' *should* interact with the wiki and what they did in practice, marking a shift in semiotic value from *core* to *periphery* and a reconstitution of boundary spaces around students' (1) social interaction and (2) collaborative knowledge construction. In the initial stages of the project, for example, the teacher provided students with brief cues relating to their wiki-based activity.

> T: What you're going to do is work at your own pace, adding as much information as you can to these links, using all of the resources that are available to all of you and, collectively, you can build something really amazing.

These comments suggest that the teacher sees the student role as autonomous, participatory, collaborative, and resourceful. In *semiospheric* terms, the combined force of these pedagogic elements and the teacher's initial design and representations of curriculum within the wiki represent the *core* semiotic value framing student engagement with the e-learning project and the digital tools available to the student, i.e., these elements are presented in close proximity to the dominant cultural contexts of the science classroom and the academic practices associated with scientific investigation.

However, it is clear, even here, that the shift from physical to digital learning space has already generated a shift in semiotic value between the individual and the social and between notions of autonomy, authority, and audience. This is evident since the previously demarcated roles of teacher, student, and knowledge domain in the pre-wiki stage now encounter a blurring of the boundaries around roles and modes of participation both in relation to the wiki environment and the contiguous pedagogic space of the science classroom. Paradoxically, it is this blurring of boundaries that serves to illuminate the cultural complexity of the classroom, the non-neutrality of technology in pedagogic spaces and the challenges these elements pose for traditional perceptions of pedagogy and literacy that underpins the *semiospheric* exploration of student boundary-crossing activities as consumers and authors of digital texts explored in the remainder of this chapter.

Students as Consumers of Digital Texts

The analysis of student consumption of digital texts in the e-learning project focuses on the processes and practices students adopted in their negotiation of available resources. The data analyzed takes the form of observational notes, *ad hoc* discussions with students as they interact with the class wiki and other resources available on the World Wide Web, as well as student group project pages on the wiki. Findings from these data suggest that student consumption of digital texts fall into four categories:

- Teacher-generated: Materials provided or suggested by the teacher.
- Other-generated: Materials obtained via the web or other digital resource.
- Self-generated: Materials previously produced by students themselves.
- Peer-generated: Materials produced or suggested by peers.

Further analysis suggests that the consumption of self- and peer-generated texts tend to occur during the authoring phase of the project, whilst a focus on teacher- and other-generated texts occurred mostly in the earlier, consumption-oriented, stages of the project. In this section, student consumption of teacher- and other-generated texts is considered in more detail.

Teacher-Generated Texts

The *core* cultural context of the e-learning project on fossil fuels was framed by student consumption of the teacher's wiki project page. For example, the learning objectives derived from the scheme of work outlined in the introductory (Figure1) section of the teacher's wiki page framed the scope and thematic content of the enquiry.

In response to these learning objectives, students were required to contribute definitions of key terms and to supply descriptive examples about fossil fuels. Student response to these teacher-generated links was dominantly textual and brief; although, even here, there is evidence of a cross-cultural informality in one student's use of slang and a digital emoticon to indicate positivity. First defining scientifically "What a fossil fuel is," this student adds, as an example: "There is also oil. Oil rules." These additional elements are indicative of a boundary-slippage between the formal contexts of the science classroom and the perceived informalities of digital spaces.

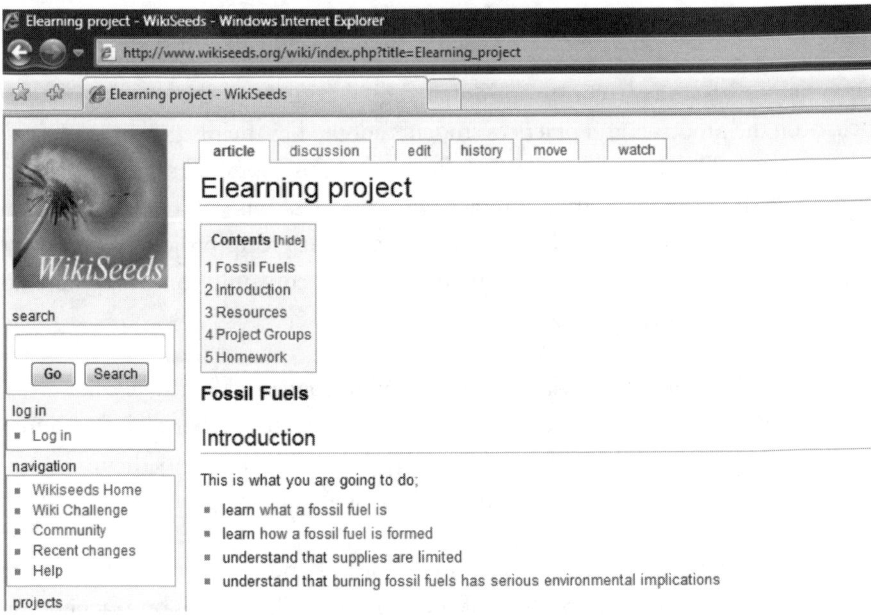

Figure 1: Learning objectives.

As also can be seen from this example, students did not wholly grasp the collaborative affordances of the wiki in this activity and rather than combining definitions, contributed individually and separately. Further, only a handful of students contributed to this space, despite the fact that an attempt to explain the notion of collaboration was made by the teacher beforehand.

> T: Can you see how it's a sharing of resources? We know who has done what, alright? So, it's not a question of, oh, I can't get credit for it because we're all sharing it, it's a question of pooling all our resources together…by putting all our work together, we all benefit from the sum of the parts.

It is possible that lack of student understanding of these learning objectives may be due to reasons highlighted by the teacher, namely, *lack of ownership* and/or *credit*. It is equally possible that the autonomy given to students led to their spending more time on their group project pages than on the individual and collaborative activities set up by the teacher. At the same time, this apparent hesitancy and lack of feeling for the collaborative and co-operative construction of knowledge suggests that issues around ownership, credit, and assessment are important boundary markers in student engagement with collaborative activities and that this is an area students sometimes find difficult to transcend in the school setting.

Another interesting factor in student consumption of teacher-generated material is the relationship between teacher talk and student comprehension of materials. For example, where alternative resources were referenced on the wiki but not explicitly discussed or referred to by the teacher, e.g., a website containing useful and relevant resources on a range of alternative fuels for school-age learners specifically targeted at the Key Stage 3 curriculum, students ignored these, resorting instead to a set of already-established semiotic strategies linked to their existing experience of digital culture and individually established repertoires for the appropriation of other-generated texts and web-based texts in particular.

Other-Generated Texts

In the student consumption of other-generated texts, the first port of call for the majority of students was Google, closely followed by Wikipedia. In fact, many students had set Google as the default start page in their browser, reorienting it from the school's default start page, the school's website.

The dominance of these information sources is illustrated in the following exchange the student owner of such a laptop made while observing her interactions with these other-generated resources.

S1: First, I would go to the Internet, and then I would type in the word; for example, petroleum, which is what I was doing, and maybe look on Wikipedia and have a look at something that it has got in there and use some of the facts that it has. And then I'd use another website....

In her elaboration of the practices and processes she engages in, this student demonstrates she is combining an existing repertoire of digital literacy practices not specifically associated with the science classroom, e.g., "going to the Internet," "looking at Wikipedia" alongside others specifically related to the task in hand, e.g., use of the key word "petroleum" as a search term, which she has extrapolated from a teacher-facilitated presentation delivered to the class and stored on the wiki for additional review. Here, using a *semiospheric* lens, we see an oscillation between *core* and *periphery* in relation to the semiotic values of the science classroom when confronted with digital technologies as a resource for learning and, in particular, in relation to the learner's critical literacy practices and the validation of knowledge across domains, which we will return to later in this chapter.

Other-generated texts were also multimodal. For video, the first port of call for almost all students was YouTube, although one student, who was particularly motivated by audio-visual materials, extended her search to include Google Video and other video sites such as Broadcaster.com and Brightcove.tv. In student school-based interactions with video sites, and YouTube in particular, we see another example of tension and boundary-crossing activity insofar as student access to YouTube was blocked by the school's filtering system. Nevertheless, students were motivated to use these materials and so populated the wiki with relevant clips at home. Further, the students became sufficiently adept at adjusting coding "blind" within the school context, in the sense that while the students could not view the clip in school, they could still see the relevant coding and were sufficiently satisfied, given existing constraints of the school context, to view their work as part of a student showcase at the end of the project, using the teacher's "filter-free" laptop and a projector. It is clear from this, however, that filtering and blocking of embedded content is an issue where the potential for innovative knowledge exchange is reduced due to school's boundary-setting and the blocking of other-generated texts in a manner that disrupts students' potential to negotiate new meanings and prevents learners from making useful connections between the scientific and the everyday. This is an area that would benefit from further exploration if an effective understanding of digital literacy practices in and beyond the school setting is to be achieved.

Despite this, there is evidence of students gradually moving away from teacher-recommended texts to self-selected resources of a re-interpretation of curricular goals and the generation of more open-ended responses to the topic under investigation, e.g., the selection of a video clip from YouTube,[1] which is only tangentially related to the subject matter being studied and this through an oblique reference in the lyrics of the song *It's a Man's World*, a geographical reference to a nearby town and the theme of global warming. It is suggested, however, that the multimodal mix of lyrics, visuals, and music can support a different, *generative* style of learning as students were encouraged to make creative leaps between oblique linguistic references to fossil fuels and renewable energy (in the lyrics) against a background of visual narratives (fast motion traffic, day and night, energy source, and countryside) that spoke more directly to the issues under investigation.

There is an interesting notion in the link between student consumption of teacher- and other-generated texts and the idea of semiotic flow or the "journey of the sign" as students draw on the teacher-generated texts of the wiki not so much in terms of what the students need to learn *from* them but rather in terms of what students need to *take* from them in order to progress to the next level. In this sense, students as consumers may be seen as moving away from the single source (textbook) and probe (question) model towards the multi-source, multi-narrative, multi-discursive model of the *prosumer* (Toffler, 1980). In other words, students may be seen as consuming with an eye to self-production for an extended audience (local and global) and in modes (audio, visual, and hyperlinked) that are far from the traditional text-dominant (written and formally published) texts of the classroom.

In order to visualize this confluence of formal and informal learning spaces, it may help to consider a metaphor used by Lotman to describe the semiotic space of the *semiosphere*, which he likens to a river populated by powerful currents flowing at different speeds and on different levels, sometimes calm, sometimes turbulent (Lotman, 2009). In this way, it is possible to see student increased agency in self-selection and remediation of available resources as the semiotic flow of the classroom shifts and expands in student encounters with "external" cultural spaces such as those of popular music, global politics, and peer-referenced commentary. This, in turn, requires a new understanding of student evolving literacy practices and of the permeable nature of the overlapping boundary spaces of digital and physical knowledge networks.

Students as Authors of Digital Texts

Analysis of student-authoring practices serve to emphasize this notion of permeability across and between digitally mediated learning spaces, highlighting student simultaneous negotiation of the science curriculum on the one hand and multi-discursive experiences of digital culture (Gere, 2002) on the other. Three particular practices were revealed that merit further investigation here: (1) collaboration/co-operation, (2) criticality, and (3) copy-and-paste culture insofar as these illustrate the utility of the *semiospheric* approach for identifying negotiated meaning spaces, the emergence of boundaries and student boundary-crossing activity.

Collaboration/Cooperation

Students were asked to collaborate on the production of a set of wiki definitions and to produce a group wiki page on the topic of fossil fuels. Student groups were self-selected and self-named. The group activity was intended to be both collaborative and co-operative (Parker & Chao, 2007).

Observations of student interactions with the wiki reveal that students did not respond well to the collaborative activity on wiki definitions. As individuals, students found it difficult to grasp the concept of a shared production. This reaction echoes earlier findings (Grant, 2006) on the use of wikis in the school setting and student perceptions of ownership and relevance of content to classroom contexts and cultures. However, where shared ownership was assumed by a self-selected group, as in the second task, this was not deemed a problem. While this disparity could be the result of the simultaneity of task allocation via the wiki instigated in this particular study, it appears from observations and discussions with students and teacher this is not the case. Rather, the issue appears to relate to student inability to grasp the meaning of a "whole class" production related to the definition of key terms, which proved disruptive of the norms previously set for that type of activity in the traditional classroom setting of writing definitions in exercise books. It may also be the case, however, that students identified more strongly with the group activity through the process of naming and identifying the group project page as their own space. In this sense, it appears that students attach a high semiotic value to ownership of their individual and group learning spaces, in contrast to those that are teacher-designated.

Criticality

A majority of students demonstrated low levels of criticality in their selection and remediation of digital sources. While most students were able to identify texts, images, and video clips that were relevant to the topic of fossil fuels, these were not always appropriate for the target audience and purpose. For example, student productions frequently incorporated facts and figures from non-UK sources—for instance, a graph showing energy consumption in the U.S.—and used these inappropriately or in a manner deemed out of context for the target setting. This blurring of the boundaries between local and global resources suggests a need for the cultivation in students of a deeper awareness of context in relation to the appropriation and reuse of digital sources. Students rarely referenced sources, although they demonstrated a willingness to do so when prompted; for instance, listing "websites we used."

Interestingly, students *did* apply a higher level of criticality to the design and layout of their wiki pages and to selection of video clips. In this and in relation to issues of copyright, plagiarism, etc., there is a marked difference in perceptions regarding the semiotic value attached to content by students and teacher. Discussion with the teacher, for example, reveals that she initially considered issues of referencing, copyright, and selection of appropriate content (in terms of audience and purpose) to be the responsibility of the English and ICT departments rather than the Science department although this is a position she subsequently reversed in dialogue with students during their showcase session at the end of the project. This suggests there is scope for the cross-curricular framing of particular skills and competencies relating to use of digital media in the school setting (for further discussion of plagiarism, see the chapter by McFarlane in this volume).

In terms of content, the teacher's concerns initially focused on student engagement with key data relating to fossil fuels and alternative energy and their implications, i.e., information viewed as *core* to the pursuit of scientific knowledge, as opposed to aesthetic or other contextual considerations. One interesting example of a mismatch between student aesthetic reflections on digital texts and the teacher's focus on scientific content emerged in relation to a video clip about biofuels from YouTube.[2]

While both teacher and students focused on the scientific content of the video clip, students based their acceptance of it on quality values more fitting with the context of the ICT classroom.

R: Can you tell me what you were doing with these videos?

S1: The first one had good music and some good information, but we thought the problem might be that you can't really see the writing really clearly, but the pictures and the diagrams are good. The second one doesn't really get to the point that we're after because it says we need to use more energy. The third one is a whole load of people saying what they think about fossil fuels.

There is also evidence in this extract of student selection of materials at multiple levels of discourse, including popular music and dialogue from peer communities outside the school setting (those clips discussed here relate to teenagers attending a pop concert themed around global warming)—elements not generally associated with the knowledge domain of the science classroom. In this sense, there is a mismatch of semiotic values attributed to the remediation of other-generated texts caused by student boundary-crossing activity in the exchange of meanings across disparate cultural contexts, i.e., classroom and rock concert. Using Lotman's notion of *semiosphere* and its sub-themes of core, periphery, and boundary enables a multi-discursive examination of the relationships between disparate meaning spaces and highlights the potential points of positive crossover between the two. This process, in turn, serves to re-contextualize the narrowly defined scientific concepts of the classroom and to identify crossing points within the academic setting, as well as areas of potential mismatch between specific knowledge delivery and student cross-contextual critical awareness of disparate knowledge domains and the validation of knowledge transfer across these domains.

Copy-and-Paste Culture

The empirical data reveals a copy-and-paste culture in student-authoring practices with digital texts. However, there is also evidence of ambiguity in student perceptions of this activity. While it was clear that at least some students recognized the need to synthesize materials, few did so in practice. The following exchange between students and teacher during the student showcase sheds some light on these practices and the meanings attributed to them in the school setting.

S1: Did you copy and paste all that?

T: No, that's the thing, they haven't copied and pasted it, they've written it up.

S2: Yeah, we've written *some* of it up but we used different websites.

T: So it looks like a *real* wiki…

S3: We used different websites.

T: When you look at that, it's really professional. […] They haven't copied and pasted, they've actually written all this.

S2: Well, we've taken some of the stuff from different websites.

Student 1's comment appears to have been generated by the look and feel of this group's wiki page (Figure 2), which resembled those of Wikipedia.

Here, by contrast to the example about the biofuels video clip from YouTube mentioned above, the teacher is impressed with the aesthetic quality of the page and places a higher semiotic value on the *form* of students' work than its *content*, which, although relevant, is largely cut and pasted from elsewhere. Student 2, by contrast, demonstrates an awareness of the need to synthesise information, but signals her understanding that the teacher has a different perception of this synthesis by repeatedly commenting that her group "used different websites" and that they had "written *some* of it up."

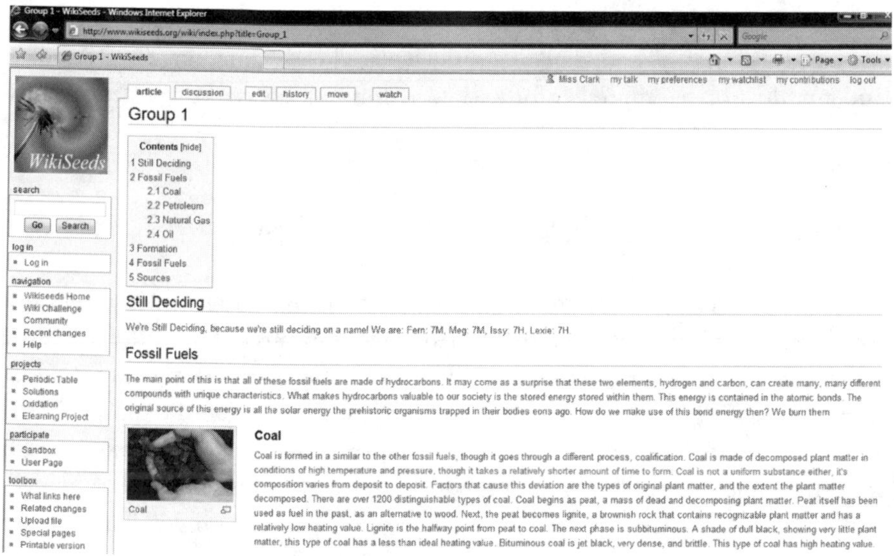

Figure 2: Student wiki page

Student-Generated Digital Texts and the Shift from "Written" to "Productive" Composition

What is interesting in this exchange is the mismatch between the teacher's perception of "writing up" and the students' perception of this activity. For the teacher, "writing up" suggests that the students have *written* the content themselves. For students "writing up" appears to mean that they had *produced* the content themselves, i.e. planning, researching, retrieving, and organizing information appropriate to the task.

The contrast between these perceptions of "written composition" and "productive composition" are interesting in terms of how these perceptions frame notions of semiotic value around literacy practices, traditional and digital, both in the science classroom and generally. While the teacher's perspective is clearly situated in the "old," student perspective points to a shift in understanding around notions of composition, away from essay-style writing to the remediation and reconstruction of knowledge contexts as shaped by an array of digital texts. The former echoes a tradition of teacher, textbook, and tuition while the latter frames an emergent conceptualization of the technology-mediated classroom as a learning environment populated by always on, instantly retrievable, multi-voiced, and multimodal information sources. These ideas are further echoed in discussion with students around their perceptions of ownership, accessibility, and use of information where it appears their view of digitally mediated information is that it "does the job," can be "found again easily" and, if not, is "easily replaced with something else." As such, students do not see digital information as limited, specialised, or inherently valuable.

Student-Generated Texts and the Semiospheric Turn

In these examples, we see both teacher *and* students oscillating between *core* and *periphery* in terms of their understanding of what it means to know in the context of the science classroom and the class wiki. At times teacher and students are close to the *core* semiotic value, framed by curriculum and the scientific topic of fossil fuels; at others, they are on the *periphery*, focusing on interdisciplinary practices such as aesthetics, literacy practices, and the social construction of knowledge, which, in the technology-mediated classroom, extends beyond the individual and the locale to incorporate the voices of the many and the global.

The shift in semiotic value generated by student boundary-crossing activity between these spaces generates a chain of intersecting boundary spaces around internal and external semiotic space relative to the *core* culture, which, here, is the science classroom. By contrast the wiki, as *semiospheric* text, bridges internal and external semiotic space and, in so doing, illuminates and emphasizes the continuities and discontinuities in the overlapping meaning spaces made explicit through technology-mediated learning and its insertion into the science classroom as a traditionally conceived pedagogically bounded space.

Conclusion

This chapter has used the lens of *semiosphere* to illustrate the complex semiotic spaces of the science classroom and the need for these to be adequately contextualized if the learning community (teacher, learner and institution) are to make appropriate and effective use of open learning spaces afforded by new developments in digital technology such as the participatory web. While earlier work (Grant, 2006; Lund and Smørdal, 2006; Forte and Bruckman, 2007; Parker and Chao, 2007) has identified processes, practices, and issues involved in wiki use in the classroom, what remains lacking is a suitable method for identifying the complex intersections of disparate contexts and cultures negotiated by students in their construction of meaningful knowledge across disparate contexts and the instability of semiotic value in the flow of meanings across and between contexts via increasing ly permeable boundary spaces.

In response to this gap, this chapter has introduced the concept of a *semiospheric* approach to digitally mediated literacies through which lens the demarcating notions of *core, periphery*, and *boundary* may be used to frame and illuminate the complex semiotic spaces negotiated by teacher and students in their interactions with technology in and beyond the formalization of educational knowledge content and contexts.

The study reviewed in this chapter also reveals the Janus-like interface of wiki architecture, which, viewed through the conceptual framework of Lotman's *semiosphere*, has the potential to act as a hub for cross-cultural learning, enabling teacher, students, and institutions to generate alternative approaches to knowledge-building and facilitating cross-contextual dialogue, creative debate, and the potential for new meanings to emerge within scientific knowledge domains.

The implications of open learning spaces such as wikis, blogs, and of the increasingly wide set of participatory technologies going under the banner of Web 2.0 are (1) formal educational contexts require a much more focused agenda for digitally mediated literacies and cultural competencies (Dorr & Besser, 2003) in the technology-mediated classroom, and (2) traditional pedagogies need to adapt to open context models within which learning is viewed as a collaborative, co-operative continuum within which the individual teacher is not the only expert and the "closed" curriculum is not the only model.

Notes

1. http://www.youtube.com/watch?v=vJQe735zFCo Lewes Transition Town and the End of Cheap Fossil Fuels
2. http://www.youtube.com/watch?v=mQjF4mtzQ&e Team AX-S Technology—Biofuels

References

Bowers, C. A. (1988), *The cultural dimensions of educational computing: Understanding the non-neutrality of technology*. New York: Teachers College Press.

Bowers, C. A. (1998), "The paradox of technology: What's gained, what's lost?" *Thought and action,* Spring 1998, 111–120.

Boyd, D. (2007), Why youth (heart) social network sites: The role of networked publics in teenage social life. In D. Buckingham (ed.), *MacArthur Foundation Series on digital learning—youth, identity, and digital media volume*. Cambridge, MA: The MIT Press.

Buckingham, D. (2007a), *Beyond technology: Children's learning in the age of digital culture*. Cambridge: Polity.

Buckingham, D. (2007b), Media education goes digital: an introduction. *Learning, media and technology, 32,* 111–119.

Buckingham, D. and Willett, R. (eds.) (2006), *Digital generations: Children, young people, and the new media*. Philadelphia: Lawrence Erlbaum.

Clark, W., Logan, K., Luckin, R., Mee, A. and Oliver, M. (2009), Beyond Web 2.0: mapping the technology landscapes of young learners. *Journal of Computer Assisted Learning, 25,* 56–69.

Désilets, A. and Paquet, S. (2006), Wiki as a tool for web-based collaborative story telling in primary school: A case study, *World Conference on Educational Multimedia, Hypermedia & Telecommunications.* Montreal, Canada: Ed-Media.

Dorr, A. and Besser, H. (2003), *Re-evaluating the bridge! An expanded framework for crossing the digital divide through connectivity, capability, and content.* Los Angeles: CA: UCLA.

Engeström, Y. (1987), *Learning by expanding: an activity-theoretical approach to developmental research.* Helsinki: Orienta-konsultit.

Forte, A. and Bruckman, A. (2007), Constructing text: Wiki as a toolkit for (collaborative?) learning, *WikiSym 2007.*

Gere, C. (2002), *Digital culture.* (1st ed.). London: Reaktion Books Ltd.

Grant, L. (2006), *Using wikis in schools.* Bristol, UK: Futurelab.

Green, H. and Hannon, C. (2007), *TheirSpace: Education for a digital generation.* London: Demos.

Jenkins, H., Clinton, K., Purushotma, R., Robison, A. J. and Weigel, M. (2006), *Confronting the challenges of participatory culture: Media education for the 21st century*: The MacArthur Foundation.

Jewitt, C. (2006), *Technology, literacy and learning: a multimodal approach.* London: Routledge.

Jewitt, C. (2008), "A multimodal perspective on textuality and contexts." *Pedagogy, Culture & Society, 15,* 275–289.

Klamer, A. and van Heusden, B. (1996), The value of culture: A dialogue between Barend van Heusden and Arjo Klamer. In A. Klamer (ed.), *The value of culture: On the relationship between economics and arts.* Amsterdam: Amsterdam University Press.

Kress, G. (2004), Learning, a semiotic view in the context of digital technologies. In A. Brown and N. Davies (eds.), *Digital technology, communities, and education.* London: RoutledgeFalmer.

Kress, G. (2007), Thinking about meaning and learning in a world of instability and multiplicity. *Pedagogies: An International Journal, 2,* 19–34.

Kress, G. and Bezemer, J. (2008), Writing in multimodal texts: A social semiotic account of designs for learning. *Written Communication, 25,* 166–195.

Kull, K. (2005), Semiosphere and a dual ecology: Paradoxes of communication. *Sign System Studies, 33,* 175–189.

Livingstone, S. (2007, 6–7 September 2007), *Engaging with media—a matter of literacy?* Paper presented at the Transforming audiences: identity/creativity/everyday life, University of Westminster, London.

Lotman, Y. (1990), *Universe of the mind: a semiotic theory of culture.* London: I. B. Tauris.

Lotman, Y. (2005), On the Semiosphere. *Sign System Studies, 33,* 1–15.

Lotman, Y. (2009), *Culture and Explosion* (W. A. Clark, Trans.). Berlin: Mouton de Gruyter.

LSE. (2006), *The mobile life youth report 2006.* London: London School of Economics (LSE)/Carphone Warehouse Group Plc.

Luckin, R. (2006), *Understanding learning contexts as ecologies of resources: From the zone of proximal development to learner generated contexts.* Paper presented at the Proceedings of World Conference on e-learning in Corporate, Government, Healthcare, and Higher Education 2006.

Luckin, R., Clark, W., Graber, R., Logan, K., Oliver, M. and Mee, A. (2008), *Learners' use of Web 2.0 technologies in and out of school in key stages 3 and 4*. Coventry, UK: Becta.

Lund, A. and Smørdal, O. (August 21–23, 2006), *Is there a space for the teacher in a WIKI?* Paper presented at the WikiSym '06, Odense, Denmark.

Marchant, G. (2007), Mind the gap(s): discourses and discontinuity in digital literacies. *e-Learning, 4,* 241–255.

Papastergiadis, N. (2002), Restless hybrids. In S. Cubitt, Z. Sardar and R. Araeen (eds.), *The third text reader on art, culture and theory* (pp. 166–176). London: Continuum.

Parker, K. R. and Chao, J. T. (2007), Wiki as a teaching tool. *Interdisciplinary Journal of Knowledge and Learning Objects, 3,* 57–72.

Richardson, W. (2006), *Blogs, wikis, podcasts and other powerful web tools for classrooms*. London: Sage.

Toffler, A. (1980), *The third wave*. London: Bantam.

Young, M. (September 11, 2005), *Schooling the digital generation: Popular culture, new media and the future of education (professorial lecture)—David Buckingham [Seminar Notes]*, Institute of Education, London.

Zhao, Y., Pugh, K., Sheldon, S. and Byers, J. L. (2002), Perspectives on culture, technology and communication. *Teachers College Record, 104,* 482–515.

3

Content in Motion

Remixing and Learning with Digital Media

Ola Erstad

Every word has been permeated, as every image has been transmuted, through the imaginative intensity of one compelling creative act, "Consider it well," says Abt Vogler of the musician's analogous miracle:

> Consider it well: each tone of our scale in itself is nought;
> It is everywhere in the world—loud, soft, and all is said:
> Give it to me to use! I mix it with two in my thought:
> And, there! Ye have heard and seen: consider and bow the head!
>
> Give Coleridge one vivid word from an old narrative; let him mix it with two in his thought; and then (translating terms of music into terms of words) "out of three sounds he (will) frame, not a fourth sound, but a star." (Lowes, 1930, p. 330)

Introduction

During the last five years we have witnessed a change in content production, distribution, and mixing. The re-use of culturally produced content is of course not new to human history (Miller, 2008), but the introduction of Web 2.0 technologies represents a dramatic change in the possibilities for content creation. We are now in a situation where potentially everybody with access to computers and the Internet can produce and distribute content, which others again can reuse. The actual implications of this for cultural production and development are still in the making.

One example is the album made by Kutiman, a young man living in Jerusalem. He has created a website with the album at www.thru-you.com consisting of seven tracks within different musical genres. Each track is made out of a remix of many different YouTube postings made by everyday people, where they record themselves on video, either a young boy blowing a horn for five seconds, a professional drummer demonstrating a specific beat, or a young girl sitting in her room simply singing a song (*Just a Lady*), which she has posted on "Songdreamer" on YouTube. Kutiman has ultimately edited together different postings he has found on YouTube, and which are not copyright protected, to create something new: a musical expression where different video clips of people playing different instruments are edited so the clips are linked to each other. For each of the seven tracks, all the credits are shown so we can click to see the original.

Much of what can be seen online on sites—such as YouTube, Facebook, Twitter, or Wikipedia—is based on activities where content is mixed together. Content is thus not fixed and static, but rather moving from user to user and from context to context. This "content in motion" is an interesting process to study, along with how we conceptualize content production as a cultural process. It is the user and creator of digital content who will be the main focus in this article and not the content itself. My main interest is how such a process of content in motion raises critical issues concerning one specific agency in our society, that of education and learning. To approach such issues, this chapter consists of two main parts: one that gives a short historical outline and recent perspectives on remixing, and another that relates content creation among young people using digital media and content in motion between people and platforms, to literacy, learning, and schooling as social practices.

Dada and After

A modern version of the perspective stated here began with the Dadaist movement around 1916, at the Cabaret Voltaire in Zürich (Richter, 1978). The relevance of the Dadaist movement is the mingling of ideas and artistic exploration of content and objects already available in culture, but reframing them and putting them into new contexts. These artists of the movement—for example, Tristan Tzara, Kurt

Schwitters, Jean Cocteau, Marcel Duchamp, and Raoul Hausmann—used many different expressive sources, often combining them in performances.

An interesting development within Dadaism for the issues discussed in this chapter is "photomontage." Of course, manipulation of the photograph is as old as photography itself. However, with Dadaism it became a genre of artistic expression, especially among the Berlin Dadaists, just after World War I, as a name to describe their new technique of introducing photographs into their works (Ades, 1986). Ades explains that "the Berlin Dadaists used the photograph as a ready-made image, pasting it together with cuttings from newspapers and magazines, lettering and drawing to form a chaotic, explosive image, a provocative dismembering of reality" (ibid. pp. 12–13). The artists also stressed the difference between montage and collage, where the latter—for example, among the Cubists—was seen as an exploration of realism, while montage was moving beyond its representational qualities. Similar ideas about montage were expressed by the Russian filmmaker and film theorist Sergei Eisenstein (1986). For the points raised in this chapter, the contribution of Eisenstein is the practical way of making movies using montage techniques along with his theories drawing our attention to the editing process.

An important development leading up to our situation today is the way music has been made and expressed in recent years, which began with sampling techniques and the role of DJs in creating music towards the end of the 1980s. Several of the contributions in the book *Unbound Sound. Sampling Digital Music and Culture* (Miller, 2008) demonstrate how digital media have had profound effects on the ways music is performed and distributed today and also how this relates to a broader cultural analysis of developments within art, where content within one context is reused within another context. The digital media have created a new platform for thinking about music production. As D. Keller explains:

> Early sonic collage, in the analog era, was painstaking and labor-intensive. It took John Cage a year to make his four-minute-long "Williams" Mix. William Burroughs spent untold hours constructing cutups with razor blades and tape. Digital recording technology revolutionizes and democratizes this recycling process, making complex manipulation of recorded fragments easy and relatively affordable. And the Internet and other digital communications media bring a treasure trove of recorded sound directly to the sonic cannibal. Contemporary music, from the top 40 to the most obscure live DJ set, reflects this technological change, taking the music that came before as raw material for reuse and reconfiguration…., this cultural practice profoundly blurs the line between creators and consumers of culture, turning listening itself into a platform for creative production and performance. (2008, p. 135–136)

Of course, the copyright laws that regulate the market of music production and distribution today are at stake. Legal disputes about copyright issues have increasingly surfaced due to technological developments that create new practices evolving outside the regulated market. Lawrence Lessig (2008) has been a key spokesman for the need to challenge the established copyright regime, trying to develop other means of handling copyright issues in his initiative on Creative Commons.

Another point is that "In an era of intensely networked systems, when you create, it's not just how you create, but the context of the activity that makes the product" (Jordan & Miller, 2008, p. 97). The interesting aspect is how reusing content and manifesting new expressions can be redefined in different contexts. Besides the more artistic ones mentioned above, the ways young people experiment with and explore the potentials of digital technologies for creative practices of participation are of special interest. This can be seen as a new way of understanding a production mode in our culture.

Constructing the Content Creators

During the last 50 years there has been an increased interest in how young people use different media. Most of this research has been directed towards the consumption of media content by young people. There is also, however, some research on media production and young people: Before the introduction of digital media, this was most often done as organized activities inside and outside of schools due to the cost and availability of equipment for recording, editing and so forth. Drotner (1991), for example, demonstrates how a group of young people were involved in aesthetic practices in their everyday culture and the aesthetic production that was going on in these practices.

Within research on media education, the production practices using different media and modes, and their framing within media education in and out of schools, have been a key focus (Buckingham, Grahame & Sefton-Green, 1995; Buckingham, 2003). With the coming of digital media, it has been explored how these technologies have had an impact on the ways students and teachers produce content in classroom settings (Buckingham & Bragg, 2007; Burn, 2009).

The turning point for young people as content creators came with the introduction of digital media on a broad scale throughout the world. Since the introduction of digital media and the growing access to such media at home (DV cameras, MP3 players, computers, and Internet access), and especially since the introduction of Web 2.0 technologies that make it possible to share and build on others' content online, the interest in young people's production practices and content creation has been growing. In the emerging participatory media culture (Jenkins, 2006), digital media has increasingly blurred the distinction between production and consumption; for example, as demonstrated by Mizuko Ito (2006) in the peer-to-peer exchange surrounding Japanese animation media mixes that rely on a combination of various analogue and digital media forms.

The main focus in this chapter is on user-generated content creation. Some have defined this as a key characteristic of a new "digital generation." Thus, Tapscott (1998) argued that young people's use of digital media creates a new generation in the way they use these technologies for different purposes. This argument has been followed up in books by Tapscott (2008) and by Palfrey & Gasser (2008), both books supposed to be based on a number of interviews with young people all over the world, even though it is not specified clearly with whom and how this has been done. These books represent the popularized version of the impact of digital media on young people's lives. In that sense they celebrate these practices and see them as expressions of future competencies of importance for our whole society. One point that has come out strongly is the emphasis on content creation as a new social practice among youth. Palfrey and Gasser (2008), for example, see this as a key feature of what they call "the first generation of digital natives."

In an American context the new emphasis on content creation has also come out in other research initiatives. As part of the Pew Internet and American life study, several studies have been made especially on user-generated content creation. In one report (Lenhart, Madden, Smith & Macgill, 2007) the researchers summarize their findings in the following points:

- Content creation by teenagers continues to grow, with 64% of online teenagers aged 12–17 engaging in at least one type of content creation, up from 57% of online teens in 2004.
- 35% of all teen girls blog, compared with 20% of online boys, and 54% of wired girls post photos online compared with 40% of online boys.
- Boys dominate one area: posting of video content online. Online teen boys are nearly twice as likely as online girls (19% vs. 10%) to have posted a video online where someone else could see it.
- Many teen content creators do not simply plaster their creative endeavours on the web for anyone to view; many teens limit access to content they share.
- There is a subset of teens that are super-communicators—teens who have a host of technology options for dealing with family and friends, including traditional landline phones, cell phones, texting, social network sites,

> instant messaging, and email. These teens represent about 28% of the entire teen population, and they are more likely to be older girls.

From a more qualitative perspective, Mizuko Ito and her research group have studied creative practices among youth using digital media, "the Digital Youth Project." They show how digital media create new possibilities for young people in their expressive practices, and how young people use social media to pursue interests and to build "friendships" (see http://digitalyouth.ischool.berkeley.edu/). In this way young people develop a collaborative strategy of communication and production of content, from simple SMS to complex multimodal expressions.

There are important cultural differences in how common these practices are (see Wildermuth's chapter in this volume). The U.S. data presented above is not supported by data from a Norwegian context. Even where access to technology is good, we do not see the same amount of young people being active producers of content in Norway. In one study of young people in the age group 16–24, only 5% answered that they wrote blogs or posted pictures and videos on the Internet, while about 50% were looking for information on different sites online (Futsæter, 2008).

In this sense, we should also be careful in the way we describe young people as a digital generation (Buckingham, 2006). Digital media is part of growing up today, but at the same time it varies a lot how young people use these media for different purposes. Still, despite variations in the amount of young people that can be described as active content creators, the way some young people have taken up these media as creative tools raises important questions about social practices among youth and especially how these developments challenge basic conceptions about education, schooling, and learning.

Localizing Literacy and Learner Identity

There is currently a growing body of research on the interrelationship between different media and the concept of literacy (Lankshear & Knobel, 2006). As defined by the New London Group (Cope & Kalantzis, 2000) "literacies," in the plural, has increasingly moved towards how people relate to multiple text formats, what the New London Group term "multiliteracies" (ibid.) and "multimodality" (Kress, 2003). These new literacy studies are located at the intersection of sociolinguistics, anthropological theories of language, and educational and learning theory using mainly ethnographic and discourse analytical methodologies. These studies open up broader conceptions of what it means to "read" and "write" using available cultural tools (Hull & Schultz, 2002; Coiro, Knobel, Lankshear & Leu, 2008) and how learning in schools relates to production practices that young people are involved in outside of schools.

Going back to the now classic text by Scribner and Cole (1981), Lankshear and Knobel (2007) describe literacy in terms of "socially organized practices that make use of a symbol system and a technology for producing and disseminating it" (p. 236). The important aspect is to look upon literacy not as something static, but as changing over time. Literacy is not about being able to read and write a particular kind of script. It is more a matter of "applying this knowledge for specific purposes in specific contexts of use" (ibid.). And as Lankshear and Knobel explains: "Literacies call us to generate and communicate meanings and to invite others to make meaning from our texts in turn." (2007, p. 4). From this point of view, it is necessary to look at and extend the notion of literacy practices to include social and cultural practices in different settings. In their ethnographic studies of literacy practices among adults in one community in England, Barton and Hamilton (1998) link literacy to a more general understanding of the social practices of the community, emphasizing how literacy is embedded in people's daily lives. These everyday literacies, or "vernacular literacies" as Barton and Hamilton call them, are learned informally, rarely separated from use and reflect the logic of practical application. Moreover, the vernacular literacies are more than an individual activity; they also serve as a vital community resource.

During the last decade, multimodality has gained attention within research on new literacy practices (Kress, 2003). In relation to the argument in this chapter, multimodality does not really grasp the processes of content creation itself. As developed by Kress and others, this approach mainly draws attention to the textual expressions and the different modalities involved. In order to study "content in motion" and content creation among young people, we, therefore, need to develop another conceptual understanding.

During the last few years the concepts of "remix" (Lessig, 2008; Lankshear & Knobel, 2006) and "media mixes" (Ito, 2006) have attracted attention in the research literature on the implications of Web 2.0 technologies. This represents a shift in the ways we conceive of content and content creation, away from a situation where content is treated in a regulated way through copyright laws, as well as bounded by located media forms such as the book or film scrolls, and where the distribution apparatus is controlled by commercial agencies such as publishing companies or the record industry. As we know today, these ways of dealing with content and content creation are challenged in several respects due to key functionalities of Web 2.0 technologies such as editing pieces of content together, the availability of information sources, and the possibility of uploading to the web and share content with others.

I have earlier defined digital production and re-mixing as implying the "selecting, cutting, pasting, and combining semiotic resources into new digital and multimodal texts (bricolage), which is achieved by downloading and uploading files from different sources (Internet, iPod, DV-camera, digital camera or sound recording devices)." (Erstad, Gilje & de Lange, 2007). The concept is also used by authors from different perspectives. For example, Manovitch (2007) writes about remixability as part of the language of new media; Ito (2006) relates it to cultural phenomena such as manga, mash-up, machinima; Lankshear and Knobel (2006) relate it to phenomena such as fan fiction among groups of young people; and Lessig (2008) to copyright issues and new ways of "writing" in a cultural sense.

A concrete example of such processes is videos made by a young Norwegian, posted on YouTube, which have generated a following, especially among Norwegian youth. In one of his videos, called "Amateur" (www.youtube.com/watch?v=JzqumbhfxRo), the artist in question tries to play on a drum set, without succeeding very well. The video then turns into a stop motion animation where he edits together small clips of hitting the different drums so that it makes familiar drum beats and gives the impression he can play the drums. He compensates for his lack of being able to play the drums with his competence in editing on the computer. The question then arises to what extent this is really playing drums, or another literate practice, similar to playing drums, but still different.

Another example is the interrelationship between online and offline activities by youth (Leander & McKim, 2003), also illustrating content in motion. For example, the jumping techniques down steps, over walls, down from buildings, and so forth under the heading of "Le Parkour.'" On YouTube, there are many videos where young people film each other performing these jumps for others to see and contribute with their jumps, in different countries (www.youtube.com/watch?v=IjQxIRWZu0c). At the same time, there are examples where young people film themselves playing games online in which they can experiment with jumps in a virtual world (www.youtube.com/watch?v=BMncHzK20mI).

These examples also point to another aspect of content in motion: the issue of identity and agency. Identity is here seen as multifaceted and something that changes over time and is played out in different contexts (Holland, Lachicotte, Skinner, & Cain, 2003). In much content creation among youth today, identity plays critical role in the process of making such content and in the content this youth can produce. Diakopoulus (2005) has related this to issues of authorship, where, in his analysis, we have moved from a romantic conception of the author producing content such as a book, towards what he describes as "remix in the wild," where different people contribute in different ways, building on different sources of content to produce new content, also for others to re-use.

The Pedagogy of Content Creation

The digitization of a wide range of media, computer capability, and broadband access to the Internet imply that more students can work with photos, sound, text, and moving images with standard software. Sefton-Green stresses how the software influences the digital editing process. Several studies show the value of digital editing software in terms of the opportunities it provides for learners to revise their work (Buckingham et al., 1995; Sefton-Green, 2005).

Such developments do not only represent new resources for school learning, but challenge the basic understanding of learning and education. Primarily, this is due to the change in how relevant content is defined, not as something pre-specified, but something to be discovered and worked on. One example is the way digital storytelling has been implemented as a new method of learning in school settings, where students in a personal way utilize digital technology to share stories with others (Erstad & Silseth, 2008). Below are two snapshots from different research projects on digital storytelling that illustrate these points.

Snapshot 1: Creating content about the other

This example is taken from a project taking place between two lower secondary schools, one in the Eastern part of Oslo and one in the Western suburbs. At each school a group of students (about 20 in the East, 13–14 year old, and about 40 in the West, 14–15 year old) took part in the project during a two-week period. The school in the Western suburbs had students from families with a high socio-economic status with only one student who was non-white and adopted from Chile. At the school in the Eastern inner city part of Oslo, the students came from many different cultural backgrounds with about 65% of the students from minority-language-speaking families and with low socio-economic status. The teachers, after discussing this with the students, decided that the collaborative project between the students should be about prejudices about living in the east and the west of Oslo and that the students should use digital technology as a central part of the collaborative work.

In the project the students used different digital tools to create an online newspaper, one for each school, which consisted of reportages about the students on the other side of town, their community, and their school. In each group the students divided themselves into an editorial board with responsibilities for different sections of the paper—on culture, religion and ethics, sport, statistics about their communities, and interviews with inhabitants. The students sent questions to each other, using a collaborative online platform and MSN. Halfway through the project, a group of students from each school, without teachers, used public transportation to visit the students at the other school. None of the students had ever been in the area of the other school. To document this visit, each group made a video film to use in their own production.

Throughout the project the students worked with different modalities and information sources in the making of the online newspapers. The students shifted on working individually on different computers looking for images, statistical data, graphs, illustrations, written texts, or editing audio interviews with players from the local soccer team, editing the video films to put on the web, and then negotiated how to integrate and remix the different content sources into something new in their online newspaper. The two online papers turned out very different: The one from the west of the city possessed different visual effects, with a high quantity of images on the front page and with links to other sections of the paper consisting of more text and images. The online paper from the eastern school was simpler in the aesthetics on the front page and with more video material; for example, featuring video interviews with students at their own school and with students from the other school recorded during their visit.

The content in motion is captured through the searching for information and sending content between the two schools, and also the students learning about the lives of the other students (through the uses of meditational processes), and further exploring and then drawing on their own life situations in their community. This was exemplified in the ways the students combined different Internet content with their own work, either through collaboratively written texts or audio and video tapes. The editorial group at each school had the last word concerning how elements should be presented in the online newspaper. Video observations of the two groups demonstrate an intense and creative process among the students working with different materials and sending them between the two schools. Often there are rapid changes in the way they relate to content; for example, when one of the Muslim girls at the school in the eastern part of Oslo describes why she is wearing a veil. This resulted in a host of questions from the students at the other school on what this meant in everyday terms such as what she did during gymnastics lessons, did she have ethnic Norwegian friends, what were her interests in music or films, or what did her parents think about her growing up in Norway? In documenting this life story, the students remixed different materials they found on the Internet regarding Islam and world incidents connected to religious conflicts and then connected them to this girl's personal narrative, which was then presented on the online newspapers of both schools. As demonstrated above, the students involved in this project were engaged on a personal level, drawing on experiences from outside the school, yet reworking such experiences within a school context. In negotiating the differences and similarities between the two communities in Oslo, the students appear to reflect on their own lives, which is reflected in the chapters they wrote in the online newspapers.

Snapshot 2: Opening the learning space for content creation

This lower secondary school is situated in an area with families of lower socioeconomic status and characterized by many social problems. An important aspect of the school's vision on teaching and learning is to create a learning environment where students can become better at what they are already good at. This implies an approach for creating better self-esteem for learning among the students. Time is spent on finding a subject area where the developmental potential of each student is high. The school also emphasizes the need for students to produce knowledge and present this to other students.

The students were organized in groups of 40 (all 13–14 years old), with a team of five teachers. In the projects, the students always worked in smaller groups of three or four. The teachers and students decided together on the main focus of the project themes.

In one specific project, the students used iMovie to make an animation movie on the theme "the changing features of water." Even though the basis for the project was natural science, it had an interdisciplinary approach since the students used elements from other subjects such as English. Student discussion at the computer indicated the students were active participants in negotiating different solutions among themselves. Collaboration was an essential element in working with such a knowledge production focus. By working together, the students supported each other, even though conflicts did arise. Many researchers argue, however, that disagreements with other students serve to highlight alternatives to their own point of view. This can foster progress in understanding (Littleton & Light, 1999).

The use of ICT created new and unexpected situations for the students and teachers. From the students' point of view, the biggest change was that the teachers didn't provide as many instructions as before. In relation to the work with the animation movie, the students said:

Boy1: Editing is the most fun thing to work on. Because we do things ourselves, there are no teachers who stand and point and tell you what you should do. You get to choose yourself and sort out what you think is best.

Girl: There are no specific assignments, "now you have to do that," we decide what we should do and how we should do it.

Boy2: The teacher does not let us give up.

Girl: If we need help, then it is available. But if we want to, we can do everything ourselves, if we can.

Boy1: That we do it the right way.

Girl: If we need help, they are there for us.

Boy1: The teachers do not give us a lot of information, like they used to do in primary school. They give us an assignment, and then we should find the information we need to complete the assignment ourselves.

iMovie turned out to be an effective artifact that gives flexibility to the creative process and, at the same time, may result in a quality, professional product. The visual focus changed how the students relate to their own learning process, and it helped create a new framework for engaging the students in different subject-oriented activities. It generated creativity and gave an opportunity for experimenting with different solutions and putting together different components of knowledge.

The visual focus also made it easier for the students to relate to a challenge, partly because they could use a broader repertoire of their own competence, and partly as it helped focus their attention. The students became more independent as a consequence of using a learning resource with many opportunities. This stimulated their motivation as well as their focus on the academic content. As one of the teachers said: "The advantage with visual presentation is that the students have to study the material well, if not, they will not be able to create a movie." The students themselves said they remembered more of what they learned because they had to know the material well to be able to present it to others. It was through academic discussions that the students demonstrated they truly understood a field of knowledge.

iMovie became an important tool for producing knowledge and created a better awareness of how to put information together in a meaningful way:

Boy1: It is more practical, so this way we learn more by doing things more than just to sit and write stuff.

Girl: I think it is much better. I think I learn more by doing it on the computer than just sitting and reading about it. When you just sit and read or write then it becomes boring, and then you don't get it in. However, when you have to do something to get it right then you have a better grasp of it.

Boy2: You forget things more easily when you just sit and read.

Boy1: You just read, take a look in the book; write the assignments, without any of it going through the brain.

This sequence demonstrates that the students gained room for negotiation and took an active part in their own knowledge production. The student discussion also shows how important it is that the assignments were practical and appeared meaningful to them. The use of photos and videos in the student work process contributed qualitatively to knowledge construction and presentation.

Good and poorly performing students benefited from working with the computer in this way, but especially the poorly performing, according to the parents and teachers. A strong statement came from the mother of twins in this group:

> My girls are academically weak because they both have dyslexia, and during the years in primary school they have struggled all the time with not being able to prove themselves in any subject-oriented way. I think it was incredibly positive for them to come here…to be able to work on computers and film and edit and such things. They have done a bit of that at home before, so they had knowledge that the other students could get from them, and through that they got a higher status in the group. So for them it has been like…I don't know…almost like a new life. It is very important that they gain ownership of their work. I think that is one of the keys to create engagement. For adults it is like this, and I do not think this is different for children.

Critical reasons for these positive learning outcomes are a combination of giving the students a belief in their own potential for learning and the flexible opportunities that the use of ICT makes possible. The project teacher also confirmed this when he talked about the same students:

> Suddenly these students come into a learning environment where they have experience related to a new tool that becomes available for them without only focusing on reading and writing. But also for the students that are clever and learn things fast, this seems to give them more. Also for them it is a growth environment to produce good results.

Heterogeneous grouping, which was employed in this project, has been positive for students at all levels. It was found this could ensure that low-performing students played a significant part in the group's work, especially when using ICT for visual communication. The learning environments were challenging and stimulating, which gave good results for student performance and learning progress.

Even though learning has not been the prime focus of this article, both of these snapshots indicate learning outcomes for the students in different areas. In the content area, the students in the first snapshot gained insight about differences in living conditions and their consequences, on immigration and Norway as a multicultural society. In the second snapshot, the students dealt with knowledge primarily within natural science. These learning elements are evident in assessments made by the teachers and the products made by the students. In addition, in the interviews with the students, they emphasized that the active engagement of content creation motivated them for learning, even though such statements should be interpreted with caution. Still, this was supported by observations of the fluid process of working with subject content in this way, remixing different modalities, sharing and collaborating with other students, online and offline. Most important, however, was the reflection on this process of content creation, with critical remarks on information sources, on questioning content made by other students and deciding on a final product.

Remixing School Practices

The snapshots mentioned above are not examples where Web 2.0 technologies are prevalent. The last snapshots were also done before such technologies were in common use. However, it is also due to the fact that such technologies have not yet been used widely in educational practices in schools, even though young people are familiar with these technologies outside of schools (see the chapter by Clark in this volume). Still, these snapshots illustrate ways of working with content that use the affordances made available by digital media.

As such, the notion of content in motion challenges the role of the learner in schools in fundamental ways, because new digital tools give new possibilities and change how we define knowledge production and creation. Content is not something predefined and fixed in school books, written by one author, and fixed over longer periods of time as something everybody in a group of students should relate to. Content is dynamic, something students search for and evaluate from different sources, something they themselves are active producers and creators of, under the explorative and questioning guidance of teachers, something they share with others, both familiar and unknown, and something that changes over time.

One implication is also to question the traditional way of conceptualizing learning (Bereiter, 2002). This chapter has tried to define learning more as a process of creating content than as an end product and has argued that content creation and knowledge building are a collaborative effort, where people share and contribute in different ways. Such developments are supported by digital media as new cultural tools (Erstad & Wertsch, 2008).

In this way, content in motion also creates an interrelationship between content creation inside and outside of schools. Digital technologies, and the development of Web 2.0 technologies especially, support and stimulate such activities. As such, they become an important educational issue, beyond the present day discussions about computers in schools.

The argument in this chapter has implications on different levels. First, it has consequences at a personal level. The students in the snapshots mentioned above said they had positive experiences of working in open learning environments and working on content creation in this way. These students changed their opinions about the school and their own perceptions of learning. Second, when the students used different digital artifacts, such as iMovie, they used their cultural competence in other areas than before they started working with this technology. So, the students received a broader comprehension of knowledge and its relevance outside the school. Third, the student acquisition of academic content changed direction in the two cases; weaker and stronger performing students appear to do better in these environments. In both cases, academic content is defined as interdisciplinary, and knowledge is problem-based and related to real life as defined by the students. New digital artifacts, and especially the potentials of working with content as process, have the potential of transforming our conceptions of learning towards what is needed for the twenty-first century.

References

Ades, D. (1986). *Photomontage*. London: Thames & Hudson.

Barton, D., & Hamilton, M. (1998). *Local literacies: Reading and writing in one community*. London: Routledge.

Bereiter, C. (2002). *Education and mind in the knowledge age.* Mahwah, New Jersey: Lawrence Erlbaum.

Buckingham, D. (2003). *Media education. Literacy, learning and contemporary culture.* Cambridge: Polity.

Buckingham, D. (2006). Is there a digital generation? In D. Buckingham & R. Willett (Eds.) *Digital generations. Children, young people and new media.* Mahwah, NJ: Lawrence Erlbaum.

Buckingham, D., Grahame, J. & Sefton-Green, J. (1995). *Making media. Practical production in media education.* London: The English and Media Centre.

Buckingham, D., & Bragg, S. (Eds.) (2007). Special issue: Media education goes digital. *Journal Learning, Media and Technology.* London: Routledge.

Burn, A. (2009). *Making new media. Creative production and digital literacies.* New York: Peter Lang.

Coiro, J., Knobel, M., Lankshear, C. & Leu, D.J. (2008). *Handbook of research on new literacies.* Mahwah, NJ: Lawrence Erlbaum.

Cope, B. and Kalantzis, M. (Eds.) (2000). *Multiliteracies: Literacy learning and the design of social futures.* London: Routledge.

Diakopoulos, N. (2005). *Remix culture: Mixing up authorship.* Retrieved online at http://wwwstatic.cc.gatech.edu/~nad/Remix%20culture%20mixing%20up%20authorship.doc Retrieved on 1 August 2009.

Drotner, K. (1991). *At skabe sig-selv. Ungdom-æstetik-pædagogik.* Copenhagen: Gyldendal.

Eisenstein, S. (1986). *The film sense.* London: Faber & Faber.

Erstad, O., Gilje, Ø., & de Lange, T. (2007): Re-mixing multimodal resources: multiliteracies and digital production in Norwegian media education. *Journal Learning, Media and Technology.* Special Issue: Media education goes digital. D. Buckingham & S. Bragg (Eds.). London: Taylor & Francis. *32*(2), pp. 183–199.

Erstad, O., & Wertsch, J. (2008). Tales of mediation: Narrative and digital media as cultural tools. In K. Lundby (Ed.) *Digital storytelling, mediatized stories: Self-representation in new media.* New York: Peter Lang. pp. 21–40.

Erstad, O., & Silseth K. (2008): Agency in digital storytelling—challenging the education context. In K. Lundby (Ed.) *Digital storytelling, mediatized stories: Self-representation in new media.* New York: Peter Lang Publishing. pp. 213–231.

Futsæter, K. A. (2008). *Medieutviklingen med focus på sosiale medier.* Retrieved at: www.tns-gallup.no/arch/_img/9082007.ppt on 1. August 2009.

Holland, D., Lachicotte, W. Jr., Skinner, D., & Cain, C. (2003): *Identity and agency in cultural worlds.* Cambridge, MA: Harvard University Press.

Hull, G., & Schultz, K. (Eds.) (2002). *School's out. Bridging out-of-school literacies with classroom practices.* New York: Teachers College.

Ito, M. (2006): Japanese media mixes and amateur cultural exchange. In Buckingham, D. & R. Willett (Eds.) (2006): *Digital generations. Children, young people, and new media.* Mahwah, NJ: Lawrence Erlbaum. pp. 49–66.

Jenkins, J. (2006). *Convergence culture: where old and new media collide.* New York: New York University Press.

Jordan, K., & Miller, P. D. (2008). Freeze frame: Audio, aesthetics, sampling, and contemporary multimedia. In Miller, P.D. (Ed.) (2008). *Sound unbound: Sampling digital music and culture.* Cambridge, MA: The MIT Press. pp. 97–108.

Keller, D. (2008). The musician as thief: Digital culture and copyright law. In Miller, P.D. (Ed.) (2008). *Unbound Sound. Sampling digital music and culture*. Cambridge, MA: The MIT Press. pp. 135–150.

Kress, G. (2003). *Literacy in the new media age*. London: Routledge.

Lankshear, C., & M. Knobel (2006). *New literacies, everyday practices and classroom learning*. New York: Open University Press and McGraw-Hill.

Lankshear, C., & Knobel, M. (Eds.) (2007). *A new literacies sampler*. New York: Peter Lang.

Leander, K. M., & McKim, K. K. (2003). Tracing the everyday "sitings" of adolescents on the Internet: a strategic adaptation of ethnography across online and offline spaces. *Education, Communication & Information*. *3*(2), July 2003, pp. 211–240.

Lenhart, A., Madden, M., Smith, A., & Macgill, A., (2007). Teens and social media. Retrieved at: http://www.pewinternet.org/Reports/2007/Teens-and-Social-Media.aspx.1 August 2009

Lessig, L. (2008). *Remix. Making art and commerce thrive in the hybrid economy*. New York: Penguin.

Littleton, K., & Light, P. (Eds.) (1999). *Learning with computers. Analyzing productive interaction*. London: Routledge.

Lowes, J. Livingstone (1930). *The Road to Xanadu*. London: Houghton Mifflin, p. 330.

Manovitch, L. (2007). *What comes after remix?* Online at http://remixtheory.net/?p=169 Retrieved 1 August 2009.

Miller, P. D. (Ed.) (2008). *Sound unbound: Sampling digital music and culture*. Cambridge, MA: The MIT Press.

Palfrey, J. & Gasser, U. (2008). *Born digital: Understanding the first generation of digital natives*. New York: Basic Books.

Richter, H. (1978). *DADA, art and anti-art*. New York: Oxford University Press.

Scribner, S. & Cole, M. (1981): *The psychology of literacy*. Cambridge, MA: Harvard University Press.

Sefton-Green, J. (2005) Timelines, timeframes and special effects: Software and creative media production. *Education, Communication & Information 5*. pp. 99–110.

Tapscott, D. (1998). *Growing up digital: The rise of the net generation*. New York: McGraw-Hill.

Tapscott, D. (2008). *Grown up digital: How the net generation is changing your world*. New York: McGraw-Hill.

4

Developing Crossmedia and Interactivity for Edutainment

Conclusions Drawn from "The Space Trainees" Project

SIMON STAFFANS & ANNIKA WIKLUND-ENGBLOM

Interactive media and crossmedia have, for a long time, been the subject of much hype. The gradual implementation of interactive television services at the end of the last decade were seen as an event heralding the coming of a new age of multimedia, where anyone could interact with anything, where everything would be ever so much better, and a media nirvana was just around the corner. Almost 10 years on, and although many things have changed, this golden age seems as distant as ever.

The new technologies, the improving interfaces, and the expanding possibilities for getting hold of content have, however, brought with them the possibility to enrich the user experience in many ways. One of these possibilities is to offer new and more exciting ways of learning or training, through interactivity and crossmedia solutions.

In this chapter we will focus on such a project, the edutainment crossmedia show "The Space Trainees," a project that originated in interactive television and moved over to a broader crossmedia solution. It is a project that our development team has been working on—on and off—for three years, and through development work, pilots, and extensive tests of user experiences, we have gained knowledge about how edutainment and crossmedia work.

"The Space Trainees"

The project "The Space Trainees" originated in 2005, when the development team at MediaCity decided to explore the possibilities of developing an educational format for interactive television. Finland is among the countries to have embraced the DVB-supported MHP (Multimedia Home Platform) solution as the tool for interactivity via set-top-box. Set-top-box interactivity can be defined as interactive television where the viewer interacts via his/her remote control and a set-top-box equipped with a return channel and the required software, in this case MHP (Multimedia Home Platform). An initiative from the Finnish government led to the initiation of the ARVID-program, with the aim to support the development of solutions and formats for interactive television. "The Space Trainees" was among the projects to benefit from the ARVID-program.[1]

From the outset, the aim of the project was to create and develop a format that would combine an educational value with an entertaining form. The subject decided on was language learning. This decision was partly based on a survey conducted by the European Commission in 2001, which showed that 93% of all parents within the EU considered learning another European language integral for their children.[2] The decision was also partly based on the growing experience of the development team, which had worked on another interactive project: the first interactive quiz show to be broadcast in Finland, a show called "Enigma."

"The Space Trainees" project developed rapidly during the first few months, with several ideas created, included, or discarded for various reasons. At one point, the project was written as a drama, at another point it moved to the basement of a medieval castle, without any possibilities of solving all the challenges with respect to interactivity, edutainment value, or overall attractiveness of the format.

In the summer and autumn of 2005, the project was accepted into the Pygmalion Programme, a development workshop for children's media supported by the European Commission. During the development weeks at Pygmalion, several key points were agreed upon:

- A strong drama setting was needed, to put the interactivity and the television show into one logical entity.
- This drama would be set in space, to give as much freedom as possible to the developers ("In space, anything can happen!").
- MHP-based set-top-box interactivity was not necessarily the best way forward for the project.
- A crossmedia approach to the project would enable the production of better content, as well as a more logical approach to the interactivity within the format.

Several pilot shoots, extensive user experience testing, and audience research and further development work followed (see below). "The Space Trainees" of today is a crossmedia format involving television and Internet, with the crossmedia aspect and solutions integrated in a logical way, striving to make it a natural step for users and viewers to switch between the different media.

As noted, "The Space Trainees" is set in space. A gigantic space ship, the *Babel*, is orbiting Earth, filled with databases of all the Earth's languages. A virus has breached the databases and is destroying the languages. The task of rescuing the languages is given to the students at the International Space Academy, the Space Trainees. They will travel to *Babel* to rescue as much of the languages as possible via playing various language games. The best team gets to go on to the next mission and is handsomely rewarded.

The viewers at home can sign up at the virtual Space Academy on the Internet to become Space Trainees themselves, train for the same games, practice their language skills, interact with fellow Trainees and, at the end of each semester, take part in tests, where the best Trainees have the chance to go on a real mission—i.e., take part in a television show in the next series.

The games the teams play on the television show—while the teams navigate the labyrinths of the space ship *Babel*, trying to rescue the language(s)—are coded in Flash. Adobe's Flash software is a multimedia platform used to add animation and interactivity to web pages.This means that the same games, looking much the same, are implemented as a part of the web portal, the Space Academy on the Internet. The major difference is that the games on the television show are developed to activate the teams and their members physically, while the games on the Internet are more sedentary. In the games on the television show the kids must run to the game screens, they must actively choose on touch screens—the idea is to get them moving, in order to achieve better television. This is not the case with the games online, as they do not require any running or jumping; just that the user concentrates on the games

Learning Through Edutainment?

Edutainment is a mix of education and entertainment. There are many examples of edutainment throughout media history, some successful, some not. Learning through edutainment has been a topic of controversy, with critics pointing out that edutainment promises a fun learning environment, and learning does not have to be fun all the time (Okan, 2003). Supporters or more neutral commentators have said that games, digital learning, and edutainment can be valuable learning and training methods if used and applied correctly (e.g., Hogle, 1996; Becker, 2007). Children of today, as researchers note, are often on a different level of digital literacy than the teachers teaching them, or even their own parents. Marc Prensky coined the term "digital natives" to describe children growing up in a digital environment, in stark contrast to earlier generations, which he calls "digital immigrants" (Prensky, 2001). By offering learning through different media in a setting based on a strong drama, not unlike many computer and online games of today, we are aiming at motivating the children to engage themselves to a higher degree in language learning activities.

Within the scope of "The Space Trainees," we encountered the problem of validating the learning outcomes and the pedagogical value of the television show and the interactive and crossmedia applications. Did the viewers learn something? To address this issue, we have actively involved professors and researchers of pedagogy and didactics at the Åbo Akademi University, who have been evaluating the game concepts and suggested improvements throughout the project development. Our own research (described in greater detail below) further suggests that while the web portal is designed to be the major form for interaction, viewers also play along in their own minds while just watching the show, thereby taking part and training languages themselves (unpublished study).

From the beginning, "The Space Trainees" was developed with a multiple language aspect in mind. Game participants can try to rescue their own native language. Alternatively, participants can try to rescue a foreign language, or there may even be two teams of trainees speaking two different languages, attempting to rescue a third language. In this last setting, a "real world" approach to communication is often taken, where people with different mother tongues attempt to understand each other by using a third, common language.

Furthermore, "The Space Trainees" crossmedia format offers teachers the possibility to register as a professional user on the web portal. Teachers can tailor a unique sequence of games and, for instance, edit the content of these games to fit in with the current curriculum and subsequently invite their students to play and practice on the web portal.

Interactive Elements of "The Space Trainees"

As noted, the teams on the television show play games in order to rescue as much of their languages as possible. These games are designed to (a) train the team members in a language, either by making them combine or construct letters, words, and sentences or by finding missing words and parts of sentences in different settings. These games are also developed to (b) physically engage the team members on the show, which is intended to heighten the suspense and the action of the television show. At the same time, the games should (c) work as Flash games on the web portal as well, where a computer is used to play the games.

One example is the Lyrics Game. One part of the databases on board *Babel* contains all songs ever recorded. As the virus has entered that database system, it is now scrambling the lyrics of the songs. The task is to find the correct missing words to the songs.

On the television show (see Figure 1), the playing field is separated onto several large screens. The team, consisting of three children, has to run around, shout, and cooperate to find the correct answers. Figure 1 is taken from the user experience test described later in this chapter. The colored areas indicate the viewer's eye fixations on the screen. Red areas show the most often viewed area, yellow areas represent fewer fixations, and green the even less viewed areas.

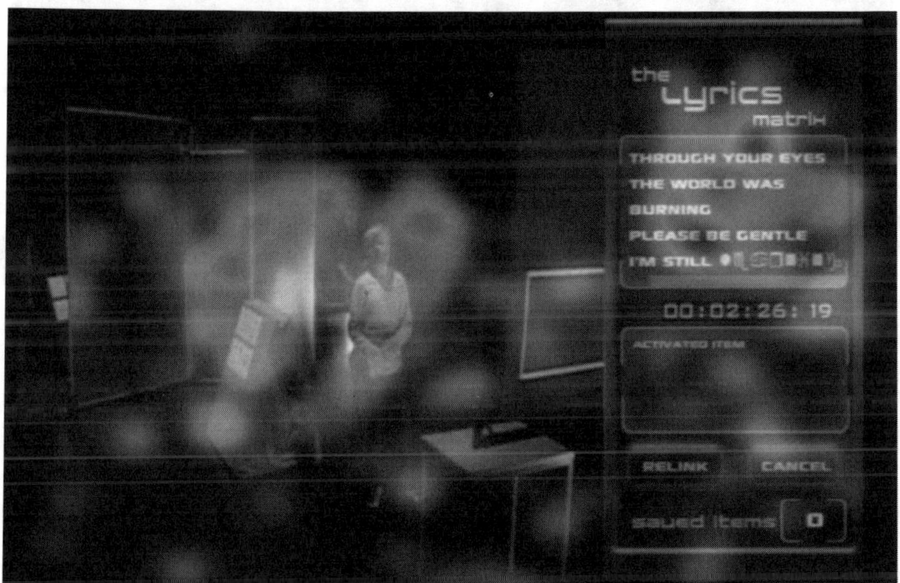

Figure 1: Screen shot of the TV show during the Lyrics Game *visualizing eye fixations of the viewer.*

On the web portal, the same game is concentrated to one screen, enabling it to be played by one user. This can be seen in Figure 2. Otherwise, the game is similar to the one on the television show.

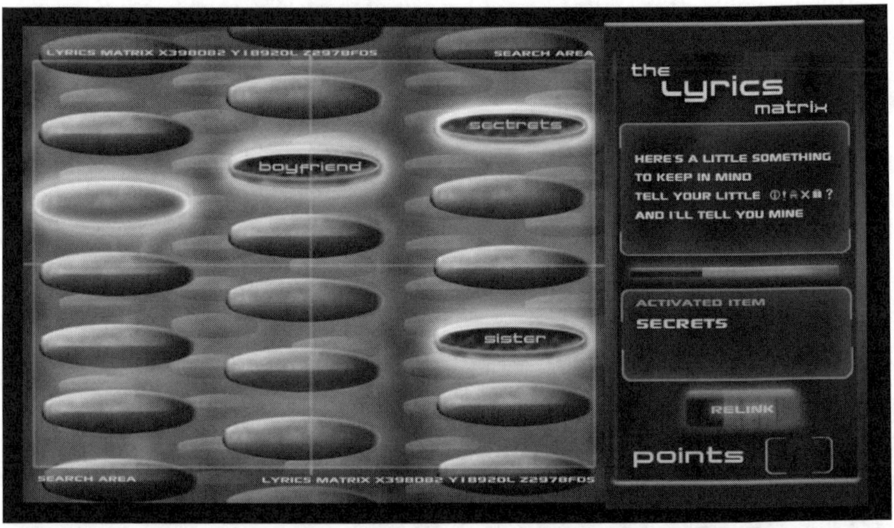

Figure 2: Screen shot of the Lyrics Game *featured on the web portal.*

The Lyrics Game works well as an edutainment game, as it focuses on popular music and lyrics, which themselves have entertainment value. Education-wise, the game trains the players and team members to find the correct words in sentences, sometimes drawing on memory but more often drawing on rhyming words, logical sentences, etc.

Other games include the Recycling Centre, where letters must be combined into words to be rescued back to the databases, or the Opposites Matrix, where opposite words must be found, descrambled and re-typed. All in all, over 15 different games have been developed to date.

Why Crossmedia? Why Not Interactive Television?

As stated, the original aim of the project "The Space Trainees" was to create an edutainment language-learning television format for interactive television based on MHP (Multimedia Home Platform) technology. However, the development team decided to re-evaluate this stance and subsequently move the project into another direction, that of crossmedia, combining television and web. The reasons behind this decision are as follows.

First, the team experienced severe restrictions on the development process while working in the MHP environment. Television is a media that thrives on exciting pictures, sound effects, music, and well-woven stories and strives to attain the suspension of disbelief among viewers. It is a media that we wanted to use for exactly those purposes. By using MHP technology, however, this simply was not possible.

Second, the market for MHP receivers in Finland (as in many other countries) remained extremely small. At the end of 2005, there were only about 20,000–30,000 MHP set-top-boxes in Finland (Miettinen, 2006) and only about 1,000 of these had their return channel properly connected, to allow for interactivity.

Working within the limitations of the MHP technology, the content created was thus not up to our desired standard. Furthermore, we believed we would be producing this sub-par content for a non-existent market. Instead, we re-thought and opted to go for the crossmedia solution of combining television and web. In doing so we liberated the project noticeably, allowing the strengths of the different media to support each other. The television show adds excitement and pulls viewers in, pushing them onwards to the web portal, which in turn allows for seamless interactivity and pushes the users back to the television show.

The aim of the development team was thus to create a crossmedia format that would reach the level of bridge-building crossmedia (Hayes, 2006), where the content of one media bridges into another media, later bridging onwards to a third media or back to the first media.

As "The Space Trainees" now stands, this has been achieved, and the television part of the format has its own purpose while the Internet-based part has another clear purpose:

Table 1: Fundamental Elements of the Crossmedia Design of "The Space Trainees"

Television *Linear Audiovisual Storytelling*	Internet *Virtual Environment for Personal Interactivity*
• Add visibility	• Individual experience
• Entertain	• Engage
• Inspiration for interactivity	• Individual learning
• Inspiration for learning	• Social interaction
• Push viewers to the interactive platforms	• Influence the linear storytelling

We have also, as indicated in the box above, researched into the possibilities of branching out "The Space Trainees" to mobile devices. The possibility exists and would be an ideal addition to the format but is currently on hold as we are concentrating on the formats for television and Internet.

Tests and Research Aiding the Development

When developing edutainment formats there are always two sides of the coin: the end product has to be both entertaining and educational. To cover these two dimensions, expertise from various fields of knowledge must be involved. It is also critical to study the end-user's actual learning experience and enjoyment at various phases of development; i.e., to look at the experience from the user's perspective. Therefore, we have considered it essential to continuously test "The Space Trainees" concept on the target audience throughout the entire development process. For this purpose, the design team has co-operated with iDTV Lab (the audience research unit within MediaCity) and conducted several studies to support the development process.

During the development process several pilot episodes and tests of game solutions and stage-setting solutions were filmed in a television studio to help aid in the development process and to give further information on the workings of the format and the crossmedia aspects involved. Beta versions of several MHP applications and later on two Flash games were also produced and integrated into the pilots and tests.Ultimately, the development, tests, and research amounted to a collaborative creative developmental project, involving an extensive design process. During this process there were many factors that needed to be considered regarding usability and user experience of the system being created (e.g., Bevan, 2008; Hassenzahl, 2008). The usability concerns led us to consider whether the games functioned at a practical level and whether the aims of the games were achieved (functionality, efficiency, and effectiveness). The user experience research targeted a subjective evaluation involving the user's satisfaction during interaction, his perceived pleasure and entertainment, as well as his perception of learning outcomes. Questions we sought answers to include: What is fun about watching the game show on TV? What is fun about playing the games on the computer? What factors contributed to the user's negative experiences? Do users feel that this is a good way to learn? Why? How? How does the collaborative dimension of the games contribute to their experience of learning and entertainment?

The research involved in the creation of "The Space Trainees" was conducted in close connection with the design phases (see Figure 3), and hence the aims were always pragmatic. Different variables were of interest at different phases of development. In the following, we will briefly summarize how research has been and continues to be involved in the development process. Figure 3 illustrates the crossmedia content development process of "The Space Trainees" in relation to the research studies conducted so far, as well as the studies planned for the rest of the development.

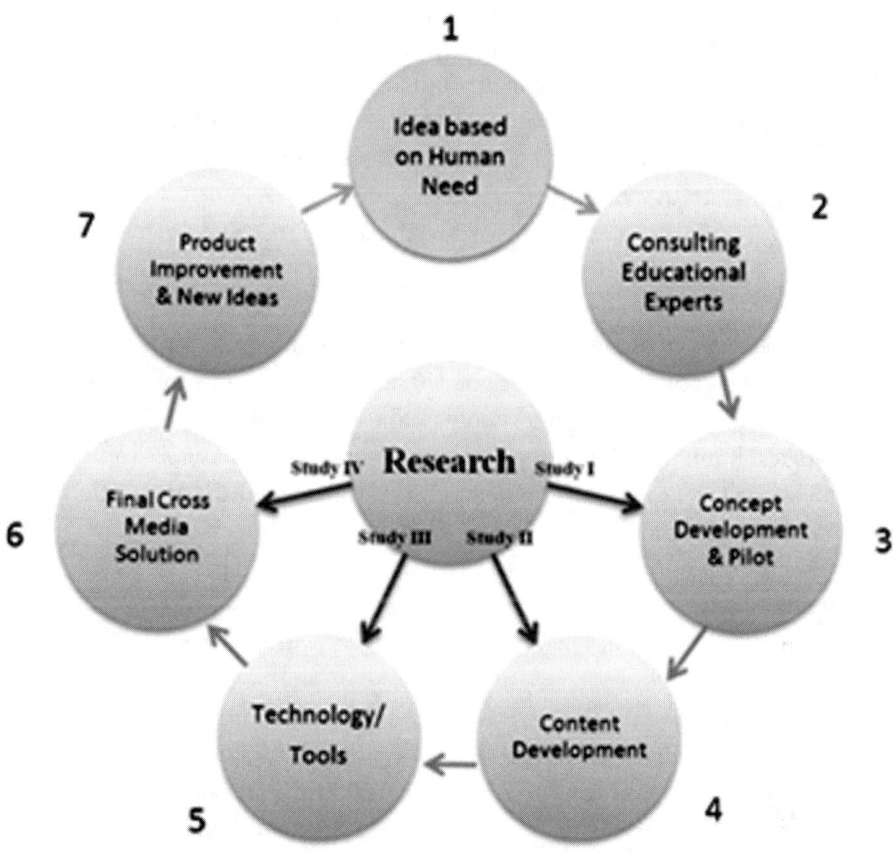

Figure 3: Illustration of research as an integrated part of the design phases of the edutainment format development

In phase 1 (*Idea based on Human Need*), the idea for an edutainment format emanated from the theory that children learn naturally through play and that academic learning is enhanced by involving the fun of play. This is an assumption of the basic human need of motivation as a base for facilitating learning. This is the thesis guiding edutainment solutions. In phase 2 (*Consulting Educational Experts*), the idea for an edutainment TV show was thoroughly elaborated on together with educational scientists.

Phase 3 (*Concept Development & Pilot*) was an intensive period of developing the concept further and creating a pilot episode that could be tested on children, used as a tool for further development, and also used as a marketing instrument to sell the format. The concepts needed to be tested on the targeted population. Twelve children were subjected to study (unpublished study, 2006). In this research both usability issues as well as user experience issues were examined. The demo used during these tests is an edited version of the pilot shot earlier, with interactive MHP games added. The basic storyline of the overall concept—the television series, the online portal and the background story—was to a certain extent the same as the one featured in the cross media format "The Space Trainees" as it stands today, but many details were still sketchy at this point. The featured games were relatively easy and simple, as more complex games could not be included due to the MPH's severe technological limitations (including weak processing power in the set-top-boxes of the time as well as slow connections that limited the size of the applications that were possible to download to the set-top-boxes within a reasonable timeframe). This study gave indications that the interactivity was well received by viewers and users. The overall concept also received support. Interactivity via set-top-box, however, brought some negative issues that contributed to the switch to crossmedia solutions instead.

Phase 4 (*Content Development*) continues to be an intensive period of design, testing, redesign, and further testing. Paper versions of the games were tested on a group of children (N=12) (unpublished study, 2008). The main issues examined were the logic of the games: how they worked, how the children understood them and enjoyed them, and how the collaboration between participants functioned. The games were evaluated from the children's point of view concerning usability and user experience at a phase where modifications to the games could still be made. This study of the further-developed versions of the concept, involving the content development phase, gave much needed information on the set instructions, the games themselves, and the collaboration between the children on the television show, and contributed to changes made during the later development phases.

Currently, we are at the point where the formats have been developed and test ed in order to meet standards required for creating an entertaining TV show. The language-learning games have also been tested regarding content and whether they match the expected level of knowledge of the targeted population. Phase 5 (*Technology Development*) is the next step, when technology developers will code the final Flash games to be used in the TV show and on the web portal. The Flash games will then be tested during the coding phase to detect usability issues. Phase 6 (*Final Crossmedia Solution*) involves testing the finalized games for user-experience issues on the targeted population on both forms of delivery: the TV show and the web portal. The final crossmedia product is planned to be released in the fall of 2009, when the TV show will be aired by the TV channel YLE FST5. The final product will be further subjected to extensive research targeting its value for learning and entertainment. The aim of this research is to build know-how for the crossmedia design team for future edutainment projects (Phase 7), but also to investigate further into the educational perspective on combining learning and play, in which educational scientists will be involved.

Results from the Research

The results from the different tests were encouraging for the development team and also gave substantial food for thought. All the pilots featured Swedish-speaking children training in English. In the first pilot, featuring MHP-based interactivity, Finnish-speaking children were also involved, training in English.

While testing the first full pilot with the earlier MHP-based interactivity, nine of the 12 children involved thought the program was "pretty good" or "very good," while eight would recommend it to others as well. One 11-year-old girl, commenting on the overall impression of the show, said, "it was exciting and it was great to be able to play along." Another girl, age 13, said, "I would say that it was exciting, and you can learn English through it." There were some usability issues, however, mostly with children not quite understanding the instructions of the games. The idea of interacting via a set-top-box also raised issues, particularly among the children more acquainted with computers. One boy, age 12, said, "...it's not as fun to sit with a small remote control and play. I would probably go to the computer after a while instead." Some of the children watched the show as a regular television show, without interactivity. It became clear that they, too, would have liked to get involved, or as one boy, age 13, said, "...I would have liked to help them out...otherwise, it could have become a bit boring." All the children participating in the interactive part of the test did, however, express delight at being able to play along (unpublished results).

Later, having opted for crossmedia solutions, several smaller pilots were shot to test the logic and functions of different games. The subsequent test involved seven 12-year-old children. These children watched the show as a regular television show, as there was no real-time interactivity featured. Instead, the aim was to create interest amongst the viewers to continue to the other part of the crossmedia concept, the web portal on the Internet. Half of the children[3] did, however, play along in the games "in their own heads" while watching the children on the show play the games. The other participants concentrated on the children playing instead of on the games themselves. One child said of the show: "It was fun to watch. It wasn't too hard and not too easy. You had to exercise your brain when the words were in English, and I didn't quite know how to spell them. And the short time and the false letters add to the excitement." Later, adding when asked whether he would watch it on television, he said, "It was fun. It sort of 'brightens up your day.' So I would watch it. Because it is a competition with children my age and it was just fun to see if I can do as well as they do." (unpublished results)

Drawing on these results and our own evaluation of the overall concept, we conclude that our initial assumptions were correct. Viewers want to interact—if the interaction can be made logical and appealing enough. A strong background story can help in that sense, by setting the stage for the viewers to crossover to different media and rewarding them with new experiences and possibilities when doing so.

Conclusions

Interactivity and crossmedia are ideal tools to complement and add to "normal" training and learning. As the development team realized while working on "The Space Trainees," there are, however, many pitfalls in the development process. What is needed from the outset is a clear vision of the desired end results as well as the flexibility to re-evaluate these visions and results if the development process or other aspects change the course of the project.

It is also critical to understand the properties of the different media involved—be it television, mobile, Internet, or any other media. The best way of making crossmedia solutions work is to build on the strengths of the different media involved, while allowing other media to cover for the parts that are not so strong. The crossing over between media should furthermore be developed in such a way that it feels not only natural to cross over to a new media, but even logical, for the user. This in contrast to so called "slap-on" crossmedia or interactivity, where the main content is developed and produced first and add-ons are added at a later stage without having been a part of the development process from the outset. Such interactive solutions are potentially more harmful than helpful to a project.

Finally, it is essential to involve experts from targeted fields in a cross-disciplinary project such as "The Space Trainees." As this project includes a television show, a web portal, a number of Flash games, and an educational resource for language learning, experts from all these fields were involved in the project to provide feedback and assist the development team. Without expert input, "The Space Trainees" would never have become what it is today.

Notes

1. "The Space Trainees" is at the moment (August 2009) in post-production for a run of a first series of 12 episodes, to be broadcast in Finland on the public service broadvaster YLEs Swedish-language FST-channel starting October 2009. The first series is English-training for Swedish-language children, aimed at the Swedish-speaking minority in Finland. A second series has been commissioned, to be produced in late 2009, featuring Swedish-language training for Swedish speaking children.

   Finland has two official languages, Finnish and Swedish, with media, including television broadcasts in both languages, due to the historical fact that Finland was a part of Sweden for several hundred years, so that the Swedish language has strong roots in Finland.

   The format has so far been optioned to production companies in the territories of Poland, Australia, China, and New Zealand.
2. http://ec.europa.eu/public_opinion/archives/ebs/ebs_147_summ_en.pdf
3. 3/7 during the first game, 4/7 during the second

References

Becker, K. (2007). Digital game-based learning once removed: Teaching teachers. *British Journal of Educational Technology, 38,* 478–488.

Bevan, N. (2008). UX, usability and ISO standards. Proceedings of CHI 2008, Florence, Italy.

Hassenzahl, M. (2008). User experience (UX): Towards an experiential perspective on product quality. Keynote in IHM 2008: Proceedings of the 20th French-speaking conference on Human-computer interaction in Metz, 2–5 September.

Hayes, G. (2006). Crossmedia—what audiences want. Retrieved March 3, 2008 from http://www.personalizemedia.com/index.php/2006/11/13/cross-media-what-audiences-want/

Hogle, J. G. (1996). *Considering games as cognitive tools: In search of effective "edutainment."* University of Georgia, Department of Instructional Technology

Miettinen, J. (2006). *Havaintoja digitv:n ensimmäiseltä 10-vuotiskaudelta Suomessa.* Viestinnän laitoksen tutkimusraportteja 1/2006.

Okan, Z. (2003). Edutainment. Is learning at risk? *British Journal of Educational Technology, 34,* 255–264.

Prensky, M. (2001). Digital natives, digital immigrants. Retrieved August 13, 2008 from http://www.marcprensky.com/writing/Prensky%20%20Digital%20Natives,%20Digital%20Immigrants%20-%20Part1.pdf

II

Competence Formation through Digital Content Creation

Personal Voice or Commercial Coercion?

5

Where Money and Meanings Meet

Theorizing the Emergence of New Values in Media and Education

John Hartley

Recent developments in technology, globalization, and consumer activism have challenged the "broadcasting model" of nationally bounded, vertically integrated, monopolistic, expert-paradigm media industries, dedicated to supplying leisure entertainment to more or less passive consumers. Instead, attention has turned to globally traded formats, social network markets, consumer-created content, multiplatform "publication," and a semiotic long tail where niche representations can be as valuable as blockbusters.[1]. Such changes are just as much a challenge to education as they are to business models. And education, both formal and informal, is a dynamic agent in these processes. Thus, the constant changes wrought in and by media technologies, processes, participation, and creative content require a rethink of "studies" just as much as of "media."

This chapter reviews the changes and challenges in the scholarly field, to ask some questions about education more generally. Going forward, what disciplinary methods and traditions will provide an adequate explanatory framework for a dynamic, changing, and emergent field? Given advances in evolutionary, complexity, and games theory, has the time come when the study of culture needs to shift from "critical" values to testable models—from the humanities (cultural studies) to the sciences (cultural science)? Should media *education* (as opposed to schooling) shift from a provider model to a demand-based model, propagating creativity in informal (entertainment) contexts, rather than in formal institutions?

Such questions are prompted by the fact that, historically, formal disciplinary knowledge has had some difficulty in coming to terms with rapidly evolving technologies of communication. Both humanities and social-science approaches to mass publishing and broadcast media, for example, began as aversion therapy. Literary and cultural studies criticized the aesthetic and cultural values of popular culture; social sciences sought to measure their behavioral or structural shortcomings. Both literary critics and social scientists studied media in terms of negative effects. It has been a long time since the "effects model" held undisputed sway in either the cultural or the behavioral sciences (although it certainly remains active in the latter), but, nevertheless, the study of broadcast media—especially in education—is still largely organized around critique rather than creativity and competence.

However, post-broadcast media pose a challenge to this paradigm. Old-style media industries are evolving into emerging social network markets, (Potts et al., 2008a; Potts et al., 2008b; Hartley, 2009), for which an adversarial approach is no longer sufficient. New frameworks of investigation are required to explain the convergence not only of different technologies but also of entire value systems; in particular, the convergence of economic and cultural values, producer and consumer productivity, money and meanings. This is the project of cultural science (http://cultural-science.org/) that will be referred to later in the chapter.

A New Paradigm for Digital Literacy

First, what kind of paradigm shift is this? Because of accelerating technological affordances and economic growth from the 1960s to 2008, there are now burgeoning possibilities for both professional and popular uses of multimedia, notwithstanding the financial crisis of 2008, for by this time social networking technologies had become reliable, cheap, and ubiquitous. Both non-market and market-based activism and social-network formation achieved a significant component of bottom-up or consumer co-creation, while at the same time attracting major commercial investment and entrepreneurship. Given that user creativity and commercialized intellectual property rights management are all mixed up, it is proper to ask whether these commercialized uses of digital literacy are evidence for the progressive potential of self-directed popular agency (bottom-up consumer co-creation) or for the success of manipulative corporate populism (top-down expert exploitation)?

Doubtless both of these conditions can be present simultaneously. However, the idea that intellectuals or educators can stand aside from or opposed to the productivity of digital culture can no longer be sustained, despite noisy attempts (e.g., Keen, 2007). It is no longer an option, if it ever was, to criticize popular culture from the outside, because the boundaries between that domain and the domains of formal, intellectual, critical, scientific, journalistic, and imaginative knowledge are dissolving. You can *navigate* the online environment to choose social networks or entertainment over science or Project Gutenberg, but these choices are not *structured* by the system, which allows ordinary people simultaneously to partake of popular entertainment and purposeful growth of knowledge and to decide among themselves, peer-to-peer, what they need, rather than relying on providers who may have pecuniary, ideological, or other ulterior motives. This has been described in the business press as a "fundamental change in behaviour": "*A social trend in which people use technologies to get the things they need from each other, rather than from traditional institutions like corporations*" (Li & Bernoff, 2008, p. 3). The "things they need" include education—and social networks and online media technologies are there to help.

The challenge then is not to oppose populism in the name of some regulatory intellectualism that knows in advance what's good for people, but to capture the energy of consumer productivity itself and to promote the development of consumer entrepreneurship within a complex system of market-based self-actualisation. Not enough critical attention has been paid to what ordinary people need to learn, either from an expert or from each other, in order to attain a level of digital literacy appropriate for *producing* as well as *consuming* digital content; thence to participate in the mediated public sphere, to pursue their own private imaginative desires, to contribute to the growth of knowledge, or to develop enterprises and create value (cultural and economic) in commercial or community contexts. Such mass productivity is evolutionary in character. It extends to whole populations the process of trial-and-error experimentation, failure, adaptation, and niche-filling that industrial innovation reserves to the corporate lab. Hence, scaling up the creative capacity of consumer-users goes beyond the satisfaction of individual or even commercial needs; it extends to the development of national and international innovation systems.

A reappraisal of humanities research is overdue. The field needs to reconfigure its understanding of the conditions of a consumer-led society. This is an open, investigative, critical, scientific task—a task for cultural science—as well as an opportunity to engage with creative enterprise and culture. The humanities to date have worked in an intellectual climate that favors culture and the arts (meanings) over mass-media forms (money), and critique over productivity. Because of a lingering media-effects model that positions audiences as behavioral effects of corporate causation (Gauntlett, 1998; 2005), that perspective is sceptical at best about the productive and progressive capacities of the popular audience. Equally, the creativity of the commercial sphere is doubted, and the possibility of achieving intellectual or political freedom in a commercial environment is treated with something close to contempt. These two critical moves confine creativity and productivity to the specialist (and restrictive) domain of the arts and intellectuals.

This approach now needs revisiting in the face of a cultural environment in which innovation arises out of public and private endeavours (Rifkin, 2000, p. 24–9, 82–95) and from individual and institutional agents and enterprises. That nexus, where money and meanings meet, is consumer co-created content or user-led innovation (Zittrain, 2007). Consumers are influencing and disrupting former patterns of media production and distribution and now, as Henry Jenkins puts it, "consumers may gain power through the assertion of new kinds of economic and legal relations and not simply through making meanings" (Jenkins, 2004, p. 36). Now that every user is a publisher, consumption needs to be re-thought as action not behaviour and media consumption as a mode of literacy: that is, an autonomous means of communication in which writing is as widespread as reading; something that was never possible during the era of broadcast, one-to-many, passively received mass communication. The implications are far-reaching, encompassing intellectual debates on the impact of new technologies, the sources, types and outcomes of innovation, and the role of consumer- or user-led innovation, as well as informing policy and industry development in the services sector of the knowledge economy.

In a contested arena, there's a need to understand what links opposing viewpoints, such as corporate and community approaches to creativity, to combine critique of power with the promotion of participation—creative industries with culture jamming (Lovink and Rossiter, 2007, pp. 204–16). The industrial era was characterized by concentrations of power based on ownership and control of capital, plant, and physical resources. In the creative industries, power is concentrated, instead, via control over access and distribution of information. This change results in the emergence of new sites of contestation; for instance, around intellectual property and copyright law, branding, cyber-democracy, the open-source movement and consumer rights (including consumer labor rights). As contemporary cultures transform from the industrial (mass) era of broadcasting and entertainment towards consumer-led interactivity and customization, there is a need to identify areas where regulation or intervention by state or international authorities is warranted and where the potential exists to broaden the social base of communications and enterprise, or where increased capacity in semiotic systems resulting from new technologies may encourage new forms of popular literacy in multimedia communications, or what Henry Jenkins called convergence culture using participatory media (Jenkins, 2003; 2006).

Such an endeavour must also be part of an attempt to understand longer-term changes in knowledge (Lee, 2003). Knowledge, culture, communication, and consumption are dynamic fields of evolutionary adaptation. They concern the growth of human relationships, values, identities, and desires, in complex interaction with the forces of political power, economic and institutional organization, market coordination, and technological invention. Meanings interact with money, economic values with cultural values, the political with the personal. At the micro level of ordinary experience, we feel and form these forces, interactions and changes as part of the unpredictable immediacy of everyday life. This is exactly the generative edge of growth (Zittrain, 2007), but it is rarely experienced at the time as part of a larger pattern.

However, larger patterns can be discerned at the macro level of systems and networks, which themselves interconnect and change over time. Indeed, the growth of knowledge seems to display a tendency, over long-term historical epochs, to cluster most intensively around successive links of the value chain of meaning (Figure 1). That is, in pre-modern (feudal) times the most productive source of knowledge was found at the *producer* end of the chain; during the modern (industrial) era its source shifted to the *commodity* (the text, document, or object of empirical investigation); while in the current postmodern (globalized) era the source of knowledge seems to have shifted ever more decisively to the *consumer* or *user*. Such a shift seems also to be part of a broad pattern—or paradigm—of related changes, as demonstrated in Figure 1, where the who, what, when, where, why, and how of communication all seem to be subject to historic shifts along their respective value chains, resulting in three characteristic paradigmatic clusters corresponding to production/author, commodity/text, and consumer/audience (columns 1, 2, and 3 in Figure 1).

At this macro scale, it is evident that different aspects of knowledge, culture, power, communication, and identity share important features and that these amount to a paradigm (in the semiotic rather than the Kuhnian sense) that characterizes particular eras. The present period does seem to be one of rapid change, arguably from a modern to a global paradigm. This macro level shift is partly responsible for the hostile reception that modernist critics sometimes give to phenomena arising in the global one—there's a kind of parallax error involved in assessing the values associated with one paradigm from the point of view of another (this partly explains the vehemence of the denunciation of postmodernism by modernists, for example). If this is the case, then such critical hostility is not necessarily the last word. Instead, the various different components of the global paradigm

Paradigm/Era:	**1 Premodern**	**2 Modern**	**3 Global**
Value chain ...			
... of merchandise	origination/production	commodity/distribution	consumption/use
... of meaning	author/producer	text/performance	reader/audience
When, where, who (time, place, population)			
When	medieval	modern	global
Where	church	public sphere	private life
Who (population)	the faithful	the public	DIY citizen
Who (intermediary)	priest	publisher	marketing
How (regime)			
Theorist	Bible	Marx	Foucault
Subjectivity	soul	individual(ism)	experience/identity
Power	pain of death/	war	administration of life
Sovereign	monarch/divine	nation-state	self
Armed force	knight/crusader	conscript/volunteer	terrorist
Enemy	peer/heretic	country	civilian
State	Hobbesian	Machiavellian	Kantian
Why (knowledge)			
Philosophy	revelation	scarcity	plenty
Epistemology	theology	empiricism	plebiscite
Educational reach	elite	mass	universal
What (form)			
Systemic form	household/family	industry	network
Interpretive form	exegesis	criticism	redaction
Creative form	ritual (liturgy)	realism: science/journalism/novel	reality (TV)
What *for* (communicative politics			
Mode of literacy	hear only	read only	read & write
Mode of address	to convert	to convince	to converse
Who says (choice control)			
Source of control	"Him"—divine control	"Them"—expert control	"Me"—self control
Source of choices	no choices	publisher/provider	navigator/aggregator
Who says (agent of Knowledge)			
Knowing subject	cleric	reading public/media audience	consumer entrepreneurs
=	**= fundamentalism**	**= modernism/Marxism**	**= globalization**

Figure 1: The value chain of meanings: The ascribed source of meaning in different epochs in the modernizing West.

should be analyzed on their own terms, simply in order to grasp how they interconnect and what these manifold shifts to the consumer end of the value chain might amount to overall. Thus, digital literacy needs to be understood in light of the large-scale paradigmatic changes of which it is a part.

Multimedia Literacy: Print, Media, Critical, Digital

Multimedia popular entertainments pose a challenge to formal education, but it is not the challenge feared by modernist critics, that of dumbing down, where aesthetic, scientific, and political values alike are being overrun by rampant commercial populism. However, the real challenge posed by the postmodern or global paradigm is of a different order: it is that compared with the modern paradigm, creativity and expertise are more widely distributed, the growth of knowledge faster, productive agency more individual, and knowledge more likely to be exchanged in a market. So rather than devaluing knowledge, commercial culture may be *outpacing* formal schooling in promoting creative digital literacy via entrepreneurial and distributed learning. It may indeed be that those in need of a creative makeover are not dumbed-down teenagers but know-all teachers. If we do live in a commercial but humane democracy, then the popular media, especially in the form of social network markets, are a chief means for interconnecting the human and the democratic parts of the community and for linking experts and specialists in government, business and the professions to the general population of ordinary people.

Thus, it seems timely for a new attempt to be made to understand these forces in relation to the *uses* to which both lay populations and expert elites put their media literacy. One important change is the extent to which media literacy itself has evolved from read-only (broadcast, one-to-many) to read and write (interactive, peer-to-peer). Early media theorists compared broadcasting with the pulpit or soapbox, where a single message was shouted from the perspective of some institutional vested interest. The role of the populace was to stand around passively and soak it up. However, in the last few years and at gathering pace, non-professionals have taken up these media as an autonomous means of communication for themselves. Writing is catching up with reading.

Here media literacy is merely following the historical pattern set by print literacy. In the early modern period, the use of reading spread well before that of writing, and even if people could write, they tended not to have much use for that skill in everyday intercourse and commerce. Only when a significant proportion of people began to write as well as read (around two-thirds of adults) did Western society produce journalism, the Enlightenment, the Industrial Revolution, the novel, and democracy. It was at that point that the social activists and emancipationists of the day realized what a friend they had in literacy and so began the long haul to invest in it sufficiently, via public schooling and private propagation, for everyone to be a participant and for the skill to be put to useful ends. Ever since, universal print literacy has been a measure of advanced status for any country wanting to compete in the modern world.

In contrast, when the electronic (broadcast) media got going during the first half of the twentieth century, the intelligentsia were under the influence of high modernism on the cultural side and the spectre of demagogic totalitarianism on the political side. It was a climate in which few policy activists believed a new literacy was at hand, much less one that needed to be taught. Instead, following critical theorist T.W. Adorno or literary critic F.R. Leavis (depending on where they stood in the disciplinary and political spectrum), they policy-makers believed ordinary people needed to be armed against the influence of such media, which was seen as a threat to print literacy and the rational and imaginative values it was said to promote (see also the chapter by Herr-Stephenson in this volume). Just as no special training beyond native curiosity and scepticism was needed for people to appreciate stage shows or to listen to sermons, so the new world of entertainment and persuasion (political and commercial) seemed to need no special literacy. If it was involved at all, it needed to be a critical literacy, dedicated to counteracting rather than extending the reach and sway of what were thought to be powerful and unscrupulous forces acting upon the people.

This is what was taught in schools: not how to make the most of the electronic media but how to make the least of them. It did not occur to many commentators that the general run of humanity might use these new media as they might use a pencil or their own voice to express and to share their own identity, relationships, and ideas. Those who did think about the emancipationist potential of radio and cinema—such as Berthold Brecht (1979/80), Humphrey Jennings (1985) or Hans Magnus Enzensberger (1974; 1997)—tended to think about media literacy in class terms rather than personal ones: the masses could represent themselves via new media, but mainly *as* masses.

With the popularization of online media in affluent economies, the notion of media literacy needs to be extended beyond the defensive notion of critical reading and media literacy as taught in schools, towards what ought to be called digital literacy—a form of hands-on productive expression, taught by and within the milieu in which it is deployed, using multiplatform devices to write as well as read electronic media; a literacy that goes beyond access, understanding, and use, to encompass creativity, innovation, and change. The history of print literacy suggests that the political and cultural impact of new communicative competences is at its most dynamic when between one third and two thirds of a national population is literate. Thus, the English, French, and Russian revolutions all occurred when their societies were in this dynamic state of transition between popular non-literacy and mass literacy (Stone 1969: 101; see also Kaestle 1985). Influential commentators have seen political democracy as a consequence of literacy (Goody & Watt, 1963). This is when a technology or medium escapes from the intentions of its inventors and the control of established interests to achieve its own potential among whole populations.

The read/write capability of digital literacy has not yet reached this level.

However, there has been little call for the kind of investment (especially public investment) in its propagation—not to mention its uses—that accompanied print literacy. Some schools and education authorities seem to be focused as much on limiting as on extending its effects. Hence, creative or generative digital literacy is primarily taught on a peer-to-peer, informal basis. The investment is almost all private, seeking to develop markets rather than citizens. It is a demand-side rather than a supply-side model of literacy propagation, and for that reason it has attracted less attention than it warrants from educational and cultural thinkers, who tend to cluster around publisher/provider models and not to know enough about how digital literacy is learnt (by doing) in informal contexts or how it is used among untutored populations.

After its invention in 1450, printing by movable type remained for a time largely tied to instrumental purposes: religion (ideology), commerce (private profit), and government (control). The gap between elite and lay populations was marked by a distinction between those who could and did read and write for all purposes including personal expression, on the one hand, and a larger population who were taught a read-only version of print literacy. The latter could read but did not write, especially not for publication. At a societal level, print literacy was geared to the needs of closed expert systems: clerical, scientific, government, commercial. Print was rarely used by ordinary folk for leisure consumption (let alone production), personal expression, the maintenance of communities of interest, or for the imagination (literature). It took a long time for print literacy to escape from instrumental purposes and to enter the life of the demos. This was achieved by a combination of *public* investment in *acquiring* print literacy through universal schooling, and *private* investment in *using* literacy though popular culture (Hoggart, 1957).

It was here, in the popular media, not through formal education, where the gap between elites and popular readerships began to be filled with non-instrumental (albeit read-only) literacy (Eco, 1986). The common folk received sensationalism (radical and commercial) along with their science and sermons. In other words, and more accurately, a demand-led or market element was established in the economy of literacy, in addition to the public or supply-side provision. Richard Hoggart (1957) was the first modernist critic to notice that these demand-led uses of literacy were both quite different from expert or instrumental uses and also worthy of serious inquiry. Hoggart was interested in mass entertainment from the point of view of the popular readership. Famously, he found it wanting, at odds with self-made working-class culture. That is why his work is associated with the valorization of critical literacy, which means an astute readership trained to resist rather than embrace the attractions of commercial culture.

But times have changed. The difference between the print and digital eras is that digital literacy—which assumes and supplements but does not supplant print literacy—allows for universal uptake of writing as well as reading, of publishing as well as sitting back and enjoying the performances of others. In the era of one-way, broadcast communication and supply-side providers, there was little room for a popular uptake of *publishing*. The broadcast media, focused on audience maximinsation and, therefore, on delivering content *to* consumers, failed almost completely to promote published writing *among* wide sections of its newly acquired mass readership: the mass media mode was B2C, not p2p. So the asymmetry inherited from print, between expert producers and ordinary consumers, was made more extreme, even while broadcasters gathered whole populations into their textual webs; the lag between reading and writing remained. People could enjoy stories, but not publish their own. This is what has now changed. Digital literacy opens up the possibility for universal publication. And it is within popular entertainment and leisure culture, rather than in formal education, that the potential of digital self-representation, user-led innovation, consumer-created content, and do-it-yourself publishing is being most actively explored.

Towards Cultural Science

Limited ambition is primarily holding cultural studies back at the moment, amounting sometimes to defeatism, of its own practitioners, who excel at in-close micro analysis of local specificities without reaching for an adequate macro level of conceptualization to replace the long-dominant but increasingly abandoned modernist/Marxist framework. In other words, cultural studies, born of paradigm 3 (Figure 1; and see Lee, 2003), has not fully emancipated itself from the prejudices of paradigm 2, and even of paradigm 1, as is attested by the collective fetishization of the producer, designer, author, or other creative originator. Given the incredible energy and productivity of popular culture itself, this failure to develop a concerted strategy of theory-formation and conceptual framework development, to understand how new media, popular sense-making, and global commercial enterprise may extend cultural and economic productivity (meanings and money) to whole populations, thereby contributing to the overall process of the growth of knowledge, is damaging, to say the least. The productivity of popular culture—of open digital literacy among non-specialist agents and enterprises—is now such that it demands a more systematic response than can be achieved by maintaining a resistive stance to culture and media.

The failure to think *systematically* at the macro level seems to result in part from the capture of cultural studies by culture war partisanship, where ideologies and values have become more important than description and theorization. Such partisanship is quite understandable, especially at times when neo-cons stalk the corridors of power and the airwaves, but it makes for poor science. Cultural studies have become most strongly established at the values end of the disciplinary spectrum, the polar opposite of the quantitative sciences. It is becoming the secular successor of that branch of clerical training concerned with sermonizing—using rhetoric, textual exegesis, and moral precepts to guide the young in public values, personal comportment, and a vision of ethical living. This is, of course, valuable and useful, but it is a long way from science; even as modified by the creative destruction of complexity and cultural studies (Lee, 2003), and even if the most progressive definitions of science are used; for instance, that the word describes not "positivist empiricism" but more broadly "self-correcting knowledge" or "contested knowledge." In cultural studies, there is often too much contestation and not enough knowledge. It is often difficult to contribute to the process of self-correcting knowledge without engaging in it directly; that is, by self-correcting the domain of cultural studies itself.

Oddly enough, this is exactly where cultural studies came in. Richard Hoggart himself saw the need for his own field—modernist literary criticism—to engage with the social sciences; this was his project in the early days of the Centre for Contemporary Cultural Studies (CCCS). He sought the input of sociologist Alan Shuttleworth, who presented a paper on "Max Weber and the Cultural Sciences" (Shuttleworth, 1966). This theme was later picked up by another pioneer of cultural studies, Raymond Williams. In 1973, Williams made a speech to the Council for National Academic Awards (CNAA), the body charged with the modernization of the higher-education curriculum in the United Kingdom via the new polytechnics, whose degree schemes were validated by the CNAA.[2] Williams used the occasion to propose something new—a risky enterprise, as he knew only too well from working in the old humanities, where:

> You can go on doing, in effect without challenge, virtually anything that has ever been done, but if you propose anything new you are lucky if your integrity escapes whipping; your intelligence and sensibility will have been long given up as dead (Williams, 1974).

Undaunted, Williams went on: "The approach I want to describe is that of cultural studies, which is English for 'cultural science.'" Williams traced the study of culture from early modern attempts to understand it as general human development driven by spirit or consciousness, to the Marxist notion of culture as material production. He wanted to move on, to identify the central problem of cultural science as "the relations between different practices," and thus to see communication itself as a practice amenable to analysis by cultural science. He borrowed the term from continental sociology after Weber and Dilthey. It is worth noting here that the binary split between arts and sciences that bedevils Anglophone disciplines is unknown in continental traditions, where the human sciences are part of science, because science refers to knowledge in general, not only to white-coat experimentation. Williams was attracted to the *openness* of cultural science and this is what he wanted to translate into English as "cultural studies":

> Out of this argument, about the relation between practices, came the new concept of cultural science and with it a significant part of modern sociology...Now the spirit of this whole inquiry—to which literally thousands of people have contributed—is profoundly open, alert, and general. It has had its bitter and even its squalid controversies, and this is understandable; but in temper and approach, it is in a wholly different dimension from what seems our own small world of small cultivators, heads down to their own fields...
>
> I recall the spirit of cultural science because I am interested in its heirs—who will change its methods but will still inherit its vigorous and general humanity... The work will be done because I think there are now enough of us who want to work in these ways to survive the defences of special interests, the general drizzle of discouragement, and even the more deep-rooted inertia of contemporary orthodox culture, to announce in effect an open conspiracy: that in new ways, by trial and error but always openly and publicly, we shall do this work because it needs to be done (Williams, 1974).

An open conspiracy among those thousands of people and their heirs who, systematically in theory but by trial and error in practice, and in a spirit of vigorous and general humanity, seek to study the *relations between different practices*: this is the prolegomena for cultural science still, even though the project itself must necessarily be updated and refined to study *evolutionary change* in practices and not just their *structural relations*. Thus, cultural science now is described in this provisional statement, in which I had a hand.

A provisional mission statement for cultural science

- *Creative productivity* has always emerged from *human interactions*, but it is increasingly *mediated by technologies* that promote subjective mental representations as *networks*, in which space and time are compressed through the continual dissemination and retrieval of *stored events*.

- The interaction of people within this *social network economy* creates a continual flux of *ephemeral communities* and *novel entrepreneurial opportunities*, with *unforeseen consequences* being the norm rather than the exception.
- This process of *creative destruction* is best addressed by the humanities allying with the dynamic science of *evolution*—the study of continual change through variation, interaction, selection, and drift.
- Cultural science, therefore, seeks an *evolutionary understanding of a knowledge-based society past and present*, in order to map the possibility space of future scenarios for creative productivity (both market-based and in community contexts) to which public policy and business strategies must adapt (<*cultural-science.org/*>).

The need for cultural studies to return to its cultural-science roots is the more urgent because the field risks being overtaken, displaced, and supplanted. A long-term trend can be observed in which disciplines once located in the humanities have drifted ever more firmly into the mathematical sciences—biology (once natural history), geography, economics, and psychology to name a few. Some of these, especially psychology and neuroscience, are becoming ever more confident about explaining culture. So, too, are the evolutionary sciences: game theory, complexity theory, and evolutionary theory. Indeed, it is evolution—the adaptation of complex dynamic systems to change—that can bring the humanities and sciences back together—in particular, evolutionary economics, cultural studies, and the creative industries. The cutting-edge of research on creativity lies in the triangulation of three domains: evolution, complexity, and creative innovation. This interdisciplinary interface is counterintuitive but highly productive:

- Creativity can be understood as reflexive adaptation to unpredictable change within complex systems.
- Complexity studies explain how social network markets are a vital enabling technology for the distribution of choice.
- Evolutionary theory focuses on the dynamics of change in the growth of knowledge.

Cultural science combines approaches from the humanities and the evolutionary sciences, and it focuses on the structures and dynamics of:

- *creativity*, understood as both generative and institutionalized;
- *identity*, understood as a property of agency in systems;

- *relationships* (as Williams prescribed), understood as complex communicative connectivity in *networks*;
- the growth of *knowledge,* understood as evolutionary and open.

Cultural science identifies patterns of action in complex social networks; their past evolution and possible future scenarios, including paying attention to unintended consequences of choices at any given moment. Some of that work must involve mathematical modeling, computational research power, large-scale data-collection, and much greater attention to robust empirical methodology than has been evident to date. All of these developments can assist those coming from the humanities—including cultural studies, ethnography, and the creative arts—to rethink creativity as a property of agency in dynamic systems. But there will be pain for some: practitioners of cultural science must engage with another kind of digital literacy: mathematics. As the pioneer of artificial intelligence John McCarthy says in his tagline, "He who refuses to do arithmetic is doomed to talk nonsense."[3] Harsh—but increasingly true—even for those who work in humanities.

Reflexive creativity is what enables human culture to adapt and change, a process that—despite some 'mass extinctions' of entire knowledge systems (e.g., hieroglyphics, Latin) throughout the millennia—has resulted in an exponential growth in knowledge and in the creation of new values, economic and cultural. Culture can no longer be seen as the preserve of artists. It is made up of the activities and productivity of the millions who interact in the social networks that are now dispersed among whole populations. With the growing ubiquity of digital media and consumer content creation, these are becoming a more dynamic source of productivity than industrial innovation, and it is here that we will find the most important uses of digital media. The open-source social network swarm outperforms the expert lab, protected by patents and intellectual property rights, and at twice the speed.

One of the best examples of how that sort of innovation works is in science itself; astronomers and physicists use digital networks to increase the scale and speed of their calculations. But the same model works in the fashion system, where constant innovation is equally imperative and a complex social network market determines individual choices in a culture that relishes risk. Such systems can be analyzed using in-close contextual techniques from the humanities and computational power to map social networks of choice and change in the way people perform their cultural identity and relationships (themselves and with others), a process that is well under way in Internet and network studies. Theory-building is also vital to model how such actions are patterned in complex adaptive systems and how agents and enterprises navigate those systems.

What does this mean for digital literacy and its uses? Individual creative innovation, which cannot be practiced without digital literacy, can be modeled as part of a large-scale, population-wide process—the growth of knowledge. This needs to be analyzed at all three levels of scale: the macro or system level, the meso or institutional level, and at the micro level of individual agency (Dopfer & Potts, 2007). Some of the most critical problems in this context are clustered around participation, of both agents and enterprises, in a context where industrial-age expertise (education) competes with population-wide access and use (entertainment). Thus, an urgent research problem is the question of expertise itself: the changing balance or tension between certificated expertise as currently understood and distributed expertise, which includes crowd sourcing, groundswell, the wisdom of crowds, etc. In other words, digital literacy is by no means an individual attribute or skill only; it is a property of systems and can be expanded and exploited by institutions and enterprises.

Further, digital literacy in circumstances of consumer productivity can be assumed to include non-proprietary or non-instrumental expertise, as when individuals with particular professional or craft skills put their expertise in the service of community- or locality based groups rather than (or as well as) hiring it for wages or profit (see the chapter by Löwgren in this volume). The point for educators and analysts to grasp is that digital literacy is a means whereby the productivity of the system as a whole can be enhanced; it is not simply training for specialist careers. Nonetheless, such careers will increasingly depend upon it.

From this perspective, the creative industries and new digital media can be seen as a kind of creative wrecking ball, or experimental lab, in relation to existing models of economic growth and cultural participation. The creative destruction (i.e., the improvement by unforeseen innovation) of the modernist knowledge paradigm is overdue in economic and cultural analysis; while the emergent global paradigm should form an important focus for research, both empirical and theory-forming, over the coming years.

Some challenging ideas are already in play; for instance, the Santa Fe Institute's attempts to produce a computational science, or even physics, of society.[4] In the face of such expansive confidence among the enabling sciences, it is important for humanities-based researchers and educators to establish principles and directions for work in the field of cultural and economic values, leading to a new cultural science. The empirical focus is on the shift from closed expert process (professional production in vertically integrated firms) and structural analysis to an open innovation system and complex adaptive networks; for example, investigating social network markets. At present that shift is more evident in informal networks and among entertainment media than it is in formal education.

The fundamental problem to be addressed is how knowledge is evolving in a dynamic and complex open system that unifies the economic and cultural spheres and harnesses the energy of all the agents in the system, both individuals and enterprises. This is a domain in which money (commercial markets and entertainment media) and meanings (public culture and knowledge) will meet—in the numberless but networked ideas, actions and creative innovations of the population at large.

Notes

1. See: www.thelongtail.com/
2. The CNAA validated Britain's first degree courses in communication studies—first at Sheffield City Polytechnic (1975–76) and second at the Polytechnic of Wales (1977), where I was a member of the course committee led by John Fiske.
3. See <en.wikiquote.org/wiki/John_McCarthy>; and see <www-formal.stanford.edu/jmc/>.
4. See <www.santafe.edu/research/topics-dynamics-human-behavior-institutions.php>.

References

Brecht, B. (1979/80). Radio as a means of communication: A talk on the function of radio. *Screen, 20*, 24–28.

Dopfer, K., & Potts, J. (2007). *The general theory of economic evolution*. New York: Routledge.

Eco, U. (1986). *Travels in hyperreality.* San Diego & New York: Harcourt Brace Jovanovich.

Enzensberger, H. M. (1974). *The consciousness industry: On literature, politics, and the media*. New York: Seabury Press.

Enzensberger, H. M. (1997). *Critical essays*. London & New York: Continuum Books.

Gauntlett, D. (1998). Ten things wrong with the "effects model." In Dickinson, R., Harindranath, R., & Linné, O. (Eds.) *Approaches to audiences—A reader.* London: Arnold, accessible at: www.theory.org.uk/david/effects.htm

Gauntlett, D. (2005). *Moving experiences, 2nd edition: Media effects and beyond.* London: John Libbey.

Goody, J. & I. Watt (1963). The consequences of literacy. *Comparative studies in society and history, 5:3,* 304–345.

Hartley, J. (2009). From the consciousness industry to creative industries: Consumer-created content, social network markets and the growth of knowledge. In Holt, J., & Perren., A. (Eds.) *Media industries: History, theory and methods*. (231–244). Malden, MA and Oxford: Wiley-Blackwell.

Hoggart, R. (1957). *The uses of literacy*. London: Chatto & Windus.

Jenkins, H. (2003). Games, the new lively art. In Goldstein., J. & Raessens,. J. (Eds.) *Handbook of computer game studies*. Cambridge, MA: The MIT Press.

Jenkins, H. (2004). The cultural logic of media convergence. *International Journal of Cultural Studies,*

7(1), 33–44.

Jenkins, H. (2006). *Convergence culture.* New York: NYU Press.

Jennings, H. (1985). *Pandemonium: The coming of the machine as seen by contemporary observers.* London: André Deutsch/Picador.

Kaestle, C. F. (1985) 'The History of Literacy and the History of Readers.' *Review of Research in Education, 12,* 11–53.

Keen, A. (2007). *The cult of the amateur: How the democratization of the digital world is assaulting our economy, our culture, and our values.* New York: Doubleday Currency.

Lee, R. E. (2003). *Life and times of cultural studies: The politics and transformation of the structures of knowledge.* Durham, NC: Duke University Press.

Li, C., & Bernoff, J. (2008). *Groundswell: Winning in a world transformed by social technologies.* Cambridge, MA: Harvard Business Press.

Lovink, G. and Rossiter, N. (Eds.) (2007). *My creativity reader: A critique of creative industries.* Amsterdam: Institute of Network Cultures.

Potts, J., Hartley, J., Banks, J., Burgess, J., Cobcroft, R., Cunningham, S., Montgomery, L. (2008a). Consumer co-creation and situated creativity. *Industry and Innovation, 15(*5), 459–474.

Potts, J., Cunningham, S., Hartley, J., Ormerod, P. (2008b). Social network markets: A new definition of the creative industries. *Journal of Cultural Economics, 32*(3), 167–185.

Rifkin, J. (2000). *The age of access: How the shift from ownership to access is transforming modern life.* London: Penguin.

Shuttleworth, A. (1966). Two working papers in cultural studies: A humane centre; and Max Weber and the "cultural sciences." *Occasional Paper No. 2.* Birmingham: Centre for Contemporary Cultural Studies.

Stone, L. (1969). 'Literacy and education in England, 1640–1900.' *Past and Present. 42,* 69–139.

Williams, R. (1974) Communications as cultural science. *Journal of Communication, 24*(3), 26–38.

Zittrain, J. (2007). *The future of the Internet—and how to stop it.* New Haven, CT: Yale University Press.

6

Media Production and the Problem of Consumption

BECKY HERR-STEPHENSON

In May of 2006, U.S. National Public Radio (NPR) reported on the popularity of the snack food Flamin' Hot Cheetos among American youth. Describing Hot Cheetos as a new "red menace sweeping the nation" in its introduction, the radio package featured interviews with a Southern California elementary school principal and several students from her school, as well as commentary from a food psychology expert and an executive from Frito Lay, the company that makes and distributes Flamin' Hot Cheetos. The NPR package focused on conflicts between student and adult opinions about the availability of snacks and beverages with minimal nutritional value (junk food), in schools.

A longstanding issue for many school communities, concerns about students' eating habits had, at the time, escalated due to increased attention to the role of diet in America's "epidemic"[1] of childhood obesity. In her interview, the principal focused on the nutritional value (or lack thereof) of the food, while other school officials called the snack a "janitorial nightmare" because of the red cheese dust often left on kids' hands (and, by extension, on desks, walls, and other school property) after eating Hot Cheetos. The students interviewed in the package expressed a different opinion on the product, unabashedly declaring their love for Hot Cheetos. One student even did so in song. The conflict captured by this brief radio segment is emblematic of larger disconnects between adult-centered and youth-centered discourses about consumption.

At the same time that schools across the United States were banning the "red menace" from their lunchrooms and corridors, the politics of junk food was raised as an issue for the Hot Cheeto aficionados with whom I was spending time while conducting participant observation in two special education classes in a Los Angeles, California, middle school. These students were tasked with producing a five-minute documentary video on the topics of childhood obesity and the California "junk food ban," which prohibits schools from selling on campus foods that do not adhere to particular nutritional guidelines. Observing the process and product of the junk food documentary project was an interesting opportunity to understand how young people in a school setting navigate increasingly blurry divisions between consumption and production. The project was designed as a remix of digital media assets found online, a type of production that necessitates particular approaches to consumption throughout the production process (e.g., finding and reappropriating media assets) (see also the chapter by Erstad in this volume).

At the same time, the documentaries took as their subject young people's consumption habits in relation to food; in this way, the project asked students to consider and (re)produce discourses about consumption. In both the content and the production process, unanticipated tensions surfaced. The first significant tension arose from a disconnect between student recreational practices with digital media and the ways in which they were expected to use digital media to research and produce the documentaries. The different ways in which students approach and/or use digital media can be understood as types of consumption, processes of active reception (often intertwined with production) in which students work to find, understand, and leverage digital media in particular ways. A second tension was evident in the ways students interpreted and responded to the content of the project, which reflected a clear position on the subject of consumption. The junk food documentaries were created under the guidance of state-mandated health curricula during a moment in which childhood obesity has been declared an epidemic threatening American children; in this context, the message and ideological goals of the assignment seemed obvious. For the students, however, the anti-consumption message of the assignment did not overshadow their own feelings and beliefs about consumption. This chapter explores these tensions in an effort to better understand the relationships between consumption and production in the context of classroom media production and how media production might be used to help students view consumption through a critical lens.

Schools, Technology, and Consumption

The use of technology in classrooms can be seen as a response to a number of discourses about media, technology, and consumption. In the USA, the primary discourse that has driven the wiring of schools is that of the digital divide, which is fundamentally concerned with equal access to sources of information and modes of communication facilitated by the Internet (Lax, 2001; Warschauer, 2003). As technology has proven transformative in many areas of social life, work, and education, concerns have shifted from providing basic access to information to facilitating opportunities for participation in social and cultural activities that occur online; as such, access issues are more frequently discussed in terms of "digital inclusion" (Livingstone & Helsper, 2007) or the "participation gap" (Jenkins, Clinton, Purushotma, Robinson, & Weigel, 2006).

In addition to these discourses focused on equal access to online media and resources, media and technology are discussed in educational environments as opportunities and resources for increasing student motivation. This way of understanding digital media recognizes its importance to young people and aims to use digital media as a hook to draw students into spaces and activities they might otherwise overlook. This discourse is particularly strong in educational environments such as libraries and afterschool programs (Agosto, 2007; Casey & Stephens, 2008). As the case presented in this chapter will show, it is also a powerful force behind classroom uses of digital media.

Whether constructed as a tool for basic access to electronic resources and information, a space for involvement in mediated forms of social/cultural life, or an incentive for participation, uses of digital media and technology in school settings reflect a tenuous relationship with school positions as gatekeepers for cultural capital. Pierre Bourdieu (1984) posits educational institutions as purveyors of institutionalized capital (i.e., educational credentials), which operates in concert with objectified and embodied capital (i.e., appreciation and association with high-status objects and knowledge) within a three-pronged structure of cultural capital. Thus, educational institutions have a vested interest in protecting objectified and embodied capital in order to maintain their status as grantor of institutionalized capital. Reflecting a particular legacy of cultural theory that privileges "high" culture (products and practices associated with elite segments of society) over "low" or "popular" culture (e.g., Horkheimer & Adorno, 1944/2002), many schools focus on teaching an established, vetted literary canon and traditional modes of literacy and expression. As Jeffrey Duncan-Andrade and Ernest Morrell (2008) note, the omission of particular works from the canon is often more problematic (particularly for urban students) than are the pieces that are included. Describing aspects of their work as secondary-level English teachers, Duncan-Andrade and Morrell highlighted the implicit and explicit messages their students received from school curricula "about which texts were aesthetic or intellectual…in ways that excluded, even condemned, the traditional and new media texts that they interacted with daily" (pp. 53–54). As these authors note, the exclusion of texts that are salient to student life experiences is highly problematic, not only in terms of missed opportunities, but also for its direct effects in disempowering students and discouraging participation and learning (see the chapter by Hartley in this volume).

Popular culture is also excluded from schools through discourses of commercialization, which positions consumption of popular culture and mass-produced goods (such as junk food) in opposition to the types of consumption that are sanctioned by the school (Molnar, 1996). For example, reading can be understood as a type of consumption (or reception) that is validated by schools. Similarly, some pedagogical models posit learning as a process of consuming (or processing) information transmitted by teachers and educational materials. It should be noted that such models have been critiqued and found to be problematic by educators committed to critical pedagogy and multicultural and liberatory education, as they construct learners (and particularly learners from non-dominant groups) as having knowledge deficits that must be repaired through the school's conveyance of dominant ideology. Commercialization interferes with the reproductive functions of schools by introducing other, competing, ideologies, which can be distracting or subversive.

Consumption (framed as commercialization) is particularly problematic for schools given a school's role in cultivating future citizens—a function long understood as one of the key purposes of public education in the United States. Public schools, a product of early nineteenth century concerns about the impact of industrialization, immigration, and class stratification on community and national identity, aimed to produce informed, rational citizens for participation in democratic society. These goals were met primarily through standardized (or "common") instruction for all children as well as the provision of necessary social services to the community (Reese, 2005). The type of citizens schools aim to create are citizens in a traditional and political sense, a definition that Sarah Banet-Weiser (2007) describes as "revolv[ing] around the conventional notion that citizenship is a political category, represented and constituted not within the world of commerce but rather in direct opposition to…material interests" such as those that are represented in popular culture (p. 7). Just as schools aim to produce a particular kind of citizen, so, too, does the market. Using the children's cable channel Nickelodeon as an example, Banet-Weiser describes this as a kind of consumer citizenship, through which young people are empowered to participate and develop identity through consumption.

As media and technology expand, converge, and become increasingly embedded in aspects of civic and social life, it becomes much more difficult for schools to police established borders of cultural capital and citizenship. The diverse forms, uses, and symbolic meanings of digital media challenge established modes of identifying and reproducing cultural capital. Digital media are at once products of popular youth culture and essential resources for civic and cultural participation; mediated spaces such as the Internet are both spaces for playful recreation and spaces for serious endeavors. Given this convergence, discourses of commercialization are threatened by possibilities for empowerment through consumer citizenship.

The junk food documentaries provide fertile ground for understanding some of the tensions that exist between schools, cultural capital, commercialization, and digital media production. As remixes, producing the documentaries required that students engage with both practices of digital media consumption and production. At the same time, the project was designed to push students to think critically about their own consumption habits and the potential outcomes of such practices for their current and future selves. Additionally, focusing on the context of production—specifically, that the videos were produced by a group of students placed in special education due to challenges with traditional, school-sanctioned modes of consumption and production (reading and writing)—raises interesting questions about how digital media can be used to challenge existing notions of literacy, cultural capital, and educational achievement.

Producing the Junk Food Documentaries

The junk food documentaries were one of eight digital media production projects undertaken by students in two mixed-grade (6th, 7th, and 8th) special education classes in a public middle school in the Los Angeles Unified School District. Students worked on media production projects in their Science/Health class (taught by Ms. Abel[2]) and their Language Arts class (taught by Mr. Davidson). Multimedia production was introduced to these students as part of a year-long professional development program in which their teachers were participating. The classes were small, on average 12–14 students (although students joined and left the class throughout the year), and evenly split between male and female students. The majority of students in the class were Latino. The students had been placed in special education primarily because they were several years behind in reading and writing ability; anecdotal reports from teachers and parents indicate that several students had been placed in special education due to behavioral challenges.

The teachers and administrators at the school saw digital media (and specifically, media production) as a unique opportunity for special education students and put much faith in its power as a motivating and transformative pedagogy. As Ms. Abel stated in an interview at the beginning of the school year:

> ...sometimes our students get lost in the shuffle. Special ed. students aren't the ones that are usually considered first for this kind of project [media production]. It's usually the gifted students, or the regular ed. students, so I'm very excited that they have this opportunity...because if they don't learn anything else in the whole school year, I know that this project is going to be one that they remember...

Indeed, the media production projects provided an opportunity to engage with content in a different, accessible, and interesting way. Students who had never completed a written assignment were able to articulate an argument in video form. Although media production skills were framed as valuable in and of themselves, the production process purposefully resembled the steps involved in crafting a written essay, an ability the teachers believed students would develop in parallel to media production. Whereas some of the media production projects were designed to focus on self-expression and creative writing (for example, two poetry-based projects completed in the students' Language Arts class), the junk food documentaries prompted students to think critically about consumption in relation to their current and future health. In this way, the junk food documentary project was similar to many other media education interventions, which aim to deconstruct media messages and/or articulate (counter-) arguments through media production.

For all the success the project had in motivating student participation and in scaffolding reading, writing, and media production skills, it was less successful in teaching and encouraging critical consumption. Students struggled to approach dominant discourses about a coveted object of popular culture (junk food) in a critical way. In addition, students experienced difficulty and frustration completing the required Internet research for the project, which asked them to approach digital media in a way quite different from their previous experiences with media and technology. As the remainder of this chapter will discuss, when media production is introduced as a classroom activity, disconnects between the ways in which students enact their roles as consumers in school and outside of school may be accentuated—particularly when media production is framed as an opportunity for students to voice their own knowledge, experiences, or opinions.

The case study presented in this chapter was researched using ethnographic methods, including participant observation and interview. Throughout the 2005–2006 academic year, I worked as part of a three-person team of qualitative researchers conducting participant observation in three Los Angeles middle schools. Schools were selected based on teacher participation in a year-long professional development program focused on multimedia production. Participant observation involved regular visits to the classrooms, during which I acted as an observer and classroom assistant, as well as regular interviews with teachers and collection of artifacts such as lesson plans and student work. In May and June of 2006, we supplemented the school-based research with a set of home visits and interviews with students and their parents.[3]

For most students in the class, the junk food documentary project was the second multimedia assignment of the school year. The previous project, produced in the student Language Arts class, tasked them with writing a structured poem about themselves and pairing lines of the poem with images downloaded from the Internet or scanned family photos. The junk food documentaries were a significantly longer and more involved production, requiring that students write a script based on factual research, find and combine digital images to illustrate the script, and record and edit video clips.

Each student began the production process for his documentary on paper. Ms. Abel distributed an outline for the project, which recommended a standard structure for student productions. Having a clear outline that broke down the project into small steps was intended to prevent students from feeling overwhelmed by the scale of the project. As struggling readers and writers, the idea of starting a sustained narrative project such as this one from scratch would likely have been frustrating and anxiety-provoking, encouraging disengagement from the assignment rather than motivation to complete it.

The documentary scripts were broken into six parts: 1. Introduction; 2. Definition of obesity; 3. Effects of obesity; 4. The school junk food ban; 5. Pros and cons of junk food sales on campus; and 6. Conclusion.

The first four sections of each documentary were constructed with images downloaded from various websites, blocks of text written by the students (with assistance from Ms. Abel or the classroom aide), and a voice-over reading of the same text. For this project, the students used their textbooks to find the information for each section. For images, they relied on Google Image Search, which was the teacher's preferred method for finding images. Certain Google Image Search tools appeared to make the research process easier, safer (in terms of preventing students from encountering unsanctioned content), and more consistent in image quality.

For example, Google Image Search allows users to turn on a feature called "safe search," which deters the search engine from returning results that have been tagged as containing "adult content." Combined with the school's firewall, which blocks many sites, some of which may contain problematic content, safe search meant that the teachers did not have to monitor students searching as closely, giving the students a degree of freedom to explore and allowing teachers to attend to other parts of the project.

The class used Apple laptops and iMovie software to complete their productions. At the time of this research, the teachers and students had access to two Apple MacBook learning labs, mobile carts outfitted with approximately 20 laptops, a wireless router, a printer, and a projector. Although the carts were shared among several classes, the teachers were able to reserve a cart for several days or weeks at a time, enabling classes to work on media projects for extended periods of time in their own classroom. Ms. Abel's class had the additional advantage of a flexible schedule, which allowed the students to spend several hours at a time working on their media projects. Further, the laptop carts enabled each student in Ms. Abel's class to work on their own machine and to use the same laptop throughout a project. Being able to save directly to the machine's hard drive, to import music or scanned images, and to do so with (relative) certainty that the data will remain on the laptop throughout the project is not often a condition of production in schools, where machines are locked down and drives are regularly (and often automatically) wiped clean after each student's use or at the end of the school day.

This variation of one-to-one computing was a particularly exciting opportunity for the students in Ms. Abel's class because most students did not have a computer at home. This is not to say the students were entirely unfamiliar with the technology. Through various channels (that included friends, family members, and public and school libraries), most students had garnered enough experience surfing the web to have familiarity with a few websites, often sites that featured free casual games. This experience of the Internet is quite different from that of other young people who have more time and resources for interest-driven, independent online exploration and play (Ito et al., 2009).

To produce the final two sections, students worked in teams to record short interviews with members of the school community using a digital video camera. In addition to talking with teachers, administrators, and staff, students were instructed to record a clip of themselves expressing their own opinions on the subject, which formed the conclusion to the project. Once the video clips were recorded, students imported the clips and integrated them into their project timelines.

As with the content of the project, the production process was broken down into small, sequential steps. Designed in this way, the project was manageable for students new to media production and offered regular benchmarks for assessment. Because reading and writing were challenging for the students, they received one-on-one assistance in preparing their scripts and adding text to their video clips from Ms. Abel and the classroom aide assigned to the class. I also assisted students, but tended to focus on helping them with the more technical parts of the project, such as finding images or troubleshooting the iMovie software. Although the project was intended as an individual project, students worked together informally, sharing images and music, helping one another find resources, and commiserating over technical difficulties.

Consuming the Internet: The Challenges of Online Research

Despite the careful design of the project and the assumption that using digital media would be motivating and make the project more accessible, the junk food documentary project was not a popular assignment among Ms. Abel's students. As Michelle, a 12-year-old seventh grader, told me in her interview:

> ...none of us liked it. Sara [a classmate] didn't like it. I didn't like it. No one liked it. Because we had to do research about that [topic], and then we had to go interview and stuff like that. I liked the interviewing part, though.

As with Michelle, most of the students saw the project as consisting of two distinct parts: research and production. Using the video camera (for the first time for many students) was an exciting new skill, particularly in comparison with the "grueling" work of research. In trying to understand why students struggled with the Internet research component of the project, both the students' prior experience of research and their prior experience searching for information online become important considerations.

As described above, the first four sections of the video were composed of digital images, text, and voice-over. As such, students searched online to find pictures of obese people that emphasized the health impacts of obesity and frequently shared the ones they found the most grotesque with the rest of the class. Similarly, they searched for images of healthier foods and happy, thin people eating healthy foods to provide a visual counterpoint. The students tended to conduct their research hastily, often choosing the first result of a single search rather than digging in to the research by conducting multiple searches, scrolling through pages of results, or collaborating with classmates on search strategies. This resulted in several of the student documentaries containing the same images as well as some visual malapropisms. For example, Felix, a 12-year-old Latino sixth grader, featured the Apple Computer logo to illustrate the recommendation that people choose fruits and vegetables over junk food to avoid obesity because it was the first image result for his search for "apple."

Many students also struggled with identifying and spelling appropriate keywords for their searches. For example, one student I assisted with the research started her image search with the phrase "fat lady eating a greasy hamburger." Although this phrase accurately described the image she wished to find, the search produced few usable results. I tried to explain to the student that using a specific and carefully chosen keyword would likely yield better search results than the phrase she had used. She listed keywords that she thought might work: "hamburger," "fast food," and "obese woman." When we tried the first two keywords, we waded through images from corporate websites (which, obviously were not a "fat lady eating a greasy hamburger") and were unable to find suitable images. The keyword phrase "obese woman" yielded better results, but still required sifting through images to find higher-resolution images not already printed with (advertising) text. Several times during this process, the student wanted to give up on the research because she was not finding the information she wanted.

One interpretation of student lack of interest and critical attention in their research could be that they were unwilling to put the necessary effort into conducting careful research for their projects. Although it is true that several of Ms. Abel's students disengaged from this project early on in the production process due in large part to the research demands, this explanation does not seem to encompass the whole picture. Instead, I emphasize the disconnect between students' prior experiences with research—both traditional library research and online research—and the searching enabled and required by multimedia production for the junk food documentary project.

In *The Internet Playground*, Ellen Seiter describes the experience of finding information online as "more like a mall than a library" (2005, p. 7) for people without specialized resources and practiced research skills. The mall metaphor is appropriate in considering the role of consumption in relation to media production. Just as in a mall, the online environment is filled with retailers (some of which have brick-and-mortar counterparts) and advertisements for consumer goods; spaces are organized to draw user attention and to provide a comfortable, interesting, and interactive experience. Within online spaces, digital media are commodities and are frequently used by young people to express identity online. For example, layouts for social network sites can call attention to particular interests, while icons, screen names, and avatars can be used to highlight personal features or associations. Often times, these digital objects/displays are remixed from other popular culture objects—movie stills, screen captures, song lyrics, or character names, for example. These practices can be understood as a process of conversion, which Celia Lury (1996) posits as a type of consumption endemic to consumer culture through which people take consumer goods and make them their own, thus continuing the production process by transferring or transforming their meaning and symbolic value.

The junk food documentary project can be described as a remix, in that it pulls assets from different places and combines them to make a new meaning. Ola Erstad (2008) has described classroom media production in terms of "trajectories of remixing," calling attention to the processes through which students learn to make media at school (see also Ola Erstad's chapter in this volume). Erstad notes that remix can be seen as a challenge to the structures of power in schools, as it challenges established notions of authoring and ownership and provides an activity in which students may come to the classroom with existing experience and abilities and are often motivated to take the lead on instruction.

The online research required for remix projects is qualitatively different from other types of research in that the goal of the research is not to find written information to be used as background or cited in a written essay, but rather to find media assets for remixing. Searching for multimedia resources can, in many ways, be more difficult than searching for textual information. In addition to the issues related to the scope of resources available and the lack of prescreening by teachers and librarians, students must be expert consumers to find assets that represent the correct information in a way that is appropriate and aesthetically pleasing and must keep in mind technical constraints such as the size of images, the quality of video clips, etc.

Unlike library research with which students may have been familiar, consuming online information online involves sifting through an array of resources that have not necessarily been vetted by an expert such as a teacher or school librarian for relevance or reading/comprehension level. While the diversity of resources available online is, in most cases, not a hindrance to research or media production, it does require students to attend to the source of the information (or, in this case, image) in a different way than do more traditional methods of research seen in schools. Some guides for online research designed for teachers and students discuss strategies for assessing the validity and truthfulness of information found online, suggesting that students look for markers such as a URL ending in .edu or authorship information on a page (e.g., Stebbins, 2005). While such guidelines work for assessing credibility on some websites, Web 2.0 sites, where content often changes and where authorship may be multiple, distributed, and difficult to discern, require different strategies for assessing credibility.

Until starting the multimedia projects at school, searching online for information was a task students had done infrequently due to a lack of access to the technology or lack of need. When students did look for information online, they reported doing so in a more informal manner, searching only occasionally and primarily looking for entertainment or for information related to specific interests such as cars, music, games, or celebrity bios. This type of searching is characteristic of what the Digital Youth Project[4] has called "Messing Around" (Ito et al., 2009), one of several genres of participation that structure young people's participation with digital media. Messing Around favors trial-and-error problem-solving and inquiry, whether in learning a new skill (such as video production or mastery of a particular move or level in a video game) or fortuitous searching, finding websites that provide the information or experiences desired. Answering questions by Messing Around is a different process than that emphasized in information literacy and traditional library instruction, which tend to focus on linear search strategies. Indeed, Messing Around can be seen as consuming information in a way closer to browsing mall shops than searching through library shelves.

Critiquing Cheetos: Media Education and Discourses of Consumption

In addition to the research and video production skills involved in the junk food documentary project, the assignment was designed to help students engage critically with information included in the state content standards for science/health. As a health intervention, the project aimed to inform students about the health risks of consuming junk food—ostensibly in an effort to discourage its consumption. The project can also be understood as an exercise in media education, as students learned to craft persuasive messages using multimedia tools. Media production is a powerful tool for media education; by creating media, students have an opportunity to understand media intimately—to understand the language of cinematography and the process of editing. By producing their own media, students can observe how stories can be shaped in multiple ways using the same footage and how elements such as transitions, sound effects, and music and graphics can contribute to shaping the message in ways that written words alone cannot achieve.

Examining the history of media education reveals shifting attitudes towards consumption. Media literacy in the United States has predominantly taken a "deficit approach" to media literacy, addressing media as a problematic influence and media consumers as lacking the skills necessary to defend themselves against its influence. Douglas Kellner and Jeff Share describe this protectionist impulse of media literacy, as one that "emerges from fear of media and aims to protect or inoculate people against the dangers of media manipulation and addiction" (Kellner & Share, 2007, p. 6). From this point of view, media is viewed as a cause of moral depravity and violence, reinforcing racism and sexism, and encouraging unchecked consumerism. The concerns addressed by the deficit model of media literacy have primarily focused on the impact of television due to its pervasiveness as a broadcast medium and its placement within the home. These factors, combined with its widespread appeal for information and entertainment make it a major threat to traditional education and civil society (see the chapter by Hartley in this volume). Roger Desmond identifies decreased academic skills (reading, concentration, and attention), increased aggression, exposure to stereotypes, and the development of poor consumer habits as the key concerns of the deficit model of media literacy (Desmond, 1997).

In contrast to deficit models of media education, David Buckingham (2003) describes an emergent approach to media education based not on protection but on preparation. This "preparatory" approach acknowledges the polysemy of media messages and moves away from the idea of media as culture industry or one-way flow of (potentially dangerous/incorrect) information. The new paradigm addresses children as an autonomous yet critical audience and seeks to build upon the repertoire of skills for understanding media that kids develop through informal exposure. Importantly, this new paradigm recognizes the pleasures of media and the sense of ownership of popular culture and new technology felt by young people.

Whereas the influence of new less defensive approaches to media education can be seen in the use of remix and the relative freedom students experienced in conducting research for the project, the influence of deficit approaches to media education can be seen in the way the subject of the documentaries was framed. The beginning sections of the videos, which leveraged statistics about the rates of obesity in the United States, descriptions of medical conditions related to obesity, and information about the state junk food ban, present information aligned with institutional interests and that endorse a particular type of discipline. This part of the assignment reflects the common assumption that if students are given the "right" information, they will come to predetermined conclusions or enact desired behaviors. In terms of media education, Buckingham (2003) describes this approach as "demystification." As production continued on the junk food documentaries, however, it became apparent that the message of the project neither reflected most of the student beliefs about junk food nor changed their opinions on the subject. Like the students in the National Public Radio segment mentioned at the beginning of this chapter, the students in Ms. Abel's class were Hot Cheeto aficionados. As Justin, a 12-year-old African-American sixth grader in the class described, "Those Cheetos are famous! Everybody likes 'em." While Hot Cheetos were particularly coveted at the time of this research, students also enjoyed many other foods categorized as "junk," including candy and sugar-sweetened beverages. Despite the efforts of the teachers in conveying the content dictated in the curriculum and in designing the junk food documentary project, the structure of the assignment and the conditions of production did not appropriately encourage students to look critically at either the adult-centered, discipline-focused discourses about consumption or their own youth-centered discourses, which focused on sharing tastes and experiences with friends and the pleasures of consumption.

For most of the students in the class, the decision to consume (or not to consume) junk food was first and foremost an economic issue, as such snacks fit within a student's limited allowances. Further, consuming junk food was not viewed by students as problematic in terms of taste; they did not understand junk food as lacking cultural capital due to its low nutritional value, the ways in which it is marketed, or its pervasive presence as a mass consumer good. Generally, in fact, student opinions on junk food were quite the opposite—they loved it; they bought it whenever possible; they wished the school would continue to sell it. Although Hot Cheetos were certainly not the only favorite food in the class, they are a particularly vibrant example of the ways in which the realities of children's consumption are often in conflict with dominant adult-centered discourses about children's consumption.

One could describe "adult-centered" discourses about children's consumption as ways of thinking about consumption that emphasize discipline. In the realm of food, adult-centered discourses tend to emphasize nutrition, quality, and the importance of a balanced diet. This kind of disciplined consumption is also encouraged by certain adult-centered discourses about media, which promote time limits, age-appropriateness, and restrictions on content. Clearly, these discourses are intended to protect children from physical and psychological harm and to teach children habits that will lead to the production of healthy, disciplined future selves. Whereas adult-centered discourses about consumption thus tend to emphasize discipline and quality, youth-centered discourses tend to emphasize aesthetics, popularity, and fun. Food advertising is a prime example of such youth-centered discourses about consumption. Ellen Seiter (1999) has written about children's commercials as presenting a utopian image of the world, in which empowerment comes through consumption. Within this utopian world of food commercials, food products (cereal and candy in particular) are advertised as not only delicious, but also fun and liberating. A current advertising campaign for Cheetos in which consumers use the snack food to take revenge on others who they find annoying (by sullying a neat-freak co-worker's desk with cheesy fingerprints) provides excellent examples of the (fantastical) ways consumption is positioned as liberating in youth-driven advertising. Although such advertisements are produced by adults, they construct and address young consumers in a fundamentally different way than do adult-centered discourses about consumption, fostering a sense of empowerment, and development of a consumer identity.

The tensions between adult-centered and youth-centered discourses about consumption were particularly apparent in the final section of the junk food documentaries. The final one to two minutes of each documentary were intended to incorporate interviews with members of the school community (teachers, administrators, other staff), in which interviewees answered one primary question: "Are you for or against junk food on campus?" After recording several of these interviews, students recorded a clip of themselves stating their own answer to the same question. This section of the video, in its efforts to provide opportunities to consider alternative viewpoints and to encourage self-reflection and expression, reflects characteristics of Buckingham's preparatory approach to media education. Students worked in pairs to record brief interviews and were instructed to include in their final cuts interviews with one person who expressed a pro-junk food position and one with an anti-junk food position before concluding the documentary with the clip of the students' own opinion on the subject.

When students set out to record the interviews, it quickly became clear that the division of opinion was not black and white. Very few of the adults interviewed responded to the question of junk food on campus with a clear "yes" or "no" answer. One of the only direct answers students received was captured by Carlos in his interview with the classroom aide who was working closely with the class on the project. In her interview, she said she was whole-heartedly against junk food on campus, remarking: "I see you guys drinking soda and eating Hot Cheetos for breakfast. I am concerned about your health. I am concerned about your hearts… You are *growing children*. You need to fill your bodies with really good things to eat…" It is possible she phrased her answer in this way because she was aware of the kind of answer students needed to complete the assignment. The adult-centered discourse in her response echoes the facts students discovered through their online research, reinforced clear boundaries between adults and children, and emphasized the importance of kids taking responsibility for the health of both their current and future selves.

More frequently, the responses students received from staff were more ambiguous, focusing on the relationship between student consumption of junk food and their behavior and performance in the classroom. However, most campus staff emphasized a kind of *lassiez faire* attitude toward consumption, noting that students need to learn to regulate their own consumption. In reviewing the videotaped interviews shot by Carlos for his documentary, I was struck by his expressions of surprise each time a staff member responded to his question in a way that was not clearly an "anti-junk food" response. Such statements seemed to violate his expectation that adults would respond with "standard" adult discourse.

The responses from adults on campus were quite different from the ways in which students represented their own opinions on the matter of junk food. First, most students positioned themselves as firmly pro-junk food. For example, in his interview, Felix stated, "I think junk food is good. Your body needs to have a little bit of sugar. And it tastes good. And all the kids like it." Felix's response combines a version of the factual information used in the first section of the video (the body's need for sugar), with language similar to that used in food advertisements directed at children, which emphasizes taste and unanimous approval among peers. Even when students did not position themselves as clearly on the pro-junk food side of the issue, they tended to emphasize the pleasures of consumption. For example, as Carlos noted in his interview, "I'm in the middle…because I like to eat junk food, but there are consequences, and the consequences could be that I could have a heart attack…" Carlos describes a possible negative outcome of junk food consumption that is extreme and uncommon in childhood, rather than describing more immediate consequences such as weight gain. One interpretation of this response is an attempt to distance the issue from himself—or, at least, from his current child self—protecting the idea that junk food is an innocent pleasure that he shares with his friends. In both Felix's and Carlos's video conclusions, the conflict between youth- and adult-centered discourses about consumption is evident.

Although tensions between adult-centered and youth-centered discourses about consumption were evident in the production and product of the junk food documentaries, these tensions were, by and large, left unexplored during the project. Instead of embodying a truly preparatory approach to media education by encouraging critical assessment of the issue of consumption, it remained closely aligned with established discourses in relation to both food and technology consumption. In the final section of this chapter, I propose a few strategies to help teachers and students maximize the critical potential of classroom media production by leveraging more textured understandings of consumption.

Conclusion

Classroom media production has great potential as a pedagogical strategy that is motivating and empowering for students. As the case study presented in this chapter demonstrates, however, achieving those outcomes can be a challenge, requiring great effort and time on the parts of teachers and students alike. Through this description and analysis of the junk food documentary project, we can see that disconnects between student consumption practices (understood both as reception and participation in the market) and the ways consumption and production are understood in school settings can be key factors complicating classroom media production. Learning from the challenges and successes of the junk food documentary project, it appears that a more careful understanding and a critical embrace of consumption might contribute to more meaningful student media production. To this end, I make three recommendations to educators committed to using media production as a pedagogical method within a preparatory model of media education.

First, educators must understand that students are consumers for better or for worse. As such, students bring with them to the classroom a particular set of experiences and beliefs related to consumption, popular culture, and participation. Many students will come to the classroom with a strong consumer identity, manifested through personal style and expressions of preferences and tastes. Consumer identities and practices extend as well to media and technology use. Most students will come to the experience of classroom media production with a number of prior experiences as media consumers and producers. (It is helpful here to think about production broadly, not just in terms of making digital media projects, but also in terms of everyday uses and reappropriations of media.) Given these strong associations and prior experiences, the goal of deficit models of media education—in this case, to bring students to enlightenment about media or consumption—is unlikely to be easily accomplished, if it is even possible at all. This leads to my second recommendation, which echoes Duncan-Andrade and Morrell (2008), who write: "Our purpose as educators is not to replace one dominant ideology with another…The goal is not to make them slaves to a different (and more politically correct) ideology, even if it happens to be one that we agree with" (p. 53). Just as young people are subject to dominant ideologies around consumption and technology in American culture, "commercialization" and assumptions about the negative effects of popular culture on the accumulation of cultural capital are dominant ideologies in many educational institutions. While it is difficult to argue that the junk food documentary project (or the teacher) was somehow disingenuous in the effort to encourage students to learn about nutrition, we can see in the example of the junk food documentaries an effort to exchange one ideology for another. If the goal of education, and media education in particular, is to teach students to be critical consumers and producers of media and information, replacing one dominant discourse with another is not the answer.

Finally, educators who are undertaking media production in the classroom are encouraged to think carefully about the structure of media production assignments and the conditions of production from the outset of the project, including ways to work with a student's existing experiences and knowledge of consumption and production. This might involve building in extra time to media production assignments to allow for Messing Around, rethinking the balance of individual and collaborative production activities, or being open to new and experimental genres of media production. In addition, it will likely require that teachers familiarize themselves with the popular culture that is important to their students as well as with youth-centered discourses about consumption and production. Consider, for example, how the junk food documentaries might have worked if, instead of gathering images to support a straightforward, adult-centered argument about childhood obesity, students were asked to remix commercials from their favorite foods in order to critique the claims made in the advertisements.

Classroom media production has the potential to be an important tool for learning and expression. However, as with all technological tools, its value comes through the ways in which it is put to use. The recommendations here do not call for new technologies or more digital media in schools. Rather, they encourage a shift in the way students and teachers think about themselves and each other as consumers and producers. Through this shift in thinking, classroom media production may move a step closer to reaching its potential as a tool for critical, transformative teaching and learning.

Notes

1. I use quotation marks around the word "epidemic," not because I do not believe that childhood obesity is a serious health problem facing American youth, but to indicate that discussions of the topic have reached the level of moral panic (Cohen, 2002). For additional discussion of moral panic around childhood obesity, please see Herr Stephenson and Banet-Weiser (2007).
2. All names are pseudonyms.
3. For additional information regarding the professional development initiative and methodol-

ogy of the full study, please see Tripp, L and Herr-Stephenson, R. (2009).

4. The Digital Youth Project was a three-year, multi-sited, ethnographic investigation of American young people's social and recreational uses of digital media. The research study described in this chapter was affiliated with the Digital Youth Project, which funded the home-based interviews and observations. The researchers who conducted the school-based research described in this chapter also participated as members of the digital youth team and are co-authors (with Mizuko Ito and others) of *Hanging Out, Messing Around, Geeking Out: Living and Learning with New Media*, (The MIT Press, November 2009), which details the findings of the study.

References

Agosto, D. (2007). Why do teens use libraries? Results of a public library use survey. *Public Libraries, 46*(3), 55–62.

Banet-Weiser, S. (2007). *Kids rule! Nickelodeon and consumer citizenship*. Durham, NC: Duke University Press.

Bourdieu, P. (1984). *Distinction: a social critique of the judgment of taste*. Cambridge, MA: Harvard University Press.

Buckingham, D. (2003). *Media education: Literacy, learning, and contemporary culture*. London: Polity.

Casey, M., & Stephens, M. (2008). Embracing service to teens. *Library Journal*, 28.

Cohen, S. (2002). *Folk devils and moral panics* (2nd ed.). New York: Routledge.

Desmond, R. (1997). Media literacy in the home: Acquisition and deficit models. In R. Kubey (Ed.), *Media literacy in the information age: Current perspectives* (pp. 323–343). New Brunswick, NJ: Transaction.

Duncan-Andrade, J. M. R., & Morrell, E. (2008). *The art of critical pedagogy: Possibilities for moving from theory to practice in urban schools* (Vol. 285). New York: Peter Lang.

Erstad, O. (2008). Trajectories of remixing: Digital literacies, media production, and schooling. In Lankshear, C., & M. Knobel (Eds.), *Digital literacies: Concepts, policies and practices* (Vol. 30, pp. 177–202). New York: Peter Lang.

Herr-Stephenson, R., & Banet-Weiser, S. (2007). Super sized kids: Obesity, children, moral panic, and the media. In J. Bryant & J. A. Bryant (Eds.), *The children's television community: Institutional, critical, social systems, and network analyses*. Mahwah, NJ: Lawrence Erlbaum Associates.

Horkheimer, M., & Adorno, T. W. (1944/2002). The culture industry: Enlightenment as mass deception (E. Jephcott, Trans.). In G. S. Noerr (Ed.), *Dialectic of enlightenment: Philosophical fragments*. Stanford, CA: Stanford University Press.

Ito, M., Baumer, S., Bittanti, M., boyd, d., Cody, R., Herr-Stephenson, B., et al. (2009). *Hanging out, messing around, geeking out: Living and learning with new media*. Cambridge, MA: The MIT Press.

Jenkins, H., Clinton, K., Purushotma, R., Robinson, A. J., & Weigel, M. (2006). *Confronting the challenges of participatory culture: Media education for the 21st century*: The John D. and Catherine T. MacArthur Foundation.)

Kellner, D., & Share, J. (2007). Critical media literacy, democracy, and the reconstruction of education. In D. Macedo & S. R. Steinberg (Eds.), *Media literacy: A reader* (pp. 3–23). New York: Peter Lang Publishing

Lax, S. (2001). Information, education and inequality: Is new technology the solution? In S. Lax (Ed.), *Access denied in the information age* (pp. 107–123). London: Palgrave.

Livingstone, S., & Helsper, E. (2007). Graduations in digital inclusion: Children, young people, and the digital divide. *New Media and Society, 9*(4), 671–696.

Lury, C. (1996). *Consumer culture.* New Brunswick, NJ: Rutgers University Press.

Molnar, A. (1996). *Giving kids the business: The commercialization of America's schools.* Boulder, CO: Westview Press.

Reese, W. J. (2005). *America's public schools: From the common school to "no child left behind."* Baltimore, MD: The Johns Hopkins University Press.

Seiter, E. (1999). *Television and new media audiences.* Oxford: Clarendon Press.

Seiter, E. (2005). *The Internet playground: Children's access, entertainment, and mis-education.* New York: Peter Lang.

Stebbins, L. (2005). *Student guide to research in the digital age: How to locate and evaluate information sources.* New York: Libraries Unlimited.

Tripp, L., & Herr-Stephenson, B. (2009). Making access meaningful: Latino young people using digital media at home and at school. *Journal of Computer Mediated Communication, 14*, 1190–1207.

Warschauer, M. (2003). *Technology and social inclusion: Rethinking the digital divide.* Cambridge, MA: The MIT Press.

7

Creating a Digital Self

Impression Management and Impression Formation on Social Network Sites

NINA HAFERKAMP & NICOLE C. KRÄMER

As Walther pointed out in 1993, the opportunity to form impressions of other people has been advanced by many new communication technologies. Users are able to meet via chat rooms, write emails, and participate in computer-mediated discussion groups. Since the mid-1990s, people are also able to present themselves via the digital content they create on a personal homepage.

Nowadays, with the help of the new Web 2.0 platforms, further opportunities are given to present oneself online. For instance, users can create a personal online profile on social network sites (SNS) such as Facebook, MySpace, or the German StudiVZ (www.studivz.net), which offer various forms of interactive and static features for creating one's own web space: Here, users can put a photo on their online profile or list their friends, display personal information as well as participate in groups. With the help of these features, users inevitably form and manage impressions of their self.

These new possibilities of self-portrayal question the extent online impression management resembles that shown in offline i.e., real-life encounters (Jacobson, 1999). For example, one aspect of "online impression management" that differs from managing impressions in everyday life refers to the control users have over their published information: An online self-presentation can be based on longer and more systematic considerations than in vivo self-presentations, which are often needed unexpectedly and thus warrant spontaneous, automatic, and thus unconscious impression management (Krämer & Winter, 2008; Leary, 1995). Therefore, it can be assumed that users of profiles can engage in more strategic impression management than in face-to-face situations (Ellison, Heino, & Gibbs, 2006).

Furthermore, we have to consider that these profiles are not addressed to a specific target group or even a single person, but rather to a broad and—in most cases—unknown audience. Unlike in face-to-face communication, users are, therefore, unable to engage in "packaging," i.e., tailoring the impression management to the specific addressee or situation. Consequently, profile owners have to create an online profile that fulfils various self-presentational goals (Krämer & Winter, 2008). The user of an online profile has to show different facets of his life and personality when using the profile elements on social networking sites. In addition to basic information given by the portfolio of the user (name, age, field of study, relationship status, etc.), profile photos, groups, as well as information about personal preferences (with regard to music and movies), offer the opportunity to use subtle descriptions, which allow a more individualized and detailed presentation of the profile owner.

However, it is still an open question whether the users of social network sites are consciously aware of the possibility to control and reassess the information they put online. In other words: Are they choosing the information about their person in a conscious and selective manner? Or, on the other hand, do they not consider possible consequences that may arise by placing certain information on an online profile that can be viewed by a broad and notably unknown audience? Furthermore, we have to ask *what* impression people would like to form if they are selecting the information intentionally and which profile elements would help them to achieve their objectives for self-presentation.

Next to the production of network profiles, consider the reception of network site users: how do producers evaluate the impression management of other profile owners and which features (number of friends, groups, and photos) are relevant for their impression formation? To answer these questions, we conducted in-depth interviews with users of the social network site StudiVZ, the German equivalent of Facebook, and, additionally, we called on the interviewees to think aloud about different profiles we presented to them. We inquired about their impression management strategies, the meaning of profile elements as well as their evaluation of several strangers' profiles to achieve a first in-depth understanding of the phenomenon impression management and impression formation on SNS.

Impression Management by Means of Social Network Sites

Scholars from various fields of research have investigated SNS in order to get an understanding of the associated phenomena concerning its usage and effects (Boyd & Ellison, 2007). While the first studies on these sites concentrated on the general motivations of users to have an online profile (e.g., Haas, Trump, Gerhards & Klingler, 2007; Harrer, Krämer, Zeini, Haferkamp, 2008; Papacharissi, 2002a, 2002b; Raacke & Bons-Raacke, 2008), current research increasingly focuses on *psychological variables* that affect the usage patterns. For example, one area of research examines user attitudes towards self-disclosure and privacy (Reinecke & Trepte, 2008). Studies reveal that regular users of SNS are more willing to self-disclose, but at the same time are aware of the potential consequences of an inconsiderate abandonment of information.

Furthermore, Buffardi and Campbell (2008) analyzed how narcissism is manifested on SNS. They found that narcissism is related to a measure of website activity derived from the number of friends and the number of wall posts (i.e., messages) posted between friends. However, it is not related to the length of self-description. Furthermore, they demonstrated that narcissism is associated with self-promoting information about the self as raters were able to identify the degree of narcissism with the help of the self-promoting information on the network profile.

In line with this study, a considerable body of research has been conducted on the more general question of how people use their online profiles for *impression management*. For instance, Banczyk, Krämer, and Senokozlieva (2008) analyzed the relationship between self-esteem, personality traits, and impression management of members of the online community MySpace. The authors found that users with a high self-esteem tend to use more words to describe themselves on their webpage and used more pictures of celebrities. Also, research by Krämer and Winter (2008) highlights the personality characteristics of SNS users. The authors examine if personality variables such as self-efficacy and extraversion influence people's impression management and the design of an online profile respectively: While self-esteem is not related to the way people present themselves and extraversion is only mildly correlated, self-efficacy with regard to self-presentation has an impact on numerous aspects of the actual design of the profile. Users with a high self-efficacy tend to present an extensive self-description on their profile, while users with a low self-efficacy prefer to use more common ways to design their own webpage.

With regard to the real-life equivalence of the profiles, some studies find that people are not always honest when they are publishing information about themselves and that they tend to exaggerate. In one of her earliest studies, boyd (2006) analyzed Friendster (www.friendster.com) and found that there are so-called "fakesters" who publish fake information on their online profile. The objective of these fakesters is to appear more attractive, more successful, or just more interesting than they really are. Also, Jung, Youn, and McClung (2007) emphasize the possibility to switch between a "real" self and a "fake" self at a social network site. In accordance with this, Marwick (2005) showed that users emphasize different aspects of their self on platforms and therefore highlight certain aspects of their personality.

On the other hand, studies that concentrated on the effects of online profiles report that people who observe a stranger's online profile do not receive a false impression of the profile owner and evaluate them as if they knew them from everyday life (see Gosling, Gaddis, & Vazire, 2007; Vazire & Gosling, 2004). Evans, Gosling, and Carroll (2008) analyzed the effectiveness of the various profile elements in conveying information about the profile owners. They found that the majority of profile elements showed no impression agreement between the profile owner him/herself and a stranger's rating of the user's personality. However, when profile owners made statements about "their spirituality, beliefs, joys, embarrassing or proud moments, heroes and when they gave links to funny videos," the impression agreement increased. In summary, it can be said, therefore, that impression management as well as impression formation may be affected by specific elements (e.g. personal information) on the online profile.

Additionally, research demonstrates that a personal webpage allows a more detailed self-description than a face-to-face interaction and that people make use of it in order to emphasize certain aspects of their "true" self (Bargh, McKenna, & Fitzsimons, 2002). These partly contradictory results raise three questions that will serve as research questions for the interviews:

RQ1: Are people aware of what they are publishing online or do they not consciously consider their "online impression management"?

RQ2: What impression do profile owners want to form?

RQ3: Which features of an online profile are meaningful for impression management?

Furthermore, we wanted to know what profile owners think about the self-description of other people and which features they use in order to form an impression. As Walther, Van der Heide, Kim, Westerman, and Tong (2008) point out, postings of friends affect the evaluation of the profile owners. The statements have a significant impact on observer ratings of the social attraction and credibility of the profile owner. For instance, the authors show that postings suggesting excessive drinking and philandering decrease favorable ratings of targets. Moreover, the physical attractiveness of profile owner's friends that are visible on the wall postings affects the evaluation of the profile owner. Hence, observers evaluate the profile owners based on the presented information (Walther et al., 2008). This assumption can also be supported by Gosling et al. (2007), who demonstrate that people evaluate others based on their profile, and compare impressions that people have formed after regarding a foreign profile with descriptions of people who know the profile owner from everyday life. The results signify that Facebook-based personality impressions show some consensus for the two groups.

Research already demonstrates that a large number of friendship links seems to be an important aspect for impression formation. This importance is based on the assumption that people evaluate a person more positively if he is connected with many other people (Baumeister & Leary, 1995). Also, research by Kleck, Reese, Ziegerer-Behnken, and Sundar (2007) underlines the assumption that the number of friends presented on one's social network site profile triggers positive social judgments in this way. The authors present different online profiles with 15, 82, or 261 listed friends. Results show that the number of friends has an impact on participant evaluation of the users, who differentiated between low and high friend conditions on several ratings; for instance, popularity and pleasantness are greater when profile owners have a higher number of linked friends as opposed to having a low number of friends. Other features may also support impression management at SNS: The profile photo, for example, which is almost always showing the person himself, is one of the most dominant features on the online profile. In line with research on the importance of physical attractiveness (see Henss, 1998; Eagly, Ashmore, Makhijani, & Longo, 1991), it can be assumed that attractiveness will play a major role with regard to the impression formation. Furthermore, the profile has several categories for user textual self-description. For example, people can use the category "previous career." Additionally, people can become a member in and participate in different groups. The names of the groups often reflect certain interests and philosophies of life and, therefore, can also be used for self-description. To achieve an understanding of the meaning of profile features for impression formation, our fourth research question is as follows:

RQ4: How do profile owners evaluate other users and what features are most important for their evaluation?

Method

Design and participants

In May 2008, we conducted 12 in-depth-interviews with six female and six male participants who are students of the University Duisburg-Essen in Germany and all own an online profile at the German social network site StudiVZ. The interviews were recorded with a voice recorder and then transcribed into a text-document.

Measures

The interviewer used a field manual with questions derived from the empirical background depicted above.

Social network site usage

The first part of the field manual consisted of general questions concerning age and social network site usage. We asked the participants: a) why they decided to host their online profile, b) how often they update their profile, c) why it is important for them to have an updated profile, d) how often they use SNS, e) which of the features they are using most frequently, f) and why they are using SNS.

Impression management

Next, we asked the interviewees what was important for them concerning the design of their online profile and what kind of information they were ready to publish and what should not appear in public. Based on the self-efficacy scale with regard to impression management by Mielke (1990; see also Bandura, 1997) and the public and private self-consciousness scales by Fenigstein, Scheier, and Buss (1975), we asked the participants what impression they would like to foster with their online profile and inquired about the relative importance of positive and truthful impression management. We asked them if they think other users would present themselves realistically by means of their profile. Also, we wanted to know if the creation of the profile makes them think about their own person to a greater extent.

Profile photo/friends/groups

The third part of the interview focused on the features of every online profile: the personal profile photo, the number of linked friends as well as the groups that people can join. First, we asked participants about their physical appearance on their profile photo: how important it is for them to look good on the picture and if they have the opinion that other people also like it. Concerning friends, we wanted to know how important it is for the participants to have a large number of friends in their profile list and if they are doing something to increase the number of virtual friends. Concerning groups, we wanted to know how they are selecting groups and which meaning these groups have for the users.

Evaluation of other online profiles

The last part of the interviews concentrated on the perception and evaluation of other online profiles. We asked the participants which elements are most important for evaluating a person. Additionally, we showed them three different online profiles. Male participants were to evaluate profiles of male users and female participants those of female users. In both groups, the first profile showed a "beautiful person" with a significant number of friends and groups (Figure 1). The second one was an "average profile" with an average number of friends and groups and an inconspicuous profile photo. The last profile was also average except for the information about the career of the persons (the male profile owner has already worked as a pilot; the female as a journalist). During inspection of the profiles, the participants were instructed to use the think aloud method.

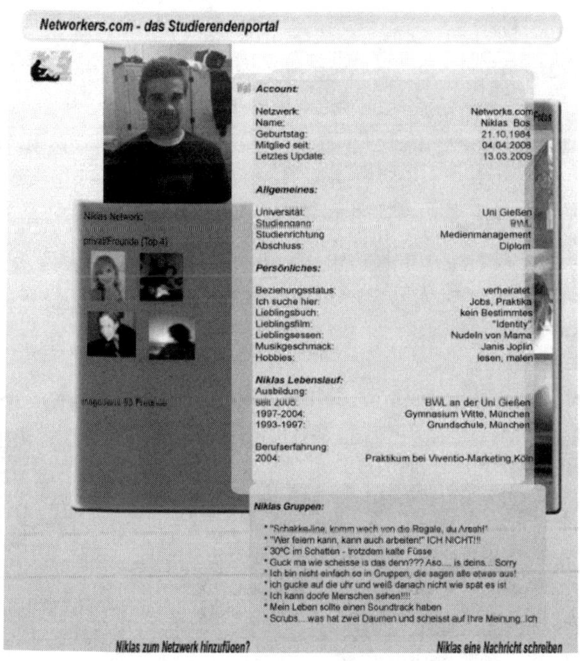

Figure 1a: Example of online profile on StudiVZ.

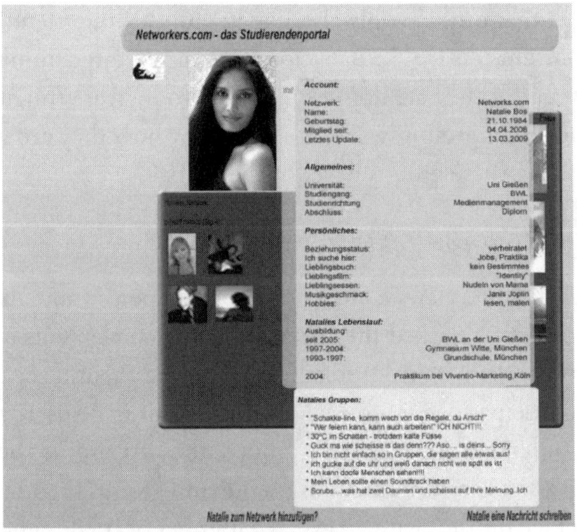

Figure 1b: Example of online profile on StudiVZ.

The analysis of the transcribed interviews was conducted with the help of ATLAS.ti (www.atlasti.com), a workbench for the qualitative analysis of large bodies of textual data. It supports the aggregation and the coding of the recorded data. The evaluation of the textual data was organized according to Mayring (2000) who suggests three separate analytical procedures. First, the data had to be summarized in such a way as to preserve the essential content and by abstraction to create a manageable corpus which still represented the whole information. Next, the material had to be explicated, explained, and clarified, especially when something seemed contradictory or unclear. Last, the text had to be structured according to content, form, and scaling. The categories were formed after regarding the whole textual data. Furthermore, the field manual with its questions helped to separate different aspects as regards content. We obtained four categories that were used to answer our research questions:

1. Consciousness of self-presentation: This category summarizes all statements that deal with the degree of consciousness with regard to impression management. We selected all the statements for this category that demonstrated to us how aware or unaware people are of what they publish online.
2. Nature of impression management: This category summarizes all statements that point out what kind of impression people would like to form and manage with their online profile. It, therefore, deals with the nature of user self-portrayal.

3. Features for impression management: This category summarizes all the statements that deal with the relevant profile elements for impression management.
4. Impression formation: This category examines the reception of online profiles. It deals with the evaluation of foreign profiles. We also consider the most important profile elements for impression formation that were mentioned during the interviews.

Results

All 12 participants (mean age = 23 years; SD = .091) report that other students recommended them to have an online profile on StudiVZ. Ten of these users update their profiles more often than quarterly, seven of them even change their online photographs more than once a month. According to the interviewees, the most important features of the social network site are the mailing function and the possibility to create virtual photo albums. We also asked the participants why they were using the social network site in general. Altogether, the participants only mentioned four different main motivations for using online profiles: The first motivation was *curiosity*. Seven of the subjects (six women) report they are curious and want to know what other people put on their online profile. Additionally, five of them assume that an online profile provides an insight into the everyday life of the profile owners.

The second motivation (*contact*) refers to the mailing function. People like to write messages to stay in contact with fellow students. However, they are not interested in becoming acquainted with a stranger; they rather want to contact students they know from everyday life. Online profiles are—according to the interviewees—an alternative to email or chat tools such as Skype:

> "On the one hand, I am just curious and I want to know what other people have experienced recently, which photos they put online and what they look like on these photos. On the other hand, I'd like to communicate with other people whose email address or telephone number is not available" (female, 24 years).

Three of the five participants whose primary motivation is to contact other students via StudiVZ were men. They note that StudiVZ has become the most important platform for a communicative exchange with others "because it is so easy and simple to put a message on the pin board or to write a private message" (male, 26 years).

Next to curiosity and communicative exchange, *entertainment* and *passing time* were also mentioned twice.

Furthermore, we were interested in the self-presentation-techniques and their implications for the evaluation of self and other people. Next, we present the results of each category with the appropriate research question and underline the results with some quotations of the participants.

RQ1: Are people really aware of what they are publishing online or do they not intentionally think about their online impression management?

RQ2: What impression do profile owners want to form?

First, we asked the participants how important it is for them to form a positive impression on their online profile and if they are finally content with the impression they form with their profile. Eight of 12 respondents report they intentionally try to form a positive but realistic impression and that they think a lot about their published data. The others mention they simply publish information without thinking about a certain impression management. The eight other persons emphasize they want to give an impression that is identical to the impression they want to make in everyday life. For instance, a 23-year-old female points out that she wants

> "…to show others who I am. This is also the reason why I use a lot of different information about myself. I pick out specific information that makes others know who I am. I don't want to cheat on somebody and I don't want to show something that doesn't belong to my personality."

Female profile owners (N=6) especially point out it is important for them not to deceive the profile's observers, which is, in their opinion, easy to achieve by using posed pictures or certain group names. A 22-year-old female states that she wants to "create a realistic impression, nothing exaggerated. For instance, I would not publish photographs which might set somebody on the wrong track."

The other four participants are all men, and they are not as reflective as the female participants. According to their statements, one can again assume that they do not give a high priority to an intentional impression management: "I don't want to give a specific impression. If the people are interested in my profile then they are interested. Otherwise, I don't care about their comments"(male, 23 years). A 26-year-old male even states that "if somebody takes a look at my 'alcohol-photos,' I wouldn't possibly be evaluated positively. But I wouldn't delete them, I like them, they are funny, aren't they? Who should care?" Three of these four men answered to a previous question that dealt with their motivation to use online profiles that they only have an account to get in contact with other people.

Finally, we asked the participants if the creation of their online profiles made them more aware of themselves in order to test the limits of self-reflection during impression management via online profiles. The eight students who already responded to a previous question that they intentionally put information online agreed. Five of them report that it took them quite a long time to create their profiles because they had to think about the most important aspects of their life and their personality. A 23-year-old woman states that she thought about her life and information that makes her stand out from the crowd: "I mentally summed up my life. Who I am? And what represents me? I realized that group names were important for my self-description." It became apparent that users of SNS are reflective and act intentionally when it comes to self-description. However, the four men mentioned above deny that the production of their online profile made them more self-reflective. One of them states he "just quickly arrange the information and then put it online" (male, 24 years).

RQ3: Which features of an online profile are meaningful for impression management?

To further differentiate the importance of single features, we asked the participants about their rationale for using specific features (photographs, friend list, and groups).

Concerning the personal profile photograph, the six women point out that their profile photograph was selected intentionally and that it should show the profile owner in a positive but realistic way. In line with this, five of the female participants emphasize that they want to control which kind of personal photos appears on the Internet and that they feel ashamed if somebody connects them to a photo. "I choose a photo which shows me in a positive way. It is very important for me that I like the picture. Otherwise, I wouldn't present it to others" (female, 24 years). However, the men appear to not be that concerned about the choice of photograph. Three of them state they are unconcerned about online photos, which can be regarded by strangers. Here, a 26-year-old male participant states that he is "totally unconcerned about my photo. Nobody knows if I am the person on the photo. What should happen?"

As Boyd and Ellison (2007) already discussed, the list of friends on the social network site seems to be another meaningful feature for personal impression management. However, our interviews do not reveal the importance of friends who are linked to a personal webpage at first sight. Seven of the interviewees state that the number of friends does not say much about a person and his sociability. In general, all of the interviewees deny that they try to increase their number of friends by intentionally searching for people who want to connect their profile with theirs. One possible reason for the irrelevance is—according to the participants—the impossibility to check if these friends are also offline friends or only persons the profile owner contacted via StudiVZ to increase his personal number of connections. The phenomenon to "boost" the list of friends on the personal profile has been labeled with the term "friends-collector." Four of the interviewees mentioned this expression during the conversation with regard to the list of friends on one's webpage. Furthermore, none of the participants stated they increase the number of friends for a more positive impression management. "The number of friends should not be overrated because you can't control what kind of connection two persons have: they can be friends but also strangers" (male, 32 years). However, two women report they would feel uncomfortable with a small number of friends: "I would be embarrassed if other people who look at my profile think that I have only 19 or 20 real friends" (female, 23 years).

Next, we asked the participants about the personal information (name, address, previous career, favorite music, film etc.) that one person can leave on the profile. Four male participants stated that it is "*quite important*" for them to have an appealing portfolio whereas women do not put a high priority on the information because "these facts do not tell much about a person" (female, 23 years). For four female users, other profile elements such as photos or even friends are more important.

Additionally, we inquired about the importance of the groups one can join in StudiVZ. Nine of the interviewees explain that groups are important for self-presentation and have to be chosen cautiously. The importance of displaying the group names on their profiles was mentioned by all of the participants, independent from their sex. The group membership is important not due to the wish to actually participate in group activities and discussions but in order to show other people one's philosophy of life or personality characteristics. Three of the interviewees even assume that a group name reveals more about a person than the private information one can leave on one's online profile. This is why users are worried about their groups and the question if they represent them adequately. "I think about the groups a long time: Do they represent me or do they represent another person? (female, 24 years).

RQ4: What features are most important for impression formation by means of other users' profiles?

After asking the participants about the self-presentation and important features for self-description, we were also interested in their evaluation of other people's online profiles. Ten of the interviewees assume that other people tend to deceive others by means of their webpage. They assume that other people exaggerate or use false information when they construct their personal profile. For instance, a 24-year-old female student claims that "some of the users present themselves more positively than they are in reality." A male participant (23 years) suggests that a lot of people use StudiVZ for self-display "with a lot of distortion and faked information." The interviewees do not trust the information they get from other people: "The information is never comparable to reality, I would never trust it" (female, 23 years).

To get a better understanding of the evaluation of other self-presentations, we showed different StudiVZ profiles to the interviewees. During all interviews it was confirmed that the photos as well as the groups are the most important information for the evaluation of a person. In general, all the participants state that the same elements they use for their own impression management are also important for the evaluation of unknown people: Whereas men put a higher priority on the personal information of a profile owner ("especially the career reveals much about a person"; male, 24 years), women put a higher priority on photos and groups. In doing so, profiles were evaluated most negatively when the profile photo shows an attractive person, independent from the sex of the interviewees. A 23-year-old female says she does not believe in the presented attractiveness of the profile owner: "I think that this girl is not as beautiful in reality as she is on the picture. This is exaggerated." If a profile presents an average person who was not that attractive and successful, respondents assumed the owners tell the truth about their lives and personal characteristics.

Finally, we asked the participants how confident they feel with their evaluations of others. Ten of the 12 persons state they feel confident with their estimations. They assume their estimations match with reality—independently of whether they thought the person presented himself adequately—and they even feel well prepared for meeting the persons in reality.

Discussion

In this section we compare our findings with previous studies and derive research questions for further studies. Our first objective was to analyze to what extent people intentionally manage impressions of their self. Respondents reveal they consciously select information for self-description. This result supports investigations of previous studies that deal with impression management and SNS (Krämer & Winter, 2008; Banczyk et al., 2008). In our qualitative interviews, women, especially, report they intentionally pick a profile photo and select information that is suitable for them.

A larger part of the male respondents do not seem to be that reflective; the respondents are less interested in a conscious impression management. When comparing the motivations of the participants to use the profiles, it becomes clear that those male participants who only use SNS for communicative exchange are not that reflective concerning their impression management. They rather regard an online-profile as a communication tool. Furthermore, we asked the participants what kind of impression they want to foster by means of their online profile. Nearly all of them put a high priority on a self-presentation that preferably reflects a realistic copy of their "everyday" self. They emphasize they are not interested in a faked profile that presents an idealized version of a person rather than describing real characteristics. These statements are supported by the results of Gosling et al. (2007) who found that strangers are able to describe a person correctly just by regarding his online profile. If people would not stick to a realistic self-description and tend to exaggerate, participants of the Gosling et al. experiment would not have been able to assess a profile owner's character.

Next, we analyzed the meaning of a profile's features for self-presentation and observed that group membership and photos play, especially for women, the most important role for impression management as well as impression formation on the basis of strangers' websites. Males put a higher priority on personal information such as career. Surprisingly, the number of friends was not that important for users. Nevertheless, two women report they prefer not to have a small number of friends due to the negative effect this could have on other observers. In general, the result is contrary to the results of Walther et al. (2008) who points out the importance of virtual friends for social judgment as well as to the results of Kleck et al. (2007) who also found that the number of friends has an impact on a participant's evaluation of the profile owners. One possible reason might be that the meaning of this list of friends has changed in the meantime: Users of SNS have realized that the number of friends is not meaningful by now because observers cannot distinguish between real friends and people the person only knows online.

For the evaluation of other profile owners, we found that interviewees assume other users tend to put false and especially exaggerated self-descriptions on their profiles. They believe that others would manipulate their profile in a way that is advantageous for them. For instance, they believe users would publish a profile photo that presents them in a more attractive way than they are in reality. This result is remarkable insofar as most of the interviewees explicitly stress they strive to present themselves as realistically as possible. Moreover, it contradicts the results of Gosling et al. (2007), who assumed that by inspecting online profiles, people form an impression that is comparable with their face-to-face impression. The assumption that others are more "seduced" by possibilities of the new media than by one's self is reminiscent of the popular "third person effect" of Davison (1983). His third-person effect hypothesis assumes that people believe that others are more influenced by persuasive effects of the media than they are themselves. Although the formulation of the hypothesis does not exactly fit our investigations (because the interviewees did not refer to persuasive media effects but the possibility to manipulate information on a website), the reported distrust of the respondents towards the profile information of others while excluding this tendency for their own behavior should be analyzed in further studies.

In sum, it can be stated that users are intentionally creating online profiles and they tend to present themselves as realistically as possible. Women think more about their impression management than men and show a higher degree of reflection with regard to the creation of an online profile. The profile photos as well as group membership seem to be most important for them for forming a self-presentation, while men put a higher priority on factual information such as regarding career. Most users state that the number of friends is relatively unimportant for managing an impression. Concerning the reception of others' profiles, photos and group membership are essential for the evaluation of a profile owner. People preferably use photos that the profile owner is linked to in order to form an opinion about the person. Given that users state they present themselves realistically, it is surprising they assume that other users fake information for self-description. They do not trust the published information of other people, especially when these people appear to be physically attractive.

Conclusions

In general, SNS opens up a new era of impression management, and there are still a lot of open research questions to be answered in order to achieve a broad coverage of this social web phenomenon. The study we present here is only a starting point for further investigations that use social psychological theories and concepts such as impression management or social comparison in order to explain the usage and effects of these applications. For instance, we have to ask what effects virtual impression management might have for the observer as well as the producer; for instance: do people compare their own impression management with that of other users? We thus have to investigate the observed reactions with the help of implicit measurements based on social psychological concepts and theories in order to receive more trustworthy information about the user intention to present themselves realistically and their assumption that other users do not.

References

Banczyk, B., Krämer, N. C., & Senokozlieva, M. (2008). "The wurst" meets "fatless" in MySpace. The relationship between personality, nationality and self-presentation in an online community. Paper presented at the annual meeting of the International Communication Association, May 2008, Montreal, Canada.

Bandura, A. (1997). *Self-efficacy: The exercise of control.* New York: Freeman.

Bargh, J.A., McKenna, K.Y., & Fitzsimons, G. M. (2002). Can you see the real me? Activation and expression of the "true self" on the Internet. *Journal of Social Issues, 58* (1), 33–48.

Baumeister, R.F., & Leary, M.R. (1995). The need to belong: Desire for interpersonal attachments as a fundamental human motivation. *Psychological Bulletin, 117* (3), 497–529.

Boyd, DM. (2006). Friends, friendsters, and top 8: Writing community into being on social network sites. *First Monday,* 11 (12), Retrieved July 1, 2007, from http://firstmonday.org/issues/issue11_12/boyd.html.

Boyd, DM., & Ellison, N.B. (2007). Social network sites: Definition, history, and scholarship. *Journal of Computer-Mediated Communication, 13* (1), Retrieved June 20, 2007, from http://jcmc.indiana.edu/vol13/issue1/boyd.ellison.html.

Buffardi, L., & Campbell, K. (2008). Narcissism and Social Networking Web Sites. *Personality and Social Psychology Bulletin, 34,* 1303–1314.

Davison, W. P. (1983). The third-person effect in communication. *Public Opinion Quarterly, 47,* 1–15.

Donath, J., & Boyd, D. (2004). Public displays of connection. *BT Technology Journal, 22* (4), 71–82.

Eagly, A.H., Ashmore, R.D., Makhijani, M.G., & Longo, L.C. (1991) What is beautiful is good, but ...A meta-analytic review of research on the physical attractiveness stereotype. *Psychological Bulletin, 111*(2), 304–128.

Ellison, N., Heino, R., & Gibbs, J. (2006). Managing impressions online: Self-presentation processes in the online dating environment. *Journal of Computer-Mediated Communication, 11* (2), article 2. Retrieved June 30, 2007, from http://jcmc.indiana.edu/vol11/issue2/ellison.html

Evans, D., Gosling, S., & Caroll, A. (2008). What elements of an online social networking profile predict target-rater agreement in personality impressions? Paper presented at International Conference on Weblogs and Social Media, March 2008, Seattle.

Fenigstein, A., Scheier, M.F., & Buss, A.H. (1975). Public and private self-consciousness: Assessment and theory. *Journal of Consulting and Clinical Psychology, 43,* 522–527.

Gosling, S. D., Gaddis, S. & Vazire, S. (2007). *Personality impressions based on Facebook profiles.*

Retrieved July 7, 2007, from http://www.icwsm.org/papers/3—Gosling-Gaddis-Vazire.pdf.

Haas, A., Trump, M., Gerhards, M. & Klingler, W. (2007). Web 2.0: Nutzung und Nutzertypen. Eine Analyse auf der Basis quantitativer und qualitativer Untersuchungen. *Media Perspektiven, 4,* 215–222.

Harrer, A., Krämer, N.C., Zeini, S. & Haferkamp, N. (2008). Ergebnisse und Fragestellungen aus Psychologie und Informatik zur Analyse von Interaktionen in Online-Communities und Potenziale interdisziplinärer Forschung. In A. Zerfaß, M. Welker & J. Schmidt (Hrsg.), *Kommunikation, partizipation und wirkungen im social web. Band 1: Grundlagen und Methoden: Von der Gesellschaft zum Individuum* (S. 301–326). Köln: Herbert von Halem Verlag.

Henss, R. (*1998*). Type nouns and the five factor model of personality description. *European Journal of Personality, 12,* 57–71.

Jacobson, D. (1999). Impression formation in cyberspace: Online expectations and offline experiences in text-based virtual communities. *Journal of Computer-Mediated Communication, 5,* 1. Retrieved May 18, 2000, from http://www.ascus.org/jcmc/vol5/issue/jacobsen.html.

Jung, T., Youn, H., & McClung, S. (2007). Motivations and self-presentation strategies on Korean-based "Cyworld" weblog format personal homepages. *CyberPsychology and Behavior, 10* (1), 24–31.

Kleck, C.A., Reese, C., Ziegerer-Behnken, D. and Sundar, S. (2007). The company you keep and the image you project: Putting your best face forward in online social networks. Paper presented at the annual meeting of the International Communication Association, TBA, San Francisco, CA Online. Retrieved 26 June 2008, from http://www.allacademic.com/meta/p172756_index.html.

Krämer, N. C., & Winter, S. (2008). Impression management 2.0. The relationship of self-esteem, extraversion, self-efficacy, and self-presentation within social network sites. *Journal of Media Psychology, 20,* 3, 96–106.

Leary, M. R. (1995). *Self presentation. Impression management and interpersonal behavior.* Madison, WI.: Brown & Benchmark Publishers.

Marwick, A. (2005). "I'm more than just a Friendster profile: Identity, authenticity, and power in social networking services." Association for Internet Researchers, Chicago, IL. Retrieved June, 2005, from http://www.tiara.org/blog/?page_id=299.

Mayring, P. (2000). *Qualitative Inhaltsanalyse. Grundlagen und Techniken* (7. Auflage, erste Auflage 1983). Weinheim: Deutscher Studien Verlag.

Mielke, R. (1990). Ein Fragebogen zur Wirksamkeit der Selbstdarstellung. *Zeitschrift für Sozialpsychologie, 21,* 162–170.

Papacharissi, Z. (2002a). The presentation of self in virtual life: Characteristics of personal home pages. *Journalism and Mass Communication Quarterly. 79* (3), 643–660. Retrieved June 2002, from, http://www.blogresearch.com/articles/papacharissi_JMCQ.pdf

Papacharissi, Z. (2002b). The self online: the utility of personal homepages. *Journal of Broadcasting and Electronic Media, 46,* 346–368.

Raacke, J. & Bons-Raacke, J. (2008). MySpace and Facebook: Applying the uses and gratifications theory to exploring friend-networking sites. *Cyberpsychology & Behavior, 11*(2), 169–174.

Reinecke, L., & Trepte, S. (2008). Privatsphäre 2.0: Konzepte von Privatheit, Intimsphäre und Werten im Umgang mit, user-generated-content. In A. Zerfaß, M. Welker & J. Schmidt (Hrsg.), *Kommunikation, partizipation und wirkungen im social web. Band 1: Grundlagen und*

Methoden: Von der Gesellschaft zum Individuum (S. 205–228). Köln: Herbert von Halem Verlag.

Vazire, S., & Gosling, S.D. (2004). e-Perceptions: Personality impressions based on personal Websites. *Journal of Personality and Social Psychology, 87*, 123–132.

Walther, J. B. (1993). Impression development in computer-mediated interaction. *Western Journal of Communication, 57*, 381–398.

Walther, J., Van der Heide, B., Kim, S.Y., Westerman, D., & Tong, S.T. (2008). The role of friends' appearance and behavior and evaluations of individuals on Facebook: Are we known by the company we keep? *Human Communication Research, 34,* 28–49.

III

Institutional Ramifications of Digital Content Creation for Learning

8

Digital Creativity

Editing versus Cheating and How You Learn the Difference

Angela McFarlane

When we examine the rhetoric of the knowledge society and the impact of computers followed by the impact of information and communication technologies (ICTs) over the last three decades, there have been countless predictions of a major impact on the nature of knowledge and, hence, on the processes of learning and teaching. In reality, however, the experience of learning in the classroom has little changed (McFarlane, 2003a). Models of learning in the Anglo-American tradition, widely adopted in the many areas influenced by that tradition, are still predicated on assumptions of a body of common content to be assimilated by an individual learner. In the learning cultures affected, the effectiveness of schooling as well as the performance of the learner may well be evaluated through the results of statutory tests. This inevitably leads to a focus on the facts and figures to be taught and then tested (McFarlane, 2003b).

A range of initiatives, usually with a genesis outside the statutory framework, have recast the curriculum as skills rather than content-based. Some of these projects are gaining purchase in the UK, especially in lower secondary schools where attempts to show improvements in learning gains have proved remarkably unsuccessful. However, the dominant model is still one where the uninitiated are inducted into a body of knowledge by a more expert other, in batches that are primarily based on the date of birth of the learner with some modification according to prior success or its absence. It is difficult to see much that is novel or innovative in the underlying paradigms of teacher and taught in the formal school system.

The impact that computers and ICTs have had on learning and teaching has been the subject of research and policy development since the 1970s. Much of the literature that addresses the interplay of digital technologies and learning, or teaching, addresses those technologies as though they are one variable. There has been relatively little work that theorizes or studies the various affordances of these technologies and breaks down the mangle of technology-enhanced learning into discrete scenarios where the content, context, pedagogy, task type, learner attributes and all the other variables that make up the complex event that is a learning opportunity are considered. Papers and journals are devoted to the use of information technology (IT), information and communications technology, computers or computer-assisted learning and so on. This approach, the monoculture of technology-enhanced learning, is somewhat problematic since, unless we consider the actual functions a particular technology can offer to support which aspects of learning, it is difficult to theorize the possible variants in the interplay of learner, task, and media and predict what, if any, impact there is likely to be on each of the actors, outcomes, or processes (McFarlane, 2003a). A particularly powerful variable here is the definition of what will count as evidence of learning.

Armed then with only the rather high level and vague models of technology-enhanced learning and encouraged by policymakers and educational theorists alike, teachers are expected to design and manage technology-enhanced learning tasks that must inevitably combine a particular pedagogical approach and specified content/topic and make available an appropriate range of media and tools for learners to use to accomplish the task.

The learning outcomes may be the result of any combination of the process and product of performing the task. The process of learning and teaching using a particular technological tool or tools becomes a black box where these resources are assumed—if only through the default of a lack of analysis—to be neutral. Incorporation of digital technologies as different from one another as an interactive whiteboard and a web-enabled handheld device, a museum website and mathematics practice software, information management systems, and instant messaging, are all treated in the mix under the catholic umbrella of ICT. The use of these is assumed to be innovative and positive, and moreover, uncontested. In much research and evaluation using the ICT tool set is compared to not using that tool set or the use of a tool is assumed to be uniform. There are often pragmatic reasons for this comparison even where the researchers know it is less than desirable.

In an attempt to gather a definitive answer to the vexing question of what value

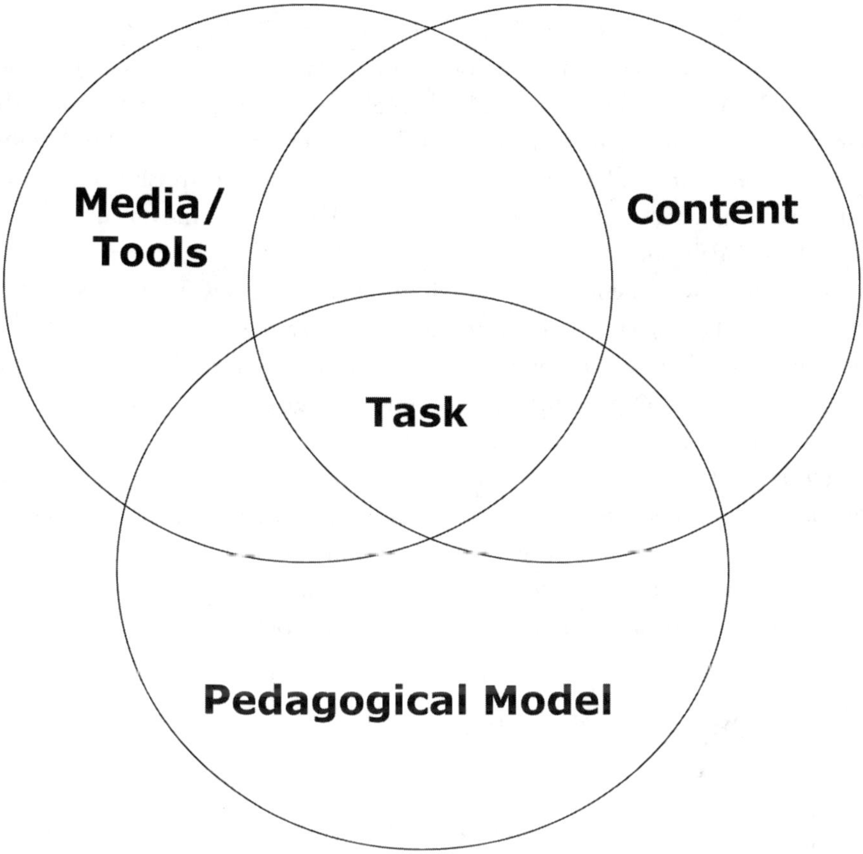

Figure 1: The interplay of tools, content, and pedagogy to frame a learning task.

the high investment in ICTs for schools had yielded in terms of improvements in test results, the UK government commissioned a two-year study in some 60 schools identified by government inspectors as users of ICTs. The ImpaCT2 study that resulted made valiant attempts to collect detailed data on use of ICTs by teachers and students, but in fact it was as much as could be achieved to record if and when an application was being used let alone what it was being used for (Becta, 2002). Large-scale studies, where there is greatest hope of finding generalized results, suffer from the fact that any learning context is remarkably complex, its ICT tools rich and flexible, making it difficult to collect all the relevant data. Smaller case study research offers more opportunity for detail, but is always then open to the criticism that it lacks scale.

However, the use of ICTs as a single variable in research is like using paper as a single variable—only arguably more absurd since the possibilities are even more varied. Aggregating data on "use" risks losing the very significant differences that are likely to arise from varied applications of the same technology. Moreover, the impact on learning is most often sought through the learner's performance on tests that are not tailored to any theorized interplay of content, process, and technology or the likely learning benefits that could accrue. It is not surprising, therefore, that convincing data on the impact of the use of ICT in learning on educational attainment remains illusive.

The UK's government agency for educational technology, Becta, has led the development of a self-review framework for schools to assess their progress with the integration of ICT into their practice. There is evidence that schools are finding this useful, not least to give them a common language to speak of their development plans (Labbe, unpublished thesis). However, at no point does this framework differentiate between forms of ICT or the different ways that they might be used, nor does it offer many examples of specific tasks that include a commentary on pedagogical models. Innovation is encouraged but not defined. The result is that the effects of the use of the framework depend heavily on local interpretation of the model of task design shown in Figure 1, and its execution.

Attempting to Establish a Context

In this chapter, we will look at a particular kind of task, albeit a generic one, and some particular uses of ICTs within it. The task type I have chosen is commonplace, if not frequent, in most school systems. This task requires the learner to produce content, which is most usually in the form of a written essay or in some cases may be a multimedia, video, audio, or animated text. The pedagogical model used here is constructivist, where the individual learner is invited to construct a representation of her own understanding of a narrative, explanation, or description that might be fictional or factual in nature. The learner is likely to be using a range of primary or secondary sources to inform her own thinking, but the purpose is to create a text that represents a view of what the learner knows, understands, or believes on a given theme. This kind of task in itself is far from new or original or unique to the knowledge age. Setting learners a task that involves writing an account of a given subject they have researched is generally a well-established practice in schools. What has changed is that these tasks are now set against a context where schools are encouraged to move from a traditional, mainstream, paper-based culture to one that is innovative, ICT-enabled, and screen-based, in effect from the bottom left to the top right of the axes shown in Figure 2. In fact, most practice has moved some way across the bottom of this grid, from paper-based to digitally enabled without noticeable innovation in pedagogy or outcome. Students may well use a word processor to produce an essay, and use the Internet—particularly sites such as Wikipedia—rather than pencil and paper and the family encyclopedia, but the nature of the end product and the process by which it is created is much the same. In some cases, the word processor is still used merely to create a presentable copy of something that originated, traditionally, on paper.

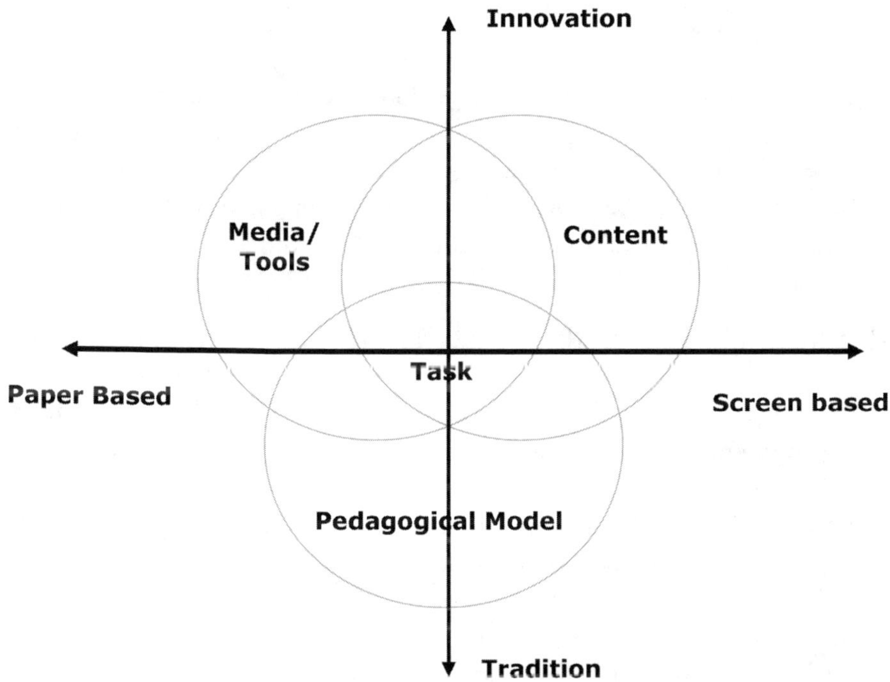

Figure 2: Axes of change.

So where is the problem? The task type remains valid—to create a text—and the tools being used to do it are now relevant to the technology-rich culture the learners do and will inhabit. The end result is largely more visually impressive than what the learners could produce with non-digital tools, not least because mistakes can be easily edited. But the process of assembling the text is little changed; the text is more than likely a standard written work and the skills developed are limited to those traditionally associated with writing essays. And yet this is against a background where those stakeholders who have a vested interest in employment-ready students emerging from the education system seek learners with a range of skills that go beyond this traditional practice of individual essay writing. These skills include the ability to:

- Find, evaluate, analyze and use information effectively
- Communicate what they know effectively
- Apply new and old knowledge to novel situations
- Be flexible
- Make decisions with an incomplete set of information
- Work in a team

This skill set begins to represent the ways of knowledge building and application that are essential to an active and successful engagement with the knowledge society. Faced with unparalleled access to information in a range of rich media and, critically, other people, via the Internet, this skill set becomes essential to building and communicating an individual's understanding of the world.

The Implications of the Knowledge Society for Pedagogy

There are those who argue that the advent of information technologies has changed the nature of knowledge and of knowing (Lyotard, 1984; Lankshear et al., 2000). Indeed there are those who believe the way the mind works when using such technologies is different. A key premise for this difference is the identification of this technology and information-rich era as the "information age," which underpins the knowledge society, a society where knowledge creation fueled by unprecedented access to information is or is predicted to be the basis of wealth and economic growth in developed nations for the first half of the twenty-first century. As a result of this, there are widespread calls for the education system to change in order to prepare learners to take their place in a "knowledge economy" that supports the "knowledge society."

Many attempts have been made to capture the essence of these changes and their implications for pedagogy. One model that has informed my thinking and the research behind this paper is that of Voogt and Pelgrum (2005) shown in Table 1. This model captures the key elements of pedagogical shift that are likely to result in the kind of learning and skill development that would equip individuals and groups to be socially and commercially successful in an information-rich culture and to develop the capability to create personal knowledge. This model also echoes a range of the aspirations of those implementing technology-enhanced learning

Table 1 Overview of pedagogy in the industrial versus the information society

Aspect	Pedagogy in an Industrial Society	Pedagogy in the Information Society
Active Learners	Activities prescribed by teacher Whole class instruction Little variation in activities Pace determined by the program	Activities determined by learners Small groups Many different activities Pace determined by learners
Collaborative	Individual Homogeneous groups Everyone for him/herself	Working in teams Heterogeneous groups Supporting each other
Creative	Reproductive learning Apply known solutions to problems	Productive learning Find new solutions to problems
Integrative	No link between theory and practice Separate subjects Discipline-based Individual teachers	Integrating theory and practice Relations between subjects Thematic Teams of teachers
Evaluative	Teacher–directed Summative	Student–directed Diagnostic

interventions including objectives such as enhanced learner autonomy and collaborative learning (McFarlane, Triggs, & Yee, 2008). There is crucially a call for a move from reproductive learning, where what is learned is produced to order, to productive learning where learners create their own representations of knowledge and understanding, individually, or collectively.

Growing Up in the Knowledge Society

The call for changes in approaches to pedagogy is set against an out-of-school context where most students in developed countries such as the UK have high levels of access to a range of digital technologies: Almost all students have access to a computer outside school by the age of 14; most have Internet access and much of this is broadband; social software is popular; most have students own mobile phone; in school most get to use technology about 15% of the time; and most use digital technologies to support school-related learning out of school

However, it is dangerous to assume that this physical access equates to deep and meaningful use of these technologies. The rhetoric that proposes that all young people are so-called digital natives, enjoying rich and complex creative interactions with and through digital technologies is mere techno-romanticism.

Despite much work to the contrary (Livingstone, 2002; Facer et al., 2003; Buckingham, 2006; Drotner, 2007; van Dijk, 2009), the myth of the teenage digital native not only persists, but also continues to underpin policy development in this area. There is a prevalent view that opportunities for physical access to technology and technologically driven tools and services are sufficient to ensure widespread adoption of, and meaningful engagement with, digital content and tools. UK government-funded work by organizations such as Becta (Harnessing Technology) and Futurelab (Teaching with Games) in the UK suggests that although the digital native is not necessarily a ubiquitous model, it nonetheless represents a view of young users of digital technologies that has financial and political significance. In all of the above examples, the assumption is that provision of technological facilities leads inexorably to meaningful engagement and in turn to educational benefit. These assumptions not only overshadow much more interesting and pertinent issues about everyday use and perceptions of new media technology, they also contribute to a technologically determined account of new media technology that presumes technological provision and access are all that is needed to guarantee use and interest (McFarlane & Thornham, 2008). Moreover, it is assumed that where use does occur this can be appropriated by policy and practice for the purposes of learning in formal and informal settings and that this will be both welcome and productive (Prensky, 2001). These assumptions risk a distortion of models of technology-enhanced learning practice, thus defeating the chances of success assumed by their advocates.

In reality, we are left with a number of questions concerning actual use of digital technologies by young people. This is perhaps most clearly illustrated in the area of the new media technologies known collectively as Web 2.0. Precise definitions of this stage of development of Internet technologies are contested, but a key attribute that separates them from Web 1.0 is that in Web 2.0 there are many tools for mass participation through contribution and sharing of content by non-specialists. Blogging and social networking sites make it easy for anyone with basic skills in operating browser technology to publish content on the Internet, whereas until about 2005 this was the preserve of those with mastery of web publishing tools aimed at those with existing programming skills. However, if use of these Web 2.0 technologies by young people is common, how much of this use in or out of school is banal and trivial? Just how many are having enriching and productive experiences of digital media and online communities? It would seem that it is not the majority (McFarlane, 2007; McFarlane & Thornham, 2008). Arthur, writing in 2006, suggests that of those who do engage with user-generated content on the web, only 1% post content, only 10% are likely to comment on the content, and the majority (89%) are peripheral observers who rarely comment or produce content. A recent research study commissioned by Becta looked at Web 2.0 use by school students aged 11–16 in English schools, and found that "although most learners use the Internet for learning, there is only limited use of Web 2.0, and only a few embryonic signs of criticality, self-management, and meta-cognitive reflection" (Crook & Harrison, 2008).

This situation raises interesting challenges for schools. If there is a significant minority of young people developing meaningful skills in evaluating, creating, and sharing rich content and if these experiences, skills and knowledge developed as a result do indeed give an advantage to those who have such access, what are we/should we be doing in school for the ones who are not? In other words, what should the tasks that sit at the heart of the diagram in Figure 1 look like and how should learners be supported to enact these tasks successfully?

Developing the Iterative, Creative Task

If we revisit the idea of the task shown in Figure 1 and assume a constructivist model of learning where the learner will be engaged in creating a representation of his own understanding through a productive task—writing, making a video or animation, etc.—we can now expand this task to include a social, iterative dimension. This opens up possibilities for a spectrum of collaboration. At one end, the individual remains the primary author producing what is to all intents and purposes an individual product. However, the learner does not work entirely in isolation on the task, offering it for assessment to a teacher once she sees it as complete. Rather she creates a number of iterative drafts of the product, at each stage offering the draft for comment and critique. This feedback may come from the teacher, other learners in her group or beyond including family members. With each iteration, she decides how and whether to respond to the input from others as she develops, clarifies, expands, or edits her creation. This process of reflection and development may well be the most powerful element of the task in terms of skill and knowledge development (Gilje, 2008; Perkel, 2008; Nyboe & Drotner, 2008). It is easy to see that the degree to which others contribute to the final product may vary, indeed at what point does a commenter become a co-author?

At the opposite end of the spectrum is a context where from the outset a number of creators decide to work together to make a text; they may work co-operatively, each to create a particular part of the whole, or they may collaborate, sharing a common text on which they all work. Final editorial decisions may also be shared—or one may take the lead role. Arguably none of the positions on this spectrum is unique to digital text creation, yet clearly there are a number of ways in which using digital tools makes this process of iteration and feedback much more accessible than any use of pre-digital tools and materials. The malleability of all manner of digital texts makes the process of drafting and editing much quicker and easier than that of any analogue equivalent. The result is that this refinement becomes a natural part of the creative process rather than an onerous chore in the way that re-writing an essay by hand remains, for example.

Moreover, some digital tools such as word processors, offer a range of functions—"track changes," "insert comments"—that are designed to support an iterative, collaborative, creative process by enabling the provision of specific and detailed feedback within a text, to which the author or authors can easily respond. However, other digital formats, where these tools for editorial input do not exist, can be difficult to use to engage in this process of co-authoring through precise and targeted input. For example, when editing web pages it can be difficult to identify to the author exactly where the comment you wish to make applies; the absence of page or line numbers or their equivalents make even a separate written commentary difficult and time consuming.

Perhaps the greatest potential for collaborative development of a text afforded by digital technologies comes with the ability to copy and share digital texts, especially through networked systems. Here, many people, within or beyond the physical community of the learner, can offer comment and feedback to the learner either through direct interaction with the original text or through an associated forum where comments can be made and responded to by a wider community. With the coming of the Internet, this community can be wide indeed. Moreover, with document-hosting services becoming more accessible, it is possible to hold a single version of a text in cyberspace to which a group of collaborators have editorial rights, and for a group to work in parallel on a single text in ways that have not previously been possible. Thus, wherever a task sits on the collaborative spectrum, from commenting to full co-authoring, there are digital tools to support the process.

So we have a theoretical model of a learning task, constructivist in nature with a pedagogical model that is social and cultural, bringing in interaction with peers and experts, using digital tools that support an iterative process of content creation that allows for critical reflection and development prompted through interaction with members of one's learning community. So much for the theory—but what happens when we try to put elements of this model into practice?

"eLearning" at Home and School

One way in which networked computer systems have been integrated into the learning culture of higher education systems, and more recently adopted at school level in the UK and elsewhere, is through the virtual or managed learning environment and so-called "eLearning." These systems manage the sharing of content between teachers and members of student groups and support a range of online communications tools, the first of which was the near-ubiquitous discussion board. These tools presaged in many ways the social networking tools now available through Web 2.0 but proved less popular with users.

One ambition of the teachers who were early adopters of these systems was the use of electronic communication to facilitate some form of co-learning amongst students on a course. The rationale for this approach lies in a model of learning as socially constructed, where exchange of views and information between students can lead to an enhanced outcome for all. Such meaningful exchange cannot, however, be taken for granted, and the best known model of management of such exchanges is that of Salmon's five-step model for e-moderating where some form of social exchange is an essential precursor to meaningful interaction to support learning (Salmon, 2004a, 2004b). Nevertheless, examples of less than successful attempts to encourage learners to use online discussion to support their learning are common. Of the papers that made up a special issue of the *Journal of Computer*

Aided Learning in late 2004, no document is entirely happy tale of deep engagement or spontaneous contribution, and these examples are far from isolated (McFarlane, 2007). One recurring problem is that of non-contribution; even where this is a compulsory element of a credit-bearing course, it can be impossible to get students to post their own comments or respond to others. This reflects Arthur's observation of engagement with UGC sites in the informal context (Arthur op cit), and yet there are some contrasts to this situation found in online communities associated with a range of informal activities, such as game play and fanfiction, where many individuals voluntarily spend hours contributing their own input or offering feedback to others. The volume of output, and time taken to read content, would be the envy of anyone who has attempted to encourage online interaction as a vehicle for formal learning (Cheng & McFarlane, 2006). However, even in environments where young people are invited to share their creative content and discuss their work with like-minded novices and experts, non-participation in discussion remains a challenge (Thornham & McFarlane, in press). Even in contexts where responses are plentiful and from a variety of community members, there still remains the question of whether the nature of the feedback actually supports reflection and development of the learner who has posted created content in the first place.

Learning Conversations

In a recent study of the interactions around creative content on a BBC website designed to encourage the sharing of creative output and development of skills of a teenage audience, the related discussions were analyzed for evidence of *learning conversations* (McFarlane & Thornham, 2008). Learning conversations were characterized as discussion board exchanges that have duration and show people offering and reflecting on feedback, most usually in the form of questions or challenges to the original author and using it to change and develop what they are doing. Of all exchanges analyzed 16% could be said to represent learning or productive dialogue, 84% are statements of opinion/emotion, which close down exchange and often come from the designated mentors in the community. These mentors are seen as experts in the related field: writing, movie making, digital games, dance, etc. As such, when they offer an opinion, this is seen as definitive and rarely if ever challenged by other community members. As the Salmon (2004b) model predicts, the role of the mentor is key to developing and modeling effective feedback practices in these discussions and where they do not do this—for example, through contributing closed statements not open questions—there is little chance of a meaningful learning conversation evolving. Not surprisingly perhaps, meaningful interaction for co-learning is something we have to learn to do and does not arise spontaneously simply because we have access to others online.

And What About the Cheating?

In order for the model of the iterative, creative task theorized earlier to emerge, not only must there be meaningful and appropriate feedback from at least the teacher/tutor, but ideally also from other members of the community to aid reflection, but the content created by the learner must be authentic. It must represent the actual world-view of the author in a thoughtful way. That does not mean that every word or pixel has to be the original work of the author, but where content from other sources is used this must be done appropriately, without breaching copyright and with full acknowledgement and accurate citation, that is without cheating! The process of editing this content into a personal text is as much part of the creative act as the generation of the author's own phrases, images, etc. However, the ease with which an author of a digital text can appropriate content and assimilate it in his own work has led to possibly the single greatest barrier to the adoption of the model I am proposing here as a method for personal knowledge building in formal education: The learners may cheat.

Currently, not only are opportunities for the production of a personal text through iteration supported by meaningful engagement with teachers and other learners rare, but explicit teaching about how to source, interpret, evaluate, and incorporate other texts within one's own in a legitimate way is uncommon. A survey carried out in the UK by the Association of Teachers and Lecturers and published in 2008 shows that over 50% of their members believe that plagiarism is a major problem in student work. The greatest source of problem content is of course the Internet. Just as digital texts offer the author an easy way of editing her own content, the texts also offer ways to copy and paste other content into a personal text with even greater ease (see the chapter by Clark in this volume for examples from the science classroom). In a small study carried out in the UK through the BEEP project (www.beep.ac.uk), teachers of post 16 students report that these students lack skills in information filtering and quality assessment. In particular, students don't question the authority of information sources; they don't like to think, and they cut and paste without engaging.

If this is as widespread as suggested by this research, it raises serious questions as to how, if at all, these students are being taught to use information to develop personal knowledge. Certainly, it is difficult to reconcile this situation with one where the students are indeed being taught to use information sources appropriately. It is not just that learners should work with information sources to build personal representations of their knowledge and understanding that is important, but that they should know they are doing so; otherwise, they cannot be consciously knowledge-building. Moreover, they should be aware that this is an important and useful thing to do, an objective to be achieved largely by encouraging children to work with ideas and content that interest them and making the elements of the knowledge-building process, in particular the relevant conceptual artefacts, explicit (Bereiter, 2002). For Scardamalia and Bereiter, the process of education involves working with ideas to understand the nature of ideas, argue about and criticize them, and improve them (Scardamalia & Bereiter, 2003). "In order to work creatively, students must become constructivists and understand that knowledge is created and continually improved upon by people and that this is something they can do" (Scardamalia, 2000, p 5).

The key to this idea may be the use of the term "creatively"; indeed, this may be the bridge between the curricula that have dominated Western school systems in the late twentieth century and those that are struggling to emerge in the twenty-first. The test-driven systems prevalent particularly in the U.S. and UK are beginning to break down. Levels of achievement have stagnated, following early apparent rises and standards of pupil behavior deteriorate year after year, according to annual reports from the UK Chief Inspector of Schools published by Ofsted over the last 10 years. This latter decline clearly has causes beyond the school system; but a curriculum that offers little authenticity to learners does not help. As early as 1999, in a response to the lack of creativity in the UK curriculum, the National Advisory Committee on Creative and Cultural Education (NACCCE) offered a definition of the essential elements involved in a creative process. These are (NACCCE, 1999):

- A fashioning process
- Using imagination
- Pursuing purpose
- Being original
- Judging value

The Qualifications and Curriculum Agency (QCA) in England, drawing on a range of sources including the NAACCE report, then offered a view of the kinds of pupil thinking and behaviour that would be involved in creative learning (QCA, 2002):

- Questioning and challenging
- Making connections and seeing relationships

- Envisaging what might be
- Playing with ideas
- Representing ideas
- Evaluating the effects of ideas

It is significant that these behaviors are clearly not unique to the traditionally creative elements of the curriculum; those that deal with the arts and crafts, for example. Indeed this approach to learning could be easily applied irrespective of the subject area under study and clearly echoes Bereiter and Scardamalia's notion of working with and improving ideas. Here knowledge is something to be worked on and with, not an entity to be passively consumed or even individually constructed. Perhaps this is the most important aspect of the nature of knowledge we need to grasp in order to inform a curriculum that is both relevant and engaging for learners growing up in the knowledge age.

Moreover, this way of working with ideas is inherently social, involving as it does discussion and argument, justification and exploration. This makes school an ideal site for such learning, which is more difficult to do in isolation. Although in theory much of this interaction can also take place online in what Gee defines as "affinity spaces" (Gee, 2007); as discussed above, the reality shows little evidence of these exchanges emerging spontaneously. Bereiter (2002) suggests that the opportunity for social learning, along with childcare, may be the most powerful reason to retain schools as sites of learning in an information rich age, a point echoed by Drotner (2007). As Salmon established, there is a need for teachers to act as mentors to support the kind of exchanges between learners that are needed to develop what we have described as learning conversations (McFarlane & Thornham, 2008). Yet there is little evidence of this kind of practice emerging at school level—no iterative, productive model of learning, which has to be the centerpiece of this kind of process of interaction between learners.

Furthermore, there is a tendency in theory and practice to be overly guided by Vygotsky's model of scaffolding through support from a more competent other (Vygotsky, 1978). This leads to a failure to value the interaction with a less, or certainly no more, knowledgeable peer whose questioning can indeed help to explore and refine the thinking of both questioner and questioned. Unless this interaction with one's peer group, as opposed to that of the tutor or teacher, is recognized as valuable to learning by all involved, the uptake of opportunities for social learning on- or off-line are likely to remain under-exploited. The role of the teacher as the ultimate arbiter of learning is likely to persist, even in adult learning contexts, but this does not preclude a role for fellow learners. Not only can fellow learners be co-creators of a text, they can also question the coherence and clarity of thought and offer alternative models of representation and perspective. Indeed, explaining what you think, and justifying why you think it, to another can be one of the best models for learning and has been since Socrates.

And it is in this context of discussion and debate about the exact nature of the ideas being presented and explained where the real difference between editing and cheating becomes a lived experience. There is little room for unthinking incorporation of other people's content in the cut-and-paste culture described when you know that firstly this is likely to be evident to and exposed by one's learning community, and moreover you are likely to be challenged to explain or amplify the text you have posted.

A Way Forward

The learning model implicit in the social engagement with iterative, productive tasks described above requires the development of iterative, productive tasks where we see reflection, critique, and development as a standard part of the process of learning. Moreover, that critique is provided by the learner's active community of co-learners not just the teacher. Those co-learners may or may not be co-located. But we cannot assume that learners will naturally take to this environment, using the experiences they have acquired in the likes of Bebo and Facebook to acquire the skills and etiquette required to become successful online, or offline, collaborative learners. As with all collaboration, we have to learn how to do this successfully, which probably means a combination of exposure to successful practitioners and some explicit teaching. Where Bereiter and Scardamalia make their most significant contribution to the development of pedagogical models appropriate to the knowledge society is perhaps in the linking of theories of knowledge to models of education—moreover, models of education that do not preclude a role for defined content, or a range of existing forms of teaching such as direct instruction, but rather weave these into a fabric that builds on what is good in the current system and takes it forward. For without coherent, scalable models of what it is to teach and learn using meaningful knowledge practices, no matter how convincing the theoretical arguments, they are unlikely to influence policy or practice.

References

Arthur, C. (2006) What is the 1% rule? *The Guardian* July 20, 2008. http://www.guardian.co.uk/technology/2006/jul/20/guardianweeklytechnologysection2

Becta. (2002). The ImpaCT2 Study. http://partners.becta.org.uk/index.php?section=rh&rid=13602

Bereiter, C. (2002). *Education and mind in the knowledge age*. Mahwah, NJ: Lawrence Erlbaum.

Buckingham, D. (2006). The electronic generation? Children and new media. In L. A. Lievrouw, & S. Livingstone (Eds.) *The handbook of new media* (pp. 77–89). London: Sage.

Cheng, C., & McFarlane, A. (2006). Gaming culture and digital literacy: Inspiration and audience. *Nordic Journal of Digital Literacy, 1*(2), 91–107.

Crook, C., & Harrison, C. (2008). *Web 2.0 technologies for learning at key stages 3 and 4*, Coventry,UK: Becta. http://partners.becta.org.uk/index.php?section=rh&&catcode=_re_rp_02&rid=14543

van Dijk, J. (2009). Users like you? Theorizing agency in user-generated content. *Media, Culture & Society, 31*(1): 41–58.

Drotner, K. (2007). Leisure is hard work: Digital practices and future competences. In D. Buckingham (Ed.) *Youth, identity and digital media* (pp. 167–84). Cambridge, MA: The MIT Press. The McArthur Foundation Series on Digital Media and Learning. http//:www.mitpress journals.org/toc/dmal/-/6.

Facer, K., Furlong, J., Furlong, R., & Sutherland, R. (2003). *ScreenPlay: Children and computing in the home*. London: RoutledgeFalmer.

Gee, J. P. (2007). *Good video games and good learning: Collected essays on video games, learning, and literacy*. New York: Peter Lang.

Gilje, Ø. (2008). Googling movies: Digital media production and the "culture of appropriation." In K. Drotner, H. S. Jensen, & K. C. Schrøder (Eds.), *Informal Learning and Digital Media* (pp. 29–48). Cambridge: Cambridge Scholars Publishing.

Lankshear, C., Peters, M., & Knobel, M. (2000). Information, knowledge and learning: Some issues facing epistemology and education in a digital age. *Journal of Philosophy of Education, 34*(1), 17–39.

Livingstone, S. (2002). *Young people and new media*. London: Sage

Lyotard, J.-F. (1984). *The postmodern condition: A report on knowledge*. Minneapolis: University of Minnesota Press. Timmis and O'Leary, 2005, Alt-J (proceedings of Alt-C) http://sole.ilrt.bris.ac.uk.

McFarlane, A. (2003a). Learners, learning and new technologies. *Educational Media International, 40*(3–4), 219–227.

McFarlane, A. E. (Ed.) (2003b) Assessment for the digital age, *Assessment in Education, 10*(3), 261–66.

McFarlane, A.E. (2007). Learning and lessons from the world of games and play. In R. Andrews, & C. Haythornthwaite (Eds.), *Handbook of e-learning research* (pp. 119–38). London: Sage.

McFarlane, A. E., & Thornham, H. (2008). Alone Together? Social learning in BBC Blast. http://www.bbc.co.uk/blogs/knowledgeexchange/bristol.pdf

McFarlane, A., Triggs, P., & Wan,Y. (2008). Researching mobile learning: Interim report, Coventry, UK: Becta.

http://partners.becta.org.uk/index.php?section=rh&catcode=_re_rp_02&rid=14204

National Advisory Committee on Creative and Cultural Education. (1999). All our futures: Creativity, culture and education. http://www.cypni.org.uk/downloads/alloutfutures.pdf

Nyboe, L., & Drotner, K. (2008). Identity, aesthetics and digital narration. In K. Lundby (Ed.) *Digital storytelling, mediatized stories: Self-representations in new media* (pp. 161–76). New York: Peter Lang.

Perkel, D. (2008). Copy and paste literacy? Literacy practices in the production of a MySpace profile. In K. Drotner, H. S. Jensen, & K. C. Schrøder (Eds.), *Informal learning and digital media* (pp. 203–24). Cambridge: Cambridge Scholars Publishing.

Prensky, M. (2001). *Digital game-based learning.* New York: McGraw-Hill.

Qualifications and Curriculum Agency. (2002). Creativity pack information sheet 3. http://www.ncaction.org.uk/creativity/index.htm

Salmon, G. (2004a). *E-moderating: The key to teaching and learning online.* Abingdon: RoutledgeFalmer.

Salmon, G. (2004b). The five-step model. http://www.atimod.com/e-moderating/5stage.shtml

Scardamalia, M. (2000). Can schools enter a knowledge society? In M. Selinger & J. Wynn (Eds.), *Educational technology and the impact on teaching and learning* (pp. 5–9). Abingdon: RM.

Scardamalia, M., & Bereiter, C. (2003). Beyond brainstorming: Sustained creative work with ideas. *Education Canada, 43*(4), 4–7, 44.

Thornham, H. & McFarlane, A. (in press). The myth of the digital native: Imperial conceptions and colonial practices. BBC Blast and its teenage users.

Voogt, J., & Pelgrum, H. (2005). ICT and curriculum change. *Human Technology, 1*(2), 157–175.

Vygotsky, L. (1978). *Mind in society: The development of higher psychological processes.* Cambridge, MA: Harvard University Press.

9

Chat Interaction in Public and Commercial Domains

ANETTE GRØNNING

The use of instant messaging or one-to-one real time messaging through a web interface has been a recent object of media research attention. A special focus of this attention has been teenager use of instant messaging in different private contexts. The popularity of this particular form of interaction indicates that near-synchronous text messaging and presence awareness have captured a significant place in teenage life (Grinter & Palen, 2002). The popularity seems to carry over to the working life where the use of new technology creates new spheres for organizational[1] communication and interaction. Instant messaging generates new ways of interacting for employees and organizations, non-experts and experts.

The terms "chat" and "instant messaging" are defined in different ways. In this study, chat or instant messaging (IM) is described as: "Internet-based synchronous text chat, with point-to-point communication between users on the same system. A window is dedicated to the conversation, with messages scrolling upward and eventually out of view as the conversation ensues" (Grinter & Palen, 2002: 21). I use the terms IM, chat, and chat interaction interchangeably throughout this chapter.

Compared with other web-based communication forms, such as email, it seems that this recent technology provides users with a hassle-free and swift form of communication. IM adds speed and ease to the interaction and eliminates the time typically lost to "telephone tag" or wasted walks to someone who is absent or otherwise occupied (e.g., Handel & Herbsleb, 2002; Nardi et al., 2000).

During the last few years, several private companies and public organizations in Denmark, as well as Danish departments of global corporations, have introduced chat interaction. Some of these initiatives are targeted internally at the employees via the company's intranet or as one-to-one messaging opportunities between colleagues. Other initiatives are targeted externally at customers and potential customers of all kinds. Companies like TDC A/S (part of the TDC Group and provider of telecommunications and communications solutions), Bang & Olufsen A/S (audio products and sound systems), Dell (computer systems), and IKEA (home furnishing products) have launched external chat interaction services for their customers and are thus in the process of collecting their first experiences with chat guidance. But not only private companies and global corporations see new service opportunities in this media form; the public sector follows suit. For example, in 2004 the Danish town of Ebeltoft introduced chat interaction between citizens and municipal employees; and today, several municipalities offer chat services in various ways. More recently, citizens in Copenhagen have been enabled to engage in real-time messaging with the different mayors of Copenhagen once a month on a particular day and for a particular period of time.

At a general level, the experiences have been positive. Customers have reacted positively to the new possibilities as introduced by the above-mentioned companies, some of which have expanded the opening hours of their on-line chat services in response to customer demand. At a more specific level, the experiences are not well described. To reach an understanding of the complexity of chat interaction in working life, it is necessary to study the actual chat content, the context in which the interaction takes place and to ask the interactants how they perceive the media form; in this case, IM.

We have to do with a completely new kind of chat interaction, unlike chat used for informal talk or socializing, event planning, and school collaboration (Lenhart et al., 2001). For instance, in the context of institutional chat service, a high degree of factual problem solving is expected as the interactions have a clear goal. At the same time, issues pertaining to working time are of interest to the organisations in another way than is the case for private IM.

In this chapter, my analytical focus is on two empirical case studies of external one-to-one real time messaging, namely the Danish portal on learning opportunities and professions, named The Education Guide (in Danish *UddannelsesGuiden*), and the Danish part of IKEA's customer service.

To illustrate this kind of chat service in its commercial and public forms, ini tial findings from the two chat service analyses will be presented. The objective of the study is to explore the advantages and disadvantages of this new form of interaction in working life across sectors (public/private), branches (education/furniture), and products (intangible/tangible). The basic question is: what characterizes IM as an encounter within the two contextual frames of service guidance?

Methodological Approach and Definitions

IM, emailing, and mobile text messaging are not stable systems but moving linguistic targets. Regarding the evolution of emailing, Naomi Baron speaks of three important elements: the technological development, the number of users, and the maturity level of the communication form (Baron, 1998). Anne Kankaanranta points out that the new technologies are dynamic constructs which develop to respond appropriately to new, recurrent situations (Kankaanranta, 2005). Given that IM is a recent form of mediated communication, compared with, for example, the use of the telephone, which was made possible in Denmark in the early 1880s, and quite recent compared with email, which has been used in Danish companies since the mid-1990s, IM may be characterized as an immature media form.

This chapter draws on findings from a qualitative computer-mediated discourse analysis (CMDA) study, conducted from 2007 to 2009. The central analysis is based on data culled from a total of 436 chat sessions from the two organizations, The Education Guide and IKEA. The empirical part of the case studies comprises analyses of one week of chat interaction from each of the two contexts. Furthermore, the study includes interviews with selected employees (so-called "chat agents" in this context) as well as the results of a perception (satisfaction) survey from one of the organization's external users. The term "perception" is used here to cover the individual's (general) subjective evaluation of digital communication such as IM and thus, it is similar to the term "media attitude" (Trevino et al., 2000). The perception (satisfaction) survey comprises 270 answers from private IKEA customers.

According to Susan Herring, "relatively little methodological guidance can be found in mainstream discourse analysis literatures for researchers seeking to analyze Computer-Mediated Communication" (Herring, 2004: 2). Herring's methodological work has resulted in the so-called CMDA paradigm that should be seen as a linguistic specialisation within the broader field of computer-mediated communication analysis. Herring recommends the use of the CMD classification scheme containing contextual variables classified as "Medium factors" and "Situation factors," respectively. The scheme is presented in detail in Herring

(2007). She points out eight situational factors: participation structure, participant characteristics, purpose (of interaction, of group, goal of interaction), topic or theme, tone, activity, norms, and code. These situational factors have been observed to condition variation in computer-mediated discourse (with reference to Baym, 1995) and in spoken discourse (with reference to Hymes, 1974), but the list of factors is not presumed to be exhaustive (Herring, 2007).

Another factor to consider, as also reflected by research into teenager use of IM (Grinter & Palen, 2002), is the notion of multitasking in the participation structure. When using IM at work (in open space offices in both case studies), via programs such as Messenger, GoogleChat, Skype, or Facebook, people often do so while engaging in other computer-based activities, such as surfing on the Internet, emailing, downloading documents, checking sales systems, marking in calendars, or non computer-based activities such as talking to colleagues, speaking on the phone, sorting papers, or writing by hand.

The organizational chat for this study comprises a one-to-one form of mediated-communication in a closed system and does not include group chat. It is possible for the commercial chat agent to carry out chat sessions with three customers at a time (but still one-to-one, shifting from one to another), while for the educational chat agent it is possible to carry out chat sessions with only one person at a time. The external users of the chat service (students, customers) initiate all the chat interactions. None of the interactants (external users and chat agents) has met in physical space prior to the chat interactions. The students may invite other parties (e.g., friends or family members) to participate in the interaction, but they do not practice this.

The concept of "encounter" is defined as "a unit of social organization" and as "a situated activity" (Goffman, 1972) similar to a "joint activity" (Clark, 1996). Herbert Clark's central point is that "language use is really a form of joint action" (Clark, 1996: 3), i.e., an action carried out by people acting in coordination with one another. As a joint activity, conversation consists of a joint action comprising the individual actions by the conversational participants. Joint activities require coordination of both the content of the activity and the process by which the activity moves forward. Goffman argues that "an encounter exhibits sanctioned orderliness arising from obligations fulfilled and expectations realized, and therein lies its structure" (Goffman, 1972: 19). The interactants (conversational participants) are expected to sustain interest in a single focus of attention. The frame for this focus and for the coordination of the joint activities comprises important individual and mutual obligations and expectations as regards both the content and as the process of the encounter.

The Education Guide and IKEA: Two Contexts of Use

The empirical data is derived from the Danish portal on learning opportunities and professions, named *The Education Guide*, and from the Danish department of IKEA customer service. *The Education Guide* has been developed in connection with the Danish educational guidance reform and was launched on August 1, 2004. The Danish Ministry of Education owns and finances the portal. Its main aim is to provide accurate and up-to-date information about learning opportunities, professions and labour market issues. *The Education Guide* applies a lifelong learning perspective on education and provides education and career information for anybody who needs it, be they children, young people, or adults, citizens in general or guidance practitioners. *The Education Guide* encompasses seven regional education guidance centres across Denmark.

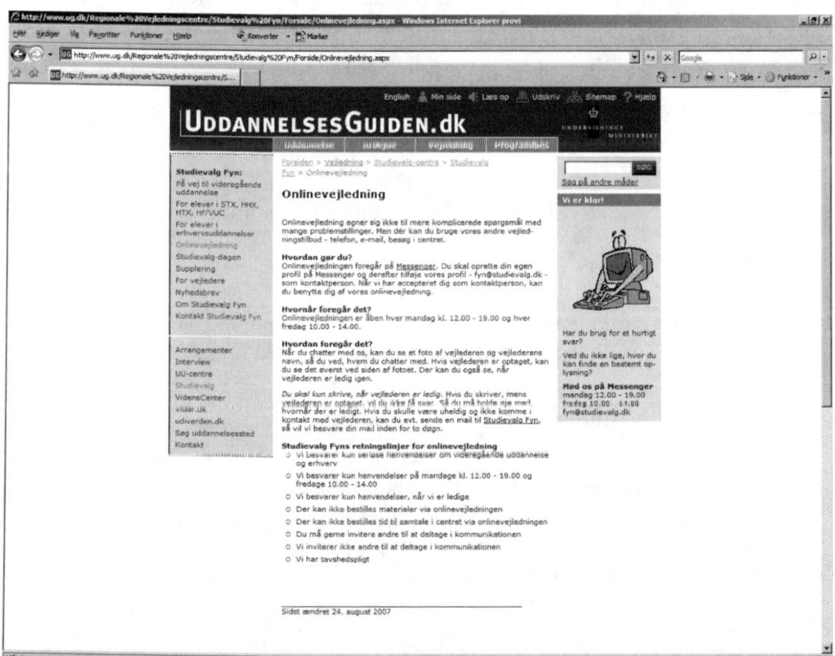

Figure 1: The Education Guide: *www.ug.dk*

In January 2006, three of the regional centers launched a chat guidance service via Messenger. For the purposes of the present study, one of the regional centres, named Funen Study Choice (*Studievalg Fyn*), was examined. From the outset, the center offered the possibility for the users to engage in chat interactions two hours per week, but in January 2007, due to popular demand, the opening hours expanded to 11 hours per week. During the second quarter of 2006, the regional centre carried out 15 chat sessions per month. One year later, the number had increased to 71 chat sessions per month. During the first quarter of 2008, the number reached 168 chat sessions per month. At the time of writing, the number seems to have stabilized, averaging 164 chat sessions per month during the first quarter of 2009. As of August 2009, it is possible to meet with the guidance consultants by way of IM throughout the opening hours (20 hours per week). The combination of a significant need for information and young people as the primary target group makes IM an obvious channel in this context.

To illustrate the actual interaction, three examples from the two contexts are reproduced in the following. The chat interactions have been translated from Danish to English as carefully as possible and all names are invented. The first example is taken from a chat session between a student and a guidance consultant at Funen Study Choice (FSC):

Lone (11:03:19):	Hi, I have a qst conc Quota Two application…
FSC (11:03:31):	Just shoot away!
Lone (11:06:07):	Is it wise to choose a stand-by place if you just want to start studying in September? I would very much like to get into journalism or business comm + media but don't have the cut for it or any special Quota Two qualifications…Therefore I have chosen Danish and English as priorities as well. There I should be able to get in. But then I shall not choose stand by for the first two?
FSC (11:07:38):	No, not if the most important for you is to start in September. If you get a stand by place you might not be able to start studying until next year. So you have to consider what is most important: to get into e.g., journalism or to start studying this year
FSC (11:08:31):	You cannot be sure of getting a stand by place just because you apply for it but if you get it you might have to wait to start till 2008 and you have to be aware that some studies introduce further specific entrance requirements which

	you have to meet then.
Lone (11:09:18):	Thanks :)
FSC (11:09:23):	You are welcome
Lone (11:10:40):	Last question, I am attending a 2 weeks course at Vallekilde Højskole in April but I don't get a certificate for this before Quota Two has to be sent. What do I do then?
FSC (11:11:44):	You write it in your quota 2 application and then you forward a confirmed copy of the certificate when you receive it. All activity until 5 July counts even if you apply by 15 March.
FSC (11:12:05):	So if you have a job until summer or you are traveling it also counts
Lone (11:12:20):	Great :)
FSC (11:12:38):	Just remember to forward your documentation 5 July at the latest
FSC (11:12:52):	It has to reach the institutions 5. July 12:00 at the latest
Lone (11:13:16):	Shall I enclose a letter about the forwarded documents etc.?
FSC (11:13:55):	No, but you could make a small arrow and write it in your application form so they know that you have everything under control!
Lone (11:14:10):	Okay
Lone (11:14:29):	Thanks for your help
FSC (11:15:08):	You are welcome—and good luck with the quota 2 applications. If you have further questions you just write
Lone (11:15:15):	Thanks a lot :)

As shown, the chat interaction lasts 11:56 minutes and consists of 19 turns. The external user/student, Lone, contributes with nine turns and the employee from Funen Study Choice contributes with 10 turns. In general, Lone is the initiator of topics throughout the encounter, and she makes use of a rather informal tone of voice: "Hi, I have a qst [question] conc [concerning] quota 2 application…" [a way of applying for further education in Denmark]. Her turns are shorter than the employee's turns, and she uses semiotic representations of embodiment (smileys) three times. In four of her nine turns, Lone is showing gratitude: "thanks :)," "great :)," "thanks for your help" and "thanks a lot :)." I will return to the substance of the chat interactions below in the discussion of my preliminary findings.

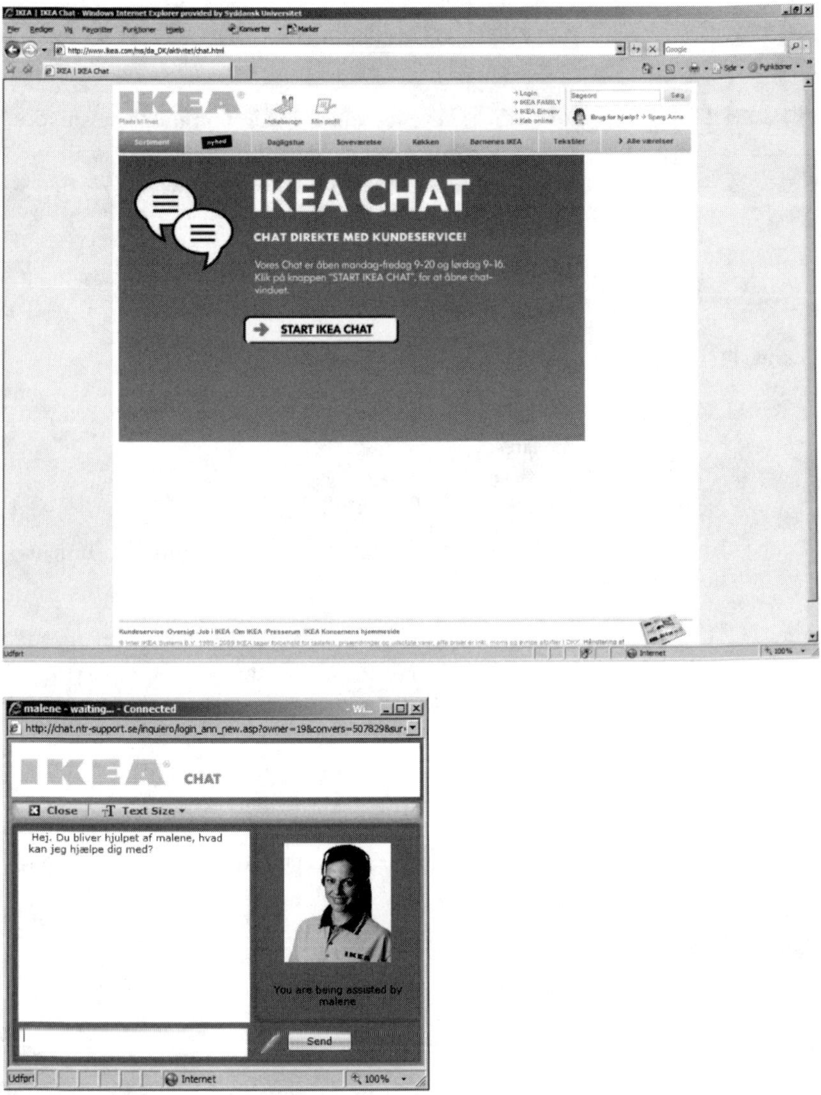

Figure 2: IKEA chat web interface—www.ikea.com/dk/da

As of August 2009, the IKEA Group has 301 stores in 37 countries. Based on successful experiences in Sweden (where the IKEA headquarters are located), a Danish version of the Swedish IKEA chat customer service was launched in April 2007, when IKEA Denmark A/S introduced online chat guidance to its private customers through its Website. Shortly thereafter, the company closed its customer email service during opening hours to motivate customers to chat or phone in. Customers can still email the company through the company's website, but now only outside opening hours. The telephone service is open during regular opening hours, and the chat initiative is used strategically, lest the customers waste their time waiting on the telephone.

At first, IKEA did not expect a lot of chat traffic due to the diversity of its customers in terms of age, gender, ethnicity, and social background. The company expected customers to continue using the telephone. But surprisingly to the Danish IKEA managerial staff, the chat guidance was rapidly accepted by the company's customers. During the first six months, 9,000 customers accessed the chat service. At the moment, 15 chat agents have what the company calls "chatting skills." All of the chat agents come from the company's telephone customer service and participate in IKEA's chat interactions on a voluntary basis. Working as chat agents in four hour shifts, the employees carry out chat sessions with a maximum of three customers at the same time. When the chat agents do not provide chat service, they answer telephone calls from the customers. Two examples between a service employee and a customer may serve to indicate the forms of interaction:

Example 1

Chat agent1 (9:33):	Hello. You are being assisted by Lars, what can I do for you?
User (9:34):	Can you buy extra upholstery for a Klippan sofa?
Chat agent1 (9:34):	Which size Klippan sofa
User: (9:35):	Two and a half seater
Chat agent1 (9:36):	As far as I can see, we have a two-seater and a four-seater. But you can buy upholstery separately, which color are you looking for?
User: (9:37):	Don't really know. Is the range shown at your website?
Chat agent1 (9:37):	When you look at the Klippan sofaen then you can see the alternatives in the drop down menu besides the photo

User: (9:38):	Ok. Thanks for your help. Have a nice day (:
Chat agent1 (9:39):	You are welcome, have a nice day.

Example 2

Chat agent1 (13:26):	Hello. You are being assisted by Lars, what can I do for you?
User: (13:28):	I would like to know when the Robin bed including frame (20064393/40064387) is back in stock in Høje-Taastrup?
Chat agent1 (13:28):	Just a moment and I'll look
Chat agent1 (13:29):	The actual frame is ordered and expected home in a couple of weeks. We don't h
Chat agent1 (13:30):	We don't yet have an expected delivery time for the bed
User: (13:31):	Thanks, regards Tina
Chat agent1 (13:31):	You are welcome Tina, have a nice day.

Encounter Patterns: Preliminary Findings

Based on the definition of IM and its conceptualization as a dynamic "moving linguistic target," chat interaction can be seen as a virtual form of conversation that has its own life, structure, and format. The following findings are based on all my empirical data and not only on the three examples shown above.

With reference to Goffman, it seems there are three different encounter patterns in the IKEA context with respect to establishing and maintaining communication. The majority of the encounters are successful in terms of keeping the contact and maintaining a serious and goal-oriented content from beginning to end of the interactions (from log-in to log-off). A small group of customers log in but present no content, and another small group of customers forget to log off and just disappear towards the end of the encounters.

The most significant features of the examined contexts are speed, semiotic representations of embodiment, and humor. With respect to speed and action, the data contain many short interactions and many meta-communicative utterances such as: "just a moment and I'll look," "I'll just check it out," "2 secs," "just hang on," "just a moment" and "I'll be right back." Two minutes without explicit interaction is perceived as an eternity by the person at the other end, and some customers lose their patience and start asking "Are you there?" "Is anybody there????" or writing "Ring, Ring, Ring, Ring" to attract attention.

The employees, on their part, explain that, having grown accustomed to this new kind of service, they perceive the chat conversations as less stressful than telephone service. Some of the customers respond that they perceive the chat interaction as a quicker and more "alive" service than other services such as phone or email service. The predominant part of the data is short-duration interactions, such as the three examples (12, 6, and 5 minutes). The shortest interaction lasts less than one minute and the longest interaction lasts 39 minutes.

The IKEA employees use a standard opening phrase: "Hello. You [second person, singular] are being assisted by [first name], what can I do for you?" By way of this opening phrase, the company tries to create the same kind of informal tone of voice as the company tries to create in other contexts, as exemplified by the fact that they are always on first-name terms with their customers. Displaying a photo (albeit a static one) of a customer service employee on the website, the company attempts to make the chat appear as similar as possible to the personal conversations of the face-to-face service interactions in their stores.

This informal atmosphere is sustained by politeness and many positive comments. As with Lone in the reproduced example from *The Education Guide,* the customers explicitly show their gratitude through expressions such as "thanks :)," "thanks for your help," "thanks a lot :)." The employees meet external user gratitude by expressions such as "you are welcome," "you are welcome and good luck with (…)," "you are welcome and have a nice day." Both the external users (students and customers) and the employees interact by employing a wide range of utterances along the lines of "have a nice day."

Another feature of chat interaction is the "quietness of IM" (Grinter & Palen, 2002:26), which constitutes an important factor in open space offices. Considering this quietness as a media feature, it seems quite interesting that the interactants make a lot of what might be called "linguistic noise." The interactants employ utterances such as the aforementioned "Ring, Ring, Ring, Ring," but also a great deal of exclamations and interjections such as: "aw," "hmm," "oops," "ugh," "whoops," "yah," and "yuck" as well as shouting by means of capital letters, e.g., when a customer asks: WHAT IS HAPPENING?

Although the chat interaction in this context is not private-to-private chat interaction, the creative and emotive play with graphics is prominent, and the body is represented in numerous ways. Different kinds of smiley and acronyms for expressing bodily reactions are particularly present. At the same time, the data contain displays of humour such as "hehe ok," "thanks for your help and lovely smile you have—know very well that it isn't you but have a vivid imagination ;-)" and other utterances featuring a virtual twinkle in the eye.

The interactions can be characterized as informal but at the same time goal-oriented. The students and the customers need an answer to a question or a solution to a problem. As mentioned, the students and the customers initiate all chat interactions. None of the interactants (users and chat agents) has met in physical space prior to the chat interactions. But how do the external participants approach the organizations and initiate the interaction? And how do they perform their requests? To illustrate the structure of the encounter openings, five examples of requests from each of the two contexts are reproduced below.

Request from customers

1. Hey, we have bought a kitchen some time ago (about half a year) and now the dishwasher has started to leak water.
2. I want to ask when Storön garden chair and garden bench will be in stock. They have been out of stock for a long time.
3. Hello Lars. We are looking at a Hemnes wardrobe—the big one—which is 200cm high.
4. Hello, I want to order a bookcase Billy DKK 269.—5) I have a question for your home page.

Requests from students

1. Hello. I wonder which admission requirements there will be for teachers and pedagogical college, respectively, in 2008??
2. Hello Tine. Are there other admission requirements than a passed exam for DJH [the School of Journalism] in Aarhus?
3. Hi….is it possible to study music at vuc [institution of further education]….without studying anything else?
4. I thought perhaps I could get some knowledge about what are the possibilities of studying psychology in England?
5. May I ask a question?

As shown, the examples represent rather different ways of approaching the employee. From the quite formal "May I ask a question?" to the quite informal "Hi….is it possible to (…)" in *The Education Guide* context, and from the formal "I have a question (…)" to the more informal "hey, we have bought (…)" in the IKEA context.

The examples above show considerable variation in the structure of the encounter openings. The opening phrases vary from goal-oriented statements such as "I want to order a bookcase Billy DKK 269" to more indirect, perhaps insecure, statements such as "I thought perhaps I could get some knowledge about what are the possibilities of studying in England." According to Erving Goffman, we, as humans, are careful to design our behavior in anticipation of what we perceive to be the recipient's expectations and standards (Goffman, 1959). We approach different persons in different situations in different ways. There is a considerable amount of variation in the style of writing in public emailing (Danet, 2001; Crystal, 2001), and the same seems to apply to public chat.

We (the chat agents and the present author alike) have no knowledge about the external user's age or social background. Based on findings from email analysis, Brenda Danet argues that younger people, especially students, use a more speech-like style than older people (Danet, 2001). Although it is dangerous to generalize, the opening phrases "hey" and "Hi" might come from younger persons than the opening phrases "Hello" and "May I ask a question." But we do not know for sure. An intriguing example comes from one of the chat agents from IKEA. One evening, she reports, she participated in a long chat interaction with a customer, who employed a rather formal tone and gave the impression of a man in midlife. To serve the customer's needs and finish the interaction as appropriately as possible, she chose to call the customer and talk to him on the phone. She was surprised to be greeted by a young man who, when he was interacting by chat, had seemed to play—to use the chat agent's expression—an older person than he actually was. With reference to Goffman, the customer chose what he thought was a convenient *usable line* based on authority and formality in order to reach his goals. The customer was under the impression that IKEA would rather please a formal and authoritative customer than other customers.

As mentioned, the objective of the study is to explore the advantages and disadvantages of IM in working life across sectors (public/private), branches (education/furniture) and products (intangible/tangible). The findings show a varied picture of the format of the interactions. Compared with non-working contexts, the focus on the part of the employees is much more time-focused, as time is considered costly in the professional context. The consultant from *The Education Guide*, as well as the customer service assistant from IKEA, create a professional face towards the students and customers. Although the chat conversations are quite informal and direct, IKEA's chat agents employ a more informal, rather jaunty, tone of voice than the consultants from *The Education Guide*. This difference might be due to the different products: furniture and future plans, age difference and/or experience of instant messaging, but this needs to be studied more carefully. None of the organizations has laid down codes of conduct for their instant messaging employees, nor have they formulated any guidelines concerning identity formation online. In the future, online branding through IM might be as important as online branding through organizational websites. But as it is the case for the content of professional emailing (Grønning, 2005), the content of chat interactions is yet to receive the management's attention.

Perceptions of Professional IM

Regarding the subjective evaluation of chat or the media attitude as such, 270 customers have given their point of view in a survey conducted in May 2007. To the question: "Compared to other ways of interacting with IKEA, how satisfied are you with chatting for your particular purpose?" the majority (84%) of the customers answers that they are very satisfied (58%) or satisfied (26%). Furthermore, these customers add that they find the chat interaction "brilliant," "very good," "smooth," "quick and easy" and that they would prefer to choose chat again if a question or problem should occur in the future. Some of the dissatisfied customers add that they prefer the telephone and that it takes too long to get an answer by way of IM.

On the other side of the screen, we find the employees who work shifts in both telephone guidance and chat guidance. The IKEA customer service employees express that they perceive the chat interaction as less stressful than the telephone interaction after a period of adaptation. Furthermore, in the experience of *The Education Guide* employees, chat interaction allows for new opportunities for reaching other groups than those who seek guidance via the more conventional guidance interaction forms such as face-to-face meetings and telephone conversations as well as those who traditionally do not seek guidance at all.

In this way, the education guidance via chat has reached a group of young men who are traditionally reluctant to contact the consultants. Another important finding yielded by the education guidance data is the fact that the consultants have received more requests from young people of a different ethnic origin than Danish, especially young men, following the introduction of the chat service. One explanation is that the young men perceive the face-to-face meeting and the telephone conversation as more claustrophobic and hence more challenging than chat interaction. For some of the young people, questions like "what do you think you are particularly good at?" or "tell me about your career plans and dreams" seem more difficult face-to-face. It seems that the chat interaction is perceived as being more anonymous, although the name (or nickname) of the student and the name of the employee are visible. This finding accords with results from research on mobile phone communication showing that young people choose text messaging because they can express things they conventionally do not dare to express (Fortunati, 2001; Laursen, 2006). Obviously, this is not an issue in the IKEA context because of the tangible nature of their furniture products and the more tangible themes in their customer interactions.

One of the biggest advantages of chat interaction in the described contexts is that it allows the customers to ask quick questions and receive answers almost instantaneously. For the customers and the students, it is much easier to participate in chat interaction than to wait on the phone. At the same time, the chat guidance service is an (almost) anonymous and non-committal way of asking questions for the customers. This might be an important advantage, especially if the subject is perceived as sensitive or private, which might be the case for some of the students whose interactions concern their talents and future plans. Besides, many customers (who are themselves employees in other companies) work in open space offices and prefer to communicate via the computer rather than talk on the phone while at work, especially if the interaction concerns a private issue such as a request for a sofa.

The rules or norms of chat interaction imply new competencies on the part of the employees, as they are required to formulate short and precise answers and messages without appearing impolite and to keep their calm and not panic in front of the computer screen. Furthermore, chat interaction requires that the interactant is capable of verbalizing on-going activity as the interactants cannot see each other during the conversation. This requires some adaptation.

For the organization, the possibility of having several current interactions at the same time is a clear advantage. This structure is not a possibility by way of traditional phone service lines or face-to-face interactions in the store. Regarding problem solving, it is easy for the employee to link to different documents or other websites, and to look at user guides or instruction manuals together with the customer during the interaction. In the same way, *The Education Guide* employees have easy online access, during the chat interaction, to links or documents that might be useful for the students. Therefore, it is reasonable to argue that the possibility of hyperlinking improves the overall quality of the virtual guidance compared with guidance over the phone.

In terms of documentation, the chat interaction can have certain practical implications as the individual customer or student must remember to save the chat interaction, dependent on the chat program used.

Among the disadvantages of chat interaction in an organizational context is that it can be a problem that the employees do not necessarily have any experience with the new interaction form and chat etiquette. The organizations have not formulated any guidelines or regulations to help the employees. However, *The Education Guide* has formulated a code of ethics mentioning confidentiality and stating that only serious requests will be processed. This code of ethics is explicitly shown on the organizational website.

The non-serious requests are, in any case, very few. Only one example is found in the current data material:

Employee:	Hello. You are being helped by Ole, what can I do for you?
Customer:	Hello do you sell pizza baking stones?
Employee:	Hello. No, unfortunately we don't have these in our assortment.
Customer:	Stupid Ole
Customer:	All the children played ball except Ole, he went to school [2]
Employee:	I have other customers who need my help for questions related to IKEA. Thanks for now.

Conclusion

In the introduction, I posed the question "what characterises IM as an encounter in the contextual frame of service guidance?" The preliminary findings from the two case studies show that organizational or professional chat interaction is different from private chat interaction in at least three ways: the interactants have never met physically before chatting; the primary use of the chat service is not everyday chitchat; and the chat sessions do not represent a community over time.

The two case studies have a number of similarities. The content of the interactions include humorous elements, linguistic noise-making as well as creative and emotive play. Seen from a user perspective, the most significant features of the first part of the analysis are speed, body representation, and to some extent an attention-demanding attitude. Perhaps surprisingly in relation to the organizational chat, the creative and emotive play with graphics is prominent, and embodiment is represented in numerous ways. Different kinds of smiley and acronyms for expressing bodily reactions are particularly frequent. Expressions displaying humour, such as "hehe ok," "lovely smile you have—know very well that it isn't you but have a vivid imagination ;-)," create a friendly tone of voice. The majority of the interactions can be characterized as informal rather than formal and at the same time goal-oriented. The customers and the students know why they initiate a chat conversation with the organizations of both contexts. Although we characterize the interactions as professional and not belonging to a private sphere, a personal and informal tone of voice can be identified.

Compared with the slower asynchronous email interaction, chat service calls for new competences on the part of the employees. The employees must have a high degree of readiness in front of the computer screen and must not be prone to panic. Furthermore, the employees must be able to formulate short and precise answers and messages without appearing impolite. As a completely new feature compared to email interaction, but well-known from telephone conversations, the interactants must verbalize what they are doing, as the co-participants cannot see each other during the conversation. If the employees do not verbalize their behavior, the customers lose their patience.

Advantages seem to include aspects such as quick problem solving, quietness in the office, the seeming ease of sharing links and documents, anonymity in a positive way, and the possibility to save time. Disadvantages, on the other hand, seem to include issues pertaining to possible extra work in terms of documentation, anonymity in a negative way, new competency requirements, and the danger of wasting time.

The two case studies also have some differences, mainly because of their very different provision of tangible versus intangible products. Furthermore, the IKEA chat interactions are longer and seem more informal and jovial.

Does IM pay in a commercial setting? We do not know yet. I presume that chat interaction in the workplace will develop much more in the future. Email changed working life routines, and chat is about to leave its mark in the same way. Recently, we have witnessed a hybridization between telephone and letter (email), between personal meetings and email (chat) and between telephone and chat (text messaging). While they challenge the sharp, dichotomous distinction between oral and written communication, these recent forms of interaction also complement each other, because they each have their own advantages and disadvantages depending on context and purposes. For public and private organizations alike, however, there can be no doubt: many managers and employees will be forced to relate to chat interaction in the future. If the organizations choose to disregard this kind of interaction, they must at least base this choice upon a certain level of knowledge about the new possibilities. Of course, this consideration will also have to be closely related to the question of whom the organizations want to address.

From the selected contexts, perhaps the most important finding is that the introduction of chat has allowed for the establishing of a dialogue with a group of young men (Danish as well as different ethnic origin than Danish), who have previously hesitated to contact the guidance professionals face-to-face. This group might constitute the most interesting subject of further analysis in relation to informal learning, as the group members, by way of using IM for guidance purposes, seem to be refining and developing competencies that they are used to bringing into play in other more socially oriented contexts, such as private chat.

Through the lens of competencies and informal learning, this kind of interaction can be understood as an important new interaction form with potential for supporting part of a learning process as well as a tool for creating content, new relations and expanding existing relations between expert and non-expert. The learning process is not structured and planned, and the learner (student, customer) might not be aware of the process going on as an act of learning. But new competencies will be acquired, and new relations might be created in pleasant atmospheres of quick and easy problem solving, as IM presents itself as a new and effective tool for students and customers seeking guidance and service. In my opinion, professional IM is relevant to consider for many different work places, settings, and contexts. With reference to Grinter & Palen's observations from their studies on teenage life, I think that text messaging and presence awareness are about to capture a significant place in professional life as well.

For future organizational communication, this will imply an openness towards a new understanding of IM (from private to professional tool), including branding issues and identity construction online. Furthermore, employees who are used to participating in IM in private settings tend to be more mature users than their non-instant messaging colleagues. This might create a new digital gap between the employees. At the moment, tomorrow's work force is in school and the "instant messaging generation" (Lenhardt et al., 2001) might be planning their further education, but soon they will need a kitchen or a sofa from IKEA as well. In this perspective, the number of chat interactions will increase significantly. Already, IKEA's experience is that, given the chance, a higher number of customers than expected prefer to communicate with the company through IM.

Notes

1. In this chapter, the terms organizational and organization include both private companies and public organizations.
2. In Danish the name "Ole" rhymes with "school" [skole] and the sentence is part of a well-known joke the same way as "All the children were normal, except Madeleine, she was insane."

References

Baron, N. S. (1998). Letters by phone or speech by other means: the linguistics of email, *Language and communication, 18,* 133–170.

Baym, N. (1995). The emergence of community in computer-mediated communication. In

Jones, S.G. (Ed.) *Cybersociety: Computer-mediated communication and community.* Thousand Oaks, CA: Sage, 138–163.

Clark, H. (1996). *Using language.* Cambridge: Cambridge University Press.

Crystal, D. (2001). *Language and the Internet.* Cambridge: Cambridge University Press.

Danet, B. (2001). *Cyperpl@y—communicating online.* Oxford: Berg Publishers Ltd.

Fortunati, L. (2001). The mobile phone between morality and writing. Paper, E-usages 3rd international conference on uses and services in telecommunications 2001, Paris.

Goffman, E. (1959). *Presentation of self in everyday life.* New York: Doubleday Anchor.

Goffman, E. (1972). *Two studies in the sociology of interaction.* Harmondsworth: Penguin Books.

Grinter, R.E., & Palen, L. (2002). Instant messaging in teen life. *CHI Letters 4(3),* 21–30.

Grønning, A. (2005). Your inbox has taken control! Perceptions of email interaction in the workplace. Peer reviewed paper for the ABC Conference, Copenhagen.

Handel, M., & Herbsleb, J.D. (2002). What is chat doing in the workplace? Proceedings of ACM Conference on Computer-Supported Cooperative Work (CSCW), New Orleans, LA, 1–10.

Herring, S.C. (2004). Online communication: Through the lens of discourse. In: M. Consalvo, N. Baym, J. Hunsinger, K. B. Jensen, J. Logie, M. Murero, & L. R. Shade (Eds.), *Internet Research Annual, Volume 1* (65–76). New York. Peter Lang.

Herring, S.C. (2007). A faceted classification scheme for computer-mediated discourse. Language@Internet, 4, article 1.

Hymes, D. (1974) *Foundations in sociolinguistics: An ethnographic approach.* Philadelphia: University of Pennsylvania Press.

Kankaanranta, A. (2005). *"Hej Seppo, could you please comment on this!" Internal Email Communication in Lingua Franca English in a Multinational Company.* Jyväskylä: Jyväskylä University Printing House.

Laursen, D. (2006). Det mobile samtalerum—om unges kommunikations—og samværsformer via mobiltelefonen. PhD thesis in Danish, University of Southern Denmark.

Lenhart, A., Rainie, L., & Lewis, O. (2001). Teenage life online: The rise of the instant message generation and the Internet's impact on friendships and family relationships. Pew Internet and American Life Project.

Nardi, B., Whittaker, S., & Bradner, E. (2000). Interaction and Outeraction: Instant Messaging in Action, submitted to Computer supported cooperative work.

Trevino L.K., Webster, J., & Stein, E.W. (2000). Making connections: Complementary influences on communication media choices, attitudes, and use, *Organisation Science, 11,* (2), 163–182.

www.ug.dk: retrieved February 24, 2009.

www.ikea.com: retrieved February 24, 2009.

www.ikea.com/dk/da/: retrieved February 24, 2009.

10

Learning Space(s)

Jenny Weight

> Space can either enable—or inhibit—different styles of teaching as well as learning.
>
> *(National Learning Infrastructure Initiative 2004, p. 1)*

This chapter explores issues that arise from combining different learning spaces in campus-based tertiary education. It uses as a case study the processes and "working conclusions" of the staff engaged with the Bachelor of Communications (Media) degree at RMIT University, Melbourne, Australia, and includes interview material from those staff.

Our degree aims to develop emerging media-makers. This is an industry that requires more than a specific technical skill-set that may quickly become dated, transferable abilities in the realms of communication and creativity, collaboration, and research. Our teaching group has responded by developing a curriculum with a novel and tailored engagement with various "learning spaces."

What Is a Learning Space?

For our group, learning is a constructivist rather than behaviorist activity. Kok (2009, p. 16) is paraphrased here to suggest some of the features of a constructivist learning paradigm:

- a process of knowledge construction rather than knowledge absorption;
- learning is highly contextual—that is, according to Harel and Papert (1990), "the idea that no piece of knowledge stands and grows by itself. Its meaning and its efficacy depend on its being situated in relation to supporting structures" (pp. 23–4);
- learning is accumulative;
- learning is dependent on distributed cognition.

In designing learning spaces, Harel and Papert (1990, p. 2) urge us to consider appropriability (the extent to which the environment can be made one's own), evocativeness (the extent to which the environment "precipitates personal thought"), and integration (the extent to which the environment can carry multiple meanings and concepts). The learning spaces we develop should also encourage "a knowledge society that is built upon distributed cognition, articulate learners, peer-to-peer learning, and incremental enhancement of information spaces by a community of practice" (Fischer 1999, p. 5).

Learning spaces may be physical environments, such as classrooms, or networked environments such as blogs, virtual worlds, wikis, etc.[1] Classrooms and networked environments can be learning spaces, although many of the latter are spatial only in a metaphorical sense. Under the right circumstances, a software package can be a learning space if it opens up a realm for exploration, experimentation, and transformative thinking (limitations will be articulated below). Even devices such as the mobile phone can be considered a learning space, depending on how the phone is used.[2] As such, I am extending the scope of the Australian National Learning Infrastructure Initiative's (NLII) 2004 white paper, which focuses exclusively on physical learning space.

A learning space only facilitates learning when it is engaged with under the correct conditions, which are generally created by learners and teachers. Learning is psychological and emotional; it is dependent on teachers and students together.

The breadth of environments considered learning spaces in this context may be controversial. It is wise to distinguish between learning spaces and learning tools. As one of my colleagues argues:

KB: Isn't software just a tool? [. . .] the software package is just the object of learning and the fact that it's on the computer doesn't necessarily mean it's in a different learning space.

KB points to a fundamental principle of our group towards the teaching of software. If a software package is the *object of learning* rather than the *means that facilitates social learning*, we question the value of that activity in degree-level education. This is a distinction between behaviorist learning environments that Rodrigues (2002) argues "provide extrinsic goals and rewards" and constructivist learning environments that 'promote an intrinsic notion of success and metacognition" (p. 50). As another interviewee, AM, proclaims:

> AM: The distinction is about knowledge discovery; about the production, discovery, and dissemination of learning. [...] Blogging, for example, is a particular sort of practice. It's not just a technical literacy, but a social literacy. Photoshop, or Final Cut [software used in media production], is about a technical competency, which is something quite separate from a social or pedagogical literacy.
>
> Our students need transferable skills for all software environments. For example, Photoshop uses layers. It is more powerful for students to learn about the principles of layers in editing. Knowing the specific menu that contains layers is not transferable. Knowing that somewhere, somehow, the software will have layers, and how to use the "help" menu to find them is a more powerful transferable skill.

Students should be uncovering transferable principles and work methodologies. According to Seimens, "the learner's challenge is to recognize the patterns which appear to be hidden" (2005, p. 17). Focusing on specific software, rather than the principles or organizing metaphors the software embeds, does not enhance understanding of a bigger, contextualized picture; nor does it help students become independent learners. We must draw out those organizing principles so they can be transferred by students to other environments. Although MB, who works in a slightly different teaching group, teaches Photoshop, she confirms:

> MB: Photoshop and blogs are completely different. I teach both narrative and design so I teach Photoshop extensively, but Photoshop is not what I would describe as a learning technology or a social technology like blogs and wikis or even Twitter or Second Life.

Those who dedicate much of their curriculum to teaching software such as Photoshop are guilty of what Papert describes as technocentric thinking (1987, p. 23). Technocentrists "reduce what are really the most important components of educational institutions—people and cultures—to a secondary, facilitating role" (1987, p 23). A learning space such as a blog doesn't do this. Papert's incites that we not ask what the learning space can do to people, but what people can do with the learning space. A learning space is merely the beginning of a whole range of changes to teaching and learning. Indeed, Papert argues, if wholesale changes do not result from a new learning space, it is not worth the computer memory or bandwidth the learning space consumes (1987, p. 25).

Constructivists would suggest that software "tools" (as opposed to the virtual learning spaces) do not actually facilitate learning at all. McDougall and Squires (1995), for example, criticize the decision to use software based on "technical and superficial features" that "fails to provide an holistic view dealing with learning, curriculum and pedagogy" (p. 93). Good learning spaces—virtual or physical—open up new horizons and expand a student's consciousness. Some of the best learning spaces are accidental; they operate beyond structured learning activities and syllabi.

Teachers explore the way different tools or spaces structure student experience in terms of course objectives and pedagogical preference. Jeong (2007) provides an example of this style of assessment regarding computer-based instant messaging:

> Benefits include a heightened "social presence" for distance-education students and a growth in collaborative opportunities, due to its millions of users everywhere. Drawbacks include adding additional layers to the learning environment, a growing expectation among students of unlimited access to instructors, and the related time issues of faculty (Jeong, 2007, p. 30).

Hrastinski (2008) goes even further. Rather than focusing on a specific technology, he compares the strengths and weaknesses of synchronous and asynchronous tools or spaces and explores the circumstances under which each should be adopted. Asynchronous communications technologies such as email allow for thoughtful, well-crafted responses on a timetable that is more flexible; synchronous technologies such as chat are more informal, immediate, and social. Hrastinski concludes that "synchronous e-learning better supports personal participation and asynchronous e-learning better supports cognitive participation" (p. 55).

It is important for teachers to progress from consideration of a specific technology or physical space to more synthetic and comparative assessments of the affordances of tools and spaces *in combination.* Learning spaces and tools operate *as a suite.* Teachers must consider the way that they *act upon each other.* Otherwise, spaces or tools may contradict and even disable each other. How learning spaces and tools work together (or not) is a particular focus of this paper.

Flexible or Blended Learning?

University teachers are obliged to engage with a variety of practical, economic, and political issues that do not strictly concern their content area or pedagogy. In Australia, for example, higher education is not free, but nor is it highly elitist. Between work and full-time study, many of our students are committed 70 hours a week. It is not surprising that students can't or won't keep up with the demands on their time, and that classes are skipped.

A question university teachers, therefore, face is the extent to which they should be responsive to the difficult circumstances under which students study. Is it appropriate to sacrifice carefully developed pedagogical principles and course activities in the name of student convenience? The belief that mass tertiary education has an obligation to address the issue of convenience is one of the rationales behind "flexible learning," which rose to prominence in Australia in the 1990s. Flexible learning is defined by Johnston (1999) as "moves towards the provision for *all* students (on and off campus) of teaching and learning approaches which are less time- and place-dependent" (p. 39). Kirkpatrick and Jakupec (1999) argue that flexible learning has become code for "a more general transformation of higher education influenced by technological change, public accountability, increased competition, restricted funding, and catering for the needs of a semi-mass rather than a semi-elite system" (p. 51).

Flexible learning has been widely critiqued over the past 15 years by tertiary educationalists who have warned against allowing technology to define the pedagogy (for example, Berry, Peterson, de la Harpe, Horvat, & Anastasiou, 2007). Perhaps the most disturbing aspect of this critique is the fact that at least 15 years of criticism remains current today. In 2007 Brabazon analyzed the language of flexibility:

> The emphasis is on individuals and choice, not communities and context. The role and function of groups and collectives—sharing a time and place—discussing the issues of the day is no longer a priority. Students become consumers, selecting generic competencies for their shopping trolley, dodging around the issues and ideas that might require more than a passing glance. Yet this truth is masked as flexibility, becomes confused with access (p. 81).

Flexible learning heralded the broad-ranging use of networked computers and software for campus-based learning. While lauded as a way to increase geographical and temporal flexibility for students, it often obscured the desire of centralised university administrations to save money (Brabazon, 2007; Chambers, 1999; Tait & Mills, 2002).

On the other hand, the concept of blended learning (also referred to as hybrid learning, see Young & Duhaney, 2008, p. 1) presents different reasons for combining a variety of learning spaces. Whereas flexible learning favors behaviorist learning *tools*, blended learning favors constructivist learning *space*. Blended pedagogies combine a variety of learning spaces to meet course or program objectives (which rarely mention "flexibility" or "economy"). Sometimes blended learning spaces can be flexible, but sometimes not. One of my interviewees argues:

> AM: All my teaching is blended, so even when I use a lot of new and emerging technologies in what I do, I've never been a believer in purely online teaching and learning. I can see its applicability in all sorts of pragmatic ways if you are living 200 kilometers away from an institution then clearly that's an advantage. If you are working full-time etc., you've got time issues I can see major advantages there. That's just good old-fashioned distance learning. It's been around in this country for—what, 100 years? And its necessary and it's valuable. But the model where we all somehow think we're going to move into these environments I just don't have a lot of faith in. I don't think it has been thought through yet, and I think that most of systems are more about student management and almost surveillance in some ways than they are about re-designing a different sort of pedagogy.

Implementing blended learning is complex for campus-based courses because the options are so varied. Many options are subtly constrained because they favor one style of pedagogy over another, or overtly constrained for legal, technical, or economic reasons. From a blended perspective, a teacher must be able to analyze learning spaces in terms of the pedagogical ramifications they entail. As AM reveals, part of this analysis requires the teacher to articulate pedagogical principles. We must discover the right sorts of questions to ask about a learning space. It may be good to have flexibility, all things being equal. However, pedagogical principles must come first, and since deep learning is simply hard work, true convenience is rarely possible.

This chapter will now propose questions that are important considerations during the design phase of blended learning spaces. I will refer to personal experience and quote that of my colleagues, mainly from the Bachelor of Communication (Media) degree at RMIT University.[3] What is represented here is a snap-shot of the continuing conversation between my colleagues and I about what are always going to be evolving learning and teaching practices under a broadly constructivist ambit.

Question 1. Is my choice of learning spaces tailored to the specific requirements of my students and my course?

Some bodies of knowledge may require more traditional teacher or expert-centered, instrumental, and behaviorist approaches to learning. In that case, software tools may assist. Other disciplines, including RMIT's media program, encourage explorative and independent learning, and behaviorist tools are less appropriate. In other words, it is not possible to implement the same tools or spaces across all content areas and for all teachers. Teachers must be actively engaged in researching the options:

MB: I think it is vital not to let the tail wag the dog when choosing technology for blended learning environments. The learning outcomes and activities always come first for me. For instance when I set up a blended environment for a transnational trans-disciplinary project I worked with the other teaching staff to find options that were suitable for the students rather than simply rely on Blackboard [a content management system designed for course delivery in distance education].

Even in similar courses, a specific learning space may not be generally appropriate. A case in point is my own and MB's experience of *Second Life*. While I have embraced it, she says:

MB: [L]ast year my students and I looked at it. Their feedback was that it was very clunky, too slow to get around, and you run into the same difficulties with chat as you do in text-based environments, which is that it's hard to keep a thread of who's talking to whom and conversations are hard.

Second Life promotes some types of learning, but not others, and the things MB was hoping to facilitate can be done better elsewhere. Teachers have to find this out for themselves by becoming expert in the proposed learning space.

PR explains his reason for choosing blogs:

PR: Blogs were chosen as our virtual space because they meet most of

> the communication and technical needs of our course. Students reflect on their work and its associated processes and also analyse and reflect on other sources similarly. They can upload stills and video to their blogs. For example, videos produced in film exercises and location stills. They look at other student blogs either by trawling through the blogroll or re-blogging select posts.

PR seems interested in what Harel & Papert (1990, p. 24) describe as the power of virtual learning space to create "direct and concrete contact with issues of representation." Representation—a conundrum that the media discipline is deeply interested in—maybe a pre-requisite for what AM calls "knowledge building":

> AM: The main reason I'm interested in using other learning spaces apart from just the traditional classroom is about knowledge building [...]. The reason I use the ones I choose to use and why I might use new ones is primarily around how I would see them as facilitating either traditional or new forms of knowledge building.

PR notes how knowledge building and representation seem to come together in his students' use of blogs:

> PR: Blogs, for example, are a valuable environment because they are relatively malleable [...] certain students will figure out new/clever ways of using them and fashioning/personalising them to their own ends.

Constructivism goes beyond the adage that "you learn better by doing" to learning "best of all by thinking and talking about what you do" (Harel & Papert 1990, p. 2). According to many of our teaching staff, blogging is a learning space that achieves this.

Question 2. Have I designed the implementation of learning space(s) myself?

Design, implementation, and assessment of learning spaces become one of the teacher's main roles in our model. The nuances involved in the design of learning spaces are class-specific. Factors involved include the course content, the sophistication of the learning group, the teacher's perception of her role, and the other learning spaces used in the course. Due to these complexities, the teacher is the only person qualified to make those design decisions. This is not only a point about the limited role of central administrations in teaching decisions, but about support to casual teaching staff. Expecting underpaid sessional staff to walk smoothly into somebody else's pedagogical vision is flawed.

It can, therefore, be seen that the flexible learning culture's centralized implementation of "one-size-fits-all" ICT learning spaces is problematic. It may be harmless enough so long as such systems are optional. Howeve,r implicit or explicit enforcement of a system has been a feature of two of the three universities in which I have worked (also see Brabazon, 2007).

Many centrally imposed ICT learning spaces and tools are alien to contemporary student experience. The Australian "Student 2.0" is routinely and recreationally engaged with social software, has learned to negotiate the risks and empowerments inherent in having a public networked identity, and has been making and publishing his own media to the Internet probably since junior high school. These environments are networked; they encourage information flow and, to some extent, are by default collaborative (we swap information about ourselves with other people; we gather "friends"). However, while the "digital native" Student 2.0 is empowered and often quite technically fluent, it does not automatically follow that he is critically articulate in the core competencies of communication and creativity, collaboration, and research. As Fischer (1999, p. 4) argues, teachers must "draw out" and "synthesize" the relevant knowledge from learners. Our group seeks to harness our student digital literacy to promote these competencies. Centrally imposed ICT learning spaces and tools may be counterproductive, because they are not sufficiently specific to course learning outcomes, and they often reference a "modernist" university culture that can only partially embrace Web 2.0.

Modernist university cultures have trouble embracing the porous nature of Web 2.0 open access systems because universities are concerned with issues of privacy, copyright, intellectual property, and even bandwidth. As a result, centrally imposed ICT learning spaces and tools tend to restrict access to the network. Such curtailment of networking freedom seems incomprehensible and frustrating to students (and staff) who are engaged with the open, "post-privacy" design-your-own identity media culture exemplified by Facebook and MySpace.[4] Rikhye, Cook, Zane & Berge argue that digital natives learn differently from digital immigrants (2009, p. 5). They proclaim that "[u]nless the language gap between the natives and immigrants is closed, or at least narrowed, it is possible that the greater part of teaching efforts will be misdirected and ineffective" (p. 3). Our teaching staff has learned to mediate between the old and new media cultures—we belong to the age group of the digital immigrants, but we have not only trained ourselves in the digital, we have learned how to translate one culture into the language of another culture. Curtailing access works against the culture of learning promoted by digitality (Siemens 2005, p. 27).

Forcing a teacher to use particular tools or spaces puts the technology before the reason to use it. A teacher must be familiar with and agree with the pedagogy implicit in a space or tool before trying to use it (see McDougall & Squires 1995, p. 94):

> AM: If you're not literate in it, then it's a recipe for disaster.

[…] The analogy is with essay writing. If essay writing is not part of your academic practice, you wouldn't get a student to write essays.
Teacher-designed blended learning spaces often support independent learning. As the affordances of such spaces are grasped and explored—and even invented—by a community of learners, the teacher becomes just one member of the learning community. Teachers in our media production courses approach what Erica McWilliam (2008) describes as a "meddler-in-the-middle":

> *Meddler-in-the-middle* challenges more long-term notions of "good" teaching in a number of ways. Specifically, it means:
>
> 1. less time giving instructions and more time spent being a usefully ignorant co-worker in the thick of the action;
> 2. less time spent being a custodial risk minimiser and more time spent being an experimenter and risk-taker;
> 3. less time spent being a forensic classroom auditor and more time spent being a designer, editor and assembler;
> 4. less time spent being a counselor and more time being a collaborative critic and authentic evaluator (p. 265).

To achieve this relationship with students, combinations of learning spaces should be fluid, inter-penetrable and evolving, and open to chance and experimentation. Teachers and students alike are together engaged in processes of discovery and creativity. Teachers who have not made the psychological adjustment to this style of teaching are wise to avoid learning spaces that thrust them into it. Furthermore, inheriting a "finished" learning space from a prior version of a course does not encourage a feeling of collaborative journey of discovery.

Teachers must take physical classroom design into account when implementing virtual learning spaces. Harel & Papert see the physical environment "as a very important factor in shaping the learning culture" (Harel & Papert, 1990, p. 3). They report on how one less structured learning space allowed them to:

> [...] bring the technology closer (physically and conceptually) to students and teachers, to integrate the computer activities with the regular classroom activities; and to facilitate movement and action around the computers; to reinforce communication and information-sharing regarding computer-based activities across grade levels and among teachers (1990, p. 3).

AM believes the physical classroom is:

> [...] important only to the extent that it supports other activities you are trying to do. In a blended mode there might be important things that might support or get in the way in the physical space. Some spaces model panoptic relationships; others are more flexible, and they support small and mid-size work groups and the ability to bring in a variety of technology. Too many classrooms seem to think all you are going to do is writing. We need room and power plugs and so on.

MB affirms "[t]hat is our job as educators—we design learning spaces—physical, virtual, and blended."[5] She has particularly adopted asynchronous learning spaces:

> MB: I have run courses online via Blackboard and found that the discussion boards are excellent for developing interaction—indeed no one has the option of sitting back in a class and saying nothing—they all have to contribute.

In terms of options—I like students to explore—I haven't used wikis but I have used blogs—have been using blogs since 2002 for teaching and find them excellent, especially for design and visual diaries.

Problems arise for blended learning if isolated engagement with a virtual learning space is required. Why would a student use a networked communications system to communicate with members of his study group if he sees them in the classroom every week? Teachers must carefully scaffold learning activities so that the absurdity of this situation does not result in students circumventing or sabotaging the learning desired. If you want a student group to collaborate only via a virtual learning space, little class collaboration time should be provided. However, this may have a negative impact on group members who are less comfortable in virtual environments and alienate them from both the teaching methodology and the course objective. Even in blended learning environments, not everything is possible. PR comments:

The relationship between the two different learning spaces [physical and virtual] is important, but in our filmmaking course it is hard to reconcile the two, especially when trying to use the virtual in the physical. It seems needed to be in a different time and place because they both demand such different ways of operating.

More phenomenological issues also arise from embedding virtual spaces in physical classrooms. What is the relationship of the self I publish using social software on the Internet to my physical self in the classroom? Should these selves "add up"? Is my public, published persona important to me? Who is my "audience"? What is private and what is public? While there may be no simple answers, it is important to acknowledge and discuss the complexity of virtual learning spaces with students, for these are complexities that are replicated in private and professional life.

The ability of the contemporary classroom to push beyond its walled boundaries and engage students with the world revolutionizes not just learning space, but learning itself. Our learning spaces become sites of exploration and experimentation. Sometimes such environments threaten a student's sense of safety and privacy, in which case we lead them through a discussion of these issues. As media students, wanting professional media careers, our students need to come to terms with public publishing. In different disciplines this may not be seen as a critical outcome. However, note Harel & Papert's (1990, p. 24) idea about the pedagogical power of representation. Representing your work to the world may be a powerful learning tool regardless of your discipline.

We can imagine a blended, almost heterotopic classroom that reduces the need for the supposed solutions that flexible learning actually fails to deliver (or delivers by reducing the value of education itself)—a classroom that, to adapt Foucault (1967, p. 20), would "juxtapos[e…] in a single real place several spaces, several sites that are in themselves incompatible." Such utopian moments will emerge more often in day-to-day learning and teaching contexts if teachers explicitly design them to be there.

Question 3. Am I continually revising my teaching style in response to the learning space?

AM answers this question:

> Yes and no. It's not so much about a revision in response to the environment, but finding environments that respond to the desired learning outcomes. However, I do adapt learning and teaching to the affordances of the environments I use. I change my teaching method to complement the learning space rather than fitting pedagogy to the environment.

AM is a teacher at the more radical end of the constructivist spectrum. Learning space implementations are constantly refined by AM from course offering to course offering. Teaching styles and learning spaces evolve together, in conjunction with the learning group. Learning spaces may even evolve in ways the teacher may not expect, in response to student creative exploration.

Constructivist learning spaces, including Web 2.0 applications, may render the traditional concept of teacher paradoxical, as students learning takes place in relation to systems and communities that only obliquely concern the course. The student learns to respond to a community of fellow social software publishers, of which, at most, the teacher is but one voice. The gain is in student inventiveness and empowerment, but teachers have to think on their toes and not be afraid to reveal their ignorance. Once again, McWilliam's (2008) meddler-in-the-middle offers a good way to positively conceptualize the relationship.

I have recently been using the virtual world *Second Life* for media production exercises in my second-year undergraduate course, for example. My use of *Second Life* is inspired by meddling. My teaching style has become much more about me being engaged in my own similar projects to the ones the students are doing. This approach alters the relationship between student and teacher.

The media program's use of blogs is another example of the way a learning space has an impact on the way we teach. Because we all have blogs, students and staff together evolve the way they use their blogs throughout student degree work, in which we engage in an asynchronous "debate" with our students and each other:

> PR: The immediacy and the feedback richness of reflection on blogs have changed the way we teach quite dramatically. Prior to the use of blogs, a report on the process of making their film would be handed in at the end of semester. At its best this could generate some deepness in reflection but its big drawback was that it was not shared and the teaching staff could not monitor through the semester.

Students thus feel they are on a journey with the entire teaching group, which can be an emotional and a communal experience.

Question 4. Have I negotiated the correct balance between control and complexity in the learning space, given the course learning objectives?

Too often learning spaces, or the inter-relationships between different learning spaces, are so complex that a significant proportion of student energy is directed to understanding how learning spaces operate. This is particularly problematic for rapidly evolving ICT and Web 2.0 applications. Some students never get past practical skill acquisition to grapple with the course learning objectives. Instead, students often flounder with unarticulated pedagogical principles or ICT issues, although they are learning neither education nor ICT. There is something to be said in defense of the conventional classroom. Although it may not be constructivist, students have been trained in how classrooms work.

AM has a particular solution to control versus complexity; however, AM's radical approach to learning space is not necessarily shared by all our staff:

> AM: The tension between complexity of a learning environment and how you use it is tricky. Either you impose teacher-directed constraints or students develop their own constraints. The constraints might be quite technical.
>
> The technologies I use often have collateral benefits. Ideally, course content concerns the learning space that students are using. Gaining literacy in the learning space therefore operates on two levels. At the utilitarian level, it allows students to pass their assessment. At the more conceptual level, it allows students to 'perform' the course content. We model a pedagogy in which theory and practice reinforce each other, via the learning spaces we implement.

By making the learning space so central, AM more radically implements virtual learning spaces into his courses than other teachers.

I am personally in favor of adapting virtual environments that are not geared specifically for education, including the range of recreational social software, which has become so powerful for amateur media production and dissemination. Although such learning spaces are often more complex and less structured, they assist students to learn to operate in the real world and are, therefore, more transparently useful. They also tend to avoid the behaviorist shortfalls of some educational software (McDougall & Squires 1995, p. 95). In other words, although more complex, recreational social software tends to be constructivist by default. Justifying learning to use learning space to students is easier with an inquiry-centered pedagogical model, which is:

> [...] concerned less to introduce people to the disciplines *per se* (understood e.g., as "bodies of knowledge") and more to identify and encourage the capacity of students to engage in the characteristic practices of inquiry i.e., those activities which constitute inquiry as well as the consequences of inquiry (Watts 2007, p. 4).

According to Watts, this approach entails "a much more reflexive engagement with the elements of good learning and teaching" (ibid). Learning about learning is explicitly articulated as an important activity. It is more difficult to justify a student's time spent learning to operate within a learning space if that student is expecting what Watts calls a transmission (behaviorist) model of teaching.

The negotiation of control and complexity depends a lot on the teacher's attitude. Being responsive to the possibilities invented by students or the pitfalls found is part of the "meddler-in-the-middle" role. We need to view diverse student behaviour as positive rather than as learning "noise." The challenge becomes how to assess it (see question 7).

Question 5. Have I structured into my teaching schedule sufficient time and support for students to learn a new learning space?

Too often we expect students to automatically absorb the affordances of a learning space. This sort of expectation can happen with physical classrooms, not just virtual spaces. One of my interviewees comments about problems caused for his honors students when confronted by culturally unusual classroom space:

> AM: [I]f you have students who don't come from a background where they've been taught, or there is an expectation of studio practice, they get a bit lost in these spaces. They don't "get" that they can move things around so they do get a bit lost in there because their preferred model would be, "If I could I'd just have a little office and shut the door and lock the world out."

Probably more common are problems implementing a virtual learning space. Learning time must be dedicated to exploring and conquering its affordances. This is a psychological point as much as a practical one. PR speaks of a need to cater for learners at different levels of competency with remedial sessions:

> AM: […] In general, they need lots of support. The analogy I always give is that students receive nine years of sustained teaching in how to write an essay. In 12 weeks you can't expect them to learn to use X or Y environment appropriately.

Teachers also have to be practical about what learning spaces they can support. For example, some learning tools require a high level of teacher availability for near-synchronous support (Jeong, 2007). While students may love this level of flexibility and availability, not only is the required level of teacher support generally unsustainable, but it encourages a level of student dependence that is counterproductive to independent learning.

One of my interviewees related a story about a student who was obliged to use her blog for written communication rather than to house and display her preferred communication medium, an audio recording (podcast). The student felt this was arbitrary and was, therefore, annoyed. The problem was not that the student did not understand the space, but it still thwarted her learning due to the teacher's attitude to it. Learning spaces are more than just technologies, and the teacher must represent them as such. They are "ways of being."

Question 6. Have I determined neither too many, nor too few, channels of information?

From the teacher's perspective, we often hear the complaint that "no matter how many times I tell my class to do X, they still don't do X." As MB points out, students learn in different ways and some will never absorb something that is just on the screen, while others switch off to speech. Students attending a non-compulsory face-to-face class are likely to be there because they feel they learn more effectively in that mode. The face-to-face affordances of the classroom should be fully used, even if it does lead to redundancy.

Often teachers combine different networked tools to ensure students receive all the information they need. While a justification may be to meet different student learning styles, that is not always the effect. Most of my colleagues share a strong belief in information redundancy, even when it is just sending the same bit of text to various devices or platforms, which manifestly does not address different learning styles:

> PR: Crucial information is pushed out in email and deposited in the course blog and blackboard. We were involved in a trial of the ultimate pushy communicating tool—SMS [short message service]. This delivered crucial information and seemed to be read by all. Crucial information is not supplied in lectures or tutes as attendance is not great in lectures and different staff teaching into different tutes can mean the information delivery is not consistent.

AM and MB broadly agree with PR. However, the high level of information redundancy that PR promotes means students feel they can skip lectures with impunity. Some students learn (or think they learn) with a minimum level of engagement. Information redundancy can spiral in negative ways, as teachers send out an ever-increasing quantity of information, and students become too bored to access the trail of emails, text messages, etc.

For example, in my own teaching, I try to limit the numbers of emails I send to the course list, so students do not end up thinking my emails are redundant. More often than not, information redundancy is a symptom of the dubious flexible learning culture, and it may lead to problems in other areas of the course.

Information redundancy needs careful thought—not only in administrative but also in learning contexts. An example of a flexible learning tool used at my university is *Lectopia*, an automated system for recording and disseminating lectures via the network. Anecdotal conversations with our students suggest that widespread use of *Lectopia* would lead to drop off in attendance at face-to-face lectures.

Many networked learning technologies such as *Lectopia* and podcasts (see Pastore, 2008) reflect or further cement teacher-centric, one-to-many information dissemination models. A "live" lecture is, to some extent interactive, whereas media such as a podcast will never be (Pastore, 2008 p. 15). Furthermore, the media quality is embarrassing. My interviewees confirm:[6]

KB: [I]t doesn't actually take advantage of the different learning environments, it's just a poor man's copy of the lecture model of delivering information rather than working with the environment [...]

PR: It's not even one-to-many, because *Lectopia* has zero interactivity, whereas even in a big lecture there's still interactivity.

According to Brabazon, the i-lecture is a symptom of Australia's financially starved university sector (2007, p. 125). That may be harsh, for it takes considerable funding to establish and maintain *Lectopia*. However, the student flexibility enabled by these systems (Pastore, 2008, p. 15) is gained at the expense of learning. The fact that students are not attending lectures that are "boring or unintelligible [and] that conspicuously lack planning or purpose" (Watts, 2007, p. 17) cannot be resolved by providing even more boring or unintelligible recordings of those lectures. While students may well be prepared to watch lectures at home, they won't automatically learn from the experience. If a networked, one-to-many means for the dissemination of lectures is required, searchable well-written lecture notes on a blog, for example, are generally easier to engage with. Furthermore, if lecture notes adequately substitute for the lecture, the "live" lecture itself is a waste of time. There is no point in such redundancy.

Question 7. Should engagement with the learning space be assessed?

Amongst our teaching staff, this is a controversial topic. AM, possibly our most extreme constructivist, is adamant:

> AM: The learning environment should always be reflected in the assessment. Not to do it is just bad teaching. For example, an essay [*qua* essay] is always explicitly assessed. When we move into other environments, there are elements that are particular to them. If there's nothing about the "blogginess" of the blog then they shouldn't be writing in a blog. All environments have particular practices that are developing around them. [...] There is a strong affinity between the technological form and the way it allows you to express knowledge, and that should be reflected in assessment.

To expand AM's beliefs, a teacher marking an essay will base his mark partly on its structural properties; that is, on the extent to which the student has mastered the form and the technologies used in its production. Students generally accept that this is an appropriate marking criteria and that however good the explication of the theme of the essay is, it is not a good essay unless structural and technical elements are also good. Presumably the same holds for other types of presentational media. However, how to assess competence with a learning space, and how to justify that assessment task in terms of course objectives is not always easy. MB says, "[l]earning to use a learning space should not be reflected in the assessment unless it is an explicit learning outcome in the course guide." PR thinks, "[o]nly if it encourages troubleshooting and showing initiative."

In my use of *Second Life*, I assess artifacts created in *Second Life* rather than directly assessing student fluency with the environment. This style of assessment is reasonably analogous to that of AM's essay example; it measures an *output* rather than a *process*. However, some of my colleagues more explicitly measure process, for example, by assessing participation.

The issue hinges largely on course content. Teachers are employed in Australia due to their expertise in a specific body of knowledge. It is expected the teacher will expend his energy and learning time on this content. Not doing so in an explicit way could break the body of knowledge "contract" between teacher and student regarding the relationship they commonly engaged in.

This "contract" is often troublesome from a constructivist perspective. According to Siemens, "[t]he pipe is more important than the content in the pipe. Our ability to learn what we need for tomorrow is more important than what we know today" (2007, p. 33). It can be difficult enough justifying to students that they should spend their limited time learning a new learning space—in effect, learning how to learn—given that our educational systems operate on the assumption that students will conquer a body of knowledge.

Assessment of learning how to learn remains contentious even within our broadly constructivist circle. In my experience, a course will be considered by students to have failed if too great a proportion of time is spent on a learning space that has only an oblique relationship to the relevant and advertised body of knowledge. Implementation of a new learning space should not be undertaken unless it can be transparently made relevant to the course content. Only then can it be validly assessed.

Conclusion

Developing powerful learning spaces not only results in explorative and personalized responses among students, but among teachers as well. Our evolving program has become an object-lesson in constructivist learning. It is the way we work.

Our group's teaching is a constant dialogue with and reinterpretation of broadly constructivist principles. There are a range of issues and questions we address and re-address. How learning spaces and tools work together (or not) in a blended learning model has been the focus of this chapter. Blended learning has strengths but also constraints. Teachers must be sensitive to both.

Learning space has become far more complex with the introduction of ubiquitous networked technologies and, in particular, Web 2.0 social software. Teachers, as course designers, have so many choices to make. Care must be taken that in our desire to empower, or create flexibility, or save money, we do not accidentally confuse, or alienate, or otherwise decrease a student's ability to learn.

As Tom, Voss, & Scheetz (2008) proclaim, "the space is the message" (p. 47). Learning spaces communicate to students in their own right. These spaces inform students about the way we see the world, about learning, how we view the teacher-student relationship, and implicitly about issues of power and democracy, ethics and creativity and self-expression. These environments send our students messages about the wider world and their place within it. A learning space should be a synecdoche for the wider world. If it is not, its usefulness is limited.

Acknowledgements

Thanks to Adrian Miles (AM), Marsha Berry (MB), Paul Ritchard (PR), and Kyla Brettle (KB) who were interviewed for this paper. My interpolations are marked []. Thanks also to Kirsten Drotner for valuable feedback.

Notes

1. Other environments, such as laboratories, can also be learning spaces, but I will restrict my comments to my own professional experience in teaching humanities and media production courses.
2. Unfortunately, most uses of mobile phones in tertiary education have been limited to sending text message reminders to students about assessment deadlines and other practicalities (Trotter, 2003, pp. 90–91). This may be valuable, but it is not a learning activity, it is an administrative one.
3. The B. Comm. (Media) introduces students to a variety of media technologies, genres, and publication paradigms. Students use a variety of social software. They make websites, interactive video projects, and explore emerging types of networked mediums such as the mobile phone.
4. See[0] Prensky (2001) on the fate of the "digital native" student, obliged to learn in learning spaces designed by "digital immigrants." These two concepts are also discussed in the chapters by Herr-Stephenson and McFarlane in this volume.
5. General principles about classroom design are outlined in NLII (2004). Edwards (2002, p. 21) identifies a range of issues to be addressed when embedding technology into a classroom. Such lists are specific to courses and technology, and must be constantly revised.
6. Some divergent points of view were expressed by the interviewees. MB appreciates the flexible options, so long as students are also attending the face-to-face version of the lecture. Anecdotal surveys of students suggest, however, that recorded version of the lecture will version.

References

Berry, M., Peterson, J. F., de la Harpe, B., Horvat, L., & Anastasiou, P. (2007, 26–28 March). Mobility and networks of learners. Paper presented at the 9th International GOR Conference (General Online Research), University of Leipzig, Leipzig, Germany.

Brabazon, T. (2007). *The University of Google: Education in the (post) information age.* Burlington, VT: Ashgate.

Chambers, M. (1999). The efficacy and ethics of using digital multimedia for educational purposes. In A. Tait & R. Mills (Eds.), *The convergence of distance and conventional education: Patterns of flexibility for the individual learner* (pp. 5–16). London and New York: Routledge.

Edwards, P. (2002). Lessons from the past: Effective learning using new technologies. In S. Rodrigues

(Ed.), *Opportunistic challenges: Teaching and learning with ICT* (pp. 9–32). New York: Nova Science Publishers.

Fischer, G. (1999). Social creativity: bringing different points of view together. Retrieved August 24, 2009, from University of Colorado: http://l3d.cs.colorado.edu/~gerhard/papers/kbs2000.pdf

Foucault, M. (1967). Of other spaces—heterotopias. (J. Miskowiec, Trans.). Retrieved January 22, 2008, from Foucault.info: http://foucault.info/documents/heteroTopia/foucault.heteroTopia.en.html

Harel, I. & Papert, S. (1990). Software design as a learning environment. *Interactive Learning Environments, 1*(1), 1–32.

Hrastinski, S. (2008). Asynchronous and synchronous e-learning. *Educause Quarterly,* 4, 51–55.

Jeong, W. (2007). Instant messaging in on-site and online classes in higher education. *Educause Quarterly, 1*, 30–36.

Johnston, S. (1999). Introducing and supporting change towards more flexible teaching approaches. In A. Tait & R. Mills (Eds.), *The convergence of distance and conventional education: patterns of flexibility for the individual learner* (pp. 39–50). London and New York: Routledge.

Kirkpatrick, D., & Jakupec, V. (1999). Becoming flexible: What does it mean? In A. Tait & R. Mills (Eds.), *The convergence of distance and conventional education: Patterns of flexibility for the individual learner* (pp. 51–70). London and New York: Routledge.

Kok, A. (2009, April). Creative design environments: A small-scale case study. Retrieved August 24, 2009, from *International Journal of Instructional Technology and Distance Learning*: http://www.itdl.org/Journal/Apr_09/article01.htm

McDougall, A., & Squires, D. (1995). An empirical study of a new paradigm for choosing educational software. *Computers & Education, 25* (3), 93–103.

McWilliam, E. (2008). Unlearning how to teach. *Innovations in Education and Teaching International, 45* (3), 263–269.

National Learning Infrastructure Initiative (2004). Leading the transition from classrooms to learning spaces. Retrieved February 2, 2009, from Educause: http://net.educause.edu/ir/library/pdf/NLI0447.pdf

Papert, S. (1987). Information technology and education: Computer criticism vs. technocentric thinking. *Educational Researcher, 16,* 22–30.

Pastore R. (2008, December). Students' perceptions of podcasts in the classroom. Retrieved August 24, 2009, from *International Journal of Instructional Technology and Distance Learning*: http://www.itdl.org/Journal/Dec_08/article04.htm

Prensky, M. (2001). Digital natives, digital immigrants part II: Do they really think differently? Retrieved August 22, 2009, from Marc Prensky: http://www.marcprensky.com/writing/Prensky%20-%20Digital%20Natives,%20Digital%20Immigrants%20-%20Part2.pdf

Rikhye, R., Cook, S., Zane L. & Berge Z. L. (2009, January). Digital natives vs. digital immigrants: Myth or reality? Retrieved August 22, 2009, from *International Journal of Instructional Technology and Distance Learning*: http://www.itdl.org/Journal/Feb_09/article01.htm

Rodrigues, S. (2002). Zones of interpretive development in education and multimedia design. In S. Rodrigues (Ed.), *Opportunistic challenges: Teaching and learning with ICT* (pp. 49–64). New York: Nova Science Publishers.

Siemens, G. (2005, January). Connectivism: A learning theory for the digital age. Retrieved June 29, 2007, from *International Journal of Instructional Technology and Distance Learning*: http://www.itdl.org/Journal/Jan_05/article01.htm

Tait, A., & Mills, R. (2002). The convergence of distance and conventional education: patterns of flexibility for the individual learner. In A. Tait & R. Mills (Eds.), *The convergence of distance and conventional education: Patterns of flexibility for the individual learner* (pp. 1–4). London and New York: Routledge.

Tom, J. S. C., Voss, K., & Scheetz, C. (2008). The space is the message: First assessment of a learning studio. *Educause Quarterly, 2,* 42–52.

Trotter, A. (2003, 15 October). Students' technology views solicited. Retrieved November 11, 2008 from *Education Week*: http://www.b-g.12.ky.us/Tech/StudentsTechnologyViewsSolicited.pdf

Watts, R. (2007, 22–24 July). Good teaching in universities? Transformation and resistance: an Australian case study. Paper presented at Learning Together: Reshaping higher education in a global age, Institute of Education, University of London, London, UK.

Young, A. E. & Duhaney, D. C. (2008, November). Hybrid learning and the principles of good practice in undergraduate education. Retrieved August 24, 2009 from *International Journal of Instructional Technology and Distance Learning*: http://www.itdl.org/Journal/Nov_08/article04.htm.

IV

Studying Digital Content Creation

New Methodological Challenges

11

Negotiating Perspective in Social Video Environments

RALPH BARTHEL, SHAARON AINSWORTH & MIKE SHARPLES

People increasingly engage with online video to view, share, and discuss audio-visual content. A recent report on Internet trends in the United States shows that interacting with online video is one of the fastest growing areas of Internet usage (Meeker, 2008). The main uses of online video include accessing of news and educational resources, but increasingly also the sharing of video resources with the age group of young adults (ages 18–29) leading the way (Madden, 2007). Increased possibilities for participation in media making through digital technologies raise the prospect of education to support and equip people to join such public dialog (Rheingold, 2007). Sharing of personal experiences through media can lead to the acquisition of new literacies (Burgess, 2006). Consequently, it has been proposed that (user-generated) online video as a creative form of expression will have an increasing influence on learning and teaching in the future (New Media Consortium, 2008). In classrooms, video is used to introduce problem situations (Barron et al., 1998), for learning and assessment based on instructional video (Schwartz & Hartman, 2007), and in project work to produce media (Levin, 2003). There are, however, fewer applications of video media as a resource in informal learning and everyday learning activities designed to support knowledge building.

More people engage daily in creative problem-solving activities at their work places (Florida, 2003), and the ability to create new knowledge and to innovate is an essential twenty-first century skill (Bereiter & Scardamalia, 2003; Prensky, 2009). Digital technologies for learning should, therefore, be designed to develop creative thinking (Resnick, 2007b) and take into account that creativity flourishes best in the collaboration of groups (Sawyer, 2006). In powerful creative learning environments, the learners have opportunities to participate in the construction of artifacts such as video or animations based on their ideas that subsequently become objects for reflection (Resnick, 2007a).

Creative knowledge work depends on the generation of new ideas and the improvement of existing ideas (Scardamalia & Bereiter, 2006). In this context the ability to show alternative and different perspectives with the help of conceptual artifacts becomes crucial. Consequently, powerful social knowledge-building environments need to enable the co-construction of different perspectives and facilitate effective discourse about different available perspectives to aid idea improvement. It is important to note there is a distinction between interaction and participation in relation to digital technologies (Jenkins, 2006). The former characterizes the responsiveness of technology to user input, but only the latter offers a degree of control, ownership, and autonomy for learners. We argue that new learning experiences enabled through participatory media are best supported by learning environments based on pedagogical models that share a common ground with participatory culture and that enable people to engage in co-construction of conceptual artifacts. Thus, software for learning through media creation should provide social tools for creating, sharing and discussing media artifacts.

We are interested in how engagement with online video can be harnessed to support informal learning processes and the creation of audio-visual public knowledge artifacts. Online video sites such as YouTube can be used to distribute and discuss lectures, video tutorials, and other instructional video and can be valuable resources for learning activities. However, a unique opportunity of participatory media is that they enable people to collaboratively create artifacts that can be used for the advancement of knowledge (Scardamalia & Bereiter, 1994) and for an exchange of perspectives in- and between communities (Boland & Tenkasi, 1995). Hence, we have carried out a design study to construct a social video environment for story creation from online video, based on Knowledge Building Theory (Scardamalia & Bereiter, 2006).

We begin this chapter with a section that outlines the foundations and principles of Knowledge Building Theory and shows its implications for the design of a social video environment. The section includes relevant outcomes from research on learning with video. We then describe the design process, which includes experience in prototyping with existing software followed by the development of iterative prototypes of a learning environment named Video Pathways.

We created Video Pathways as proof of concept of a social video environment that embeds knowledge-building principles. We present a summary of the results of an expert evaluation and of a formative usability and desirability evaluation of the software. In the final section of this chapter, we identify some of the methodological challenges in studying digital content creation processes with Video Pathways and introduce a set of research methods and instruments that we apply to meet those challenges. With our research we wish to inform both design and theory; hence, readers will find elements of design-based research practices (Barab & Squire, 2004) in our work.

Knowledge Building Theory

Knowledge building, a constructivist learning theory (Scardamalia & Bereiter, 2006), describes what is needed for students to construct new knowledge in collaboration. Knowledge building involves collective inquiry on a topic as a method for the continual improvement of ideas. The results of these inquiries are made available as public cognitive artifacts that can be drawn on by others for continual further improvements to these ideas. The 12 principles of knowledge building (Scardamalia, 2002) include idea diversity (consideration of multiple perspectives), continuous improvement of ideas, reflection and synthesis of ideas, knowledge-building discourse, democratizing of knowledge and epistemic agency.

Knowledge Building Theory thus suggests that collaborative manipulation of conceptual artifacts is a useful way to explore and improve ideas and to exchange different perspectives (Bereiter & Scardamalia, 2003; Stahl, 2000). In learning environments that are modeled after knowledge building principles, it is thus crucial that it is possible to collaboratively explore multiple perspectives and to discuss these different perspectives. Empirical studies with learning environments modeled after Knowledge Building Theory have shown that support for group collaboration (Gilbert & Driscoll, 2002) and discussion (Leng, Mai, & Law, 2008) is necessary.

The characteristics of video itself when used as an instructional medium can promote or inhibit learning. Salomon (1994), in several experimental studies, investigates the effects of video learning resources on skill activation, skill short-circuiting, and skill modeling, with results that show possible positive impacts on learning. Salomon describes a gap between what can be affected and what is typically affected by learning from video due to lack of active engagement with the media system. Further, it has been proposed (Chambel, Zahn, & Finke, 2004) that the difficulty to show different perspectives in a video medium is problematic for learning. Consequently, video as a linear medium does not lend itself directly to perspective taking because it is difficult to portray abstract concepts and to construct alternative realities through video. We propose, however, that combining online video and social software may be a way to overcome these intrinsic limitations of video for knowledge building in general and for sharing and negotiation of perspective in a video medium. Enabling co-construction of video resources as conceptual knowledge representations, in a system where alternative video resources can be related to each other and discussed, can help reduce the typical difficulties of using video for knowledge exploration.

From this analysis of Knowledge Building Theory, and based on the limitations of using video for learning that we found in the literature, we decided on the following high-level goals for the development of our social video environment. It should enable:

- the exploration of different perspectives in a social video medium,
- participation in the remediation of the video resources, and
- collaboration to create video resources.

Drawing on these basic requirements, we began an enquiry into the design of a social video environment that fulfills these aims and embeds design features that offer effective support for learners who wish to engage in knowledge-building activities based on video media.

Design Process

We chose an iterative design process for the creation of a social video environment. We began by testing a development idea inspired by knowledge building theory in a pilot study. We used existing software that, in combination with the task design, enabled us to simulate certain aspects of the experience of using the social video environment we envisioned without the need to build the software at this stage. The aim of this pilot study was thus to refine our development idea and to enquire about the possible educational benefits and constraints of such a learning environment.

Design idea: multi-path video

Knowledge Building Theory is based on the concept of "improvable ideas," with idea building and idea diversification being important elements in a knowledge-building environment. To enable this kind of activity with video, we decided to represent knowledge in the form of multi-path video. The concept of multi-path video means that users co-create multiple versions of a video by providing alternative and interchangeable clips and scenes that form different path sequences through the entire video content. Each path shows one possible alternative rendering of a video. The multi-path video created by users is viewed as sequences of linear movies of which different versions can co-exist. Users of the service create and explore different routes through alternative sequences of clips for the scenes. Each of these routes through a sequence of clips can be saved as a path, which is a linear video stream.

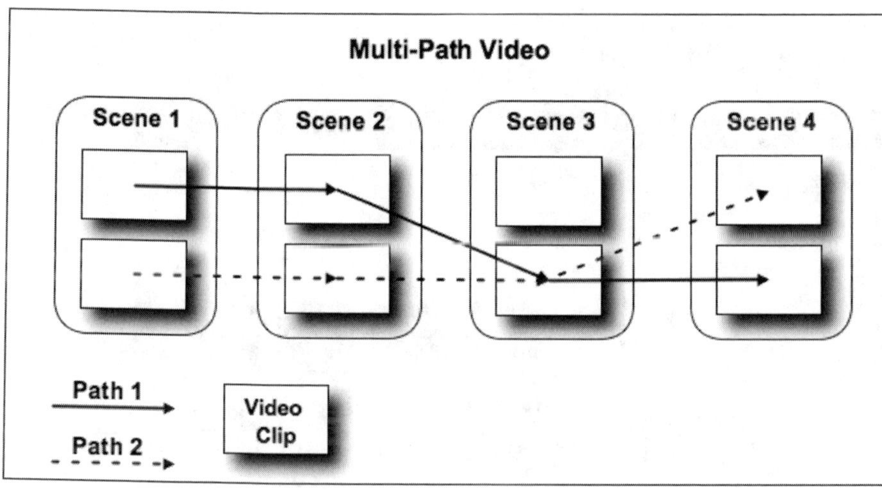

Figure 1: Schema multi-path video.

Figure 1 shows a schematic view of two alternative routes through a multi-path video project, each of which forms one path that consists of four different video clips. In the example depicted in Figure 1, the two paths share only one element in the third scene; all other elements differ. People who create multiple-path video can add or remove scenes and provide alternative video clips to refine or diversify the topical video content, and thus it becomes possible to share different perspectives and alternative representations in a video medium.

Pilot study

We tested the idea of multi-path video in a pilot study with four postgraduate students from the University of Nottingham. We asked them to co-construct a thematic video narrative using a commercial service for online video sharing and editing named Eyespot. At the time of writing the Eyespot service has been discontinued. Therefore, we will briefly describe the main features of the software. Eyespot enables users to edit online video either individually or in group collaboration. Video clips used in Eyespot must be uploaded by the users of the service. The application provides a browser interface to cut video clips, create transitions and effects between clips, and add titles and an editor to assemble a video story from the different clips. The resulting video in Eyespot is a single, linear video stream. The results can be shared and remixed by other users of this web-based service. Figure 2 shows a screenshot of the Eyespot application.

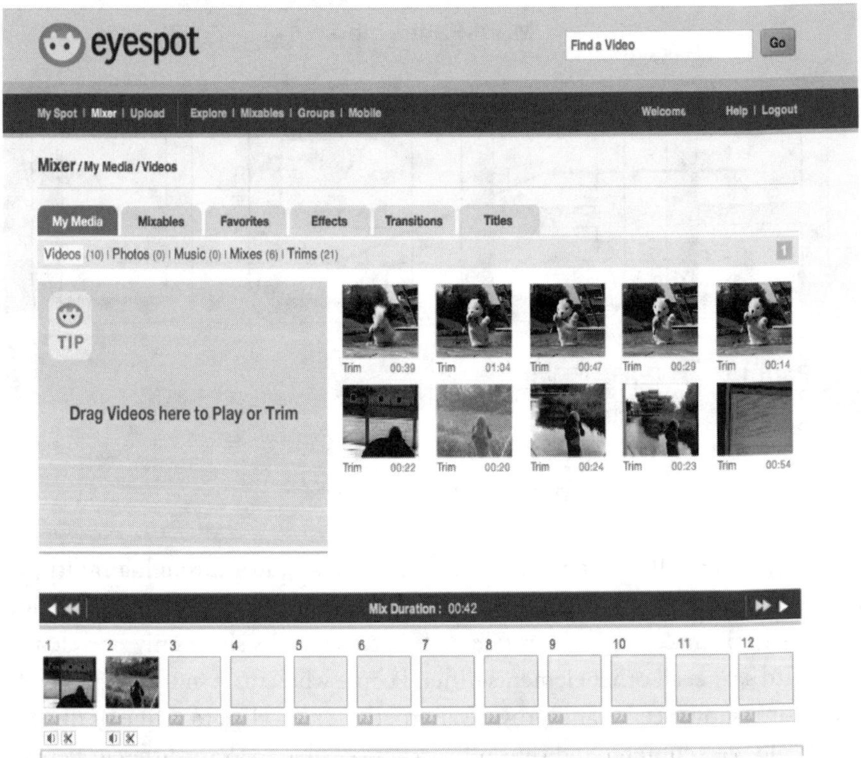

Figure 2: Screenshot of the Eyespot application

We asked our study participants to group in pairs and to record a video story that contained four different and interchangeable scenes, so that later, in the post-production, different paths could be constructed by switching between the scenes of the two groups. The theme of the video was to create a small narrative about personal fitness; the video needed to include an introduction, two fitness exercises (each one presented in a separate scene), and a closing sequence. Through this task design we were able to explore the processes of creating multi-path video. There were no further instructions given on how to produce the video. We provided access to camcorders to originate the video. The students were seeing each other on a daily basis on the University campus so that they had an opportunity to meet and discuss. Consequently, they were not constrained by the communication features of the software. The rationale for this task was to work with a topic that is accessible to everyone; it should be easy to produce a video, and we thought that the resulting video would also be useful as a small, informal learning resource. We conducted personal post-intervention interviews with each participant and held a focus group session with the whole group after the intervention.

We analyzed the data by looking at the educational potentials and breakdowns in the process of creating these multi-path videos. The main outcomes of this pilot study can be summarized as follows:

- There was a varying degree to which participants felt comfortable producing their own video clips. This was partly due to lack of perceived media literacy skills, especially related to the planning and creation of narrative video that had to follow a certain storyline (Representative participant remark: *"I have taken many videos but never created a narrative that links these videos."*) The study participants thus found planning and production time-consuming and difficult.
- The task required considerable effort to plan, reflect, and coordinate between the two pairs to make the scenes interchangeable. The coordination proved difficult as Eyespot does not have features to support group work on such a task. Thus, the study participants were required repeatedly to meet to discuss the coordination of their work.
- Participants with video editing experience with software such as Adobe Premier or Final Cut Pro wished for more editing features than the ones provided by the Eyespot application.
- Creating multi-path video was perceived as interesting and in a positive way challenging, but it was also difficult due to the constraints imposed by the software. The latter is not surprising since Eyespot is primarily an

online video editing tool and not a multi-path video editor. Hence, our participants wished for a better support to coordinate their collaboration on the task of creating multi-path video.

- Multi-path video was perceived as educationally useful for different reasons. Study participants mentioned in interviews and in the focus group session several educational use cases where multi-path video could be useful. These use cases include the scaffolding of narrative creation and improvement of narrative skills, the exploration of multiple perspectives by showing alternative narratives and scenes, the construction of visual knowledge resources from field trips, lab experiments and everyday learning episodes, and finally it was suggested that multi-path video creation could be useful in special needs education as an alternative to writing tasks.
- All participants said they wanted to present the videos to friends and access them online.

The results of this pilot study indicate that the creation of multi-path video seems to be an educationally useful activity; we took it a step further and developed a prototype that enables the creation of multi-path video.

Designing Video Pathways

Based on the results of this pilot study and our literature review, we made the creation of multi-path video stories the focal point of our research as it represents a novel way to engage with video. One constraint emerging from the study was the need for video production. The production of video for peer and public audiences has proved to be an engaging and valuable educational activity (Burden & Kuechel, 2004; Kearney & Schuck, 2006; Levin, 2003). To enable a broad range of educational scenarios, we designed our software as a mash-up service that uses popular video hosting sites as the repository for video clips. On the one hand, this enables the remediation of existing video without the requirement to produce or upload personal video clips, which proved to be a constraint in our pilot study. On the other hand, it still allows users of the service to use video they originated themselves, although the video had to be uploaded to a video-hosting site before it could be used in the system. Further, we wished to provide useful functions that are sufficient to enable the collective creation of multi-path video structures and are suitable to converse about shared multi-path video representations.

In the next step, we developed iteratively a number of prototypes of the social video environment that we named Video Pathways. Video Pathways is a web-based service that enables users to create multi-path video in a browser interface. The software makes use of video clips that are hosted on YouTube as its content resources. In Video Pathways, users can create movie projects, alter the structure of these projects and in selecting a path through these scene structures create different versions (called a path in the software) of a movie. The clips are elements of a path that can be altered in their length so that only selected parts of YouTube clips are shown. These versions of a movie can be shared so that other community users can comment and remediate these paths. Video Pathways supports group collaboration through shared movie projects. The people that share the workspace of a movie project can comment on the different available paths. With our research prototype, multi-path video stories from YouTube video can be created in collaboration. YouTube was chosen as a proof of concept for the prototype due to the stability of the service and the availability of a stable interface enabling third party applications to search and stream the clips via a standardized API (Application Programming Interface). The following screenshot shows the path editor of Video Pathways.

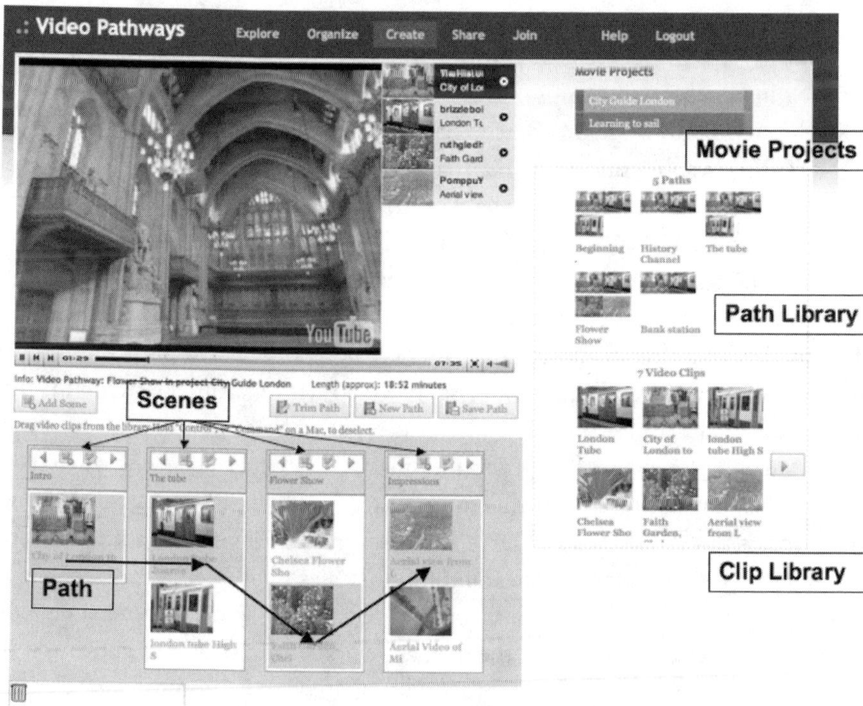

Figure 3: Screenshot of Video Pathways.

Possible learning applications of the Video Pathways service include the creation of multi-path video stories that represent a guide for a location with paths for different audiences (e.g. City Guide to London), an exploration of a topic (e.g. the Reasons for the Global Financial Crisis of 2008), or the use of the software as a pre-production tool to sketch a distributed filmmaking project before using a nonlinear video editing software.

Next, we conducted an expert evaluation of a prototype of Video Pathway. We used a customized version of a heuristic evaluation (Nielsen, 1994) with four usability experts, and we refined the system prototype based on feedback gathered during the evaluation. The customization of the heuristic evaluation was performed to capture elements such as conviviality and desirability (Benyon, Turner, & Turner, 2004) that are relevant in social software. Following this expert evaluation, we designed a first formative study with Video Pathways. The results of this study are described in the following section.

Formative Evaluation of Video Pathways

We conducted a formative evaluation of the usability and desirability of Video Pathways in which small groups of three to four students created multi-path video about the city of Nottingham (Barthel, Sharples, & Ainsworth, 2009). The study reveals positive results concerning the usability and desirability of the software and demonstrates that Video Pathways enables study participants to create coherent narratives. Participants in the study enjoyed the ease with which the video stories could be created and the access to YouTube video search and retrieval from within the system. On the negative side, there was a lack of continuity between the loading of different clips of a stream and the inaccurate playing of selected parts of YouTube clips, due to the way YouTube compresses its video stream. Some participants proposed additional features such as audio editing and the availability of transition effects. These preferences relate to the amount of prior experience with video editing of participants and were not shared by all study subjects. Since creating Video Pathways is a novel task, we evaluated usability and desirability in a separate step prior to evaluating the knowledge-building processes in greater detail.

A software tool to create multi-path video on its own is not sufficient to enable collaborative learning. For the formative evaluation of Video Pathways, the participants in a study shared a goal (e.g. to explain what caused the meltdown of the global financial systems in 2008), and they shared a knowledge representation in a workspace. The question of how collaborative learning is defined has no single answer (Dillenbourg, 1999). Often a distinction is drawn between collaborative and cooperative learning where the former is a coordinated joint activity to solve a problem, and the latter is a division of labor where each group member solves a part of a problem (Roschelle & Teasley, 1995). Collaborative learning is thus often defined as learning that happens during a joint problem-solving activity (Dillenbourg, 1999). Knowledge Building Theory suggests that the advancement of knowledge, idea improvement, discourse, and emergent understanding over time characterize learning in knowledge-building environments (Scardamalia & Bereiter, 2006). To evaluate learning in such a knowledge-building environment we need to study the joint activity (the process), the outcome (conceptual artifacts) of the joint activity, and the individual experiences (see also the chapter by Weight in this volume).

Studying knowledge-building processes in Video Pathways raises a number of methodological challenges for the evaluation of collaborative learning. First, we need to keep track of the evolution of conceptual ideas and link them to rich descriptions of the process that has led to the construction of multi-path video structures. Questions we need to answer include: How did the conceptual ideas evolve over time? How were different perspectives explored and evaluated during the joint activity? How do people who create a multi-path video structure together organize their work and how do they interact with others' knowledge representations during that process?

A second set of questions relates to the conceptual artifacts that have been created. What is the quality of these artifacts and how do we evaluate them? How can we analyze the coherence of video narratives? And, finally, we need to enquire if Video Pathways is useful to participants who use the system. In the remainder of this chapter, we focus on the analysis of process and conceptual artifacts that can prove difficult in social software environments.

Process analysis

To aid the generation of a rich process description we are using log files to visualize patterns that show user activities and the evolution of the different paths and the multi-path structure over time. To visualize the content of the log files, we are using the open-source software of the Exhibit project (Huynh, Karger, & Miller, 2007). Figure 4 shows a screenshot of a visualization of a part of a log file in Exhibit.

The analysis of log files in Exhibit can help to elicit interaction patterns that are otherwise difficult to detect in a textual log file and can be a source of information to be used together with other research methods such as interviews. We use the information from log files as prompts in interviews with study participants to follow up interesting phenomena that emerged during a study. Log file analysis has been used in recent years in research for studying online collaboration in education (Harrer, Hever, & Ziebarth, 2007).

With the increased availability of data mash-up services, more tools become readily available for researchers to create visualizations of their data. One needs, however, to define and mine for meaningful interactions that are useful for explaining knowledge-building processes in context. We have recorded approximately 50 different user interactions in log files. Single user interactions, or in some cases sequences of user interactions, can then be mapped on to knowledge-building activities such as participation in discourse or the refinement of an idea. A research narrative that explains the process of multi-path video creation can draw on this information.

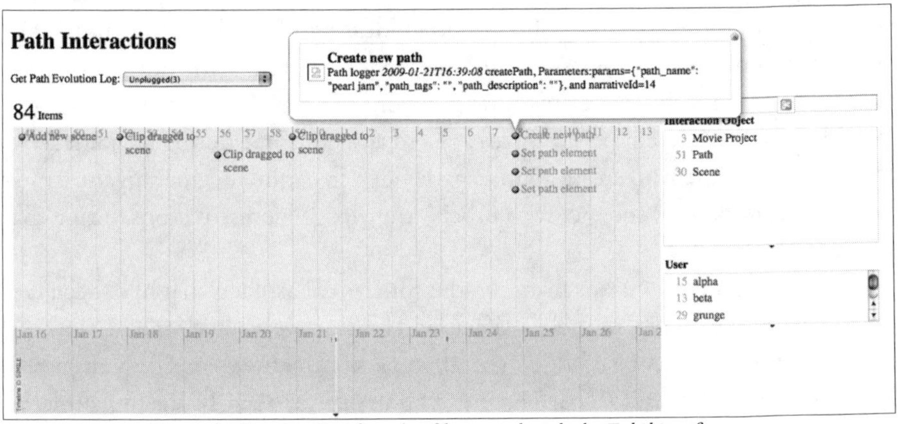

Figure 4: Visualization from log file created with the Exhibit software.

Analysis of conceptual artifacts

In a social video environment such as Video Pathways, the learners who use the service will potentially create a large number of knowledge artifacts over time. In a small-scale study it might still be feasible for a researcher to evaluate all path sequences by viewing and coding them. Even then, however, it would be desirable to see how the different paths that participants have created are related to each other. The purpose of such a comparison is to discover if participants do work on the refinement and synthesis of ideas or if the paths show video clips that are largely unrelated to each other. The similarity of paths can thus inform us to what extent different knowledge-building principles can be observed in Video Pathways.

In Video Pathways a path consists of a sequence of video clips. Each video clip in a path sequence contains two timestamps that encode when to start and end the streaming of a clip. By default, the entire clip is streamed, but users can set in and out points of the stream using an editing function in Video Pathways. This combination of clip and timestamps in Video Pathways is called a block element. A path thus consists of a sequence of block elements. This sequence of block elements can be encoded as string representation. If we want to quantify how similar the paths created by two study participants are, the similarity can be determined by using an edit distance algorithm, which is an algorithm that calculates the minimal amount of operations from the set addition, deletion, and substitution necessary to transform one sequence into another. The Levenshtein Distance Algorithm (Levenshtein, 1966), an implementation of an edit distance algorithm, has been used in education for classification of teaching approaches with an Intelligent Tutoring System (Ainsworth, Clarke, & Gaizauskas, 2002) and to adapt content for learners in a Mobile Learning Environment (Zhao, Ninomiya, Anma, & Okamoto, 2008).

Computing the edit distance between different paths enables us to quantify similarities in the paths between users who share a workspace in Video Pathways. However, this tells us only about the similarity of paths at the syntactic level. To judge the different paths at a semantic level, we carry out an additional analysis of the paths with a group of human coders. These human coders are asked to judge the narrative coherence and content quality of each video story of a path. To get an indication of the narrative coherence, the path sequences are deconstructed into single block elements and show the coders in a first step the single video clips of a path in random order. The coders are then asked to reassemble what they think was the original video sequence based on these single elements. We finally compare the order of the initial path with the reconstruction made by the coder. We then code the coherence depending on the similarity between these two path sequences. The combination of syntactic and semantic analysis of conceptual artifacts together with interviews and the process analysis as described above is useful to craft a rich description of content creation activities with Video Pathways.

Conclusion

In this chapter we have described a design study that led to the development of the Video Pathways social video environment, which aims to support knowledge-building activities through the creation of multi-path video. Knowledge Building Theory is an educational model that is well suited to inform the design of learning environments that can be used by autonomous learners in everyday learning situations. We outlined the different design steps and described how experience prototyping enabled us at an early stage of our research to identify and refine a promising concept for knowledge building with video. The results of formative evaluation of the research prototype that was subsequently built demonstrates that Video Pathways is an easy to use and desirable web service that enables users to create coherent video stories.

To evaluate asynchronous collaborative learning in a social software environment, it is necessary to use methodologies that enable a detailed analysis of process and conceptual artifacts. We have proposed that the analysis of log files and computational analysis of conceptual artifacts are methods that, in combination with qualitative research methods, are helpful to study digital content creation and knowledge building in complex learning environments. Digital technologies and participatory media enhance the agency of learners and thus it is important that the design of educational software is based on pedagogical models that harness their strength.

References

Ainsworth, S., Clarke, D., & Gaizauskas, R. (2002). Using edit distance algorithms to compare alternative approaches to ITS authoring. In *Intelligent tutoring systems* (pp. 873–882). Retrieved February 19, 2009, from http://dx.doi.org/10.1007/3–540–47987–2_87.

Barab, S., & Squire, K. (2004). Design-based research: Putting a stake in the ground. *Journal of the Learning Sciences, 13*(1), 1–14.

Barron, B. J. S., Schwartz, D. L., Vye, N. J., Moore, A., Petrosino, A., Zech, L., et al. (1998). Doing with understanding: Lessons from research on problem- and project-based learning. *Journal of the Learning Sciences, 7*(3), 271–311.

Barthel, R., Sharples, M., & Ainsworth, S. (2009). Narrative creation from online video as knowledge representation. In V. Dimitrova, R.Mizoguchi, B. du Boulay, & A. Graesser (Eds.), *Artificial intelligencein education—Building learning systems that care: From knowledge representation to affective modeling* (Vol. 200, pp. 575–577). Amsterdam: IOS Press.

Benyon, D., Turner, P., & Turner, S. (2004). *Designing interactive systems: People, activities, contexts, technologies* (illustrated edition). Harlow: Addison Wesley.

Bereiter, C., & Scardamalia, M. (2003). Learning to work creatively with knowledge. In E. D. Corte, L. Verschaffel, N. Entwistle, & J. V. Merriënboer (Eds.), *Powerful learning environments: Unraveling basic components and dimensions* (pp. 55–68). Oxford: Pergamon.

Boland, R. J., & Tenkasi, R. V. (1995). Perspective making and perspective taking in communities of knowing. *Organization Science, 6*(4), 350–372.

Burden, K., & Kuechel, T. (2004). *Teaching and learning with digital video assets 2003–2004*. Becta Government & partners. Retrieved January 7, 2009, from http://partners.becta.org.uk/index.php?section=rh&&catcode=&rid=13994.

Burgess, J. (2006). Vernacular creativity, cultural participation and new media literacy: Photography and the Flickr network. Internet research 7.0: Internet convergences (AoIR), 2007, Brisbane.

(Unpublished)

Chambel, T., Zahn, C., & Finke, M. (2004). Hypervideo design and support for contextualized learning. In *Proceedings of the IEEE international conference on advanced learning technologies* (pp. 345–349). IEEE computer society. Retrieved September 11, 2008, from http://portal.acm.org/citation.cfm?id=1018423.1020010&coll=GUIDE&dl=GUIDE.

Dillenbourg, P. (1999). What do you mean by "collaborative learning"? In P. Dillenbourg (Ed.), *Collaborative-learning: Cognitive and computational approaches* (pp. 1–19). Oxford: Elsevier.

Florida, R. (2003). *The rise of the creative class: And how it's transforming work, leisure, community and everyday life* (New edition.). New York: Basic Books.

Gilbert, N. J., & Driscoll, M. P. (2002). Collaborative knowledge building: A case study. *Educational Technology Research and Development, 50*(1), 59–79.

Harrer, A., Hever, R., & Ziebarth, S. (2007). Empowering researchers to detect interaction patterns in e-collaboration. In R. Luckin, K. R. Koedinger, & J. E. Greer (Eds.), *Artificial intelligence in education: Building technology rich learning contexts that work* (pp. 503–510). Amsterdam: IOS Press.

Huynh, D., Karger, D., & Miller, R. (2007). Exhibit: Lightweight structured data publishing. In *Proceedings of the sixteenth international world wide web conference (WWW2007)* (pp. 737–746). Banff, Alberta, Canada.

Jenkins, H. (2006). *Convergence culture: Where old and new media collide.* New York: New York University Press.

Kearney, M., & Schuck, S. (2006). Spotlight on authentic learning: Student developed digital video projects. *Australasian Journal of Educational Technology, 22*(2), 189–208.

Leng, J., Mai, L., & Law, N. (2008). Characterizing patterns of interaction in knowledge building discourse. In *ICCE 2008: The 16th international conference on computers in education* (pp. 351–355). Taipei, Taiwan.

Levenshtein, V. I. (1966). Binary codes capable of correcting deletions, insertions, and reversals. *Soviet Physics Doklady,10,* 707–710.

Levin, H. (2003). Making history come alive: Students interview holocaust survivors on camera and publish their stories on the web. *Learning and Leading with Technology, 31*(3), 22–27.

Madden, M. (2007). *Online video.* Pew/Internet. Retrieved from http://www.pewInternet.org/PPF/r/219/report_display.asp.

Meeker, M. (2008). Technology/Internet Trends. *Morgan Stanley—Institutional Services.* Retrieved February 18, 2009, from http://www.morganstanley.com/institutional/techresearch/Internet_trends.html.

New Media Consortium. (2008). *The Horizon Report—2008.* Educause Learning Initiative. Retrieved from http://www.educause.edu/ir/library/pdf/CSD5320.pdf.

Nielsen, J. (1994). Heuristic evaluation. In J. Nielsen & R. L. Mack (Eds.), *Usability inspection methods* (pp. 25–62). New York: Wiley.

Prensky, M. (2009). H. Sapiens digital: From digital immigrants and digital natives to digital wisdom. *Innovate, 5*(3), 1–9.

Resnick, M. (2007a). All I really need to know (about creative thinking) I learned (by studying how children learn) in kindergarten. In *Proceedings of the 6th ACM SIGCHI conference on creativity & cognition* (pp. 1–6). Washington, DC, USA: ACM. doi: 10.1145/1254960.1254961.

Resnick, M. (2007b). Sowing the seeds for a more creative society. *Learning & Leading with Technology, 35*(4), 18–22.

Rheingold, H. (2007). Using participatory media and public voice to encourage civic engagement. *The John D. and Catherine T. MacArthur Foundation series on digital media and learning*, 97–118. doi: 10.1162/dmal.9780262524827.097.

Roschelle, J., & Teasley, S. D. (1995). The construction of shared knowledge in collaborative problem solving. In C. O'Malley (Ed.), *Computer-supported collaborative learning* (pp. 69–107). Berlin: Springer-Verlag.

Salomon, G. (1994). *Interaction of media, cognition, and learning: An exploration of how symbolic forms cultivate mental skills and affect knowledge acquisition* (1st ed.). Mahwah, NJ: Lawrence Erlbaum.

Sawyer, R. K. (2006). Educating for innovation. *Thinking Skills and Creativity, 1*(1), 41–48. doi: 10.1016/j.tsc.2005.08.001.

Scardamalia, M. (2002). Collective cognitive responsibility for the advancement of knowledge. In *Liberal education in a knowledge society* (pp. 67–98). Chicago: Open Court.

Scardamalia, M., & Bereiter, C. (1994). Computer support for knowledge-building communities. *Journal of the Learning Sciences, 3*(3), 265, 283.

Scardamalia, M., & Bereiter, C. (2006). Knowledge building: Theory, pedagogy, and technology. In K. Sawyer (Ed.), *Cambridge handbook of the learning sciences* (pp. 97–119). Cambridge, MA: Harvard University Press.

Schwartz, D., & Hartman, K. (2007). It's not video anymore: Designing digital video for learning and assessment. In R. Goldman, R. Pea, B. Barron, & S. J. Derry (Eds.), *Video research in the learning sciences* (pp. 335–348). Mahwah, NJ: Lawrence Erlbaum.

Stahl, G. (2000). A model of collaborative knowledge-building. In B. J. Fishman & O'Connor-Divelbiss, Samuel J. (Eds.), *Fourth international conference of the learning sciences* (pp. 70–77). Mahwah, NJ: Lawrence Erlbaum.

Zhao, X., Ninomiya, T., Anma, F., & Okamoto, T. (2008). Adaptive and personalized content architecture for mobile learning system. In *Proceedings of the 11th IASTED international conference computers and advanced technology in education (CATE 2008) (pp.26–31).* Crete, Greece.

12

Design Strategies for Developing Mobile Collaborative Learning Platforms

DANIEL SPIKOL

Mobile games to support learning have recently gained a lot of attention in the educational and learning technologies research communities (Klopfer, 2008). These types of mobile collaborative learning activities seem to provide benefits for the learners by giving them opportunities to discover, create, and develop new literacies by actively working with and collaborating through new technologies (Shaffer, 2008). Although participatory design practices and other design methods have been used extensively in educational research, the issues of designing learning activities to support collaboration across locations with mobile technologies raise new challenges.

Utilizing multiple methods to produce and obtain complementary insights during the design process can be a strategy for the creation of mobile learning activities and a tool to understand the different learning processes. This chapter will demonstrate how different methods used for the design and development of a mobile learning platform, *mLearn2go*, developed out of a series of informal mobile games called Treasure Hunt (*Skattjakt* in Swedish). These games offer new strategies and benefits with regard to the development and implementation of future learning activities. Three completed versions and an authoring platform are in the first stages of commercial development. Over the last two years at the Center for Learning and Knowledge Technologies (CeLeKT) at Växjö University in Sweden, more than 200 children, along with teachers and student teachers, have engaged in research practices with the platform. In addition, another 500 people have played the games outside of research activities. These learning activities and games have provided us with valuable results that help us to think about new ways in which mobile technologies can bridge learning in informal and formal settings. The active involvement of the teachers and the learners in the design process of these mobile games has given us new perspectives regarding strategies for developing new learning activities, and this, in turn, has led to the implementation of the authoring tool or learning platform.

Games in Education

Over the last several years the relevance of mobile-based educational games has been the focus of multiple projects in research and education, and for good reason. As Kirriemuir and McFarlane (2004) illustrate, computer games develop valuable skills that include strategic thinking, planning, communication, negotiation skills, and group decision-making. Meanwhile, others (Prensky, 2007; Gee, 2007; Squire & Jenkins, 2003; Shaffer, 2007; Klopfer, 2008) point out that computer games can provide excellent means of transferring knowledge, testing hypotheses, and understanding complex systems. Computer games have become an important part of the learning ecologies for school and training. The main aim of this chapter is to reflect on these developments through a closer inspection of different design strategies employed over the last three years of work at CeLeKT to develop the *mLearn2go* platform. Such inspection, it is hoped, will help to identify, in more general terms, key design strategies for mobile collaborative learning.

mLearn2Go: a Mobile Learning Platform

The motivation for this project was the mobile game Treasure Hunt initially conceived and developed to encourage young people to get physically active by solving a mystery surrounding a castle located on the university's campus. The game has been inspired by the ideas behind treasure hunt activities and the sport of orienteering, a traditional Scandinavian running sport involving navigation with a map and a compass. The Treasure Hunt games promote physical activity and collaborative problem solving through the combination of practicing orienteering using mobile technologies. The game explores informal skills in map reading and learning across different domains and requires different degrees of collaboration between team members to solve the mystery. Multiple teams can compete simultaneously using mobile phones, as they progress through the playing field with detours for wrong answers. Generally, a strong narrative drives the players to solve a mystery with the playing field spread across relevant locations. The mobile game application provides an interactive map with the different locations marked in such a way that the players can zoom and pan to see the entire playing area. Pre-activities include a video presentation that sets the story for the game and a brief hands-on demo of the mobile client. Post-activities allow visualization of teams' different routes, results, and other player-created content presented in reflective spaces (for a technical description, see Spikol et al., 2008). Figure 1 depicts two of the game screens on the mobile device, players at a control marker working with the phone, the playing field map and detours, and the general game flow.

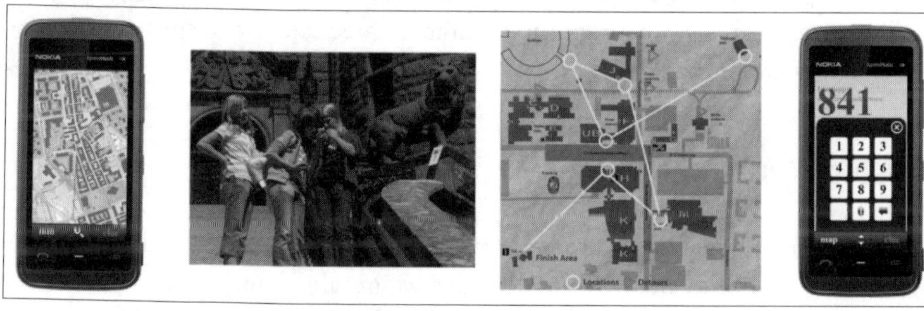

Figure 1: Treasure Hunt *Game*

Over the last two years, many students have played different versions of the Treasure Hunt game and students and teachers have designed and implemented their own games and learning activities (see Spikol et al., 2008). The need to develop a fully fledged authoring platform to enable large-scale use has been warranted and now we are in the process of releasing the first version. The objective of the platform is to create a user-friendly authoring tool for location-based educational activities with mobile devices. The *mLearn2go* platform supports multiple tasks per area and works with a simple numeric code input to allow a broad range of mobile phones. In addition, the platform is open for 2D barcodes and GPS sensors to be used for different learning scenarios. The learning platform is web-based and allows teachers and learners to quickly create activities using a library of activities from which to start. The platform allows a post-activity review that details the learner's routes and can include geo-tagged photographs, video, and other data on the a generated web-based map. The design of the *mLearn2go* platform is modular based and is open for new features to be easily incorporated from ongoing research efforts.

Similar Mobile Learning Platform Tools

Recent literature reviews of mobile technologies and learning generally break down mobile learning efforts into theory-based categories of activities (Naismith et al., 2004; Frohberg et al., 2009). Additionally, frameworks used for evaluation have explored best practices for implementing games and simulations in formal learning (Freitas & Oliver, 2006). Alternatively, a simple taxonomy can be generated that categorizes different games from a goal-based perspective that can supplement the above frameworks by identifying what special features make the learning activity specifically mobile. To present learning activities and authoring environments similar to *mLearn2Go*, we can group them into three categories: epistemic, kinesthetic, and location-based games.

Epistemic Games

Epistemic games are designed to help students think like professionals using real-world scenarios. Students become detectives, journalists, and scientists and play other roles to investigate and solve problems, applying abstract formal knowledge to these concrete problems. What makes epistemic games different from regular computer games are the clear educational goals (Shaffer, 2008).

Environmental Detectives is an early mobile game that uses personal digital assistants (PDAs). The game engages high-school and university students in a real-world environmental consulting scenario constructed to immerse players in the practices of environmental engineers, giving them a "virtual practicum" experience similar to working on an environmental research team. The main focus of the game is on planning an effective investigation that balances quantitative and qualitative data (Klopfer, 2008).

Frequency 1550 is a historical game in which groups of students compete, acting as pilgrims in old Amsterdam while trying to find a holy relic. The players communicate via videophones and use a GPS-equipped mobile phone for the game and position tracking, while members at headquarters have a laptop connected to the Internet. Recently, Frequency 1550 was tested with 250 students in a more controlled experiment where the students were divided into groups to explore how collaboration and narrative influenced learning in this mobile game (Raessens, 2007).

Physical-Kinesthetic

The physical-kinesthetic games as defined by Rogers et al. (2004) bring "physicality" into "brains-on" learning inspired by experiential learning. In this type of game, physical engagement and activity are combined with learning.

The Ambient Wood project is designed to enable children to switch between the experiences of the physical world (for example, observing a butterfly drinking nectar from a thistle) and to reflect upon the ecological processes behind this interdependency (for example, pollination). The learning experience is designed to encourage children to explore and hypothesize about different habitats found in a forest through the use of pervasive and mobile devices placed outdoors. Mobile devices and visualization tools were provided for the children to access and share contextually relevant digital information (for example, the animation of seasonal changes) when exploring the forest (Price et al., 2003).

Another example is the Savannah project, a mobile game that recreates the African savannah outside on local school grounds. The game consists of two related areas of activity. In the first, children are able to play at "being a pride of lions" outside in a playing field (100 m x 50 m), interacting with a virtual savannah and exploring the opportunities and risks to lions in that space. Children are given global positioning system (GPS) devices linked to PDAs through which they "see," "hear," and "smell" the world of the savannah as they navigate the real space outdoors. The second playing field, the "Den," is an indoor space where children can reflect on how well they have succeeded in the game, access other resources to support their understanding, and develop strategies for surviving as lions in the virtual savannah (Facer et al., 2004).

Location

Location-based games rely on situated learning, which is a general theory of knowledge acquisition based on the notion that learning (stable, persisting changes in knowledge, skills, and behavior) occurs in the context of authentic activities (Lave & Wenger, 1991).

The COLLAGE (Collaborative Learning Platform Using Game-Like Enhancements) project brings to secondary-school students and their teachers a mobile learning platform for context-dependent and location-based games. The COLLAGE platform supports the authoring and playing of a board-like game on the location of educationally interesting sites. The game is played with the aid of mobile learning technology (mainly mobile phones, PDAs, and GPS technology) that relies on direct communication with the players situated on site. COLLAGE's learning experiences are designed to support the curriculum together with an implementation guide and web-based interface for creating and designing the game (Sotiriou & Chryssafidou, 2006).

The Mobile Informal Learning Kit (MiLK) is a support tool that allows teachers and students to develop location-based activities around event paths. These paths consist of a series of SMS messages and answers that lead players through checkpoints. These paths can be designed to suit desired learning scenarios. MiLK consists of a web-based authoring tool and post-activity reflective space for students. The game runs on any mobile phone, and geo-tagged photographs can be integrated into the post-activities, which include an extensive forum for students to discuss the activities (Polson & Morgan, 2008).

How mLearn2Go Differs

The examples described above show promising results regarding the use of mobile games in educational settings. In can be easily pointed out that all the efforts mentioned have varying degrees of epistemology and physicality and a reliance on location. COLLAGE and MiLK include accessible authoring platforms; teacher- and student-created materials open up the opportunity for different learning approaches to be used. The multiple method approach we used for Treasure Hunt, combined with an active participation of the children in the different phases of the design process, offered us advantages over these games by providing us with new insights through working with the different stakeholders. This design process has had direct involvement of the different users, providing easier ways to promote innovative educational practices through informal channels in formal education. By working with the players and involving them in the creation of new game concepts based on Treasure Hunt, our aim has been to gather new knowledge related to the requirements and design of new mobile learning tools that can engage students while providing insights into the design challenges of mobile-based learning.

Design Issues

Design is a complex activity that calls for a challenging discipline of design thinking. Winograd (2006) emphasizes the importance of the dual roles of designers, as they work with the hardware and software to create artifacts with desired behavior and appropriate use of resources. In addition, the designer needs to take seri ously the perspective of the people who will live with and alongside the system, with a primary concern for their intentions, actions, and experiences. In educational practice, different methods have been used to address the needs of learning. For the development of *mLearn2go*, we have worked with multiple design practices concerned with questions of both research and practice.

The multiple role of design leaves us in something of a dilemma with regard to generating new theories and at the same time creating new artifacts such as the learning systems. This is not a new problem for human-computer interaction. Fallman (2003) elegantly points out the difference between "design-oriented research" and "research-oriented design," a difference that defines this dichotomy. For design-oriented research aims to have truth or knowledge as its main contribution that would not have been attainable without design bringing about the research prototype. The settings and the studying of the designed artifact in use result in a scientific contribution. Conversely, research-oriented design is concerned with the production of new artifacts, and the production of these artifacts is the main motivation, not the acquisition of new knowledge. In practice, this design dilemma can be used iteratively to go back and forth between theoretical investigations and artifact creation. The shifting back and forth can be analogous to "Interaction Design," which is defined as the process of designing interactive products to support the way people communicate and interact in their everyday and working lives (Sharp et al., 2007). The process of interaction design is based on the user's experience of the product in the context for which it was designed.

A theory of practice used for design-oriented research has been labeled "design-based research" (DBR). One of the primary aims of design-based research is to develop domain-specific theories in order to understand the learning process (Mor & Winters, 2007). The Design Based Research Collective group (2004) argues that design-based research blends empirical education research with the theory-driven design of learning environments. This can be an important methodology for understanding how, when, and why educational innovations work in practice. It is a suitable methodological approach for the field of mobile learning, since DBR attempts to combine the intentional design of interactive learning environments with the empirical exploration of our understanding of these environments and how they interact with the individuals (Hoadley, 2004). Design-based research follows an iterative cycle of identifying, developing, building, and evaluating similar to interaction design and introduces theory building and expansion into the cycles. These iterative and human-focused design processes form a key to understanding how to promote collaborative learning with technologies. DBR deals with the consequences of action by involving the researcher in the iterative process of design.

DBR additionally deals with real-world problems in their settings and is pluralistic in its approach.

Additionally, a technique that helps with these design challenges is to actively involve and work directly with the stakeholders throughout the design process. Co-design is one such method and can be defined as a highly facilitated, team-based process in which teachers, researchers, and developers work together in defined roles to design an educational innovation (Penuel et al., 2007). The benefits of co-design arise from direct involvement of stakeholders, which helps to ensure that the concerns and values of the users are kept in focus. The team realizes the design in one or more prototypes and evaluates the significance of each prototype for addressing an educational need. The co-design process relies on a teacher's ongoing involvement with the design of educational innovations, which typically employ technology as a central support for learning and inquiry practices. Penuel and colleagues (2007) point out some of the challenges in co-design that result in a tension between stakeholders in workplace norms and practice combined with the time-intensive processes required.

A solution for this project that helped to resolve some of these challenges and tensions between different team members was to look more closely at the start of the design process, when brainstorming techniques can be used to build a common ground for the initial concepts. In developing *mLearn2Go*, brainstorming was introduced as an associative technique helping a group of people to quickly generate and organize a large number of ideas starting from a given question or problem (Löwgren & Stolterman, 2005; see also the chapter by Löwgren in this volume). In addition, future technology workshops (FTW) were conducted primarily with different groups of students. FTW is a method whereby people with everyday knowledge envision and design the interactions between current and future technology through a series of structured workshops (Vavoula & Sharples, 2007).

mLearn2Go Description

The initial pilot was developed in the winter of 2007 together with a special project group from the local orienteering clubs. Working by utilizing co-design methods together with an undergraduate class in mobile games, we developed the initial game concept. Through a process of paper prototype testing, the game flow was developed that used four-digit codes and detours as mechanisms for the game flow. The campus of the university became the playing field of the initial version, with the narrative centered on a nineteenth century castle and the story of its residents: the former countess returns as a ghost and enlists player help to solve a mystery about her husband the count and the first bishop of the county.

The initial pilot was conducted in February 2007 with 12 players aged 12–16 recruited from an after-school program and local youth-orienteering clubs. From the success of the initial prototype, based on surveys collected from players and stakeholders, we recruited girls aged 13–15 to play the game during a week-long summer program. From the pool of 26 players, we selected 10 of the older students for a two-day workshop where they brainstormed, used FTWs, and developed two future game concepts. Through this summer school program, the research team was invited to co-run an elective course in a local school that initiated Version 2 of the game. Figure 2 depicts the brainstorming and the workshop conducted with the summer school students. In the FTW, we used custom whiteboard magnets that helped the students envision possible game flows with the help of props and markers.

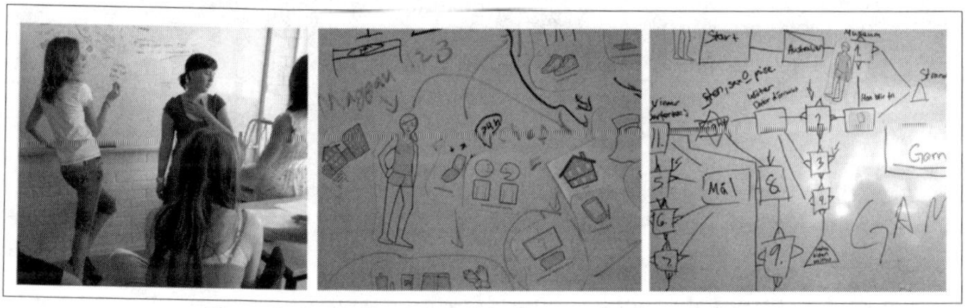

Figure 2: Brainstorming and the future technology workshop

In addition, this version of the game was played by six local middle schools (103 children) over the year, three groups of student teachers (N = 18), and regular teachers (N = 23) as part of the teaching program at the university, and by the public at an open house at the university.

Treasure Hunt 2.0

After the success of the two pilots, one of the teachers from the summer school initiated an elective course in her local middle school for the fall of 2007 and winter of 2008. Eleven students participated in a semester-long course together with the teacher and the research team. Through the design process inspired by co-design and other participatory methods that empower students to design their own learning materials, a new story and playing field were developed along with some new game features. For the new story, the team placed more focus on environment, and the narrative featured aliens who came to earth long ago and placed hidden heat transmitters around the local city; these heat transmitters contributed to global warming. The players had to discover the locations of these transmitters and solve mathematical puzzles related to the environment. In addition, we developed power-ups that enabled teams to shield themselves from other team attacks—attacks that would automatically send the opposing team on a detour. The concepts of shields and bombs were developed with a paper board game prototype and worked extremely well when we were playing the game around the board. Figure 3 shows the paper prototype as a board game, the new students playing the game, and the post-activity workshop.

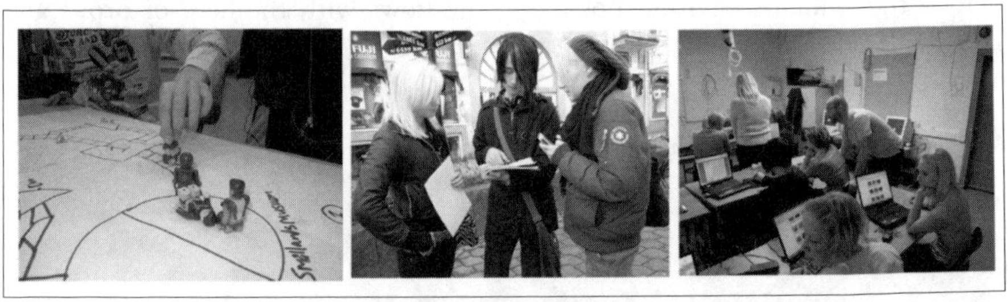

Figure 3: From board game to the game followed by the post-game activity.

Fifteen students from another local middle school were recruited to play the game. Outside, the bombs and shields had little value since the teams were spread out over the center of the town. Players were also equipped with an additional mobile phone, and to solve each task, they needed to photograph different subjects related to the environment. At the end of the game the students came together to review the photographs, which were automatically geo-tagged and displayed on video-projected web-based map, enabling the students to reflect and discuss the game and choose the best photographs.

Treasure Hunt 3.0

The 11 students from the second local school that played the second version of the game with their teacher made a new version of the game to be played in June of 2008 as part of the end-of-school-year field trips for the younger students. In this version, the students and teacher became the drivers of the design process. Together, they developed a game concept based on the popular board game Cluedo, where the players had to complete an informal task such as going through an obstacle course carrying a water glass, sort the recyclables correctly, and sing karaoke—all while being judged by other students. In addition, each team of players was split into two, and each subgroup collected up to three clues based on their performance of these tasks. Then they had to put together their clue sheets to solve the mystery. Twenty-four students played this version of the game. Figure 4 shows the teacher and the students fine-tuning the game and setting up the phones. The middle image illustrates a station the players had to complete to get clues. In this case, the players needed to sort the recyclables correctly. The right-hand image shows team members from the sub-groups comparing notes in order to make deductions for solving the murder mystery.

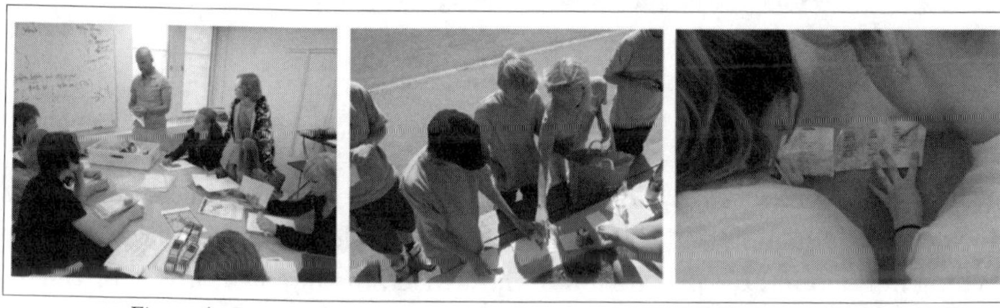

Figure 4: Game making, game playing, and group work to figure out the clues.

mLearn2Go 1.0

During the spring of 2008, the initial specifications of the authoring tool for the platform were developed. Using co-design in the traditional sense, we recruited teachers from the different trials, and over seven sessions we developed needs and goal specification, first through interviews, and then a paper prototype, followed by a screen-based prototype (Johansson & Winter, 2008). This design process resulted in the basic starting point to develop the *mLearn2Go* platform. From this initial work, combined with the experience of the three game versions, we began the design and development of the platform. Figure 5 illustrates the sketching to the product view of the web-based application.

What is clear when we reflect on these four iterations is that the focus of the design has shifted between design-oriented research and research-oriented design in each successive version. Design-based research (DBR) can be seen to be ambitious in its attempt to generate theory and provide practical innovation for education through the creation of new innovations for use in schools. This shift between worldviews can be seen as a main argument for the validity of this type of design research.

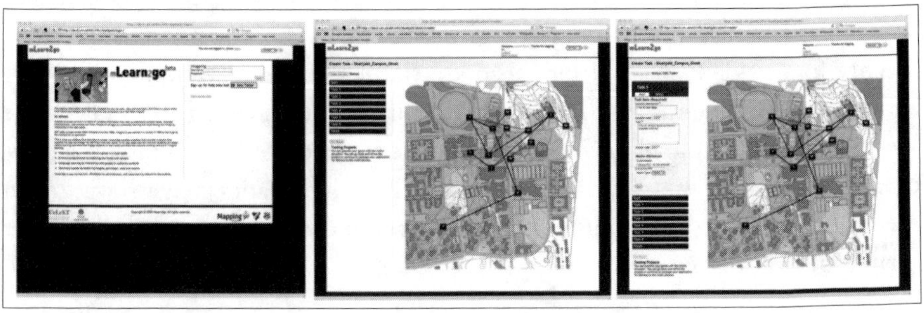

Figure 5: Authoring tool for mLearn2go *from sketch to product.*

Design Outcomes

In each of the project's iterations the focus has shifted between generating new knowledge about mobility, collaboration, and to a lesser extent learning while keeping in the mind the production of the artifact, the mobile learning platform. In version 1.0 of Treasure Hunt, participatory design drove the initial effort where researchers, programmers, and the stakeholders, the orienteering club, worked together to develop and test the game. This was done in conjunction with a university course on mobile gaming where the students worked with the team to further develop the game. Once the game was complete, we tested it on the after-school children. We surveyed and interviewed the players and the stakeholders and documented the game play with photography and video. When the summer school played the game and then worked with the game concept in a series of brainstorms and FTWs, insight was gathered about how the game could be used in different contexts between informal and formal learning, in addition to being a tool to teach students about game making. Based on the interviews from the summer school, designers reported the students enjoying the challenge of inventing the stories and the game tasks as described below: "Both making up a story and coming up with tasks for the players was fun, especially the combination. It would be great to see something similar in school."

In Version 2.0 of the game, we continued working with students and expanded the co-design practice to include learners in the process since, generally, the students are not represented in co design; although learner-centered design has strong similarities the goals can be different, with co-design concentrating on innovation while learner-centered design focuses on the learner's experience. In addition to brainstorming sessions and workshops, we developed a paper prototype in the form of a board game to test the game flow, the puzzles, and the new game features mentioned in the last section. Again we documented the process through interviews, surveys, photography, and video. Due to the challenge of developing and implementing the game without a proper authoring platform, a student designer expressed his frustration and satisfaction like this:

> The game turned out better than my hope because we had low expectations of what the game would be like when the other students played it. But once we saw the other students playing the game we were amazed.

The teacher and the students conceptually developed Version 3.0 of the game with support from the research team. Here, we supported the teacher with expertise in game design and more theoretical concepts of scaffolding. Our goal with this version was to enable the teacher and the students to work with the game concept without major intervention, enabling us to see how the game concept would develop. Post-game interviews were conducted with the students, designers, players, and teachers. From these interviews a student designer commented:

> We have thought up many ideas and I think I had the idea of having a murder story theme. It was exciting, making and seeing the students play the game and seeing that it actually worked, fitted together, and had everything we talked about.

For the design session with the teachers that set initial requirements for the *mLearn2go* platform, it was clear the teachers required a broader tool than that used for treasure hunts or mobile orienteering. They expressed the need for different types of tasks and inputs for answers. In addition, the teachers expressed the desire for inclusion of sensor data for environmental studies with media support from video, audio, and detailed text. One teacher summarized:

> What I think would be a fun idea is kind of like a treasure hunt that doesn't need to be one question on top of another. You come to an area and you do something, find out something that is required in order for you to even get to the next area. Exactly how it's supposed to be done I don't know, but I think this would be the most exciting, that there is some type of clue that leads you forward.

When we conducted the summer school session, we explored how the game could be used in the classroom as part of broader learning goals across subjects, from game design to history, math, and science. In Version 2.0, the pilot game became part of a semester-long elective class on game design. The students used their initial experience with the first game to develop a new game while learning about game design and integrating environmental awareness. For the Version 3.0, the students played the new game (Version 2.0) and participated in the reflection space with the geo-tagged photographs. From this experience, with the guidance of their teacher, they developed the third version. Expanding the concept to include other activities of which the game was part drove the overall experience of this version. The iterative process of co-designing with the teachers used for Version 4.0 has defined the current effort to develop the authoring tool, and the input cycle continues.

Discussion

The main aim of this chapter has been to reflect on the different design strategies used to develop the *mLearn2go* platform and to see what factors can be identified for designing more effective mobile collaborative learning systems. Fischer and Ostwald (2005) divide the design process into three categories: professional design, participatory design, and meta-design. In professionally dominated design, users have no input into or control over the artifact. Participatory design offers the users input during the design process, but once the artifact is in use it is difficult to fit it to new needs. Meta-design provides the users with active participation in the design phase, and during the use time they can continue to evolve the artifact to different uses. Meta-design describes how the role of users needs to shift to one of designer partners and how they become creators of their knowledge (Fischer & Ostwald, 2005). Therefore, by letting the users become key participants in the design process throughout the lifecycle of the product, they become engaged in the creation of knowledge rather than restricted to instruction or consumption of existing knowledge.

Frohberg and colleagues (2009) point out that the field of mobile learning has little consensus about terms and that research and practice suffer from this. In order to critically appraise mobile learning projects until 2007, they adapted a set of criteria based on the Mobile Learning Analysis from Sharples and Taylor (Taylor et al., 2006; Sharples et al., 2007). In this framework, context, tools, control, communication, subjects, and objectives are the categories used for analysis of mobile learning projects. Although these categories work well for the critical framework and at times for the socio-cognitive engineering design method that Sharples and colleagues (2002) have developed, in practice different factors need to be considered to achieve a sufficient level in the project size in order to utilize these approaches.

From our point of departure we will be inspired by the model of experiential learning that is generally comprised of the following four elements (Kolb, 1984):

- Action creates the experience
- Reflection on the action or experience
- Abstraction drawn from the reflection
- Application of the abstraction to a new experience or action

The application of putting learning theories into practice has proven to be a difficult hurdle in computer-supported collaborative learning (Stahl et al., 2006). One way to help solve this dilemma is to take the idea of user-driven meta-design and with the inspiration of experiential learning to create factors that can be applied to the design process and the learning goals. Egenfeldt-Nielsen (2007) makes a case for how computer games can be used successfully for education by expanding the model of experiential learning. From this theory and praxis combination, a set of factors to help design mobile collaborative learning systems can be evolved. Egenfeldt-Nielsen suggests that the concepts of action, creation, reflection, and sharing should be used as key guidelines in the initial design.

Action

Action is the first factor identified. Action is illustrated in *mLearn2Go* with the use of situated learning by placing the users in the field to perform tasks related to the environment and the learning domain. Action enables learners to explore the physical world outside and inside across the learning environments. Physical action can be used to visualize data in the real world, providing means for bringing information into the classroom from the outside or sending it back out into the world. These actions help to enable technology-enhanced collaboration that provides the means for learners to experience learning in and across different physical settings. Without being tethered to the computer in the classroom, students can be mobile, taking the tools with them as they explore, while supporting collaboration across different places. At the same time they can bring back material to be used and evolved in the classroom. Learning can be described in the mobile context as flowing across locations, times, topics, and technologies (Sharples et al., 2008).

Creation

Creation is important because it enables the learners to produce artifacts but also to own them for future use. This empowers the learners to become active in the construction of artifacts. These activities provide opportunities for tangible and valuable "meanings" happening in the learning process. Mobile technologies provide a rich toolset for this creative endeavor, enabling collaborative work between different locations. Photographs, video, audio, text, location, and additional data from geo-tagging photographs are just some of the tools presented in my work; tools that mobile and pervasive technologies have supplied. With mobile devices, the artifacts created can be collected, organized, and shared on another scale with technology. Providing tools for creation is a factor that needs to be considered in promoting and developing playful learning. Fischer and Ostwald's meta-design concept (2005) empowers learners to construct personal meaning from the design process, and artifacts lead us to the second factor, creation. In the later versions of Treasure Hunt the students used the game as a basis to first create new game concepts that were play-tested with paper prototypes and with board games. In the latest version, the students created new games that other students played.

Sharing

The creation of artifacts and physical action in the world may not be enough to support collaborative learning. Sharing enables these constructs by letting students work together on a peer-to-peer basis or with the involvement of a more capable mentor who guides the learning. Learning can be seen as enculturation, the process by which learners become collaborative meaning-makers among a group defined by common practices, language, use of tools, values, beliefs, and other norms (Hoppe et al., 2005). In *mLearn2go* projects, students and teachers shared experiences of past games when they developed the successive versions of their games. The students worked in small teams together and at times with the guidance of teachers and researchers. Collaborative knowledge building requires reflection to construct the mental meanings needed for collaborative knowledge gain.

Reflection

Reflection together with other learners as facilitated by educators provides an important factor for design that has been overlooked in mobile learning. Through the introduction to the later versions of *mLearn2go*, the design workshops, and then game-making courses, the students and the teachers began to reflect on the use of mobile learning as they designed new mobile activities. Reflection is a key part of many learning approaches, especially in computer-supported collaborative learning. Reflection allows the students to generate their own solution paths as well as helping to make them into conscious and creative members of the problem-solving community (Brown et al., 1989). In *mlearn2go*, the students generally reflect about the game in order to design the new games.

Table 1: Meta-Design Framework in Relation to mLearn2go

Project	Professional Design	Participatory Design	Meta-Design
SKATTJAKT 1.0	Designed by research team.	Stakeholders part of the design team	Players had little control of created artifacts
SKATTJAKT 2.0	Research team still controls the technology	Introduction of co-design with students and teachers	Co-creation of new activity / game played by other students
SKATTJAKT 3.0	Research team implements the game based on the students and teacher's design	Students and teacher drive the game design with input from research	Students and teachers own the concept and expand the concept
mlearn2go 1.0	Research team again drives the design	Participation is based on the input of the previous 3 iterations	Project goals need to allow for meta-design.

In Conclusion

The *mLearn2go* platform and its activities as described in this chapter suggest that meaningful learning supported by mobile and ubiquitous technologies has additional design challenges that need some initial factors to be considered before larger frameworks can be used for design and analysis.

These new challenges require different design strategies. Table 1 presents a brief overview of the *mLearn2go* platform across Fischer and Ostwald's design framework (2003).

What the overview presents is a flow between professional, participatory, and meta-design. Verganti (2006) argues that users alone will never drive innovation; rather, as a result of the collaboration and clusters of creativity, users become key ingredients in the process. While DBR strives towards the innovative educational product or process, we arrive back at the design dilemma of conducting research and designing innovation, which leaves us with a solution of iterations such as interaction design that enables us to both design and research (Sharp et al., 2007). This further leaves us with a set of initial factors of *action*, *creation*, *sharing*, and *reflection* for the design of collaborative mobile systems to support educational activities. Bollen and colleagues (2008) clearly illustrate the benefit of orchestrating learning environments with personalized devices and shared public interactive displays to overcome fragmented communication. Amiel and Reeves (2008) note that researchers need to look beyond the short-term objectives of their individual projects and technology goals and to contemplate educational ends or aims, making these explicit in the process of investigation. The challenge is to recognize that research and practice are intertwined and each carries values that must be recognized and integrated. Design-based research can provide a research cycle that promotes this reflection and a long-term foundation to investigate technological processes in education and its relationships with larger society.

Acknowledgements

This work has been partially supported by the Swedish Knowledge Foundation and Växjö University under the ICT and Teacher Training program, project Young Communication. Additional funding has been provided by the Internet Infrastructure Foundation of Sweden, project MeMiMo. In-kind support was received from Mapping Växjö, NätverketSIP, Norregaard School, and Kronoberg School. Special thanks are owed to all the players and game makers and to the research support of Sadaf Salavati and David Johansson at CeLeKT.

References

Amiel, T. & Reeves, T. C. (2008). Design-based research and educational technology: Rethinking technology and the research agenda. *Journal of Educational Technology & Society, 11*(4), 29–40.

Bollen, L., Giemza, A., & Hoppe, H. (2008). Flexible analysis of user actions in heterogeneous distributed learning environments. *Times of convergence. Technologies across learning contexts* (pp. 62–73).

Brown, J. S., Collins, A., & Duguid, P. (1989). Situated cognition and the culture of learning. *Educational Researcher, 18*(1), 32–42.

Design-Based Research Collective (2004). Design-based research: An emerging paradigm for educational inquiry. *Educational Researcher, 32*(1), 5–8.

Egenfeldt-Nielsen, S. (2007). *Educational potential of computer games*. London: Continuum.

Facer, K., Joiner, R., Stanton, D., Reid, J., Hull, R., & Kirk, D. (2004). Savannah: mobile gaming and learning? *Journal of Computer Assisted Learning, 20*(6), 399–409.

Fallman, D. (2003). *Design-oriented human-computer interaction*. Paper presented at the Proceedings of the SIGCHI Conference on Human Factors in Computing Systems.

Fischer, G., & Ostwald, J. (2005). Knowledge Communication in Design Communities. *Barriers and biases in computer-mediated knowledge communication* (pp. 213–242).

Freitas, S. d., & Oliver, M. (2006). How can exploratory learning with games and simulations within the curriculum be most effectively evaluated? in *Comput. Educ.*, 46(3), 249–264.

Frohberg, D., Göth, C., & Schwabe, G. (2009). Mobile learning projects; a critical analysis of the state of the art. *Journal of Computer Assisted Learning, 25*(4), 307–331.

Gee, J. P. (2007). *What video games have to teach us about learning and literacy* (Rev. and updated ed.). New York: Palgrave Macmillan.

Hoadley, C. M. (2004). Methodological alignment in design-based research. *Educational Psychologist, 39*(4), 203–212.

Hoppe, H. U., Pinkwart, N., Oelinger, M., Zeini, S., Verdejo, F., Barros, B., et al. (2005). *Building bridges within learning communities through ontologies and thematic objects.* Paper presented at the International Conference on Computer Supported Collaborative Learning (CSCL2005), Taipai, Taiwain.

Johansson, D., & Winter, S. (2008). *Designing authoring tools for m-learning geo-games*. Paper presented at the DREAM Conference.

Kirriemuir, J., & McFarlane, A. (2004). *Literature review in games and learning*: A NESTA Futurelab Research report, Report 8.

Klopfer, E. (2008). *Augmented learning: research and design of mobile educational games*. Cambridge, MA: MIT Press.

Kolb, D. A. (1984). *Experiential learning: Experience as the source of learning and development.* Englewood Cliffs, N.J.: Prentice-Hall.

Lave J., & Wenger E. (1991). *Situated learning: Legitimate peripheral participation*. New York: Cambridge University Press.

Löwgren, J., & Stolterman, E. (2005). *Thoughtful interaction design : a design perspective on information technology*. Cambridge, Mass.: MIT Press.

Mor, Y., & Winters, N. (2006). Design approaches in technology enhanced learning. *Interactive Learning Environments 15*(1), 61–75.

Naismith, L., Lonsdale, P., & Vavoula, G. (2004). *Literature review in mobile technologies and learning*. Bristol, UK: FutureLab Report.

Penuel, W. R., Roschelle, J., & Shechtman, N. (2007). Designing formative assessment software with teachers: An analysis of the co-design process. *Research and Practice in Technology Enhanced Learning, 2*(2), 51–74.

Polson, D., & Morgan, C. (2008, October 7–10). *MiLK: The Mobile Informal Learning Kit.*

Collaborating to design successful mobile learning applications. Paper presented at MLearn 2008, Ironbridge, UK.

Prensky, M. (2007). *Digital game-based learning* (Paragon House ed.). St. Paul, MN: Paragon House.

Price, S., & Rogers, Y. (2004). Let's get physical: The learning benefits of interacting in digitally augmented physical spaces. *Computers & Education, 43*(1–2), 137–151.

Price, S., Rogers, Y., Stanton, D., & Smith, H (2003). *A new conceptual framework for CSCL: Supporting diverse forms of reflection through multiple interactions.* Paper presented at the the International Conference on CSCL'03, Bergen, Norway.

Raessens, J. (2007). Playing history. Reflections on mobile and location-based learning. Unpublished journal article. Waxmann Verlag.

Rogers, Y., Price, S., Fitzpatrick, G., Fleck, R., Harris, E., Smith, H., et al. (2004). *Ambient wood: Designing new forms of digital augmentation for learning outdoors.* Paper presented at the Proceedings of the 2004 Conference on Interaction Design and Children: Building a Community.

Shaffer, D. W. (2007). *How computer games help children learn.* New York: Palgrave Macmillan.

Sharp, H., Rogers, Y., & Preece, J. (2007). *Interaction design: Beyond human-computer interaction* (2nd ed.). Hoboken, N.J.: Wiley.

Sharples, M., Jeffery, N., & Du Boulay, J. (2002). Socio-cognitive engineering: a methodology for the design of human-centred technology. *European Journal of Operational Research, 136*(2), 310–323.

Sharples, M., Jeffery, N., du Boulay, J. B. H., Teather, D., Teather, B., & du Boulay, G. H. (2002). Socio-cognitive engineering: A methodology for the design of human-centred technology. *European Journal of Operational Research, 136*(2), 310–323.

Sharples, M., Milrad, M., Arnedillo Sánchez, I., & Vavoula, G. (2008). Mobile learning: Small devices, big issues. *Technology enhanced learning: Principles and products, kaleidoscope legacy book.* Berlin: Springer-Verlag,.

Sharples, M., Taylor, J., & Vavoula, G. (2007). A theory of learning for the mobile age. In R. Andrews & C. Haythornthwaite (Eds.), *The Sage handbook of e-learning research* (pp. 221–247). London: Sage.

Sotiriou, S., & Chryssafidou, E. (2006). *Collage implementation guide* (Implementation Guide No. 960–6701–28-X). Pallini Attikis, Greece: Ellinogermaniki Agogi.

Spikol, D., Kurti, A., & Milrad, M. (2008). Collaboration in Context as a Framework for Designing Innovative Mobile Learning Activities. In H. Ryu & D. Parsons (Eds.), *Innovative mobile Learning: Techniques and technologies.* Hershey, Pennsylvania: IDEA GROUP INC.

Squire, K., & Jenkins, H. (2003). Harnessing the power of games in education. *Insight, 3*(1), 5.

Stahl, G., Koschmann, T., & Suthers, D. (2006). Computer-supported collaborative learning: An historical perspective. In R. K. Sawyer (Ed.), *The Cambridge handbook of the learning sciences.* Cambridge, MA: Cambridge University Press.

Taylor, J., Sharples, M., O'Malley, C., Vavoula, G., & Waycott, J. (2006). Towards a task model for mobile learning a dialectical approach. *International Journal of Learning Technology, 2*(2–3), 138–158.

Vavoula, G., & Sharples, M. (2007). Future technology workshop: A collaborative method for the design of new learning technologies and activities. *International Journal of Computer-Supported*

Collaborative Learning, 2(4), 393–419.

Verganti, R. (2006). Innovating through design. *Harvard Business Review, 48*(12), 114–122.

Winograd, T. (2006/05). Designing a new foundation for design. *Communications of the ACM, 49*(5), 71–73.302.

13

Digitally Mapping a Rhizome

Making Sense of Digital Content Creation Processes

MIKAEL KIVELÄ & JARKKO MYLLÄRI

"Well, we think that time 'passes,' flows past us; but what if it is we who move forward, from past to future, always discovering the new? It would be a little like reading a book, you see. The book is all there, all at once, between its covers."

Ursula LeGuin, The Dispossessed (1974/2002, p. 184)

This chapter presents an approach for working with multi-modal data to analyze digital content production as a process involving learning and innovation. We begin by outlining our approach's conceptual framework and describing our data with the aid of these concepts. Next, we provide concrete examples from our research to illustrate the theoretical and technical means at work. Finally, we discuss the possibilities and pitfalls of our approach to make data-supported claims, through and despite the data's transformations throughout the research process. We argue that digitality helps us benefit from complex and seemingly overwhelming amounts of data in various forms, such as video and audio recordings, still images, and text.

Despite focusing on research methodology, we touch upon general issues of understanding digital content creation, which seems to thrive on recycling and repurposing material, which is more or less intentionally shared online. In our experience, the creation, sharing, and use of user-generated content seems to be often familiar and pleasurable to primary- and secondary-school students as well as some researchers. The operations students apply go far beyond assembling web content into formal-task-driven collections of hyperlinks or copy-and-pasted texts and images. Taking into account the processes of creation and embedding, downloading and uploading, the manipulated diversity of digital materials reveals how the students shape the actual context these operations take place in and develop. To outline future pedagogies, the perspective must be broad enough to cover the methods of finding, shaping, and sharing content. There must be room for an expanding number of trajectories of studying with varying constituent parts and consistency. Concluding the chapter and underpinning the following dissections, it cannot be emphasized enough how our school approach benefits from the notion of studying as content creation. We hope the reader will contemplate how this notion's inherent convergence of materials, operations, and technical means are realized in schooling or in research.

The examples presented are from a case study aiming to discover when and in what way primary-school students use ICT skills learned outside the classroom for taking on in-school tasks. We primarily studied this deployment of skills as spatially and socially distributed activity in a longer sequential structure to find out what enabled them and how they influenced the following activities The goal was to find elements and patterns enabling or supporting such initiatives that we could then use to provide teachers with ideas and methods for tapping these resources in school tasks. We collected the data during 2008 with a class of 25 students (ages 10–12), who were creating concept maps for two geography projects. The first, Project Europe, began in February and lasted four weeks, and the second, Project Africa, began in October and finished after six weeks.

Due to its explorative nature, our research project needed to be flexible. We did not know where, when, or in what way critical events would take place. So our goal was to collect complementing and overlapping forms of data to work with and across. Amounts of data from Projects Europe and Africa are separated with a "+" in the following description.

The video data consisted of 12+11 hours of dual-camera recordings of students working in the school's computer lab and three hours of single-camera video recordings of the introduction to and concluding lessons of Project Europe. In addition, we recorded 99+142 screen capture animations from student workstations and 9+0 stimulated-recall student interviews using the screen capture animations as prompts. We augmented these with 25+25 student-produced concept maps, as well as internal recordings and log files of the IHMC CmapTools software for outlining the temporal distribution of edits performed on the actual task product. We also collected questionnaire data during Project Europe to discern the informal ICT-contexts of the students and their perceived social relations within the peer group. Finally, we experimented with short "Making of Project Africa" videos shot by the students, but the analysis was still under way at the time of this writing.

Henceforth, we support Bruno Latour's claim that "One should never speak of 'data'—what is given—but rather of *sublata*, that is, of 'achievements,'" (Latour, 1999, p.42) even though we use the term "data" in this text.

Tracing and Mapping

We have built our theoretical framework around the concepts of rhizome, map, and tracing adapted from Deleuze and Guattari (1980/2004). Here rhizome is not used as a botanical term but as a name for systems of a non-hierarchical and horizontal nature. The concept is elaborated later in this chapter. We focus first on tracing and map that are vital to the basic operations of our approach. Our reading of the many characteristics of maps given by Deleuze and Guattari is based on the following description: "The map is open and connectable in all its dimensions; it is detachable, reversible, susceptible to constant modification." When making one or more maps of the data, we want the maps to have multiple entryways and to be "entirely oriented toward experimentation with the real," instead of developing a hierarchy or stable organization. (Deleuze and Guattari, 1980/2004, p. 13) In an explorative study such as ours, neutralizing the complexity of data by structuralizing it can be counterproductive. Digital concept maps and the processes of producing them seem to allow entry from any point and movement in any direction. We look for singularities, the addition of something new, "remarkable and unrepeatable turning points in the process" (Goodchild, 1996, p. 219). To find these, we turn data into a map.

We do this mainly by tracings: turning something into an image by using restrictive procedures such as selecting or isolating. According to Deleuze and Guattari, this process reproduces only itself (1980/2004, p. 14–15). However, our strategy is to produce such a number of tracings that they start to become rhizomatic by enabling new connections and by showing directions of movement. Due to their digitality and the technical means available to us, these tracings also create entry points to the map. We see tracing as a way to translate, in that it creates "a link that did not exist before and…to some degree, modifies the original two" (Latour, 1999, p. 179). Mere quantity does not suffice to turn frames into a map. But through the tracings' connections to other forms of data—especially interviews, questionnaires, and logs—they can avoid self-reproduction and contribute to map-making. We will elaborate on this shortly. We see our data as a multiplicity, being diverse, heterogeneous, and not divisible into subjects and objects; it is not something constituted by different dimensions and lines. In our adaptation, the function of lines is to show directions of movement and points of connection. These include human lines, one for each person within reach of our recording equipment during the course of our study. We have also included nonhuman lines of software, web pages, computers, chairs, and other elements. Finally, there is the timeline: the backbone of data navigation and most tracings.

Timeline and Manipulation of Data

To explain the timeline, we must briefly return to the idea of the tracings as a means of becoming rhizomatic. Video recording is our best example of this. Technically, digital video consists of single images called frames. Each frame is a tracing of several lines within our data. Lines are used to give an indication of the relationship between objects populating the physical space of the computer lab and of their relation to the virtual space accessed via software running on the computers. For example, in one moment, a certain student sits next to her computer—let us call it computer X—with Wikipedia on her screen. The lines of this student, computer X, and Wikipedia connect at this point. A minute later, different lines cross as she stands behind another student seated next to computer Y. Even this gives some idea of movement, albeit coarsely. At the rate of 25 or more frames per second, human perception can no longer separate the frames, which results in the illusion of continuous movement perceived as directions and speeds.

Despite the smooth perception of movement, the video recording has striated time, having a starting point and an ending point. It is also divided into even metric intervals (Deleuze & Guattari 2004, p. 527–536). This provides us with a predictably segmented timeline, revealing connection points crucial for tracing and interpreting the data as rhizomatic. The timeline enables the synchronization of all our time-stamped data. The stream of images and sound from two video cameras connected to four directional microphones, screen-capture animations, and log files of the CmapTools program all become connected points of entry and traversal (see Figure 3). So, as Ursula LeGuin notes, "the book is all there, all at once" (1974/2002). We still may perceive the data sequentially, but as it becomes increasingly hypertextual by containing increasingly more links, the sequence of events or ways of perceiving them do not need to be the same.

Connections between data in different modalities are necessary to turn a heap of tracings into a map. The questionnaire data, interviews, and short "Making of

. . ." videos recorded by the students all create new connections and intertwined with existing ones. The interviews integrated the data by reaffirming and elaborating questionnaire data and explicitly linking it to episodes in the dual-camera videos and animations. The interviews also contextualize the activities and lend insight into events outside the recordings, such as how a student has learned to use a certain digital tool.

Another example would be one "Making of. . . video explaining how one student learned to save his work regularly (the student had been losing his work due to a computer restart required after an automatic update). On the "Making of. . ." video, we see the message box on the screen giving the option to restart now or later, and we clearly hear the student shooting the video say, "Go ahead and restart it." The digital concept maps created by the students are critical to our map; they are connected to one another and give a point of reference to the internal recordings of CmapTools and the videos. As we do not have a single tool capable of doing all we need, Atlas.ti software was used as the main platform for managing our data and keeping it retrievable, with the help of strict rules for file naming. We also used Atlas.ti to analyze textual data such as interview or discourse transcriptions (Atlas.ti, 2006).

Another way of eliciting different perspectives is to create alternative versions of some data segments. Everything digital is, by definition, in numerical form, enabling easy copying and mathematical processing. As tracing is a process of reduction or isolation, we find such processing useful. We can, for example, concentrate on a particular student by cropping out most of the video recording and combining it with the audio recording from the microphone closest to him. We also can manipulate time by changing the playback speed of the recordings, or we can leave out measurable time and even a lot of sequentiality, as shown in Figures 1 and 2. We call this sort of tracing *flattening*, which is a term borrowed from digital-image processing software, where it means merging several separate image layers into one.

To provide consistency between tracings, we adapted the use of three time scales from Green et al. (2007) as elaborated below. Some clarification and structure make it easier to perceive what is represented, and the project-session-episode time scale division works in conjunction with the limitations of the data. A 90-minute session is the largest unit with a continuous segmented timeline provided by the video recording, and the annotation software we used (called ELAN) is also built around the idea of one annotation database per recording session. Because some students worked from home as well as during recording sessions, a larger unit was needed for mapping. In addition, it is easier to make sense of digital content production as a process when viewing it as a whole. Episodes are needed to trace particularly interesting events within the sessions, such as student movement or the introduction and negotiation of new ideas or tools. Episode traces, such as annotations of movement or speech, mostly attach themselves to the timeline, whereas session-level traces introduce a flattening or condensing of time. An example of the latter are the edit distribution graphs, which display the temporal distribution of edits performed by each student during a session. Figure 1 demonstrates how the rhythms of the whole group as well as individual students are put together as a graph.

Before introducing mapping and decalcomania as the twofold basis for data representation, we operationalize the concept of rhizome further by its main qualities. In the process, we will also introduce the related central concepts of cartography and decalcomania.

Mapping the Rhizome

For analyzing and representing multiplicity, we have adapted the concept of rhizome as developed by Deleuze and Guattari (1980/2004). Rhizome, an originally botanical concept, can be differentiated from hierarchical interpretations such as that of a tree with roots, by its horizontal and non-hierarchical nature. For our purpose of conceptualizing, analyzing and representing, Rhizome has the following three main characteristics:

- among the points of a rhizomatic network, any point can be connected to any other point;
- the traits of a rhizomatic network do not need to be connected to the trait of a similar nature;
- a rhizome describes the nature of a multiplicity, for which there is no unity to serve as a pivot in the object or as a divide in the subject (adapted from Deleuze and Guattari, 1980/2004, p. 7–13).

We have applied the concept of rhizome to two areas of mapping the dimensions of activities in the computer lab. First, the interaction between the students within the ICT-class space happens—or at least by its physical constraints can possibly happen—in a rhizomatic way. The connections through physical movement and spoken and virtual (e.g., chat) utterances can be established unrelated to any predetermined order. Second, the process of hypertextual reading as suggested by Ruitenberg (2007) and content creation practices during our case are well conceptualized by a rhizome, where no single linear text provides the sequential structuring of different operations and related states of the student or the group. Characteristic of our approach is the ability to elicit the interconnectedness of student interactions and the possibility of hypertextual reading, which further emphasizes the rhizomatic nature of our subject of study. The context and connections for a line or point of tracing within the rhizome are defined within the multiplicity. Actors, utterances, and objects (including texts and technologies) in the active physical and virtual spaces can be connected in a multitude of unpredictable ways. Through this connectedness, the various elements engage in an interaction that shapes the stages and states of the processes as well as of the artefacts produced during a particular period of time.

We can cite an interesting, third area of expansion and application for the concept of rhizome within the cartographic nature of media presentations created by the students during our study cases. Though we will only elaborate on this area through contextualization, this third area provides us with some valuable tools. More specifically, the necessity of the researcher becoming conscious of the different styles of representation—in our case, cartography and decalcomania—is one of the implications from the application of the concepts of rhizome, map, and tracing.

Decalcomania presents the creation of a tracing as an image, an axis, a path, or a sequentiality laid on a given logic and hierarchical causality of choices. Cartographic representation in turn does not provide a single, pre-decided entry point or primary order to be perceived or communicated, but a multitude of possible ones. Cartography allows the reader to structure her own approach towards presented content. The cartographic tradition of presentation utilizes five main sign systems: a matrix of areas to mark boundaries and divisions; a network of channels to explicate flow, communication and navigation; point distribution to explicate positions of discrete objects; nested signs to explicate continuums of equality and quality of relation; and a coordinate axis to serve as a grid in which to plot the other four systems (Wood & Fels, 1992, p. 37). Our approach is an attempt to make sense of the rhizome by creating a combination of these two types of tracings that are "plugged back into the map" (Deleuze and Guattari, 1980/2004, p. 15).

By making the distinction between the two kinds of representational translations to produce non-linear and linear tracing in context with our time-stamped digital data, we are emphasizing the significance of selecting methods for processing and reconstructing time. The following three statements exemplify our method of separating and combining the non-linearity and linearity in tracings:

- A non-linear tracing of the rhizome does not define an entryway, nor does it impose any linear or chronological order for its incorporated elements to be observed in.

- A linear tracing produces an organized passage of points connecting the map's lines or the different levels of tracing.
- Hence, the linear tracings are "sustainable chains of logic and consequence" explicitly made by the researcher (Lemke, 2007, pg. 46) within or connecting the non-linear tracings.

Before portraying our approach through data examples, we pause briefly to elaborate on the usefulness of Latour's (1999) concept of actant. In mapping the rhizome, we perceive actant as a valid concept for linking agency and crossings lines.

Agency as Activity and Structural Function

While viewing the computer lab's content creation activity as a rhizome, we must simultaneously take into account the notion of agency. In our attempt to map the multiplicity of emerging patterns of interaction, connection, and operations performed on different technologies and materials, the concept of an actant provides a meaningful way to differentiate two levels of view on agency.

When observing the networks of interaction and connectedness, we can outline agency on one hand from the perspective of one point's position and function within the network. Here, the notions of node (e.g., Hanneman & Riddle, 2005) and in particular of an actant (Latour, 1999) provide us with tools for defining qualities of traced points within the rhizome. Nodes, a concept appropriated from network analysis, can be compared to one another by the sets of their connections. The basic assumptions of network analysis, seen as patterns of channels able to carry various material and immaterial resources, determine the sets of connections (Wasserman & Faust, 1994). As the nodes being analyzed by their connectedness are identified through their position and function within the network, they are best described utilizing the notion of an actant. An actant is a functional entity that exists only in relation to the network that incorporates it. By definition, an actant can be anything of which the network consists. This definition encompasses every technology and artifact, as well as the human actor constituting the traced network. Our application of this concept in tracing processes is also an attempt to focus on deep structures instead of the surface-level content of interaction and events. In doing so, it refers to Greimas' use of the concept in the context of textual narratives (Greimas, 1987)

We also define agency from the perspective human actions. The observational nature of our data-collection and analysis is hereby expanded to include the perceptions of the actors themselves. This is done by interview techniques such as stimulated-recall and semi-structured-theme interviews, both aimed to deepen our understanding of the thinking behind decisions made in the observed situation and of the background of a given sequence of events. However, we always consider the analysis of the linguistic expressions as providing yet another entryway into the rhizome and a distinct line on the map—not as something to provide us with the decisive explanations for the multiplicity. The analysis of speech is a parallel process to the other lines of analysis, and the meaning of parallel is threefold. First, the quality of interaction and events is indexed and identified through analyzing the immanent language: we understand what is happening better, because people talk about it while it is happening. The second parallel level is the simultaneity of carrying out the indexing of the data and the analysis of speech; if desirable, we can listen to the speech each time we discover interesting events, even while our main focus is on analyzing movement in the computer lab. The third parallel level is that the analysis of the interviews conducted before entering the computer lab, as well as our participation in the actual activity later, has given us insight to the events, which in turn enables us to orientate ourselves while analyzing the data: we know what to expect will happen next, and, to an extent, we know why it is happening because we were there and we remember.

Nonlinearity and Linearity of Tracings

We can best define the preceding grounds for our selection of tracings for representing research findings by introducing two of the representations from different stages and parts of analysis performed on the movement in the physical space (see Figure 2). Then we will introduce a solution for tracing the nodes visible in the graphs back to the computer lab's multiplicity. We will achieve the latter through visualizing a sequence of meaningful events through the actual digital materials organized into a figure of this text (see Figure 3). This is a concrete attempt to "plug the tracings back into the map," which, as suggested by Deleuze and Guattari, we are doing to avoid mistakenly perceiving the tracing as a reproduction of something else—here, the multiplicity of the computer lab reality—instead of the reproduction of only itself (1980/2004). In doing this, we simultaneously demonstrate the process of indexing and analyzing the video data using ELAN 3.7.1.

Figure 2 is a combination of two examples of nonlinear tracings: graphs traced from student movement from their own to another student's workstation during two 90-minute sessions in the computer lab (see A and B in Figure 2). The two sessions are from different stages of the first data-gathering period, where graph A is a tracing related to the second session and graph B to the last (sixth) session of

Project Europe. In producing the images, the connectedness of the nodes—in this case, students and workstations—has been visualized utilizing multidimensional scaling (MdS) of the nodes' length of geodesics, the geodesic being the shortest path from one node to another (Wasserman & Faust, 1994, p. 110). MdS, in turn, belongs to a larger family of algorithms designed to define relations of nodes as distances in metric space. To cut it short, the visuals provided by MdS and exported from NetDraw software are an image where nodes with similar sets of connections are positioned close to one another. In addition, in Figure 2 we have also emphasized the attraction of a node by increasing its size incrementally for each visit paid by another person to the particular resident of a particular workstation. The reshaping of observed phenomena through analysis into this kind of representations is an example of how the smoothness of the actual studied space and selected movement, as well as distances within it, are striated in the process in order to produce a novel tracing to map the multiplicity.

Comparing the two graphs reveals the substantial change happening during the project within the emerging interactional patterns of the rhizomatically operational entity, namely the group of students working in the computer lab. The graph excludes the adults displaying only student movement on the grounds of the research task for the first phase of our research, which was to focus on and elicit the nature of student self-directed actions within a formal education classroom setting that utilizes ICT in studying. The advantages of being able to compress time are obvious: the ability to crystallize the events into the graphs themselves. However, this advantage is also present within the indexing process. The analysis of physical movement can be performed while viewing the digital video at 200% speed. During the analysis of physical movement, we identified and synched with the two-camera video the significant screen capture animations to gain a deeper understanding on student movement.

We indexed the data using the ELAN 3.6 software's tier functionality (see Figure 3). Tiers were created and organized separately within a singular file dedicated to each 90-minute data-gather sessions for the individual lines of analysis (e.g., student movement, adult movement, general descriptions of classroom activity stages, specific description of the significant student-student, student-adult, adult-student interactions). The annotation schema performed on the tiers was also designed to yield suitable exports for further processing in other types of software. We used additional software, such as UCINET/NetDraw and Microsoft Excel, to construct representations such as seen in Figures 1 and 2, as well as to provide indexes for printed transcripts to be handed out in data sessions.

Data sessions are defined here as a meeting to share the video data and research find-

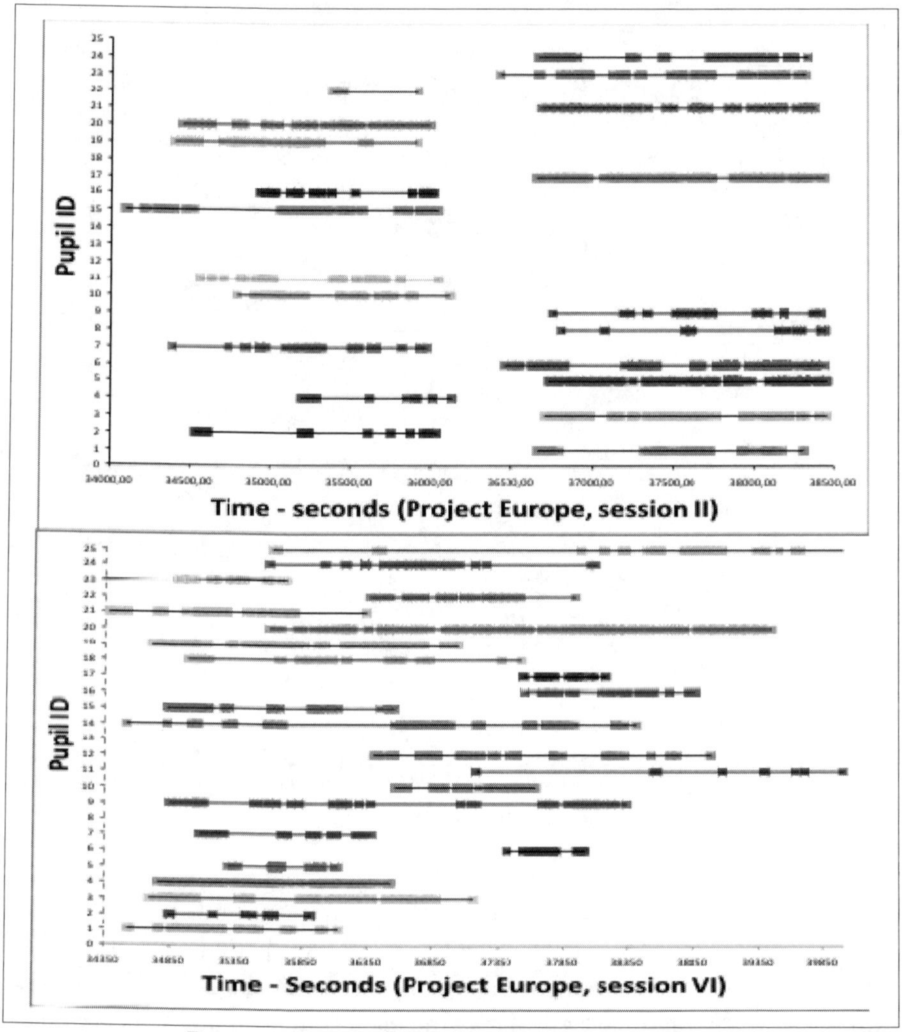

Figure 1: Edits performed by all the pupils during two sessions.

ings as well as define and adjust the analysis process. In the data sessions, the printed, line-numbered transcripts are used as a means of collective navigation and reference. The ease of navigation within the data is a crucial element in a meaningfully directed and focused discussion. When ELAN is used to present the data, its functionalities can be utilized to navigate within the annotated data; using the line numbers and/or text searches on the annotations can come in handy, as they are a good tool to get collective input from the research group focusing on the data on a flexibly and accurately selected level of detail that is simultaneously appropriate for the prevailing stage of analysis.

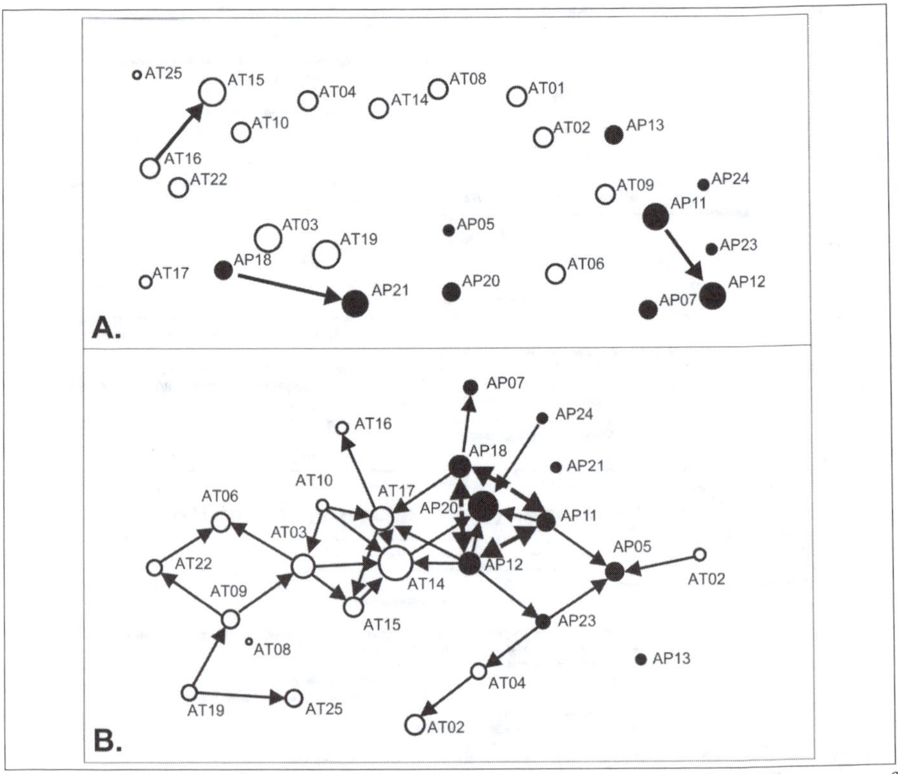

Figure 2: Student movement in the computer lab during two 90-minute sessions from different stages of Project Europe, *traced into sociographs.*

Figure 3 is a composition of a collection of digital artifacts that hark back to a significant series of events during the second data-gathering period, Project Africa. It is a profound manifestation of how our tracing approach combines the nonlinear with the linear on multiple levels. Here, the main combined levels are the image and the narrative derived from it, where the latter is supported by visualizing the sequence using numbers, letters, boxes, and arrows to anchor the narrative's successive stages. Figure 3 solidifies our integrative use of ELAN in combination with IHMC CmapTools in organizing and analyzing data.

The figure is divided into five accordingly numbered sections. Section number one (upper left) is an ELAN screen capture from one specific point in time. A girl student (AT03) has just returned to her workstation after discussing another girl's work at the other girl's workstation. Back at her own workstation, AT03 observes AT22, who happens to be operating Google Earth (GE) software, which is installed in all the lab's computers. This is the first time AT03 has seen GE in

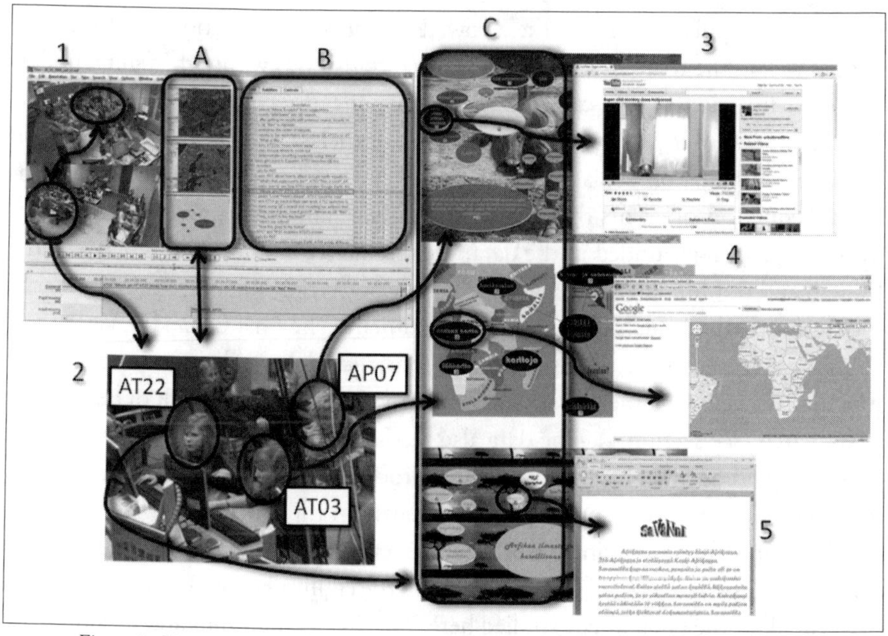

Figure 3: Linear tracing advancing from the two-camera video viewed in ELAN 3.7.1

action, and she is impressed (in the audio recording, AT03 utters, "What—is—that?!" three times during the first 20 seconds of seeing what AT22 is doing). AT03 sees AT22 using GE to "fly" from one place to another and zoom in and out. Soon, after 1 minute and 10 seconds of watching AT22 operating GE, AT03 begins learning to operate GE herself. While the two girls discuss and operate GE, other students become interested. This is particularly the case with AP07, a boy, who observes the girls' actions and talks to them over their shoulders, though he has not yet experimented with GE himself (see his screen as the bottom-most in Box A).

While studying section number one, in addition to observing in detail what happens on the students' (AT03, AT22, and AP07) computer screens (Box A) while they are talking, we also see some of the organization of the ELAN layout. This includes part of the grid (Box B) showing the indexing annotations on a selected tier, which can be seen on the bottom of the section, below the transport controls of ELAN.

In viewing the transition from section one to section two in Figure 3, it is possible to reconstruct the nature of our process of indexing the video data. We begin to map the connectedness of the rhizome through the indexing process by identifying the meaningful segments of the visible and audible parts of the recorded reality of the computer lab. Here, the arrowed transition from section one to section two, as well as the rest of the two-way arrowed transitions within the figure, underline their function as non-categorized connections of reconstructions of the perceptual process of indexing the video data. Nevertheless, the illustrated connection based on causally non-explanatory logic does not undo the element of time within the sequences of events that can be traced back and forth and built into a linear tracing. Well grounded in the data, the interactive connectedness between the human and nonhuman actors within the network yields outcomes traced as far as the final formal products of the school assignment. The final Cmap by AT03 truly contains a hyperlinked resource that is constructed by utilizing Google Map's functionality, allowing the user to build a unique URL from the result of her Google Map search (see section 4). The data also records how AT03 is the one who, after a short period of time, backtracks the GE process by prompting one of the adults to explain the process of "putting Google Earth on the Cmap."

By its incorporated principle of heterogeneity, the concept of rhizome captures some of the essential qualities of the sequence traced into Figure 3. We perceive this as essential for the phenomena studied here. Viewing sections four and five in Figure 3, we can see how all three selected students (AT03, AT22, and AP07) utilize the functionalities allowing the hyperlinking of web content. The figure also suggests that we could advance to classifying the linear tracings related to these three actants into the same category (Box C) based on their utilization of the software's functionalities. Also, when executing the process of tracing further—which, in the setting of formal educational is to the actual content of the handed-back school assignments—the content introduced by students operating GE is not present in all three final Cmaps. The Cmaps, when viewed in their final form, provide us—as well as the teacher receiving the schoolwork—with yet one more collection of entryways for initiating the construction of further tracings or lines of analysis. To illustrate the possibilities for direction selection and depth of tracing, as well as the rhizomatic connections of the hyperlinked digital content of our data, we have presented some of the Cmaps' content in Figure 3. In doing this, we have leaned against the experience of taking part in the computer lab's activity and indexing the video recordings. For example, the particular chain of logic and consequence related to AP07's choice of including a YouTube video clip (see section 3) into his final Cmap, is available to be traced and brought under observation in great detail. The same is the case for AT22's choice to pay attention to the incorporated text documents' layout (see section 5), which briefly illustrates one of the more general, collective aptitudes within student work during the data-gathering periods.

Conclusion: Multiplicity or Simplicity

Most of this chapter consists of ideas published and techniques employed decades ago. Multi-camera video recording facilitating changes of angle and magnification was used in a classroom setting already in the late 1960s in Finland (Koskenniemi, Karma & Martikainen, 1974), and this was most likely not the first time this had happened. Ricki Goldman (2007a) recounts her first plans to take advantage of computer-supported shared interpretations of videos in 1987. Digital content created by children was researched in the 1970s, if not earlier; manipulation of time to enhance the use of moving images was done in the 1930s; and approaching video data as a constellation of points was accomplished in the late 1980s (Goldman, 2007(a), 2007(b); Lemke, 2007). Landow (1997) traced the history of the term *hypertext* to the 1960s, where he quotes Theodor H. Nelson in presenting the perhaps familiar idea of a "series of text chunks which offer the reader a series of pathways" (Nelson, as cited in Landow, 1997). The idea of supplementing one's memory with technical means based on intuitive association instead of indexing and enabling annotations was published by Vannevar Bush in 1945, although he used the term *trails* much in the same way we use *traces* (Landow, 1997, p. 3–10). So why bother with our research?

The practice of traveling with the map and reconnecting tracings to it and enriching its connections are the main contributions of this chapter. The nonhuman actants for accessing and editing are easy to move around. As such, the digital rhizomatic map has travelled with us to stimulated-recall interviews, data sessions, conferences, and meetings and thrived because of it. When the goal is to explore, it is useful to retain the possibility of going in unexpected directions instead of having only a handful of tracings selected by the researcher. Reporting one's findings seems to be the difficult part, and a tracing's simplicity of telling is more comfortable than dealing with the multiplicity of maps. The need to convincingly articulate a sustainable chain of logic and consequence remains. In our study, we have found it useful to work with the whole map for as long as possible before translating it into a report. The opposite is also worth considering: Why go through all the trouble of collecting and mapping multi-modal data, if you only want to know what websites the students visited during the projects?

References

ATLAS.ti Scientific Software Development GmbH. (2006). ATLAS.ti (Version 5.2) [Computer software]. Berlin: ATLAS.ti Scientific Software Development GmbH

Deleuze, G. & Guattari, F. (2004). *A thousand plateaus* (B. Massumi, Trans.). New York: Continuum. (Original work published 1980)

Goldman, R. (2007a). Orion(TM), An online digital video data analysis tool: Changing our perspectives as an interpretive community. In Goldman, R., Pea, R., Barron, B., & Derry, S. (Eds.). *Video research in the learning sciences* (pp. 507–520). New Jersey: Lawrence Erlbaum associates.

Goldman, R. (2007b). Video representations and the perspectivity framework: Epistemology, ethnography, evaluation and ethics. In Goldman, R., Pea, R., Barron, B., & Derry, S. (Eds.). *Video research in the learning sciences* (pp. 3–37). New Jersey: Lawrence Erlbaum associates.

Goodchild, P. (1996). *Deleuze and Guattari: An introduction to the politics of desire*. London: Sage.

Green, J., Skukauskaite, A., Dixon, C. & Còrdova, R. (2007). Epistemological issues in the analysis of video records: Interactional ethnography as a logic of inquiry. In Goldman, R., Pea, R., Barron, B., & Derry, S. (Eds.). *Video research in the learning sciences* (pp. 115–132). New Jersey: Lawrence Erlbaum associates.

Greimas, A. J. (1987). *Actants, actors and figures*. In Perron P., Collins F., and Jameson F. (Eds.), On Meaning: Selected writings in semiotic theory (pp. 106–120) Minneapolis: University of Minnesota Press.

Hanneman, R. A., & Riddle, M. (2005). Introduction to social network methods. Retrieved 10/04, 2006 from http://faculty.ucr.edu/~hanneman/nettext/C1_Social_Network_Data.html#Nodes

Koskenniemi, M., Karma, K. & Martikainen, M. (1974). *DPA Helsinki system for describing instructional processes*. Institute of Education Research bulletin 42. Helsinki: University of Helsinki.

Landow, G. P. (1997). *Hypertext 2.0: The convergence of contemporary critical theory and technology*. Baltimore & London: Johns Hopkins University Press.

Latour, B. (1999). *Pandor's hope: Essays on the reality of science studies*. Cambridge, MA: Harvard University Press.

LeGuin, U. (2002). *The Dispossessed*. London: Gollancz. (Original work published 1974)

Lemke, J. (2007). Video Epistemology In- and Outside the Box: Traversing Attentional Spaces. In Goldman, R., Pea, R., Barron, B., & Derry, S. (Eds.). *Video research in the learning sciences* (pp. 39–51). New Jersey: Lawrence Erlbaum associates. Max-Planck-Institute for Psycholinguistics. (2008). ELAN—Linguistic Annotator (version 3.6) [Computer software] Nijmegen: Max-Planck-Institute for Psycholinguistics.

Ruitenberg, C. W. (2007). Here be dragons: Exploring cartography in educational theory and research. *Complicity: An International Journal of Complexity & Education, 4*(1; 1), 7–24.

Wasserman, S. & Faust, K. (1994). *Social network analysis*. Cambridge University Press, 1994.

Wood, D. & Fels, J. (1992). *The power of maps*. Mappings: Society/Theory/Space. New York, NY: Guilford Press.

V

Perspectives for Media Education in the Age of Digital Content Creation

14

Empowerment

The Real Challenge of Digital Inclusion

Norbert Wildermuth

Digital content creation by young people, which has attracted considerable attention, can be observed on a global scale and has nourished optimistic expectations regarding its potential in formal and informal education. The seeming "ease" with which young people embrace ICTs and the interactive potential of the Internet points toward potential learning processes beyond narrow delineations of e-learning as curriculum-based processes. However, the usefulness of ICTs enabling a digital environment in which these new, user-generated learning processes can evolve, demands a cultural and socio-economic context that is far from a given for the majority of young people in the Global South.

While access to the Internet and computer-facilitated practices of learning, working, leisure, and communication are a reality for the majority of children and young people in highly developed societies, the continued significance of the so-called digital divide is undeniable in large parts of the developing world. Arguably, the explosive proliferation of the mobile phone and localized applications in some of the "least developed countries" of the Global South may narrow this gap in ICT uses and appropriation in ways that we have grasped only recently. A good example is Nepal, where the number of registered mobile phones has passed 5 million in autumn 2008. In consequence, the use of mobile phones can be observed even in some of the remotest valleys of the Himalayan kingdom, providing access to a family member's, friend's, or commercial village operator's mobile phone to the majority of Nepal's 27 million strong population. Similarly, the astonishing success of safari.com's *m-pesa* service in Kenya—which allows for mobile-based money transfers, cash withdrawals, and billing operations—may serve as an example.

The digital divide, probably one of the most used phrases in academic and popular writing about the Internet, refers to the gap between people with effective access to digital and information technology and those with limited or no access at all. However, besides imbalances in physical access to technology, the digital divide further includes imbalances in resources and skills needed to effectively participate as a digital citizen. Moreover, there is not a single divide, but several, persistent inequalities that exist between the info-rich and the info-poor (Chadwick, 2006, p. 49).

Over the past decade, the digital divide has been the subject of much attention from development agencies, non-government organizations, researchers, governments, and the private sector (Potter, 2006). To overcome the digital-poor state of countries, communities, and individuals, a plethora of countermeasures and activities have been initiated. Sharing a common point of concern, an unusual alliance of academics, IT industry executives, politicians, social welfare organizations, and multilateral donor organizations has taken such initiatives. Together they are pursuing the ideal of a (more) widespread use of Information and Communication Technologies (ICTs)—albeit for very different reasons (Strover, 2003).

However, while substantial policies are being put into place and while numerous projects of digital inclusion and computer literacy are being realized, the concept of the digital divide remains highly contested and, thus, the normative role that ICTs are supposed to play in processes of social change and human development. Though a broad political consensus exists around the common goal, the digital inclusion of citizens, communities and nations, the concrete objectives and meanings of this intervention remain all too often vague and unclear due to simplifications at work in the common understanding of the whole issue, its consequences and causes (Potter, 2006; Selwyn, 2004).

In the Global South, but also amongst underprivileged communities in the "developed" world, we can by now observe a boom of telecentre projects that "target" young people by means of a state- and donor-driven ICT4D (Information and Communication Technologies for Development) approach. Financially not self-sustaining and often rather techno-centric, the resulting initiatives can be considered as problematic in several ways. To begin with, too often efforts to decrease the digital divide are (mis)guided by assumptions of what Mark Warschauer (2003, p.

31) terms "devices and conduits" approaches, the belief that overcoming the digital divide is simply about providing people with access to computers and an ISP account. As practitioners and academics have specified, the employment of such simplified notions has significant consequences for attempts at digital inclusion. Thus, efforts to "bridge the digital divide" are running a substantial risk of diverting attention and resources from addressing the deeper causes of the mechanisms of digital exclusion, the development communication consultant Roger W. Harris (2004, p. 12) among others, has warned. That is, the "conceptually oversimplified and theoretically underdeveloped" debates (Selwyn, 2004, p. 343) that surround much of the attention paid to the phenomena summed up under the term "digital divide" may misguide respective attempts at social inclusion through digital inclusion.

As will be shown here, a more differentiated understanding of the various micro- and macro-dimensions that together bring about specific forms of digital exclusion is imperative to determine how exactly systematic efforts and institutional attempts at *digital inclusion* may contribute to make a difference.

A basic idea in this chapter is that a more differentiated understanding of the social dynamics of the processes of digital exclusion begins from acknowledging that the observed inequalities in access and in ICT-related skills are best understood as the result, rather than the cause of poverty and marginalization. This is not to suggest that being excluded from digital forms of mediated communication does not aggravate preexisting forms of social exclusion; quite the contrary. However, with reference to Ling (2004), we can argue there are good reasons to pursue a "domestication of technologies" approach; a perspective devised to move beyond arguments between various forms of technological determination and social determination. The phenomena subsumed under the term *digital divide* should thus be acknowledged theoretically and explored as a concrete reflection of existing broader socioeconomic inequalities.

With Warschauer, we can state that while a basic understanding of the inequalities in physical access is essential, we also need to consider that these inequalities are "embedded in a complex array of factors encompassing physical, digital, human and social resources and relationships" (Warschauer, 2003, p. 6). While the access divide seems to be contradicted by the proliferation of Internet Cafes and telecentres in the Global South, the skills, opportunity, and computer literacy divide continues. It is, therefore, highly relevant to study and understand the totality of individual and contextual level barriers, which means that some young people are excluded from using ICTs while others do use computer and the Internet, but only in restricted (and often predictable) ways.

This chapter seeks to contribute to a grounded, inductive exploration of some of the principal barriers to a more diversified and empowering use of the Internet by underprivileged young people living in the urban centers of the Global South. In empirical terms, my arguments will be substantiated by the findings and preliminary conclusions of a field study in Recife in March and April 2008, which included a qualitative case study of the *Projeto Coque Vive*, located in one of the major *favelas* (slums) of the capital of Pernambuco in Brazil.

Specifically, I will focus on ICT employed as a means for the social and political empowerment of individuals and through them of the various communities they constitute and participate in. To this purpose I will ask: What new patterns of power and participation are digital empowerment (sometimes called e-citizenship) initiatives enabling, de facto, and potentially? Under what circumstances do respective digital empowerment initiatives contribute to the facilitation of a participative and inclusive society and under what circumstances do they fail? That is, I will seek to explore the limits of digital inclusion policies and determine some of the interactional dynamics that are a central constraint to concrete initiatives of digital empowerment, as encountered in a particular youth initiative located in North East Brazil.

As a first step, I will outline and propose a multi-dimensional framework that seeks to overcome some of the outlined theoretical and conceptual shortcomings of the digital divide debate. This framework, based on the principles of the participatory paradigm in development communication studies, advocates a focus on digital empowerment—as elaborated by Mäkinen (2006) and others—rather than on digital inclusion. It provides, in my view, a more adequate concept to designate those ICT-facilitated processes by which "people gain new abilities and ways to participate and express themselves in a networked society" (Mäkinen, 2006, p. 381). As a second step, I then will apply this theoretical frame analytically to the concrete experience of the *Projeto Coque Vive*.

Impediments to Digital Inclusion

The new digital means of mediated communication play an important role in attempts to socially include and empower young, underprivileged people. ICT offers, for example, a considerable potential for increasing people's possibility to participate in political decision-making processes. The lack of knowledge about existing problems and of a possibility to connect with other people is a major obstacle for mobilizing underprivileged persons for common action. However, without widespread mobilization it seems difficult to pressure often irresponsive and irresponsible political decision-makers to be influenced by common people's concerns. Thus, an ICT-facilitated ability "to communicate with others and to access information about the factors affecting one's life may seem like an ideal tool for overcoming problems of political mobilization" (Lanki, 2006, p. 457; see also Clark & Themudo, 2003).

Not surprisingly, then, Western democracies have, in recent years, been investing in "democratic renewal" initiatives, pursuing the re-engagement of their citizens with government political agendas. While ICTs are perceived as having a pivotal role in this "empowering" process, the participatory outcome of these "digitally enabled" attempts at new forms of political citizenship and deliberation are still highly debated and far from secured.

The contested concept of participation—central to any consideration of e-citizenship and digital empowerment—can by now be seen as fluid, moving beyond e-voting and the provision of e-government services to address, in a more radical way, the "crisis of voice" (Couldry, 2008), which is at the heart of the widely lamented "democratic participation and motivation crisis."

This common "failure" of digital inclusion initiatives for citizenship and political empowerment in the "developed" world underlines the enormous challenges faced by comparable attempts at e-participation located in the developing economies and democracies of the Global South. Not only do these initiatives usually operate in a local environment characterized by a severe lack of all kind of material resources, but commonly they also face educational prerequisites, comparable only to "Western" initiatives working with the most marginalized and socially excluded groups within society (Bure, 2005).

From this perspective, the case study here suggests that ICTs will not achieve their full potential without suitable attention being paid to the wider processes of community development that they are intended to assist and to the social context within which they are implemented. The design and implementation of an adequate media-facilitated intervention and mobilization strategy becomes in consequence a challenge that exceeds by far the mere selection of the right communicative applications and the development of adequate software and e-literacy curricula to be used with them. The real challenge exists in designing and implementing an e-participation project that is able to challenge the constraining power structure and mechanisms of marginalization constituted by an stratified and unequal society.

More specifically, I will point out and discuss some of the pitfalls and ambiguities that Brazilian social inclusion and digital empowerment initiatives are confronted with, in their struggle against a rampant culture of crime-related violence and against the social destitution it originates from. As is well known, the pervasive presence of drug trafficking and a culture of youth gangs in the environment of the Brazilian *favela* is a consequence of the inhabitants' social marginalization and their impoverished living conditions. Yet, organized crime and the insecurity it creates amongst community members and society at large should be understood not only as a consequence of but also as a cause for the continued marginalization of a majority of *favela* inhabitants.

Thus, while commonly infested with a pathos of resistance by the gang members in their self-glorifying tales of collective identification, the destructive violence and far-reaching lack of law and order encountered in vast parts of urban Brazil perpetuates the blight of the *favela* communities the gangs originate from. Hence, *a violência* (the gang-related culture of violence) constitutes a major impediment to processes of social change initiated at a local level and, in more concrete terms, to the efforts of the mentioned change agents who strive to "empower" young people by legal means. From this perspective, I will now describe how the *Projeto Coque Vive* attempts to confront the structural forces and dynamics of crime-related violence that determine everyday living conditions and diminish the prospects of social inclusion for male and female youth residing in the neighbourhood.

Digital Empowerment as the Enhancement of a Self-Expressive Participatory Citizenship

Use of ICT does not necessarily entail "meaningful use of ICT" or what could be termed as "engagement" rather than merely use where the "user" exerts a degree of control and choice over the technology and its content, thus leading to a meaning, significance, and utility for the individual concerned (Bonfadelli, 2002; Silverstone, 1996). In this sense, the consequences of engaging meaningfully with ICT could be seen in terms of the effect on individual and community "social quality"—i.e., socioeconomic security, social inclusion, social cohesion, and empowerment. Such a perspective will reflect the extent to which technology use enables individuals to participate and be part of society, i.e., the extent to which "ICTs enhance our abilities to fulfil active roles in society, or being without them constitute a barrier to that end" (Haddon, 2000, p. 389).

A digitally included person, in this understanding, feels like a full member of the community or society and has the competence to influence with or without using the new technology. An excluded person does not have these possibilities or the necessary competence. People who decide not to use digital technology do not belong to the group of disadvantaged or excluded, and neither do the people who could not substantially improve their wellbeing by using the new technology. That is, the excluded people of the information society are the ones who could increase their welfare and prospects by using the information technology, but who do not have the chance or ability to use it. Excluded people are also the ones who are weakened or deprived by the information society and its characteristics such as consequences of globalization. They are finally the ones who are only in receiving and consuming roles and who do not feel full participation in social decision-making processes (Mäkinen, 2006, p. 383f).

Participatory citizenship requires a new attitude towards cooperation and relearning new practices to act. A citizen should become visible not only for the administration but also for himself. Growing towards active citizenship not only requires learning computer (literacy) skills, but also learning to act as a subject, who has an equal role in interaction. Moreover, growing towards participatory citizenship is not only an individualistic process, where a person learns useful skills for himself but also an interactive learning process in the context of one's environment and community.

Citizen activities in society can be of different kinds and levels. People act in their communities, in civic groups, and in organizations; they may use institutional channels or try direct action. The activities can be political, concerning specific issues, communal activities in neighborhoods or participating in wider social networks. The easiest forms of online action are related to receiving and using, more demanding ones require interaction and the most demanding forms require the abilities to create and provide new contents. The essential difference between these levels is a change from receiving object to a self-expressive actor.

The more ready and capable people are to participate, the more competent they are to be influential in their society and to improve their environment. The levels of action may divide people, leaving "the receiver-users" marginalized and without being heard.

The Internet supports traditional forms of social capital, such as social networks, access to information, communal activities, and political participation. In general, empowerment and increase of social capital correlates with commitment to a community. A community can encourage an individual in an empowerment process, in which case an individual may want to commit himself to the community and work towards its aims. Hence, a community role is essential within a process of digital empowerment. The mere presence of a telecenter or community information center is not enough for community empowerment, if it does not lead to any relevant activities on a collective level.

Information technology can be applied to support individual and community empowerment or to start an empowering process in a community. By using information technology, digital inclusion initiatives can increase the competence of communities to be involved meaningfully in the information society. This can help in bridging poor and marginalized communities to enable them to become part of broader societal networks of communication and welfare. Mäkinen has aptly conceptualized this bridging as *a process of digital empowerment.*

> Digital empowerment is an *enabling process*, which proceeds like a spiral from the prerequisites to the improvements in skills and knowledge, and then to the consequences, which are empowering for the community and its members. The changes happening during this process are not just one-way improvements, but they reflect and influence each other. The spiral of digital empowerment is dynamic and changing because it keeps up with progress in the surrounding society (Mäkinen, 2006, p. 391).

After having outlined a participatory framework of social inclusion based on the digital empowerment of individuals and communities, I will now apply its principles with respect to a concrete example.

The Local Context of Recife, Brazil

The case study referred to in this paper, the *Coque Vive* project, is located in *Ilha Joana Bezerra* (commonly known as Coque), one of the major *favelas* in Recife. The area, characterized by its low human development index, is located halfway between the commercial center of town and Boa Viagem, Recife's high-rise middle- and upper-class extension along the foremost city beaches. Despite these affluent neighbourhoods, Coque has a reputation to be one of the most dangerous urban settlements in Recife, notorious for its crime-related violence and homicides[1] and avoided by motorists who have to pass this *favela*, located close to the city highway that links Recife's center with its affluent suburbs in the south.

The *Projeto Coque Vive* is run by a collective that has brought together three social change initiatives engaged with youth in Coque. Namely, the ETAPAS Consulting, Research and Social Action Team, a non-governmental organization created in 1982, NEIMFA (*Núcleo Educacional Irmãos Menotes de Francisco de Assis*), a voluntary Christian organization and MABI (*Movimento Arrebentando Barreiras Invisíveis*), a social action group formed by local youth. NEIMFA, MABI, and ETAPAS share two premises—a public library building and a "community center" located in the neighborhood—and have worked together since 2006 on the realization of various cultural, media, and educational projects (subsumed under the name of *Coletivo Coque Vive*) such as:

- *Biblioteca Popular do Coque* (2006); [Public Library of Coque]
- *Gestão e Processos Comunicacionais no Coque* (2006); [Management and Communication Processes in Coque]
- *Rede de Agentes de Educomunicação Solidária* (2007); [Network of the Agents of the Solidarity Education and Communication Initiative]
- *Programa de Formação de Agentes de Mediação Sociocultual* (2008); [Programme for the Consciousness Raising of Agents of Socio-Cultural Mediation]
- *Rede de Comunicação, Educação e Cultura: Filhos e Filhas do Coque* (2008); [Network of Communication, Education and Culture: Sons and Daughters of Coque]

These activities have included the use of photography, print media, community radio, video, fanzines, graffiti, street art, music, web logs, chat forums, and Internet exhibitions and were realized in close cooperation with faculty staff and students of the UFDP (Universidade Federal de Pernambuco), Department of Journalism.

As is crucial, the *Coque Vive* initiative is integrated with the agency of some of the non-governmental organizations (NGOs), community-based organizations (CBOs), and social movements involved with the people living in Coque. A bottom-up organizational structure goes hand in hand with a primarily volunteer-based engagement of change agents from outside and within the community. This sets *Coque Vive* distinctively apart from a more top-down institutional telecentre approach as characteristic for example for *Casa Brasil*, the federal, state-funded digital inclusion projects; a difference that results in a distinct mode of understanding and pursuing a participatory approach to development-oriented communication. That is, the *Projeto Coque Vive* seems, on the basis of its institutional mode of operation, in tune with objectives aimed at making use of ICT and other means of communication to further processes of political empowerment and collective action by local youth.

These generalized considerations put aside, the open question remains what type of marginalized young people *Coque Vive* is able to attract and to what extent the initiative manages to get these individuals engaged in its activities, and finally, how it enables them to develop personally and in their communities? Obviously, this is too broad a question to be answered here or in a single research project. I will, therefore, focus on how each of the projects has specifically dealt with the one, all-pervasive challenge to the living conditions of (young) people in Coque and Peixinhos: the omnipresent lure and threat of gang-related criminal activities that shape and affect the life trajectories of male and female adolescents in serious ways.

The main reason for this analytical focus is an acknowledgement of the fact that the crime-related activities and (often deadly) violence are a major impediment to the realization of social and human developments in the community (Freitas, 2005). Itself a consequence of the socio-economic marginalization of the inhabitants of urban Brazilian *favelas*, gang-related crime and violence perpetuates this marginalization by narrowing the range of realistic youth identity constructions, as Lucia Rabello de Castro (2006), among others, has demonstrated convincingly in her work. In an environment that denies the young the most elementary human rights, criminal activities are not only a way to gain material goods but also a source of symbolic gains, once the fear the criminal inspires is perceived as power. Such practices and behaviors are widespread in the community, being easily imitated and internalized by adolescents.

Obviously, any initiative attempting to empower young people and thus to support them in their desperate struggles for social independence and economic betterment, has to face the accompanying constraints that arise from working with young people in such an environment. The project design and implementation may be judged against the initiative's ability to work through the participatory challenges that arise under such conditions. Thus, we can ask how successful the studied social inclusion and digital empowerment initiative is, not only with regard to young people's acquisition of digital literacy competencies but also with regard to their appropriation of critical reflective and communicative abilities in general and based on these the capacity to develop into strong, self-reliant individuals—that is, youth who are able and willing to challenge the structural predetermination as victim and/or participant in illegal and illicit activities that affect, with a frightening degree of probability, youth growing up in a Brazilian *favela*.

Lessons from the Ground

A profound awareness and comprehension of the asymmetrical matrix of power relations criss-crossing a particular community—including the external relations that individual members bring into play to strengthen their relative position in the hierarchical social order of the community—is a crucial pre-condition to any attempt at community development and social change. Applied to the studied situation, one crucial matrix of power that has to be understood is the informal coercive authority created by those (young) men, who "call the shots" in the *favela*. That is the informal coercive power of those heavily armed male youth, who seem to belie the notion of the disempowered, mainly black and colored, young inhabitants of the poorest urban quarters, by the sheer potential of violence they are ready to employ.

Given the material prosperity and masculine, aggressive self-assuredness these criminals are eager to display, it comes as no surprise that the most successful gang members figure as role models to "success" in the eyes of not so few local youth (de Castro, 2006, p. 187), who almost without exception face the prospect of unemployment or underemployment and in consequence the prospect of a sustained economic dependence on their impoverished families. Identity positions in drug trafficking and crime seem crystallized and centered round easier chances to survive and become included. That is, a "logic of survival" seems powerfully at work, a logic that demands poor urban Brazilian youngsters to consume, as a "mode of inclusion" in society, in order to achieve short-term gains that narrow down "alternative" prospective visions of the self (de Castro, 2006).

In consequence, institutions of formal and informal education spanning from the local public schools to extra-curricular initiatives as offered by *Coque Vive* compete directly with the opportunity structure offered by the criminal subculture that is ever present in the daily lives of *favela's* youths. Running small, but lucrative errands for the local gangs or providing sex for favors and material gifts are more than a mere hypothetical possibility and often a first step to getting further involved. Most important, though the majority of poor Brazilian youngsters manage to stay away from illicit activities—as a "career"—the institutional spaces created by *Coque Vive* are no islands of bliss, but have to deal with the fact that a considerable number of local youngsters have intermittent links with the gangs, either to consume drugs or to earn a little "on the side." As some of the most outspoken change agents interviewed here were ready to admit, the venues of ETAPAS have become the site of occasional drug dealing. Moreover, the general security situation has meant that courses and other activities are limited to daytime hours.

One of the less obvious, but concrete barriers to the digital inclusion of young people from Coque is thus the question whether the ETAPAS/NEIMFA premises are considered to be a safe enough semi-public space for parents to allow their teenage children to participate in the project's activities. If the answer is no, parents will try to keep children away and encourage them to either stay at home[2] or to participate in other, less "dangerous" activities. Moreover, young people representing de Castro's "cautious" type of youth identities—youth who turn, for example, to religion and religious activities as a "defense" against the lure of the pleasurable (de Castro, 2006, p. 189)—may keep away on their own accord, if they feel not at ease amongst their peers frequenting the premises of ETAPAS/NEIMFA.

The fact that Coque's public library has become the occasional site of drug trafficking (as several change agents were ready to admit) was therefore seen and acted upon with great concern. What seems at stake is nothing less than the reputation of the NGOs and CBOs (community-based organizations) involved with local youth. While the general security situation has meant that courses and other activities are limited to daytime hours, the organizations coming together in the project *Coque Vive* have meanwhile decided neither to employ professional security guards nor to ask for regular police patrols. Instead they seem to have established some rapport with the local gangs, in terms of being "accepted" and afforded some guarantees of "non-interference." While the concrete processes of negotiation at work in this tenuous relation are too complex to be summed up in a few lines, it is worth pointing out the constructive role played by the local Movement for the Abolishment of Invisible Barriers (MABI) and by a number of prolific musicians and rock bands with roots in Coque and other city *favelas*, in establishing some kind of dialogue with deviant youth, who seem to be beyond the reach of state institutions and civil society organizations.

The former's "street credibility" and (sub)cultural status, brought vehemently into play in this communicative relation between young adults and adolescents, can be understood as an interactional prerequisite and counterweight to the "status" that high-profile gang members wield amongst *favela* youth. The situation in Coque compares thus to a high degree with the experiences made by the Rio de Janeiro-based *Grupo Cultural AfroReggae* (GCAR), which started in 1993 in *Vigario Geral*, one of Rio de Janeiro's most violent *favelas* and which by now has grown into one of Brazil's best known and established Community Culture Centers.[3] In an interview for *Radio Favela*, Damian Platt, the coordinator for international partnerships of Afro Reggae, has pointed out the importance of the rapport established between the musicians-cum-change agents and leading members of the local gangs:

> DP: We have always been capable of very good dialogue with the drug traffickers, AfroReggae has always, has got…one of the most important things is the reputation we have with them….The thing is, we negotiate with everyone. That is how, I think, we got this role as bringing people together, because we can negotiate with the authorities, with the police, with the media, civil society, but there in the *favelas* we talk with drug traffickers and that includes sitting down with some of Rio's most wanted and sitting over a table with them.[4]

As in the case of GCAR, the members of MABI and the musicians who have been involved in the efforts of the project *Coque Vive* seem to command a considerable sub-cultural legitimacy to address the social reality faced by local youth. With reference to Axel Honneth's (1995) well-known theory of recognition, we can state that they demonstrate the ability to occupy a crucial assertive position in their community's historic struggle for cultural recognition.

Most important, their "voice from within" is basically a non-violent, mediated articulation that challenges, by means of cultural expression, the gang members' belligerent, but poorly articulated manifestation of a self-assertive identification as marginalized and subaltern *favela* youth. As an assertive subcultural articulation, their (mediated) "voice" is powerful, precisely because they employ and refer to popular music and other forms of cultural expression in their verbal communicative exchange with local peers and youth. Essentially, theirs is an emotional and engaging way to address male and female youth, with its appeal derived from the life histories and identity positions that are culturally shared. In Silvia Ramos' (2006) generic characterization of these "new mediators":

> The texts of their songs, their clothes, the names of their groups are pronouncedly antiracist and show strong commitment with the black race. Not necessarily making part of the so-called "black movement," these young people refer in their music and in interviews permanently to the fact of being "black" and to living in *favelas*....This brings them into an opposite position to the silence predominating in traditional cultural expressions like Samba with respect to racial discrimination, and also differs from the traditional protests against racism based on the idea of victimization used by the black movement (Ramos, 2006, p. 423).

Building on their essential credibility, principles of mutual recognition and acceptance, the musicians-cum-change agents seem able to propagate powerful appeals to restraint, to "the right way" and to non-violent ways of conflict resolution, arguing not from a moral, Christian, or legal position, but trying to make sense and talk reason in a language "from below" (cf. Molde, 2002, 2003).

No less important, the involved musicians-cum-change agents, while perceived as rooted in the Brazilian *favela* culture, have been able to transgress the narrow confines of their primary audience base. Having "ghetto authenticity" and "street credibility" on one hand and a non-confrontational, universally humanistic message on the other, their inter-subjective articulations of subaltern self-respect, solidarity, and cultural identification have contributed to initiatives that are striving to bridge Brazil's social stratification by providing for a "less divided" cultural space (Ramos, 2006).

Finally, the "new mediators" qualify as central agents who invest strongly in individual careers and life histories, valuing the symbolic field of subjectivity. In counteraction to the creation of stereotypes, they seek to create powerful images of young people of the *favela* who, against all expectations, go on to become film-makers, stage actors, or musicians. They use the media and seek partnerships with the great communication corporations, appearing not only as artists, but also as leaders talking in the name of the young people from the *favelas*. In this sense, they are different from the syndicalistic and associative model of the left, where the "collective" prevails over individualistic deviations (Ramos, 2006, p. 423).

I have gone to some lengths in outlining the mediating role of cultural activists and (semi)professional artists in challenging a *favela's* predominant subculture of crime-related violence. The reason to do so is that this "history" allows us to understand the reasoning behind *Coque Vive's* decision to set up a fully fledged digital studio in 2008, aimed at musical, video, and Internet-based content production. With *Coque Vive's* insistence to include facilities for the digital recording and editing of music, whether in audio only or in audio-visual formats, the young people involved in the final decision process seek to tap into the encouraging experience made in Coque, in Recife and Brazil.

While it is still too early to determine whether this most recent, ambitious project lives up to its expectations, it makes sense to look at some of the precursors, realized in 2006 to 2008, by which *Coque Vive* has ventured into the field of digital content creation for social inclusion and digital empowerment.

Amongst these precursors the *Coque Vive* website and the related *Movimentos sociais e mídias digitais* (Social movements and digital media) blog[5] might be considered the most lasting and visible attempts. The website includes regularly updated information on ongoing activities and provides numerous links; for example, to the *Revelando O Coque* (*Revealing Coque*) Flickr photo stream[6] featuring 141 pictures, taken by participants in the *Rede de Agentes de Educomunicação Solidária* (2007) workshop. Moreover, the website provides a link to videos produced by participants of several *Coque Vive* projects and is accessible via YouTube.[7] Finally, the mentioned blog provides a link to 14 different audio streams, consisting of short interview clips (up to 3:30 minutes) with associated volunteers and change agents.[8]

However, while these web-distributed text, audio, visual, and audio-visual media products speak of the processes of personal and situational self-reflections in which the workshop participants have been engaged, it is questionable whether *Coque Vive's* "external" communication goal has been realized. That is, whether this user-generated content has reached out beyond the community in an effort to build new stereotypes that dissociate local youth from the image of criminality. Relative low numbers of viewing and the "static" appearance of the mentioned sites, emphasize respective doubts.[9] The prejudiced image of *Coque* continues to dominate reporting in local media; for example, in the daily television crime shows *Bronca Pesada* (*Heavy Quarrel*) and *Ronda da Cidade* (*Patrol of the City*) and in the regional tabloid *Folha de Pernambuco*. Clearly, the public reputation of *Coque* as "*morada da morte*" evolved and circulated in the mainstream media over several decades (Freitas, 2005, p. 274), sticks hard. To counter it demands more than the sporadic counter-representations, produced and circulated on digital platforms by a number of local youth.

Also, a detailed analysis of the *Coque Vive* website and its related blog points to some of the communicative shortcomings. Most important, it shows few contributions by local workshop participants, and the bulk of written text is produced by volunteers and change agents; for example, by Igor Cabral, a University of Pernambuco student and project volunteer (not resident in the community), who has set up and almost exclusively provided the content of the Social Movements and Digital Media blog. The dialogical features that both website and blog potentially enable are in practice insufficiently realized. In consequence, neither site has created significant forms of mediated debate. While Internet-based forms of interpersonal communication are dominated by the use of email, MS Messenger, and social network sites such as Orkut, young people from *Coque* seem to prefer mobile phones as a mediated substitute of face-to-face conversations. That is, *Coque Vive's* promotion of a localized, mediated space for chatting, debate, and social networking seem to have failed.

However, this "failure" should not induce us to state the irrelevance of digital inclusion initiatives for strategic inventions of social empowerment and change. Rather what we must acknowledge is the challenging nature of digital inclusion attempts which seek to move beyond the prevalent computer literacy approach. *Coque Vive's* self-reflexive approach to media education and digital empowerment continues to explore the role of (digitally mediated) communication, questioning the well known practices and theoretical understandings of a techno-centric digital inclusion perspective. *Coque Vive's* trial and error approach comes with failures and setbacks. However, the involved volunteers and change agents have demonstrated a high degree of critical self-reflection and thus the potential to learn from experience as they move on.

The lesson learned so far is that self-expressive, politicized, and counter-hegemonic creative media engagements that give a voice to a specific group of youth within the community—and possibly to the community within broader society—may evolve if a collective of young people working with communication in all mediated forms is formed, encouraged, and supported over a considerable period of time. To do so, digital empowerment attempts must grow from and give voice to the lived experiences and cultural identifications of the participants. Eventually, a collective group of participants may evolve who is motivated to engage consistently in the creation of a localized, transformative expressive space. ICT proficiency (including technical and communicative skills) and an improved access to information are in themselves insufficient. Given, the prevalence of "exit strategies"—fueled by mediated representations and personal narratives of a bright future "somewhere else," compared with the perceived lack of rewards and opportunities in the community—the individual bias of the skills approach might in fact encourage the most promising participants to leave their life in the community behind. This "brain drain" goes hand in hand with a narrow motivation structure, encouraging workshop participants to seek immediate personal benefits.

Digital empowerment, understood in the sense outlined here, is accompanied by widening social network improvements and by advances in learning new courses of interaction. That is, it enables (young) people to do what is important to them and enables them to grow as competent subjects who have control over their lives and surroundings by non-violent, civic means.

Final Considerations

One experience that underlines this line of thinking and gives reason for continued optimism has been the production of the *Jornal Coque*, published in print and as a free downloadable electronic version.[10] The fact that makes this project, realized in cooperation with scholars and students of the department of journalism at the Federal University of Pernambuco (UFPE) in 2006, so remarkable is the high degree of subjectivity that comes to an expression in the around 30 textual contributions to the journal, in which students, voluntaries, and workshop participants articulate their view and vision on what it means to be a young person living and growing up in *Coque*. These first-person accounts, interspersed with pictures and drawings over two dozen pages, focus on the dynamics of structural violence, political neglect, and economic marginalization, which are a main cause of the 40,000 inhabitant's harsh realities of daily life. However, to its credit, a number of contributions to the journal question also the role played by the local power structure, gendered hierarchies, and a subculture of machismo in sustaining the community's present state. This "introverted" perspective includes critical reflections on Coque's ubiquitous gang culture, on the resulting fear and silence and on the resulting limitation of life chances and identity roles, "available" to local youth.

Given these "literary" qualities, it seems plausible that the *Jornal Coque* has been widely circulated within the community and beyond. According to Yvana Fechine, a scholar at UFPE and responsible for the project, a thousand copies have been distributed initially. While we can only speculate on the public impact of this community media project, it seems reasonable to suggest that the young people involved, both those from within Coque and those from without, have gone through a mutual learning process. That is, the *Jornal Coque* project has demonstrated its potential in furthering one of *Coque Vive's* central aims: to approximate the *favela* and the middle-class, operating in both directions.[11]

A last, but not less, important lesson that can be drawn from this "success" is a realization that (young) people, in their appropriation of new communication technologies, at first seldom seize on all the new possibilities that ICTs offer. Rather, they seem to prefer to appropriate them with reference to aims and desires that are well established, but have remained unfulfilled or only partly fulfilled, due to the limitations of previous communication technologies. In relation to *Coque Vive's* experience made with new digital means of media production, distribution, and networked communication, the forte of digital inclusion efforts lies equally, in prolongation of the existing, established, and well-proven participatory communication and intervention strategies. The growing presence of ICTs and their proliferation (both market-driven and through the institutional agency of social inclusion and change initiatives) may encourage digital empowerment initiatives' focus on the advanced forms of computer-facilitated communication, popular with many young people in the Global North and amongst Brazil's middle- and upper-class. For the time being, digital content production by and for *favela* youth is most powerful and enabling when linked to and expressed in terms of the existing popular forms of cultural expression, music, dance, graffiti, *capoeira*, etc., and when tapping into the oratory power of *favela* speech.

Notes

1. With an annual average of 60 homicides in 2005–2007, the neighborhood which houses an estimated 40,000 inhabitants within an area of 1.33 sqkm, has become known as '*morada da morte*' ('homestead of death') in popular parlance.
2. For a more detailed consideration of this protective 'strategy' of parents in Recife, see Dalsgaard et al. (2008) and Gough (2008).
3. By 2006 the GCAR offered training and workshops to 2,000 youth in over 60 programs and began touring internationally. The plethora of activities initiated by GCAR includes workshops and programmes of dance, percussion, recycling, soccer, capoeira, informatics, theatre, community radio, art and video production (see http://www.favelarising.com/about-afroreggae.html).
4. Interview downloaded at http://www.ar2com.de/radiofavela-blog/afroreggae-and-urban-

connections/

5. At http://coquevive.wordpress.com/ and http://experienciaemdigital.wordpress.com/
6. At http://www.flickr.com/photos/revelandoocoque/
7. For example, *Biblioteca Popular do Coque* (6:40 min.), *Circuitos nas Escolas—Coque Vive* (4:11 min.), *Projeto Coque* (3:28 min.), Revelando o Coque (2:05 min.) and Desclassificados (4:59 min.).
8. At http://experienciaemdigital.wordpress.com/anexo-fragmentos-de-audio/
9. Between 179 and 1.247 views for the videos and less than 200 views for each of the uploaded photos (15–09–2009).
10. At http://coquevive.wordpress.com/projetos-2/jornalcoque/
11. Compare *Coque Vive: comunicação, educação e cultura*, the UFPE's project description posted 03/12/2008 at http://www.pluricom.com.br/clientes/grupo-sm/noticias/2008/12/coque-vive-comunicacao-educacao-e-cultura/?searchterm="coque vive."

References

Bonfadelli, H. (2002). The Internet and knowledge gaps: A theoretical and empirical investigation. *European Journal of Communication (17l),* 1, 65–84.

Bure, C. (2005). Digital inclusion without social inclusion: The consumption of information and communication technologies (ICTs) within homeless subculture in Scotland. *The Journal of Community Informatics* (2005). *(1),* 2, 116–133.

Chadwick, A. (2006). *Internet politics: states, citizens, and new communication technologies.* Oxford: Oxford University Press.

Clark, J., & Themudo, N. (2003). The Age of Protest: Internet-based "dot causes" and the "anti-globalization" movement. In *Globalizing civic engagement: civil society and transnational action,* edited by J. Clark. London: Earthscan Publications.

Couldry, N. (2008). Media and the Problem of Voice. In *Participation and media production: critical reflections on content creation,* edited by Nico Carpentier and Benjamin de Cleen. Newcastle upon Tyne: Cambridge Scholars Publishing.

Dalsgaard, A. L. et al. (2008). Dominant Ideas, Uncertain Lives: The Meaning of Youth in Recife. In *Youth and the City in the Global South,* edited by Karen Tranberg Hansen et al. Bloomington: Indiana University Press.

de Castro, L. R. (2006). What is new in the "south"? Consumer culture and the vicissitudes of poor youth's identity construction in urban Brazil. *Young (14),* 3, 179–201.

Freitas, A. S. (2005). *Fundamentos para uma sociologia crítica da formação humana.* Tese de Doutorado apresentada ao Programa de Pós-Graduação em Sociologia do Centro de Filosofia e Ciências Humanas da Universidade Federal de Pernambuco.

Gough, K. (2008). Youth and the Home. In *Youth and the City in the Global South,* edited by Karen Tranberg Hansen et al. Bloomington: Indiana University Press.

Haddon, L. (2000). Social Exclusion and Information and Communication Technologies: Lessons from Studies of Single Parents and the Young Elderly, *New Media & Society (2),* 4, 387–408.

Harris, R. W. (2004). *Information and communication technologies for poverty alleviation.* United Nations Development Programme's Asia-Pacific Development Information Programme (UNDP-APDIP): Kuala Lumpur, Malaysia.

Honneth, A. (1995). *The struggle for recognition. The moral grammar of social conflicts.* 1995. Cambridge: Polity Press.

Lanki, J. (2006). Why would information and communications technology contribute to development at all? An ethical inquiry into the possibilities of ICT in development. *eLearning, (3),* 3, 448–461.

Ling, R. (2004).*The mobile connection: The cell phone's impact on society.* San Francisco: Morgan Kaufmann.

Mäkinen, M. (2006). Digital empowerment as a process for enhancing citizens' participation. *e-Learning, (3)* 3, 381–95.

Molde, M. (2002). At følge den gode vej (To follow the good path). Master thesis, Institute of Anthropology, Copenhagen.

Molde, M. (2003). Storbyliv uden mure (Metropolitan lives without walls). *Jordens Folk (3),* 56–61. Aarhus: Dansk Etnografisk Forening.

Potter, A. B. (2006). Zones of silence: A framework beyond the digital divide. *First Monday (11),* 5.

Ramos, S. (2006). Brazilian responses to violence and new forms of mediation: the case of the Grupo Cultural AfroReggae and the experience of the project *Youth and the Police. Ciência & Saúde Coletiva (11),* 2, 419–428. Centro de Estudos de Segurança e Cidadania da Universidade Candido Mendes.

Selwyn, N. (2004). Reconsidering political and popular understandings of the digital divide. *New Media & Society (6),* 341–362.

Silverstone, R. (1996). Future Imperfect: Information and Communication Technologies in Everyday Life. In *Information and communications technologies: Visions and realities,* edited by W. Dutton. Oxford: Oxford University Press.

Strover, S. (2003). Remapping the digital divide. *The Information Society (19),* 275–277.

Warschauer, M. (2003). *Technology and social inclusion: Rethinking the social divide.* Cambridge, MA: MIT Press.

15

Do We Really Need Media Education 2.0?

Teaching in the Age of Participatory Media

DAVID BUCKINGHAM

The advent of digital media has been seen by many commentators to require new paradigms, in scholarship, in creative practice, and in pedagogy. "New" media is, according to some, so fundamentally different from "old" media that each requires different methods of analysis, different theoretical and conceptual frameworks, and different forms of intellectual and political engagement. In relation to education, the interactive, participatory possibilities of digital media are believed to transcend the limitations of hierarchical, top-down "mass" media, and hence to undermine what are seen as the authoritarian "knowledge politics" of traditional pedagogy. The potential which digital media offer for learners to become creators—rather than merely "consumers"—of knowledge has been seen by some as close to revolutionary.

In this chapter, I seek to interrogate these claims and assess their implications for educational practice. My specific concern is with the practice of *media education*, in what and how we should teach *about* media, rather than in the use of media as teaching materials or teaching aids (that is, *educational media*). My focus is primarily on teaching in schools, although what will be stated here has implications for the practice of media education in universities as well.

In the UK, media education has a long history, going back over 60 years. We have specialist examined courses in Media Studies, which students in most schools can follow from the age of 14; and media education is a dimension of mother tongue language teaching ("subject English") throughout secondary school. While there has been less coherent provision in primary schools, there is now a growing recognition among policy makers that all children should be taught about media as a core element of literacy education in particular (see Buckingham, 2003; Burn & Durran, 2007). As such, I speak from a context where there is already a well-established body of educational practice: media education in the UK is guided by a fairly coherent conceptual framework, and there is a good sense of "what works" in classroom terms. Crucially, in relation to the focus of this book, media education in UK schools has *always* been about creativity as well as critique: it is about making media as well as analyzing media.

Of course, this is not to say that there are no debates to be had or no areas in need of development. Indeed, there is a growing body of research that is addressing some of the contradictions and limitations of established practice in media education[1]. Much of the debate here hinges on fundamental questions about knowledge and learning: what do we imagine young people *already* know about media, what do they need to know, and how might they learn it? The advent of digital media has interesting implications in respect of these questions. As we shall see in the following, some have claimed that contemporary changes in the wider media environment require us to rethink the fundamental aims and methods of media education—not just the content of the curriculum, but also our pedagogy and teaching methods. But are such changes as fundamental as their advocates suggest? And is it necessarily the case that the age of "Media 2.0" also requires "Media Education 2.0"?

Media Studies 2.0 and the Complete Reinvention of Everything

In early 2007, there was a brief but intense debate on the UK academic Media Studies message boards focusing on the notion of Media Studies 2.0. The debate appears to have been initiated by William Merrin at University of Wales in Swansea and was quickly taken up by David Gauntlett, of University of Westminster. It was subsequently joined by various named and anonymous participants and was also commented upon in online groups of Media Studies teachers in schools and further education colleges.[2] This debate was primarily about the academic discipline of Media Studies as it is taught in universities rather than schools. There are certainly debates to be had about the pedagogy of Media Studies (and Cultural

Studies) in universities, although these cannot be addressed here.[3] My interest is in the implications for teachers in schools; despite the occasionally somewhat irritating polemical tone of this debate, it did raise serious issues that are, if anything, even more acute for those teaching young people at this level.

Many contemporary teenagers are now growing up with the ensemble of participatory media collectively known as Web 2.0—social networking, photo- and video-sharing, blogging, podcasting, remixing and mash-ups, wikis, machinima, user-generated content, online games and social worlds, and so on. These new media have not replaced old media, however: on average, young people still spend much more time watching television than they spend online (Ofcom, 2008); many of them even obstinately continue to read books. Nevertheless, if we base our teaching on forms of media that are, if not completely outmoded, then at least only part of the environment that young people are now experiencing, there is clearly a danger that what we do in the classroom will become irrelevant to their lives. This is not simply a question of *curriculum content*—of teaching students how to analyze websites as well as television ads, for example. Enthusiasts for new media typically claim it entails a distinctively different orientation towards information, a different phenomenology of use, a different politics of knowledge, and a different mode of learning. If this is the case, it has potentially far-reaching implications for *pedagogy*—not just for *what* we teach, but also for *how* we teach.

For William Merrin (2008), new media represent a fundamental challenge to our *right to teach*:

> Our fear of technology often extends to our own personal use of it. Whereas in the broadcast-era we broadly understood the basic technical principles of the dominant media and we understood their use—sharing that use with our students—today, lecturers are being left behind in their knowledge of what technologies are out there, of their technical possibilities, of how they even work, of how to use them, and of what they are being used for. Again, we no longer share a common culture with our students. Unless we can keep up with these changing technologies and uses and unless they become as integral a part of our lives as they are to our students then we will lose both the ability and even the right to teach them. In an era in which we watched and studied TV we had a right to teach it: in the future, unless we're downloading, sharing, ripping, burning, messaging, networking, playing, building and producing then we'll lose that right (Merrin, 2008: n. p.).

Questions could certainly be raised about the historical narrative that is offered here—the notion that at some unspecified time in the past there used to be a "common culture," a shared experience of media between teachers (or "lecturers") and students, that has now been lost. However, the more challenging question is about the right to teach—in effect, about the *legitimacy* of teaching in the age of Media 2.0.

The arguments developed by Merrin and Gauntlett across their various contributions hinge on a (rather old-fashioned, structuralist-style) binary opposition between "1.0" and "2.0." A summary, drawing principally on Gauntlett (2007), would look roughly as follows:

As with many such binary models, this one suffers from the tendency to deal in

MEDIA 1.0	**MEDIA 2.0**
Old (analogue) media	New (digital) media
Consumption	Production/participation
Hierarchy	Popular democracy
MEDIA STUDIES 1.0	**MEDIA STUDIES 2.0**
The media canon	Diversification of tastes
Western media	Global media
Textual analysis and political economy	Audience research
Conventional research methods	Qualitative/creative research methods
Expert readers	Ordinary audience members
People need to be taught to be critical	People are already critical

Figure 1: Media (studies) 1.0 versus media (studies) 2.0.

absolute oppositions and to conflate quite different issues. For example, the distinction between Western media and global media does not simply map onto the distinction between "old" and "new" media—particularly in a situation where the majority of the population of the Global South does not even have access to electricity, let alone broadband Internet (see the chapter by Wildermuth in this volume). There are other debates to be had about research methods and about the merits of so-called "creative" approaches to audience research (which I have pursued elsewhere: Buckingham, 2009). To some extent, Gauntlett is also replaying an old debate in academic Media Studies between political economy and audience research—a debate that, as Lawrence Grossberg (1995) and others have suggested, is itself unhelpfully polarized.

Even so, there are interesting pedagogical issues here, which go back to the point about the legitimacy of teaching. We might characterize this position as a kind of *pedagogical populism*. For example, Gauntlett is dismissive of textual analysis. A key characteristic of Media Studies 1.0, he says, is "a tendency to fetishise 'experts,' whose readings of popular culture are seen as more significant than those of other audience members (with corresponding faith in faux-expert non-procedures such as semiotics)." By contrast, in Media Studies 2.0, this approach is "replaced with a focus on the everyday meanings produced by the diverse array of audience members" (Gauntlett, 2007: 3). Likewise, Media Studies 1.0 is characterized by "a belief that students should be taught how to 'read' the media in an appropriate 'critical' style." In Media Studies 2.0, this is no longer necessary: "The patronizing belief that students should be taught how to 'read' the media is replaced by the recognition that media audiences in general are already extremely capable interpreters of media content, with a critical eye and an understanding of contemporary media techniques, thanks in large part to the large amount of coverage of this in popular media itself" (Gauntlett, 2007: 3). Obviously, there is an element of deliberate provocation here; but there are also interesting questions about learning. If ordinary people are already creating their own diverse meanings, participating and producing their own media, in the capable and critical way Gauntlett is suggesting—and he is of course by no means alone in this—then what do these people need to learn and what do we have to teach them?

The Limits of Media 2.0

The advocates of Media Studies 2.0 are clearly subscribers to what Richard Barbrook and Andy Cameron (1996) many years ago called "the Californian ideology"—a kind of populist cyber-libertarianism that claims ordinary people will somehow be empowered by technology, and that digital media is inherently liberating and countercultural. This approach is certainly apparent in the celebration of "creativity" and "participation" *for their own sake*; and in the valorizing of "ordinary people" *as opposed to* the spurious critical procedures and patronizing attitudes of self-declared "experts."

The broader problems with this approach have been widely rehearsed (see, for example, Robins & Webster, 1999; Woolgar, 2002; Buckingham, 2007), because it rests on a form of technological determinism—a view of technology as somehow autonomously producing social change. In this context, and in discussions of education more broadly, it is also implicated with the notion of the "digital generation"—the idea that technology has brought about fundamental and absolute generational change and that young people today are somehow automatically technologically savvy or media literate. As several critics have argued, this approach embodies a kind of essentialism, an "exoticising" of youth, which ignores the diversity and the inequalities in young people's experiences and the continuities across generations (Facer & Furlong, 2001; Buckingham, 2006; Herring, 2008).

A full critique of the rhetoric of Media 2.0 is beyond the scope of this chapter, although key critical questions need to be raised. The term "Web 2.0" appears to have been coined by the digital marketing entrepreneur Tim O'Reilly and his associates in 2001 (O'Reilly, 2005). Indeed, it can be seen to reflect an attempt to rebrand the Internet business after the bursting of the so-called "dot.com bubble." O'Reilly himself appears already to have tired of the idea; while others—including Tim Berners-Lee, widely identified as the inventor of the World Wide Web—have questioned whether Web 2.0 is actually any different from Web 1.0, because the basic technological infrastructure and many of the forms or genres of Web 2.0 have been around since the beginning of the Internet (Anderson, 2006; *First Monday*, 2008).

Claims about the potential of new media in terms of democratization and empowerment are by no means new. One can look back to the arguments being made about cable TV in the 1970s (Streeter, 1987), or about portable video in the 1980s (Buckingham et al., 2007)—although in fact most new media technologies have arrived amid claims about their inherently radical potential (Marvin, 1988; Winston, 1998). This was certainly the case with the "old" media of television and radio, but it was also true of the printing press (Eisenstein, 1979): all of these media were apparently going to bring power to the people, undermine the control of knowledge by elites, enable ordinary people to express themselves and have their voices heard, and create new forms of collaboration, in precisely the revolutionary ways that are now being seen as characteristic of digital media. And in each case, the ultimate effects were much more complex and equivocal than their advocates proclaimed.

One reason for this has been the uneven and indeed unequal diffusion of technological innovations. In the case of Web 2.0, statistics on patterns of use are not wholly reliable. For example, in a recent study by the Pew Foundation (Lenhart et al., 2007), 64% of U.S. teens said they had created or shared content online. While this figure appears to include profiles on social networking sites, nevertheless, 39% of teens claimed to have posted artwork, creative writing, photographs, or videos. On the other hand, figures from the market research agency Hitwise suggest that among users of YouTube—the most accessible online video-sharing site—only 0.16% actually upload material, and it is not clear how much of that material is originally produced, rather than pirated clips from commercial media (Auchard, 2007). The same study found that 0.2% of Flickr visitors upload photos, while 4.6% of users edit or write for Wikipedia (a suspiciously high figure).

One of the evident difficulties here (and indeed for this volume as a whole) is in defining "creating content." When undertaking research in the mid-1990s—early days for digital creativity—my colleague Julian Sefton-Green and I found surprisingly high numbers of young people claiming in a questionnaire survey that they engaged in creative multimedia activities on their computers; but when we probed more deeply via interviews and home visits, we found that very little of this was actually taking place (Sefton-Green & Buckingham, 1996). Most of these young people seemed to know what they could *potentially* be doing with the technology, but they mostly lacked the social or personal motivation to actually do it themselves. Even today, it appears only a small proportion of users are in fact generating original content; most are simply consuming it as they always have done.

Furthermore, there is a danger here of misrepresenting what the majority of people are actually doing when they are creating content. Jean Burgess (2006) has rightly criticized the participatory media enthusiasts for focusing on the more artistic avant-garde or post-modern manifestations of "cool"—fan-produced mash-ups, or counter-cultural political critique—while neglecting the relatively banal domestic practices of the majority. Our research suggests that most amateur video-making, for example, continues to be dominated by what Richard Chalfen (1987) calls the "home mode"—home movies of family life, children's birthday parties, or holidays on the beach. This material is rarely edited or shared and is kept as a record that people imagine will be watched at some time in the future, even if it rarely is. While home video serves particular functions in terms of memory and family relationships, people rarely see home video as having anything to do with what they watch in the mainstream media: it is a long way from the radical democratization of mediated communication proclaimed by some enthusiasts (Buckingham and Willett, 2009; Buckingham et al., in press).

Research also suggests there are striking social differences in levels of participation. Lenhart et al. (2007) suggest that young women are leading the way in areas such as blogging, while young men tend to dominate video-sharing; although the research also demonstrates that suburban teens from high-income families are most likely to be posting or sharing online. Hargittai and Walejko (2008) also point to a social class imbalance, while Warschauer (2003), in a slightly older study, points out that while people in disadvantaged communities may increasingly have computers, these people are less likely to have the multimedia capabilities and bandwidth necessary for more sophisticated content creation and sharing.

This implies "digital divides" are still apparent, although we need to differentiate between different *types* of content and access and take account of the skills or abilities (the forms of technological, cultural, or educational capital) that are at stake. These inequalities in levels of participation are clearly related to wider forms of social inequality, and they largely coincide with other differences; for example, in how families from different social classes use the educational dimensions of the Internet or participate in creative or arts-related activities offline. To a large extent, the most active participants in the creative world of Web 2.0 are the "usual suspects:" those who already have an established interest in social/political issues, and the skills and motivation to engage in political debate. Indeed, if online participation is as socially, culturally, and politically important as the enthusiasts suggest, it seems likely that, far from liquidating social inequality, it might actually accentuate it.

Finally, there is the question of the commercial interests at stake in these developments. One of the paradoxical characteristics of the Californian ideology is its appeal both to libertarian political radicals and to contemporary business gurus. Here, for example, is the media magnate Rupert Murdoch (2006) expressing his egalitarian vision of the future of media: "Technology is shifting power away from the editors, the publishers, the establishment, the media élite…now it's the people who are taking control." In fact, the apparent explosion of democratic participation in the media is being accompanied by a growing concentration of power in the hands of a small number of global companies. The political economy of Web 2.0 is still evolving—at the time of this writing, for example, YouTube has yet to generate a profit, despite being the second most frequently visited site online. Even so, the Internet is an exceptionally efficient medium for niche marketing, not least because of the Internet's potential for the targeting and surveillance of individual consumers. Indeed, much of this marketing is itself "user-generated" and "interactive" (as in the case of viral advertising).

These issues also apply to what Soren Peterson (2008) has aptly called "loser-generated content." A great deal of unpaid labor goes into the production of blogs, for example, while most of the income generated from blogs remains with the big corporations. In the case of social networking, participants typically spend enormous amounts of time working on their profiles and building networks—accumulating social and cultural capital—which they are then unable to take with them if they want to migrate to another site. What they produce effectively becomes proprietary information, owned by the company—an issue that has recently come to the fore in legal disputes over copyright ownership of images on Yahoo's Flickr site (see "Thoughts for Deletion," 2007).

Clearly, there is a debate to be had about the wider social and political ramifications of Media 2.0. It could be argued that, far from precipitating a democratic revolution in communications, these new media are merely part of much broader move towards individualization, self-surveillance, and self-promotion that are characteristic of how identities are formed and lived out in neo-liberal consumer societies. These debates are beyond the scope of this chapter: the intention here is merely to signal some of the potential limitations and criticisms of these much-celebrated developments. Despite the claims of some new media evangelists, digital media are not likely to result in a society of creative media producers, any more than the printing press resulted in a society of published authors. While there is certainly a democratic promise here, the realization of that promise will require more than technology alone.

Beyond Celebration

With this rather more skeptical view of the contemporary media environment, how might we assess the implications for education and, specifically, for media education? Here again, caution must be exercised upon reviewing some of the more celebratory accounts that typically circulate here. The Californian ideology has its own manifestations in education, where technology is widely believed to be transforming learning, changing the power relationships of classrooms, and creating autonomous, liberated learners. This form of cyber-utopianism is typically aligned with a range of fashionable but ill-defined concepts—of which creativity, informal learning, and (most recently) personalization are among the most prominent (see Buckingham, 2007: chapter 2). This rhetoric is strongly promoted by commercial technology companies, but it is also espoused by governments seeking to identify a technological fix for what are seen as the problems of public education. In such discussions, it is often difficult to tell the difference between the over-excited claims of policy-makers (and some academics) and the sales pitches of the computer companies (Buckingham, 2007).

For some apparently "progressive" educational thinkers, the technology-driven classroom is somehow the vindication of the child-centered learning theories of the

1960s and 1970s; although there are others who argue that digital technology has rendered the institution of the school redundant and that the real learning is now taking place in children's "informal" engagements with games or online social worlds. This celebratory argument typically entails a wholly positive, uncritical stance towards popular uses of technology. For example, those who extol the benefits of computer games for learning tend to ignore the commercial dimensions of games and avoid awkward questions about their values and ideologies (e.g., Gee, 2003). They also engage in a rather ill-defined valorization of "informal learning," in which formal learning is seen as something inherently bad.

Another mode of celebration that is particularly apparent in relation to media education is that of vocationalism. In the UK over the past several decades, the curriculum for 14- to 19-year olds has been the focus of a seemingly endless series of innovations apparently designed to address the problem of work in a post-industrial "knowledge economy." In the case of media, there has always been the hope that young people from economically disadvantaged backgrounds would somehow be able to "cash in" their cultural capital—to use vocational media courses as a way of turning their expertise with media and popular culture into something that can be accredited and, hence, lead to employment (Cohen, 1990). In the UK, the latest of these innovations is a series of new diplomas, qualifications that purport to cross the academic/vocational divide and to prepare students for new kinds of working situations. At present, these courses are lavishly funded by the government, although teachers are struggling to come to terms with new curriculum structures and modes of assessment, not to mention a plethora of new jargon. The courses I have seen thus far are very much aligned with Media 2.0: students are making websites, staging events in Second Life, creating photoblogs and machinima. However, the fact remains that such courses are likely to be perceived as alternative routes for those who are defined as "low achievers": they will not replace the existing high-status examinations that will continue to be sought after by the elite universities.

Such courses offer these young people a promise of employment—a seductive fantasy of cool jobs, the no-collar jobs in the technology and cultural industries of the kind that Andrew Ross (2003) has described. Yet despite the mythology, there are few instances of fans or amateur enthusiasts crossing the line from unpaid labor into paid employment—and, as Ross outlines, the conditions of work for young people in the computer games industry or in web companies are often profoundly exploitative. Indeed, it is very much in the interests of the media industries to have a large cohort of fans aspiring to become professionals, not least because it allows them considerable freedom to exploit the people who do work for them (see also van Dijk, 2009).

Addressing Digital Divides

Rather than reducing schooling to a mere irrelevance, or indeed to a training ground for the new digital economy, the advent of digital technology points to a need to extend the traditional mission of the school as a public institution. In collaboration with other public institutions, schools exist partly in order to provide young people with social, intellectual, and cultural experiences that they might not otherwise have. Of course, schools have always had functions in terms of the regulation of populations and the reproduction of social relations, but there is also a powerful modernist rhetoric about the school as an element of the public sphere that should be invoked here.

In the context of continuing digital divides, schools should play a key role in attempting to ameliorate inequalities in participation. As Henry Jenkins and others (2006) have argued, schools have to address the "participation gap"—"the unequal access to the opportunities, experiences, skills, and knowledge that will prepare youth for full participation in the world of tomorrow" (2006: 3). As in agreement with Jenkins, this is about much more than access to equipment; it is about cultural competencies, social skills, and knowledge. Jenkins offers an extensive list here, which includes skills to do with play, experimentation, and problem-solving; skills in handling different media sources and modes of communication, and navigating across and between them; skills in networking and collaborating, locating information, and interacting with others; and skills to do with judgment and critical evaluation.

While some of the skills that Jenkins and others identify are certainly new, others are decidedly traditional. This has been confirmed by research I am currently conducting with colleagues on the role of the Internet in promoting civic participation (see www.civicweb.eu). While some have looked to the Internet as a means of re-engaging young people who are currently disaffected from civic and political organizations, we have found that the usual suspects have largely taken up such opportunities. To this extent, it is possible that the Internet may accentuate existing inequalities rather than help to overcome them. If disaffected and disadvantaged young people are to be enabled to participate, they need to develop relatively traditional skills in locating and evaluating information, constructing arguments, and thinking critically; these activities depend in turn on fairly advanced forms of traditional literacy.

This is not to imply that nothing is changing—the Internet may be fostering new forms and styles of civic engagement, that are at least potentially more inclusive. But participation, in this area as in many others, also requires relatively traditional forms of cultural and educational capital. Addressing the "participation gap," therefore, depends upon addressing broader inequalities: it will not disappear simply as a result of widening access to technology.

The Place of Critique

The kinds of learning typically celebrated in discussions of digital technology in education tend to allow little space for critical reflection or the explicit development of critical skills. There seems to be an assumption that participation or creative production is good in itself and that it either stands in for, or automatically generates, critical understanding in its own right. Indeed, as we have seen, Gauntlett (2007) expresses a strong suspicion of critique, as though it necessarily represented a "patronizing" imposition of pedagogic authority. Media audiences, he argues, are "already extremely capable interpreters of media content": they do not need to be taught to be critical.

As I have argued elsewhere (e.g., Buckingham, 2003), there is some justification in this suspicion of critique. "Critical" itself is very much an "us and them" term: people who are critical are often simply people who happen to agree with us, whereas those we disagree with are hopelessly uncritical. This represents a version of what has been called the "third person effect" in discussions of media influence (Perloff, 2002): it is always *other* people who are deemed to be lacking in critical competence. There is also a danger that "being critical" becomes one of the standardized routines or language games of the media classroom—a game in which students simply give back to the teacher the forms of critical discourse they have been fed (about student's reluctance to do so, see the chapter by Herr-Stephenson in this volume). The emphasis on critical analysis can sanction a rather superficial, rationalistic approach to media—even a form of superficial cynicism—that belies the complex (and not least emotional) ways in which we actually relate to media.

However, none of this is to imply that audiences are readily capable and critical—that they already know everything they need to know. Nor does it mean that we can throw out the critical tools and perspectives used to analyze media. We can accept that audiences can be active, discriminating, and indeed "critical," while also recognizing there are ideals they generally do *not* know about media—and indeed that they need to learn. There is a body of knowledge here—about how the media work, about the media industries, about the history of media, about the uses and effects of media within society. It is a changing and contested body of knowledge, to be sure, but it is, nevertheless, a body of knowledge with shared criteria for determining what counts as truth. The danger here is in assuming that a focus on critique necessarily implies a negative effects model—that somehow criticism is about an illegitimate imposition of authority, or that it necessarily implies that "ordinary people" are stupid or deluded. This seems in turn to imply a rather old-fashioned, narrow sense of criticism as necessarily negative, or at least a notion of criticism as merely a form of defence or inoculation against influence.

Again, Jenkins and his colleagues (2006) are correct to identify another "gap" here, to do with critique. As they suggest, we need to enable young people to become active participants in media culture, but participation or creativity for its own sake is not enough. We also need young people to be *critical* participants and to develop a broader understanding of the economic, social, and cultural dimensions of media. Such critical understanding does not follow automatically from the experience of creative production. As Carmen Luke (2000) argues in relation to literacy, learners do not develop critical literacy just through the experience of reading and writing: they have to step back from immediate experience, in order to reflect and to analyze.

This leads to the complex and time-honored question of how we integrate theory (critical analysis) and practice (creative production). How does learning transfer from the domain of "reading" media to the domain of "writing"—and vice-versa? How do we promote meaningful, rather than superficial, critical reflection on what students do as participants or creators of media? How do we help them to understand those experiences in the broader social and cultural context?

Digital technology is offering us new ways of addressing this issue and of bringing theory closer to practice. For example, in the case of digital editing and image manipulation, the technology can help to make explicit the processes of choice, selection, construction, and manipulation that often seem to be "locked away" with analogue forms. As students drag and drop shots onto the timeline in a digital editing program, the experience of drafting and redrafting a sequence, and debating as the students go along makes a significant difference to the nature of the learning: the experience of editing is not just easier, but also more explicit than was the case with older analogue technology (Buckingham et al., 1999).

My colleague Andrew Burn (2000; Burn & Durran, 2006) has analyzed how teachers can use the "remixing" potential of digital media—a very 2.0 practice—to bring theory closer to practice. Quite well-established activities in media teaching, such as making a trailer to market an existing movie to a new audience (*Psycho* and *Romeo + Juliet* are two of Burn's examples), have become much more feasible and controllable than used to be the case with analogue technology. This process also provides new opportunities for analysis and reflection, although (as Burn suggests) this needs to be an explicit expectation that is built into the process.

Indeed, Burn's case studies show extensive evidence of students applying the "faux-expert non-procedures" of semiotics and political economy analysis to inform such reflection.

Ola Erstad and his colleagues (2007) and Kirsten Drotner (2008) have also recently written about this re-mixing—looking at how students search out material on the Internet for their digital design work and then process and recombine it in various ways, using what is referred to as "cut-and-paste literacy" (see also the chapter by Erstad in this volume). However, the authors also suggest there is a danger in being seduced by the superficial professional "gloss" of this kind of work, and by young people's apparent facility with the technology. Actually, there is a lot they don't know and a lot they can't do; and the activity of media-making needs to be accompanied by forms of analysis and theoretical conceptualization and a set of clear curricular aims on the part of teachers.

Finally, our own recent research on digital game-making provides further instances of this connection between theory and practice (Buckingham & Burn, 2007; Pelletier, 2009). In this project, we worked with an educational software company and a group of schools to develop a game-authoring tool: the resulting package, MissionMaker, enables users to make three-dimensional games without the necessity of programming. We learned quite quickly that, even if students are adept game-players, it does not automatically transfer to the ability to make games. Making games is difficult: it involves computational thinking, logic, and an ability to imagine a user who is not just an audience (or a reader) but a player interacting with the text. In order to move from being a player to being a maker of games, you need to take a step back from your immediate experience and engage in difficult, systematic analysis.

Conclusion

Do we really need Media Education 2.0? Perhaps we do; but we certainly still need Media Education 1.0 as well. The advocates of Media Studies 2.0 do identify key imperatives here. I would not accept Merrin's claim that we lose "the right to teach" if we are not ourselves actively participating in the whole range of contemporary media. However, I would agree it is necessary to keep pace with student media experiences and their changing orientations towards media. Nevertheless, we also need to be aware of assuming that those experiences are all the same (the "digital generation" argument); and keeping up with our students does not mean we should automatically import the latest technological gimmicks into the classroom, let alone start pimping up our Facebook profiles in some hopeless desire to be "down with the kids."

New media can offer new opportunities for participation, for creative communication and for the generation of content, at least for some people in some contexts. However, the competences that people need in order to take up those opportunities are not equally distributed, and they do not arise simply because people have access to technology. Furthermore, it would be wrong to assume that participation is always a good thing or that it is necessarily democratic, countercultural or liberating. Creative production can be a powerful means of learning—whether it involves remixing of various kinds, appropriating and adapting existing texts, or creating wholly new ones, or simply exploiting the potential for networked communication. However, all of this needs critical reflection, and it needs to be combined with critical analysis—although how that combination happens is a genuinely difficult question.

More broadly, media education itself needs to adopt a stronger and more critical stance towards the celebration of technology in education and the kind of market-driven techno-fetishism that is mistakenly seen by some as the cutting edge of educational change. There is a risk here that media education might be seen as just another way of importing computer technology into schools—or indeed as a sexy alternative to the wasteland of spreadsheets, file management, and instrumental training that constitutes most "information technology" courses in schools. There is an opportunity here, but it should not involve abandoning the traditional critical imperatives of media education—which are about much more than practical skills or the sentimental appeal to "creativity."

Notes

1. Reviews of some of this work may be found in Buckingham (2003) and Buckingham et al. (2005). More recent examples are contained in special editions of *Learning, Media and Technology* (2007); and *Media International Australia* (2006).
2. Some of this debate is archived at http://twopointzeroforum.blogspot.com/; Merrin's ongoing blog can be found at http://mediastudies2point0.blogspot.com/; while Gauntlett's work is at http://www.theory.org.uk. (Sites last accessed March 2009.)
3. Some interesting discussions of this may be found in a special issue of the *International Journal of Cultural Studies* 5(4), 2002; and in Blackman (2000).

References

Anderson, N. (2006). Tim Berners-Lee on Web 2.0: Nobody even knows what it means. Retrieved March 17, 2009, from *Ars Technica* http://arstechnica.com/business/news/2006/09/7650.ars.

Auchard, E. (2007). Participation on Web 2.0 sites remains weak. Retrieved December 3, 2007, from Reuters, http://www.reuters.com/article/internetNews/idUSN1743638820070418.

Barbrook, R., & Cameron, A. (1996). The Californian ideology. Retrieved November 8, 2008, from http://www.hrc.wmin.ac.uk/theory-californianideology.html.

Blackman, S. (2000). Decanonized knowledge and the radical project: Towards an understanding of cultural studies in British universities. *Pedagogy, Culture and Society, 8*, 43–67.

Buckingham, D. (2003). *Media education: Literacy, learning and contemporary culture.* Cambridge: Polity.

Buckingham, D. (2006). Is there a digital generation? In D. Buckingham, & R. Willett (Eds.), *Digital generations: Children, young people and new media.* Mahwah, NJ: Lawrence Erlbaum, pp. 1–17.

Buckingham, D. (2007). *Beyond technology: Children's learning in the age of digital culture.* Cambridge: Polity.

Buckingham, D. (2009). "Creative" visual methods in media research: Possibilities, problems, and proposals. *Media, Culture and Society, 31*(4), 633–652.

Buckingham, D., with Banaji, S., Burn, A., Carr, D., Cranmer, S., & Willett, R. (2005). *The media literacy of children and young people: A review of the academic research.* London: Ofcom.

Buckingham, D., & Burn, A. (2007). Game literacy in theory and practice. *Journal of Educational Media and Hypermedia, 16*, 323–349.

Buckingham, D., Harvey, I. & Sefton-Green, J. (1999). The difference is digital? Digital technology and student media production. *Convergence, 5*, 10–20.

Buckingham, D., Pini, M., & Willett, R. (2007). "Take back the tube!" The discursive construction of amateur film- and video-making. *Journal of Media Practice, 8*, 183–201.

Buckingham, D., & Willett, R. (Eds.) (2009). *Video cultures: Media technology and amateur creativity.* Basingstoke: Palgrave.

Buckingham, D., Willett, R., & Pini, M. (in press). *Home truths? Video production and domestic life.* Ann Arbor, MI: University of Michigan Press.

Burgess, J. (2006). Hearing ordinary voices: Cultural studies, vernacular creativity and digital storytelling. *Continuum, 20*, 201–214.

Burn, A. (2000). Repackaging the slasher movie: Digital unwriting of film in the classroom. *English in Australia, 127–8*, 1–19.

Burn, A., & Durran, J. (2006). Digital anatomies: Analysis as production in media education. In D. Buckingham, & R. Willett (Eds.), *Digital generations: Children, young people and new media* (pp. 273–294). Mahwah, NJ: Lawrence Erlbaum.

Burn, A., & Durran, J. (2007). *Media literacy in schools.* London: Paul Chapman.

Chalfen, R. (1987). *Snapshot versions of life.* Bowling Green, OH: Bowling Green State University Press.

Cohen, P. (1990). *Really useful knowledge.* Stoke-on-Trent: Trentham.

Drotner, K. (2008). Learning is hard work: Digital practices and future competencies. In D. Buckingham (Ed.), *Youth, identity and digital media* (pp. 167–184). Cambridge, MA: MIT Press.

Eisenstein, E. (1979). *The printing press as an agent of change.* New York: Cambridge University Press.

Erstad, O., Gilje, Ø., & de Lange, T. (2007). Remixing multimodal resources: Multiliteracies and digital production in Norwegian media education. *Learning, media and technology, 27*, 183–198.

Facer, K. & Furlong, R. (2001). Beyond the myth of the "cyberkid": Young people at the margins of the information revolution. *Journal of Youth Studies, 4*, 451–469.

First Monday (2008). Special issue "Critical Perspectives on Web 2.0" *13*(3). Retrieved 20 August 2008 from http://www.uic.edu/htbin/cgiwrap/bin/ojs/index.php/fm/issue/view/263/showToc.

Gauntlett, D. (2007). Wide angle: is it time for media studies 2.0? *Media Education Association Newsletter, 5*, 3–5.

Gee, J.P. (2003). *What video games have to teach us about learning and literacy.* Basingstoke: Palgrave.

Grossberg, L. (1995). Cultural studies vs. political economy: Is anybody else bored with this debate? *Critical Studies in Mass Communication, 12*, 72–81.

Hargittai, E., & Walejko, G. (2008). The participation divide: Content creation and sharing and the digital age. *Information, Communication and Society, 11*, 239–256.

Herring, S. (2008). Questioning the generational divide: Technological exoticism and adult constructions of online youth identity. In D. Buckingham (Ed.), *Youth, identity and digital media* (pp. 71–92). Cambridge, MA: MIT Press.

International Journal of Cultural Studies (2002). Special issue: Returning cultural studies to education," 5(4). Eds. K. Maton and H. K. Wright.

Jenkins, H. with Clinton, K., Purushotma, R., Robison, A. J., & Weigel, M. (2006). Confronting the challenges of participatory culture: Media education for the 21st century. Retrieved 27 November 2007 from http://www.digitallearning.macfound.org.

Learning, Media and Technology (2007). Special issue: Media education goes digital, *27*(2). . D. Buckingham, & S. Bragg (Eds.).

Lenhart, A., Madden, M., Macgill, A.R., & Smith, A. (2007). *Teens and social media.* Washington, DC: Pew Internet and American Life Project.

Luke, C. (2000). Cyber-schooling and technological change: Multiliteracies for new times. In B. Cope, & M. Kalantzis (Eds.), *Multiliteracies: Literacy learning and the design of social futures* (pp. 69–91). London: Routledge.

Marvin, C. (1988). *When old technologies were new.* New York: Oxford University Press.

Media International Australia (2006). Special issue: Media education, *120*. S. Bragg, D. Buckingham, & S. Turnbull (Eds.).

Merrin, W. (2008). Media studies 2.0. Retrieved March 16, 2009, from http://twopointzeroforum.blogspot.com/.

Murdoch, R. (2006). His space (interview by Spencer Reiss). *Wired* 14:07. Retrieved April 12, 2007, from www.wired.com/wired/archive/14.07/murdoch.html.

Ofcom (2008) *Media literacy: Report on UK children's media literacy.* London: Ofcom.

O'Reilly, T. (2005). What is Web 2.0? Design patterns and business models for the next generation of software. Retrieved March 17, 2009, from http://www.oreillynet.com/pub/a/oreilly/tim/news /2005/09/30/what-is-web-20.html.

Pelletier, C. (2009). Games and learning: What's the connection? *International Journal of Learning and Media 1*(1). Retrieved March 18, 2009, from http://ijlm.net/.

Perloff, D. (2002). The third person effect. In J. Bryant, & D. Zillmann (Eds.), *Media effects: Advances in theory and research.* Mahwah, NJ: Lawrence Erlbaum, pp. 489–506.

Petersen, S. M. (2008). Loser generated content: From participation to exploitation. *First Monday 13*(3). Retrieved August 20, 2008, from http://www.uic.edu/htbin/cgiwrap/bin/ojs/index.php/fm/issue/view/263/showToc.

Robins, K., & Webster, F. (1999). *Times of the technoculture.* London: Routledge.

Ross, A. (2003). *No-collar: The humane workplace and its hidden costs.* Philadelphia: Temple University Press.

Sefton-Green, J., & Buckingham, D. (1996). Digital visions: Young people's "creative" uses of multimedia technologies in the home. *Convergence, 2*, 47–79.

Streeter, T. (1987). The cable fable revisited: Discourse, policy and the making of cable television. *Critical Studies in Mass Communication, 4*, 174–200.

Thoughts for Deletion (2007). Yahoo user sues Virgin. Retrieved March 17, 2009, from http://thoughtsfordeletion.blogspot.com/2007/09/flickr-user-sues-virgin.html.

van Dijk, J. (2009). Users like you? Theorizing agency in user-generated content. *Media, Culture & Society, 31*(1): 41–58.

Warschauer, M. (2003). *Technology and social inclusion: Rethinking the digital divide.* Cambridge, MA: The MIT Press.

Winston, B. (1998). *Media, technology and society: A history.* London: Routledge.

Woolgar, S. (Ed.) (2002). *Virtual society? Technology, cyberbole, reality.* Oxford: Oxford University Press.

Contributors

Shaaron Ainsworth is an associate professor in the School of Psychology and Learning Sciences Research Institute, University of Nottingham. She has a BSc in Psychology, an MSc in Artificial Intelligence, and a PhD in Learning Sciences. Her work focuses on the roles of multiple and visual representations and on the design and evaluation of interactive technologies (e.g., authoring tools, educational games, mobile learning, CSCL). She has published over 50 journal papers, high-quality conference papers, and book chapters on these topics.

Ralph Barthel is a PhD candidate at the Learning Sciences Research Institute, University of Nottingham. He has an engineering degree in media and information sciences and is experienced in the design, development, and evaluation of Interactive Systems. He has provided consultancy to many organizations on learning technology innovation and standardization. His current research focus is the design of social knowledge systems and their application in everyday learning activities.

David Buckingham is professor of education at the Institute of Education, London University and director of the Centre for the Study of Children, Youth and Media (CSCYM), London Knowledge Lab. His research focuses on young people's interactions with electronic media and on media education. He is currently working on two major research projects: about the everyday use of video camcorders, and about the role of the Internet in young people's civic participation.

His most recent books are *Beyond technology: Children's learning in the age of digital culture* (Polity, 2007); *Global children, global media: Migration, media and childhood* (with Liesbeth de Block, Palgrave, 2007) and *Youth, identity and digital media* (edited, MIT Press, 2008).

Wilma Clark is a PhD student at the Institute of Education, University of London, and a technology research fellow at the London Knowledge Lab where she conducts research in the areas of Web 2.0 technologies and participatory design approaches to technology use in support of learners and learning. She is an editor for the interdisciplinary journal, *QWERTY: Journal of technology and culture*, of the Collaborative Knowledge Building Group (CKBG).

Kirsten Drotner is a professor of media studies at the Institute of Literature, Culture & Media Studies at the University of Southern Denmark and founding director of DREAM: Danish Research Centre on Education and Advanced Media Materials). Her 20 (co-)authored and (co-)edited books in Danish and English include *English children and their magazines, 1751–1945* (Yale UP, 1988), *Researching audiences* (Arnold, 2003; with Kim C. Schrøder, Steve Kline, and Catherine Murray), *International handbook of children, media and culture* (Sage, 2007, co-editor Sonia Livingstone). She has published in internationally reviewed journals such as *Communications, Media, culture & society, European journal of communication* and *Theory, culture & society*. Currently, she serves on the editorial board of *Communication, culture & critique* (Sage), *The International journal of learning and media* (MIT), *International journal of cultural studies* (Sage), *Journal of feminist media studies* (Sage), *Journal of children and media* (Routledge) and on the editorial advisory board of *European journal of cultural studies* and *Young: Nordic journal of youth research.*

Ola Erstad is a professor at the Department for Educational Research, University of Oslo. From 1998 until 2005, he was head of research at a national center on technology in education, studying a broad range of issues in relation to the impact of technology in Norwegian schools. At present he is head of research at the Department for Educational Research and leader of a research group called "TransAction," focusing on the relationship between formal and informal ways of learning. He has published on different issues of technology and education, especially concerning media literacy and digital competence. Recent publications include "Re-mixing multimodal resources," *Learning, media, and technology* (2007, co-authored) and "Tales of mediation: Narrative and digital media as cultural tools," in Knut Lundby (Ed.). *Digital storytelling, mediatized stories: Self-representations in new media* (Peter Lang, 2008, co-authored).

Anette Grønning is an assistant professor at the Institute of Literature, Culture

& Media Studies, University of Southern Denmark, and her work centers upon computer-mediated discourse studies. She works with computer-mediated communication in organizations, in particular email and chat interaction between employees and customers. Her PhD dissertation examines social presence in email as a factor in the interaction between customers and employees, collected from the context of Danish insurance companies.

Nina Haferkamp, Dipl. Medienwiss., is a PhD student at the University of Duisburg-Essen, Germany. She has conducted research on the usage of social networking sites in consideration of social psychological variables. Her current research interests include social aspects of computer-mediated communication within the Web 2.0. She is co-author of "Communicating within the blogosphere: Motives for reading, writing, and commenting," *Journal of computer mediated communication* (with N. C. Krämer and A. Lam-Chi).

John Hartley is professor, Federation Fellow, and research director of the Australian Research Council Centre of Excellence for Creative Industries and Innovation at Queensland University of Technology in Australia. He was foundation dean of the Creative Industries Faculty at QUT and head of the School of Journalism, Media and Cultural Studies at Cardiff University in Wales. He is the author of 18 books, including *Television truths* (2008) and *Creative industries* (2005); editor of the *International journal of cultural studies*; a Fellow of the Australian Academy of Humanities, Royal Society of the Arts and Queensland Academy of Arts and Sciences.

Mikael Kivelä received his MA in education from the University of Helsinki. He works there as an educational technology adviser in the Department of Education. In addition, he has developed video recording and post-processing techniques for classroom use in several projects as a technological expert and researcher. His fields of interest include interaction with, around, and through ICT such as computer games or virtual environments and minimally invasive recording techniques for capturing such interaction.

Nicole Krämer is a professor of social psychology, media, and communication at the University of Duisburg-Essen, Germany. Her research interests include social and emotional aspects of human-computer interaction and computer-mediated communication. Her key publications explore the socio-emotional effects of nonverbal behavior and the effects of embodied conversational agents. She is the co-author (2008) of "Avatar-assisted net-working: Increasing social presence and interpersonal trust in net-based collaborations," *Human Communication Research*, 34 (2), 287–318 (with G. Bente, S. Rüggenberg, and F. Eschenburg).

Jonas Löwgreen is a professor of interaction design and co-founder at the

School of Arts and Communication, Malmö University, Sweden. He specializes in crossmedia products, interactive visualization, and the design theory of the digital materials. In 1998, he initiated the influential two-year masters program in interaction design at Malmö University. He has published some 50 scientific papers and three books, including *Thoughtful interaction design* (MIT Press 2004, with Erik Stolterman), and a vast range of general-interest and pedagogical materials. His design portfolio comprises some 40 projects from explorative research and professional contexts.

Angela McFarlane is a professor of education at the Graduate School of Education, University of Bristol, and adjunct professor at Department for Educational Research, University of Oslo. Originally a research biologist and secondary science teacher, she is director of Content and Learning at the Royal Botanic Gardens, Kew. She was a founder of the TEEM project on evaluation of digital content in the classroom and ran a software research and development unit at Homerton College, Cambridge for over 10 years. She has designed and directed national UK research and evaluation projects on ICT and Learning and was part of the team that designed the longitudinal study of the impact of networked technologies on home and school learning—Impact2. She is currently researching mobile learning with Learning2Go, Europe's largest handheld learning project, in Wolverhampton, and Hand e-learning in Bristol. She was a member of the OECD expert group on quality in educational software and the first evidence and practice director at Becta, the UK government agency for ICT. Current research interests include the role of e-learning in professional development, personal, and mobile computing, computer games in learning and in particular the creative online learning communities they spawn.

Jarkko Mylläri received his MA in Education from the University of Helsinki. He works in the Department of Applied Sciences of Education as a Project Researcher for the Centre for Research on Teaching. His fields of interest and previous work are studies of Student's Pedagogical Thinking related to the use of ICT in teaching-studying process and cumulative knowledge building utilizing virtual knowledge-building platforms and tools.

Kim Christian Schrøder is a professor of communication at the Department of Communication, Business and Information Technologies at Roskilde University, Denmark. His books in English and Danish include *Researching audiences* (Arnold 2003, co-authored with K. Drotner, S. Kline, and C. Murray), *Media cultures* (Routledge 1992, with M. Skovmand), *The Language of advertising* (Blackwell 1985, with T. Vestergaard). His articles about the theoretical, methodological, and analytical aspects of audience uses and experiences of media have appeared in *Media,* *culture & society, European journal of cultural studies, and European journal of communication.*

Mike Sharples is a professor of Learning Sciences and director of the Learning Sciences Research Institute at the University of Nottingham. He has an international reputation for research in mobile learning and the design of learning technologies. He inaugurated the mLearn conference series and is president of the International Association for Mobile Learning. His current projects include a collaboration with the Open University UK to develop twenty-first century science learning between formal and informal settings. He is author of 160 publications in the areas of interactive systems design, artificial intelligence and educational technology.

Daniel Spikol is a PhD student in computer science at Växjö University, Sweden. He works for the Center for Learning and Knowledge Technologies (CeLeKT). His current research interests include the design of mobile learning environments that explore modes of collaboration that foster discovery. Spikol holds an M Sc from M.I.T. and a B.F.A. from Rhode Island School of Design. Forthcoming and recent publications include "Physical activities and playful learning using mobile games," in *Research and practice in technology enhanced learning*; "Exploring novel learning practices through co-designing mobile games," in *Researching mobile learning: Frameworks, methods, and research design.*

Simon Staffans has worked in the media since the early 1990s, mainly in publishing and radio. His current occupation is that of a format developer for crossmedia formats at MediaCity, Åbo Akademi University in Vaasa, Finland. His fields of interest are crossmedia, interactivity, user experience and edutainment. He has been enrolled as a speaker at numerous conferences and has had articles appear in publications such as *The Sagasnet reader* and *Mercator media forum*. He is currently studying for an MA in political science and mass communication.

Jenny Weight, PhD, teaches in the Media Section of RMIT University, Australia. With her colleagues she received a 2008 Australian Learning and Teaching Council Award for University Teaching. She has published widely about networked technology, including its pedagogical uses. She is currently part of a team of ethnographic researchers looking at the various ways people use mobile phones and other domestic media technology. Other current research interests include the "identity media" phenomenon. Her PhD dissertation was a phenomenology-inspired study of the relationship between humans and their digital devices.

Norbert Wildermuth is an associate professor in the Institute of Literature, Culture and Media Studies at the University of Southern Denmark. He has published widely on issues of media globalization, such as transnational satellite television in Asia. His recent work includes field studies in Zambia, Vietnam, Nepal, and Brazil with a focus on young people and their media uses. His current interdisciplinary and comparative research project "Youth and the city: Skills, knowledge and social reproduction" is funded by DANIDA.

Index

new literacies

AND DIGITAL EPISTEMOLOGIES

Colin Lankshear, Michele Knobel, & Michael Peters
General Editors

New literacies and new knowledges are being invented "in the streets" as people from all walks of life wrestle with new technologies, shifting values, changing institutions, and new structures of personality and temperament emerging in a global informational age. These new literacies and ways of knowing remain absent from classrooms. Many education administrators, teachers, teacher educators, and academics seem largely unaware of them. Others actively oppose them. Yet, they increasingly shape the engagements and worlds of young people in societies like our own. The *New Literacies and Digital Epistemologies* series will explore this terrain with a view to informing educational theory and practice in constructively critical ways.

For further information about the series and submitting manuscripts, please contact:

Michele Knobel & Colin Lankshear
Montclair State University
Dept. of Education and Human Services
3173 University Hall
Montclair, NJ 07043
michele@coatepec.net

To order other books in this series, please contact our Customer Service Department at:

Or browse online by series at: